READING THE RHYTHM

Reading the Rhythm

The Poetics of French
Free Verse 1910–1930

CLIVE SCOTT

CLARENDON PRESS · OXFORD
1993

Oxford University Press, Walton Street, Oxford OX2 6DP

Oxford New York Toronto
Delhi Bombay Calcutta Madras Karachi
Kuala Lumpur Singapore Hong Kong Tokyo
Nairobi Dar es Salaam Cape Town
Melbourne Auckland Madrid
and associated companies in
Berlin Ibadan

Oxford is a trade mark of Oxford University Press

Published in the United States
by Oxford University Press, New York

British Library Cataloguing in Publication Data
Data available

Library of Congress Cataloging in Publication Data
Scott, Clive, 1943–
Reading the rhythm : the poetics of French verse : free verse,
1910–1930 / Clive Scott.
Includes bibliographical references and index.
1. French poetry—20th century—History and criticism.   2. French
language—20th century—Versification.   3. Free verse—History and
criticism.   I. Title.
PQ471.F74S33 1993   841'.91209—dc20   92-44197
ISBN 0-19-815882-3

Typeset by Graphicraft Typesetters Ltd., Hong Kong
Printed and bound in Great Britain
on acid-free paper by
Biddles Ltd., Guildford and Kings Lynn

Acknowledgements

I would like to express my warm gratitude to Marie Mactavish, who typed the manuscript, for her inexhaustible patience and skill, and to OUP's editing team—Andrew Lockett, Jackie Pritchard, Elizabeth Stratford, and Jason Freeman—for their help and support throughout the production process.

Contents

Notes on the Text

Where the names of authors of books and articles are followed by two dates, as, for example, Huret 1982/1891, the first date is that of the particular edition referred to, the second the date of the work's first publication.

Asterisks mark the first appearance of those terms explained in the Glossary of Technical Terms (Appendix I). These technical terms are indexed, along with proper names, in the main index.

Appendix II contains the complete texts of poems not quoted in full in the body of the book.

Prefatory Remarks

As in *Vers Libre: The Emergence of Free Verse in France 1886–1914* (1990), I have concentrated in this book on problems of reading posed by different kinds of free-verse poem. Sometimes the poems in question have been sufficiently short for me to offer a fairly comprehensive interpretation of them; sometimes the length of a poem has obliged me to confine myself to isolated sections, so that I have only been able to sketch in, in broad outline, a possible interpretation. But my chief concern is, after all, not to provide ready-made interpretations so much as *methods* of interpretation, based primarily on rhythmic data, and methods for discovering what rhythmic data are most relevant to a given poem. My subject is the reading of rhythm, where rhythm is not some comfortable, unified entity providing, for every poem, roughly the same kind of infrastructure, but something variable and elusive, redefined and relocated with each new text. To find the appropriate rhythmic coordinates is the first task of any reader who wishes to orientate himself on the shifting map of free verse.

In line with this preoccupation and this approach, where I have made connections between poetry and the visual arts, I have done so not primarily in order to demonstrate particular debts, or establish parallels between visual and verbal techniques—although I have engaged in *some* speculation of this kind—but more to create a plausible mentality, an appropriate perceptual frame, for reading different species of free verse. I am not thereby attempting to historicize modes of reading; reading is a question of being true to one's own perceptions more than to anyone else's. But if one wishes to give shape to these perceptions, or to make works easier of ingress by the adoption of other perceptual strategies, then the contemporary visual arts are a ready repository of potentially useful models.

I should add that my approach to the relationship between the arts is one that tries to register the promiscuous ways in which we live with the arts in our present culture; we experience the crossing of boundaries between the arts as psychologically necessary, if not natural. W. J. T. Mitchell (1986: 49–50) seems to me to have the measure of the issue:

We tend to think, in other words, that to compare poetry with painting is to make a metaphor, while to differentiate poetry from painting is to state a literal truth ... My argument here will be twofold: (1) there is no *essential* difference between poetry and painting, no difference, that is, that is given for all time by the inherent nature of the media, the objects they represent, or the laws of the human mind; (2) there are always a number of differences in effect in a culture which allow it to sort out the distinctive qualities of its ensemble of signs and symbols ... Since the end of the eighteenth century Western culture has witnessed a steady stream of innovations in the arts, media and communication that makes it hard to see exactly where the line ought to be drawn.

Much of the discredit brought by structuralism on this kind of 'liberal' and uninhibited disregard of frontiers is focused on a critique of metaphorical thinking, which masks structural principles. Such a critique, however, supposes that the metaphorical itself can be defined, and that it is a categorical linguistic figure. This is clearly unsatisfactory: for one thing, metaphors can have different functions in discourse (metaphors of convenience, of shock, of habitual vision, etc.) and, for another, different kinds of discourse affect the degree to which we respond to metaphors as metaphors. In the end, it seems only reasonable to assume, as David Scott does (1988: 172), 'that the verbal/visual relationship is infinitely complex, involving an equation in which elements from one side have to be used in constituting the nature of the other'. This assumption underlies my own transferences of visual models to the perception of rhythm. But the world of the visual arts is not my only point of reference, as will be seen: the theme of the journey provides another figure for the unfolding rhythms of poetic utterance, upon which the poets in my study have richly drawn.

As in previous books I have made occasional reference to Anglo-American metrics, and particularly so in the introductory chapter, partly in the unsystematic pursuit of a comparative prosody, partly because recent years have witnessed a palpable Anglo-American influence on French metrical theory—I think of generative metrics—and partly because some of the problems I am attempting to solve may be made more accessible for English readers if approached through the native prosody.

I

Introductory Reflections on Rhythm and Metre

BEFORE the pursuit of understanding, the acknowledgement of ignorance. Metrics is not an exact science, but a speculative one. It is easy to assume, given the technicality of its data, that metrics is a stable, verifiable, describable body of knowledge whose development lies in the direction of refinement and completion. But metrical description is, on the contrary, highly unstable, constantly under the obligation to make new beginnings, as new poets and new readers become involved in verse-making.

Something of the danger of metrical institutionalization can be seen in American generative metrics, which developed out of structuralism. Even though structuralist metrics had introduced into metrical analysis a much greater attention to linguistic constituents and a more rigorous taxonomy, it remained wedded to a descriptive method, and thus to an enumeration of metrical norms and deviations from them. The immediate drawbacks of this method, in the eyes of the generativists, are threefold: (1) no significant generalizations can be derived from it; that is, the rules by which a line is metrical, and by which metricality can be predicted, are invisible; (2) it is an 'exclusive' rather than an 'inclusive' approach, in that the abstract metrical scheme is single and rigid and marginalizes, as deviations, a large number of verse-instances; (3) the list of deviations is itself meaningless, because it tells us neither what deviations can be combined and in what quantities, before a line becomes unmetrical, nor anything about differing degrees of deviation. These are the shortcomings that the generativists sought to put right. Taking over Chomsky's transformational-generative model of syntactic structure, the generative metrists suppose that every reader has an intuitive knowledge of what is metrical and what is unmetrical in a given metre, and that this knowledge can be made explicit in a set of rules, which particular metrical instances embody in either a direct or (acceptably) transformed way. Acceptable transformations of the metrical deep structure are usually called 'correspondence rules', which account, inclusively, for what otherwise would be regarded as deviations. The formulation of generative rules presupposes three things: (1) that the greater the degree of the rule's generality, the more instances it covers and predicts, the 'deeper' it is, the more valid it is; (2) that instances not covered by the rules are unmetrical; (3) that the further down the list of correspondence rules (in the direction of tolerance and, therefore, generality) a particular metrical configuration is predicted, the more complex it will be; in other words, the metrical complexity of the line is proportional to the inclusiveness (generality) of the rule which covers it.

Now, even though from the very inception of the generative approach, with Morris Halle and Samuel Keyser's 'Chaucer and the Study of Prosody' of 1966, the authors imagined their theory as relative, and predicted that it would require adjustment according to each particular context of enquiry ('One of the things which a study of later poets would show is the way that these principles have been modified by a given poet' (1970/ 1966: 411)); even though the Halle–Keyser model has attracted amplifications and revisions, chief among which are Magnuson and Ryder's alternative proposals (1970, 1971) and Kiparsky's theories of 1975 and 1977; even though Gilbert Youmans argues that generative metrical rules should be treated as normative principles rather than categorical constraints (1989: 5–6); yet generative metrics has promoted the view that all verse worth its salt is rule-governed; that the challenge for the metrist is not to relate structure to interpretation, but to find the most inclusive rule (often formulated in a particularly rebarbative manner); that consequently the 'deep structure' revealed by that rule is more fundamental than the 'surface' experience of reading a particular line of verse. Is there such a thing as an innate metrical competence, invulnerable to the perceptual relativities of changing history?

French applications of generative metrics are to be found in the work of J.-C. Milner (1974), Jacques Roubaud (1971), Roubaud and Pierre Lusson (1974), and more recently Paul Verluyten. Verluyten, for example, incorporating his argument that French words are informed by 'un *rythme sous-jacent alternant* de syllabes relativement proéminentes (s) et relativement non proéminentes (w)' (1989: 31), applies Kiparsky's (1977) notions of permissible and impermissible mismatches between the abstract metrical pattern and the verse-instance to the *caesura of the *alexandrine. Using Kiparsky's two categories of mismatch, phonological ('labelling mismatches': *discordances d'étiquetage*) and those that affect the boundaries of words and phrases ('bracketing mismatches': *discordances de parenthésage*), Verluyten is able to demonstrate by what rules a line like Catulle Mendès's

De sa chair et de la ‖ blancheur de sa pensée

can be deemed to have a medial caesura (here it is because the caesura falls between words). While seeming, paradoxically, to maintain the metrical fixity of the caesura, the generative solution throws in doubt the reasons for maintaining its fixity, by undermining its function as a point of metrical, syntactic, and intonational articulation. Indeed Verluyten should perhaps be taxed with confusing, in his account, the caesura as an accentual phenomenon *of* the sixth syllable and the caesura as a phenomenon of boundary *after* the sixth syllable. The generative solution also fails to respond to shifts in metrical perception which justify Mallarmé's call for a free-rhythmic dodecasyllable:

Les fidèles à l'alexandrin, notre hexamètre, desserrent intérieurement ce mécanisme rigide et puéril de sa mesure; l'oreille, affranchie d'un compteur factice, connaît une jouissance à discerner, seule, toutes les combinaisons possibles entre eux, de douze timbres. ('Crise de vers'; 1945/1896: 11)

It is these historical shifts in metrical perception which seem to me crucial. We simply cannot understand free verse unless we are prepared to evolve perceptually with the *verslibristes*. Generative metrics deals with history, as it deals with all differences of verse-instance, inclusively, so that a metric structure is able to maintain its homogeneity:

Nous voyons au contraire la structure métrique de l'alexandrin comme *homogène* et *fixe*: les modifications, si elles ne sont pas impossibles, sont réduites au minimum . . .

On est en droit de se demander dès lors si le modèle que nous avançons, où la structure métrique du vers est rigide, permet de rendre compte de l'évolution historique indéniable de l'alexandrin et d'éventuelles différences individuelles dans la versification d'un poète à l'autre, voire d'une période à l'autre chez le même poète. Nous démontrerons ci-dessous que notre modèle parvient à intégrer cette évolution . . .

Avant cela, nous devons préciser la distinction entre le niveau *prosodique* et le niveau *métrique* car, selon nous, les différences historiques ou individuelles mentionnées résident, non pas en une modification du système métrique de l'alexandrin (à une légère exception près), mais en une série de changements dans la *relation* entre ces deux niveaux (Verluyten 1989: 46).

This integrative strategy fossilizes metrical thinking, as it fossilizes an albeit increasingly tolerant metrical structure. It is inconceivable that the history of metrics should involve only a staged intensification of tension between prosody and metre, or to use our previous terms, between verse-instance and abstract metrical pattern, and that with such compliant consistency; it is inconceivable that metrical priorities should not change, that change should not involve concomitant revisions of the significance of different metrical resources. But the integrative view makes least historical sense when it comes to free verse; generative metrics have signally neglected free verse, presumably because free verse threatens to be all surface structure without deep structure, all performance without competence, and this because the versification of free verse derives more from the physiology of its subject, or the psychophysiology of its creator and consumer, than from some available pattern-book. The integrative view must either assume some cataclysmic break between regular verse and free verse, or it must assume that, for example, those twelve-syllable lines or units which still appear in free verse are still alexandrines in all but the company they keep, and that the distinction between an alexandrine and a free-rhythmic dodecasyllable is bogus.

But underlying this quarrel with the kind of metrical mentality which too easily develops out of generative metrics and which, it seems to me, makes the tackling of free verse either inconceivable or of traumatic complexity, is a quarrel of another kind: the generative metrist, with the pertinent correspondence rule as his quarry, approaches the text too much as a metrist, too little as a reader. This is part of Derek Attridge's objection to generative metrics (1982: 34–55), reflecting his wish to revalidate the temporal dimension of metre, metre as rhythm unfolding, rather than as static structure.

In highlighting the perspective of the reader, Attridge is insisting that scansion must have a literary/interpretative 'pay-off' and that it must be 'commensurate with' the reader's perception—for example, metrical complexity is not, as the generativists would have it, an absolute quality, pre-defined by a set of rules, but relates to the reader's particular expectations in a particular verse-context. In other words, Attridge is made uneasy by the generativists' single-minded pursuit of explicitness, which overlooks perceptual and psychological factors, and by the extreme abstraction of their theories. He has returned to these charges in a later paper (1989), adding a plea for intuitive judgement:

For whatever reason, the tradition of generative metrics, while strongly asserting the theoretical value of the model of generative linguistics, and in particular its use of native-speaker judgements to provide more insightful evidence than can be obtained from a corpus, actually proceeds in quite the opposite direction, mistrusting the poetry-reader's intuitions and placing enormous emphasis on what can and cannot be attested on the page, regarded as evidence for the writer's metrical intuitions. (p. 193)

It is a peculiar neurosis of metricians perhaps that they feel bound to justify themselves by a theory, rather than by the appropriate observation of metrical features, or interpretation of metrical data, as an aid to the reading of a poem; which is to say that little attention has been given to a functional metrics, user-friendly, which would enable the reader to determine what features are peculiarly relevant to the metrical investigation of a particular poem. For surely every poem has the capacity to insinuate a scansion with slightly different emphases and permutations of features? What kind of allowance can be made in metrical description for perceptual and psychological variables? In the end, one must feel that the primary concern of a metrical theory should not be with definitional reliability (the elusive and illusory ability to say, categorically, what is metrical and what is unmetrical), but with the range of metrical features it can bring into operational use for the 'average' reader, and with the range of the relationships between those features it can show to be rhythmically significant.

If metre is experienced as constraint, then it must be pre-existent to the text and complied with to a sufficient degree to function as a constraint. Because metre is not a constraint immanent to the language, it is arbitrary and cultural rather than motivated and textual (see Wheatley 1988). Within this proposition are two further implications. First, metre is arbitrary and yet is regarded as *the* underlying determinant of textual structure; either, then, the attention we give to metre is in excess of what it can reveal about a text; or the very arbitrariness of metre is what makes it peculiarly revelatory, is a crucial part of the 'making strange', or the expressive potentiation, of language—in which case it would be perverse to envisage any metrical theory which allows for the 'naturalization' of metre. Secondly, scansional systems should be constructed on particular verse-instances alone, so that the fusion of metrical analysis and 'rhythmic' analysis is more complete, and so that each poem may be in a position to promote its own metrical variation, its own redisposition of metrical emphasis.

There should be nothing remarkable about this last proposal for French prosody, given the minimal nature of its metricity. We should remember that in the regular alexandrine, graphically representable as:

$$\_\_\overset{(\prime)}{\_\_}\_\_{}^{\prime} \parallel \_\overset{(\prime)}{\_\_}\_\_\_{}^{\prime}$$

only the number of syllables (twelve) and the accents on syllables 6 and 12 are metrical; the 'secondary' accents, usually one within each *hemistich, and marked here with brackets because they are both optional and mobile (can appear on any of the five unoccupied syllables of the half-line), are not metrical; they are nonce rhythmic products of the syntax, whose position may vary from hemistich to hemistich, line to line. And it is only in the alexandrine that the caesura is fixed, medially; in other lines articulated by a caesura (nine syllables or more), the caesural position is established rhythmically, by each particular poem, and becomes a convention for the duration of that poem only (although certain dispositions in the relatively popular decasyllable were standard for certain periods of its development: 4 + 6 or 6 + 4 for the classical decasyllable, 5 + 5 for the nineteenth-century decasyllable).

Let us suppose that we began reading Lamartine's 'Le Lac':

> Ainsi, toujours poussés vers de nouveaux rivages,
> /ɛ̃/si/tu/ʒur/pu/se/ver/də/nu/vo/Ri/vaʒ/ 2 + 4 + 4 + 2

What appears to us to be the principal structuring device? Is it the number of syllables in the line, according to most accounts the primary metrical determinant? Surely not. First it might be the phonetic insistence of /u/, and the semantic appropriateness of the conjunction of 'toujours poussés' and 'nouveaux'. Secondly, it might be the modulating consonant and vowel closures of the rhythmic groups—/si/ > /se/ > /vo/ > /vaʒ/—and the process of expansion and contraction encoded by those groups 2 > 4 > 4 > 2: the sense of setting out on the open sea and then homing in on a destination. We hardly have any need to specify the caesura, since structural devices already noted put it in place. One further acoustic twinning, that of /ʒ/, will also encourage us to lift out the central topos: time ('-jours', '-age').

If we entertain the idea that a line like this is an array of other effects before it is an alexandrine, we might be accused of putting the cart before the horse, the effects before what makes them possible. But we should take note of Cornulier's view that an alexandrine needs a context of other alexandrines to achieve its metrical identity as an alexandrine:

La définition que les métriciens dits générativistes donnent du vers en tant que 'réalisant' un certain *schéma abstrait* est donc insuffisante, puisque, pour qu'une expression soit un vers, il ne suffit pas qu'elle 'réalise', par exemple, 'le schéma abstrait × × × ×' (en ayant 4 syllabes); il faudrait compléter cette définition en ajoutant—et c'est l'essentiel—qu'elle doit réaliser le même schéma métrique que des vers voisins . . . Un vers n'a pas à 'réaliser' un schéma préexistant dans un ciel des idées et des mètres: en général, la structure métrique est *immanente* au texte. (1982: 39)

Cornulier does not take sufficient account of intertextuality and of the necessary externality of anything experienced as a constraint; but even if allowance is made for such factors, there is still a powerful plausibility in this argument.

This brings us to the second feature of metre mentioned above, namely the cultural. We may argue that lines of verse, as paradigms or exemplars, have certain structures, certain kinds of availability to accentuation and intonation, certain possibilities of syntactic development, and thus certain indelible connections with particular kinds of discourse. But it is only in stanzas or in stichic sequences that these connections can be realized, and these larger configurations are themselves the bearers of the ideologies buried in genres and forms. The alexandrines which alternate with octosyllables (*rimes croisées) in the satiric *iambe (from Archilochus), in a dialogue between the stern or stoical, public-voiced amplitude of the one, and the more urgent, more unpredictable, private voice-tones of the other, are very different from the alexandrines borne along by the unremitting, self-generating momentum of *terza rima; equally the decasyllables of the ode have only their length in common with the decasyllables of a *ballade. In one sense, of course, this is to underline the intertextuality of metre: metre is motivated culturally by the sum of its uses and, in particular, by its generical imprinting. But it is also to insist that lines, both in their metrical presence and in their cultural dimension, only become visible to the reader when they occur in significant combination.

So we return to Cornulier and the proposition that French lines are not inherently metrical, but are only so by mutual confirmation, circumstantially and translinearly (strophically). Such a view would invalidate all those discoveries of chance 'alexandrines', 'octosyllables', and other verse-fragments in prose, as an index of its greater or lesser poeticity. Such a view would imply that the scansion of French verse normally operates within too limited a verse-environment. This has a further implication for the function of rhyme. It is often argued that rhyme was treated as indispensable to French verse until the end of the nineteenth century, because it had a metrical or near-metrical function; put another way, the heavy metrical loading of the last syllable of a line naturally attracted rhyme, since rhyme is rhyme as much by virtue of its line-terminal position as by its acoustic properties. The positional significance of rhyme is exploited to mark the end of the syllabic string; the acoustic fore-grounding that accompanies rhyme intensifies the line-terminal accent, reinforcing the boundary and the intonational cadence of the line. But Cornulier (1981) is much less convinced of rhyme's line-demarcative function than he is of its stanzaic function, which might be described as twofold: rhyme-schemes are rhythms of recurrent acoustic units, patterns of interval, sometimes complicated by syllabic variations in the line (heterosyllabic stanzas); rhyme-schemes are also patterns of intonation— the last two lines of an *abab* stanza tend to repeat the intonational configuration of the first two at a slightly lower pitch, while an *abba* stanza produces an intonational suspension in its third line, with the fourth line providing a more definitive cadence. If French metre is context-derived, then rhyme is metrical not because of its line-demarcative function, but because it is the agent by which lines are built into the metrical context and by which other metrifying forces are activated, such as rhythmic combination, intonation, and acoustic patterning.

How then does our first line from Lamartine's 'Le Lac' fit into the larger metrical frame of the stanza?

Ainsi, toujours poussés vers de nouveaux rivages,	2 + 4 + 4 + 2
Dans la nuit éternelle emportés sans retour,	3 + 3 + 3 + 3
Ne pourrons-nous jamais sur l'océan des âges	4 + 2 + 4 + 2
Jeter l'ancre un seul jour?	3 + 3

A phonetic transcription will make the acoustic field more visible:

ẽsi | tuʒuRpuse ‖ vɛRdənuvo | Rivaʒ
dɑ̃lanɥi | etɛRnɛl ‖ ɑ̃pɔRte | sɑ̃RətuR
nəpuRɔ̃nu | ʒamɛ ‖ syRlɔseɑ̃ | dezaʒ
ʒətelɑ̃kR | œ̃sœlʒuR

Moving on from our initial observations, we might propose that /u/ reinforces the rhyme-scheme: this phoneme, the 'nous' perspective, is line-internal to lines 1 and 3, and line-terminal to lines 2 and 4. As a rhyme, it takes up the relentless linearity of time, denying both the cyclical and the pausing. We might argue that /ʒ/ is also a feature of the first and third lines, though it appears twice in the fourth line. This last should not surprise us since the fourth line is not merely the fourth line of two pairs, but the summation, acoustic and semantic, of all previous lines. Similarly /ɑ̃/, which appears as a measure-initial feature in the second line, is picked up in the fourth line, where it also echoes, however, the single accentuated (measure-terminal) occurrence of the phoneme in the third line ('océan').

The structural reinforcement of the *rimes croisées* is even more apparent in the rhythmic configurations: 2 + 4 or 4 + 2 belong to the odd lines, 3 + 3 to the even. At first sight this might look like an oscillation between vicissitude and equilibrium, the fundamental movement of elegy; and indeed it might have that effect, establish that modality, in this liminary stanza. But more important, perhaps, it draws our attention to two structural cruces in the stanza. First, we might enunciate the following principle: the stanza of 'Le Lac' is governed by an opening measure of 2 or 4, largely because each stanza is an attempt to parley with time, to negotiate a respite; if 3 + 3 is the mode of homogeneous temporal flow, then 2 or 4 will be the manner in which one disrupts this flow, makes an intervention, and these interventions take the form of exclamations, apostrophes, optative subjunctives, interruptive adverbial phrases. The twelve stanzas of 'Le Lac' which concern us—I leave out of account the four stanzas (VI–IX) of Elvire's address, which have a different structure—open in the following manner: I: Ainsi (2); II: O lac! (2); III: Tu mugissais (4); IV: Un soir (2); V: Tout à coup (3); X: Temps jaloux (3); XI: Hé quoi! (2); XII: Éternité (4); XIII: O lac! (2); XIV: Qu'il soit (2); XV: Qu'il soit (2); XVI: Que le vent (3). Three of the twelve stanzas, therefore, do not comply with our principle, but their syntax ('Tout à coup', 'Temps jaloux', 'Que le vent') keeps them within the overriding rhythmic/syntactic expectations.

We then might move on to enunciate a second, structurally more far-reaching principle: the first hemistich of the third line will tend to be 2 + 4 or 4 + 2 rather than 3 + 3. How far is this borne out by the facts? The same twelve stanzas have the following first hemistichs in their third lines: I: 4 + 2; II: 2 + 4 / 3′ + 3 (where 3′ means treating 'Regarde!' with a *coupe lyrique*—'Regarde! | . . .—rather than with a *coupe enjambante*—'Regar: | de! . . .'); III: 2 + 4 / 4 + 2; IV: 3 + 3; V: 2 + 4; X: 2 +4; XI: 2 + 4; XII: 2 + 4; XIII: 2 + 4; XIV: 4 + 2; XV: 2 + 4; XVI: (2 + 4) (the bracket) indicates that the first accent (on 2) is weak and that the whole might be encapsulated in a single measure of 6). What are the reasons for making this supposition? The short, hexasyllabic last line of the stanza has two structural/rhythmic consequences: first, the second hemistich of the third line tends to run on to it, either by explicit enjambement or by semantic indicators of speed, erasure:

> Ce temps qui les donna, ce temps qui les efface,
> Ne nous les rendra plus.

> (st. XI)

or urgency:

> Gardez de cette nuit, gardez, belle nature,
> Au moins le souvenir.

> (st. XIII)

This means that the more insistent juncture, which would normally have occurred at the end of the third line, 'regresses' to the middle of the line, in an exchange of function; and the greater expressive pressure which is now put on the caesural accent must be justified by an uneven combination of measures in the first hemistich, as a symptom of emotional turmoil or vicissitude. The second consequence concerns the final line and its **coupe*, which in its turn is put under unusual pressure; for this *coupe* must act both as a buffer for the momentum generated by the second hemistich of the previous line, and as a moment of self-collection, so that the stanza can come to an orderly close. This entails a hexasyllable whose early syllables are permeated by haste or impatience or stress, and whose final syllables are measured and wistfully protractive. Sometimes the tide running from the third line cannot be stemmed, as above in st. XI, or in st. XII:

> Parlez: nous rendrez-vous ces extases sublimes
> Que vous nous ravissez?

and an uninterrupted measure of 6 results. But more frequently, there is a *coupe* which transforms loss into poignant revisitation:

> Regarde! Je viens seul m'asseoir sur cette pierre
> Où tu la vis s'asseoir.
>
> (st. II)

> Que le bruit des rameurs qui frappaient en cadence
> Tes flots harmonieux.
>
> (st. IV)

This latter example is the nearest to being the exception which proves the rule: the 3 + 3 + 3 + 3 of the third line bespeaks achieved memory momentarily unconscious of loss, so that even though we move without resistance into the final line, the *coupe* here—

> Tes flots | harmonieux

—is only the necessary hesitation to ensure a more complete savouring, or that moment which precedes a satisfying synthesis of sensory data in an undifferentiated aesthetic experience.

This analysis of the 'Le Lac' stanza has necessarily been rudimentary and truncated. But I hope that it has enabled us to entertain the following possibilities: that metrical constraints can be text-generated and text-immanent to a greater or lesser extent; that the alexandrine is not a single thing, but something which performs differently in different verse/stanzaic contexts; that different locations in stanzas are metrically motivating in different ways—in other words, a first-hemistich 2 + 4 in a first line has an altogether different mode of action and of meaning from the same measure in the first hemistich of a third line; that metre is inevitably a *product* of syntax, however much syntax may be constrained by it, and that, therefore, syntaxes themselves may be viewed as metrically determining; that the proper function of scansion is not that of checking up on a text's degree of obedience to metre, but of exploring the expressivity of a text's linguistic schema; that, therefore, any separation of metrical imperatives and rhythmic ones is justified neither interpretatively nor by the nature of French prosody itself, which is minimally metrical; that rhythm is a multilevel phenomenon (Cureton 1985), and that what levels are relevant, or what hierarchy of levels operates, depends on the modes of meaning of each particular poet or poem. Without acknowledging these things no scansion of free verse can begin, because, for one thing, to apply to free verse a mode of scansion which is peculiar, and I think inadequate, to regular verse, is clearly impertinent.

But one further point needs to be underlined by this analysis of the first stanza of 'Le Lac'. If we translated the alexandrine's activity into a free-verse arrangement, according to the principles we have extrapolated, then we would come up with something like:

> 2 Ainsi,
> 10 Toujours poussés vers de nouveaux rivages,
> 12 Dans la nuit éternelle emportés sans retour,
> 4 Ne pourrons-nous
> 2 Jamais
> 9 Sur l'océan des âges jeter l'ancre
> 3 Un seul jour?

This is not idle amusement. It reveals, viewed from the side of the original alexandrines, that the metrico-rhythmical subtext of a sequence of alexandrines is a complex synthesis of different expressive drives, of impetus and braking, of units with different semantic and grammatical densities, syllabic weights. This begins to look like that late nineteenth-century argument that a sequence of alexandrines is already free verse:

Le vers polymorphe! Mais l'alexandrin est le vers polymorphe par excellence! Le poète qui sait son métier peut en varier les formes à l'infini, à l'aide de la brisure, de la césure et de l'enjambement. Nous pourrions prendre dans Ronsard, dans Régnier, dans La Fontaine, dans Racine, des exemples à n'en plus finir. Contentons-nous d'en prendre un dans Chénier, dans son admirable idylle de *Néère*:

> Mon âme vagabonde à travers le feuillage frémira.

N'est-ce pas pour un symboliste un très beau vers de seize pieds?
  Mais Chénier a écrit:

> Mon âme vagabonde à travers le feuilage
> Frémira.

C' est un alexandrin avec un rejet de trois pieds! (Heredia in Huret 1982/1891: 256–7)

One must regret that only with the advent of *vers libre* did the polymorphousness of the alexandrine become visible, generating a new, positive attitude towards its flexibility and resourcefulness: René Ghil found it an adequately 'organic' medium for his verbal-instrumental *Œuvre* in the 1890s and Jules Romains, supplementing its versatility with his 'théorie des accords',[1] used it to express the richly polyphonic experience of *La Vie unanime* (1908) and *Un être en marche* (1910). More recent commentators have restated this case.[2]

But looked at from the point of view of *vers libre*, this rewrite indicates something more disturbing: if we identified the second line as a 4 + 6 decasyllable, or the sixth line as an enneasyllable, we would, in the terms of the original, be mistaken. How determining are the line boundaries in a free-verse poem, how reliable is the scansional strategy of treating free verse as a patchwork of fragments of regular verse, how far should free verse be treated to processes of reconstitution? These are questions to which we are bound to return in ensuing chapters. Let us in the mean time formulate the following caveat: the description of rhythmic units in free verse is more reliable the smaller those units are; once one starts combining those units in larger configurations, one is tempting oneself to choose wrong.

This issue of metrical identification leads on to two further points which will be important in our investigation of free verse, two points which concern two rarely discussed differences between English and French versification: namely processes of metrical amplification and re-duction, and the metrification of pause.

---

[1] See Claire Vanderhoft's article 'Problèmes de métrique dans la poésie unanimiste: La Théorie des accords' (1989).

[2] I think particularly of Robert Champigny (1963: 61): 'Au fond, le moule le plus "libre", celui qui permet sans dommage la plus grande variété dans l'arrangement des mesures, c'est peut-être bien la séquence d'alexandrins qui le fournit.'

In Pound's 'Shop Girl':

> For a moment she rested against me
> Like a swallow half blown to the wall,
> And they talk of Swinburne's women,
> And the shepherdess meeting with Guido.
> And the harlots of Baudelaire.

the poet seems to set a two-line Imagist encounter (ll. 1–2)[3] against, in resistance to, the literarizing, universalizing tendency of critical table talk (ll. 3–5)—the relentless, all-engulfing prolixity of the latter is fixed in the line-initial co-ordinating conjunctions. At first this division might be missed, for after all, if through-read, the poem produces a sequence of pretty regular, but presumably ironic, anapaestic trimeters (× × ⁄ × × ⁄ × × ⁄). Just as the first two lines must resist the last three, so the poem as a whole must resist this unremitting metricality, this concession to Swinburnian rhythms, this convenient encapsulation. It does so by its laconic flatness of tone, which allows the sturdy phrasal configuration to emerge and redispose the continuous metre into a diversity of rhythmic elements:

> For a moment | she rested | against me
> Like a swallow | half blown | to the wall,
> And they talk | of Swinburne's women,
> And the shepherdess | meeting with Guido.
> And the harlots | of Baudelaire.

So we discover that the Imagist introduction is essentially triphrasal as well as trimetric, and that the following literary inflation is, in line with its slacker, self-extending discourse, biphrasal. We might suppose that the triphrasality of the first two lines would endorse their trimetricity, but this is not so. What we have in the first line, in classical foot terminology, is a third paeon (× × ⁄ ×) followed by amphibrachs (× ⁄ ×) and, in the second, a third paeon followed by an iamb and an anapaest. The diversity of 'foot' is partly to be explained by the tensions between repose and instantaneity, reflective fullness and confusion which inform the encounter: the event lasts only a moment, but the verb 'rested' exudes a collectedness, a leisurely control, which the jostling crowd would not

---

[3] Closely comparable with 'In a Station of the Metro', 'L'Art 1910', 'Women before a Shop', or 'The New Cake of Soap'.

seem to allow; the shop-girl may well be catching her breath, recovering her balance, but she does so with a certain classical calmness and ingathering of herself. But then, the swallow, which may evoke grace in its speed, is marked here by an erratic, buffeted flight; while 'rested' suggests a voluntary act, 'half blown' suggests both the involuntary and the incomplete. We might then want to propose that the amphibrach is the core of quietness, stillness, self-collection, and that the addition of an initial weak syllable, in the third paeons, upsets this balance, produces volatility, and that the iamb and anapaest of the second line are failed attempts to recover the stability and symmetry of the amphibrach. Alternatively we might look upon the third paeon as the metric motor of the poem; it is the figure of the image ('Like a swallow') and of its instantaneousness ('For a moment') ('An "Image" is that which presents an intellectual and emotional complex in an instant of time'), and it is the rhythmic figure which includes and synthesizes the 'complexity' of the other feet. And this third paeon is the agent of the incipient redemption of the final three lines; for, if lines 3–5 represent the kind of poem that Pound is glad not to have written, poems in which encounters, with a heavy sensual flavouring, are expressly set up to act as instruments of vicarious pleasure for an unidentified group of *cognoscenti*, there are signs (in the intimate first-name address of Cavalcanti and the fact that his shepherdess is freely chanced upon rather than part of his poetic baggage (cf. Swinburne's women), in the framing and focusing of the last line by the full stop at the end of l. 4) that the poet also parallels his encounter with those of other poets deep in his affections. The 'and' of infinite predication, of the meaningless multipliability of resonant instance (as against the poet's own unique, uncounterfeitable moment with the shop-girl) then becomes the first element in a third paeon which is trying to re-emerge, and in fact, in the final line, does emerge.

The length of this commentary is necessitated by what it is meant to demonstrate: that in Anglo-American free verse the elasticity of the measure (complex foot/phrase) is a crucial source of expressive modality; the integrated complexity of an experience, or stance, grows naturally from the foot's ability to expand and contract, to adapt itself, in the unfolding line, to changes of tone, association, and so on. In other words, it is not difficult to argue that a poem like Pound's 'Shop Girl' is based on a single foot or rhythmic configuration, and that the freedom of its free verse lies in the transformations that this single measure can undergo without entirely losing its identity; one would want to say the same thing about the ⁄ × × ⁄ × ⁄ figure which subtends Pound's 'The Return'. In comparison, French verse finds its various rhythmic units peculiarly isolated from each other. Just as an alexandrine and a decasyllable only relate to each other as fundamentally different metres, with different metrical constraints and degrees of constraint applying to them (particularly in relation to the caesura), rather than as expanded or contracted forms of each other, so the difference between a hexasyllable and a pentasyllable is the apparently unbridgeable incompatibility of a *vers pair* (line with an even number of syllables) and *vers impair* (line with an odd number of syllables), whose radical separation is enforced by a whole ideology enshrined in a polarized terminology:

On pourrait, en schématisant un peu exagérément, dire que la 'force de persuasion' du poème [*Anabase*] vient des mètres pairs et la 'force de séduction' des mètres impairs. L'un lui donne sa vigueur, sa rigueur, son caractère stable; l'autre l'instabilité, l'imprécision, la douceur. L'un est plus statique, l'autre plus dynamique. L'un confère au langage la solennité, la régularité, l'équilibre; l'autre provoque la mobilité, la vitalité, le frisson. (Favre 1977: 25)

Cornulier (1989: 82) warns us against becoming an easy prey to this kind of metrical indoctrination; each case should be judged on its merits:

souvent, non content de caractériser *l'ensemble* des derniers vers de Rimbaud par les quelques 55% de vers qui s'y trouvent impairs, on caractérise esthétiquement tous ces vers impairs, de longueurs diverses, d'un seul coup d'un seul, par des qualifications censées valoir pour tous—forcément, puisque, croit-on, *un* vers de nombre (total) impair incarne *le* mètre impair en général. On puise donc dans un stock connu d'épithètes du genre: *insaisissable, impalpable, déséquilibré* ou même *boiteux* ou *irrégulier* . . . si par *mètre insaisissable* ou *impalpable* on entend *mètre difficilement perceptible*, alors cette catégorisation n'est pas également correcte pour tous les vers à nombre syllabique total impair; et elle n'est pas également fausse de tous ceux à total pair.

It cannot be denied that the kinds of quality attributed respectively to the *pair* and to the *impair* played an important part in the polemics and hermeneutics of late nineteenth-century metrical affairs, and with some justification. After all Leconte de Lisle did say that 'le vers français vit d'équilibre, il meurt si on touche à sa parité' (Huret 1982/1891: 239); after all the *vers impair* has all the look of a *vers faux*, does raise doubts in the reader's mind about numeracy; after all, even if enneasyllables sometimes look like dissolving decasyllables, sometimes like amplified octosyllables, and if the hendecasyllable sometimes strikes one as a hypoalexandrine and sometimes as a hyperdecasyllable (Scott 1990: 86), the fact remains that this metrical ambiguity looks more like a deliberate act of sabotage, a disrespectful carelessness, of the *pair* lines on either side, than a development out of either, an extension of their resources.

What is quite clear, however, is that this kind of debate, and these kinds of conditioned attitude, are entirely inappropriate to free verse, where there are no guarantees that a string of syllables really add up to the ten one wants them to—particularly if they involve doubts about *synaeresis and *diaeresis, or about the status of the *e atone*—or that, if they do, it is appropriate to identify them as an instance of that traditional entity, the decasyllable, with its specific metricality, which must be differentiated from the metricality of the enneasyllable and hendecasyllable at all costs, if it is to maintain its identity at all. But the view to take about syllabic ambiguity in free verse (*e atone*, synaeresis/diaeresis) is surely not that the poet has failed to make his wishes clear and that therefore we should take it into our hands to try and ascertain his policy, but that he has quite consciously left the matter open, not only to create what Jean-Pierre Bobillot calls 'élasticité métrico-prosodique', allowing one text to produce several rhythmic versions of itself (Bobillot, for example, finds three texts in Apollinaire's 'Les Colchiques', 1990), but also to break down the barriers between different line-types, between *pair* and *impair*, to ease transitions between them, so that processes of amplification and contraction of a single measure can be seen to take place in the manner described in our treatment of Pound's 'Shop Girl'. It is no coincidence that those prosodic commentators who have come closest to providing some kind of account of Saint-John Perse's rhythmics, based on notions of expansion and contraction, have resorted, quaintly perhaps, to classical feet as their units of measurement (iamb, anapaest, and fourth paeon (× × × ⁄, called just 'péon') (see Bateman 1976; Favre 1977).

For the second aspect of this comparison, pausing, we need to turn back to Coventry Patmore, and his 'Essay on Metrical Law' (1878). Like Hopkins after him, Patmore subscribed to an *isochronous view of metre, i.e. that each measure (foot, *dipode, etc.) of a given metre is equal in duration—not *exactly* equal, but perceived as approximately equal; according to Patmore, isochrony is 'the primary condition of metre in all languages' (1894/1878: 249). This means that syllables need to be treated more as values, like musical notes, than as stress-factors; it further means that, as readers, we should be aware of the contextual acoustic input to a syllable's value.

Patmore's insistence on isochrony underlines two other convictions in his work. First, that the reading mind constantly works to restore regularity. If the relationship between the reader and metre is to be an active and involved one, then the reader, like the poet himself, must work to construct the metre rather than passively obey it: 'The best poet is not he whose verses are the most easily scanned . . . but rather he . . . who, in his verse, preserves everywhere the living sense of metre, not so much by unvarying obedience to, as by innumerable small departures from, its *modulus*' (1894/1878: 223). The regularity of metre is not a regularity imposed, but a regularity restored (by complex processes of compensation) out of the irregularities which themselves have served to enliven metre.

Secondly, and consequently, that metre is not a sequence of physical events, but of mental adaptations of physical events, and that these adaptations operate within fairly wide margins of tolerance. Modern generative theorists have the virtue of trying to describe metre in terms of margins of tolerance; but for them, metre is a question of linguistic fact rather than of mental percept, and thus their margins of tolerance are located elsewhere, in linguistic rules rather than in negotiations of the ear. Patmore's metrical theory is novel inasmuch as it tries, implicitly at least, to revise poetics: verse is not simply a certain kind of linguistic structure designed to maximize acoustic and semantic productivity; it is a certain kind of linguistic structure which activates in the reader processes of compensation and supplementation, which take him/her directly into the text's invisible inside and underside, acoustic as well as semantic.

In view of these convictions, it is not surprising that Patmore should wish to establish the metrical reality of pause. The basis of Patmore's case is provided by two propositions: first, that grammatical stops and metrical stops are very different things, metrical stops being more significant and usually longer; secondly, that the pauses at the caesura and line-ending are measurable because they are constituted by the absence of one or more syllables or feet (*catalexis). Patmore goes on to propose that the six-syllable iambic 'is the most solemn of all our English measures . . . the reason being, that the final pause in this measure is greater, when compared with the length of the line, than in any other verse' (1894/1878: 243). He quotes the first stanza of his own 'Night and Sleep' as an example:

> How strange it is to wake × ∕
> And watch, while others sleep, × ∕
> Till sight and hearing ache × ∕
> For objects that may keep × ∕ . . . etc.

If the catalectic feet of the line-terminal pauses were 'filled up', the verse would change from the slowest and most mournful to the 'most rapid and high-spirited of all English metres' (p. 243), the octosyllabic quatrain, the only truly *acatalectic (not syllabically deficient) metre in English. Hopkins declared himself convinced by these arguments. Like the white paper which surrounds the poem, pauses in verse are embedded in its substance, full of speechless expressivity, of acoustic and semantic reverberation. Any metrical theory which ignores pausing as part of the metrical framework risks nullifying one of the crucial, genre-specific resources of verse. The metrification of pause acknowledges the fact that the reading of verse is a continuous experience, from beginning to end; metrical awareness does not proceed by a series of caesurally and line-terminally interrupted spasms, but informs the whole process of our inhabitation of the poem.

If we turn back to Pound's 'Shop Girl', in the light of the foregoing arguments, and if we opt, for the moment, for the third paeon ($\times \times \prime \times$) as the metrical constant, then we might scan the first two lines thus:

$$
\begin{array}{lll}
\overset{\times\ \times\ \prime\ \times}{\text{For a moment}} \overset{(\times)}{} & \overset{\times\ \times\ \prime\ \times}{\text{she rested}} \overset{(\times)}{} & \overset{\times\ \prime}{\text{against me}} \overset{\times}{} \\
\overset{\times\ \times\ \prime\ \times}{\text{Like a swallow}} \overset{(\times)}{} & \overset{\times\ \times\ \prime}{\text{half blown}} \overset{(\times)}{} & \overset{\times\ \times\ \prime}{\text{to the wall}} \overset{(\times)}{}
\end{array}
$$

I do not want to embark here on an analysis of what these metrical pause-inserts signify in detail, but it is clear that the very rhythm of the placement of these silent off-beats itself constitutes much of the psychological and emotional dynamic that lies hidden beneath the words.

It is not certain whether Claudel had read Patmore's 'Essay on English Metrical Law' or not, but his attraction to the English Catholic poet's irregular odes, some ten of which he translated, is not surprising:[4] his interest in Pindar would explain it, as would his notion of the 'iambe fondamental'. But more particularly Claudel is wedded to the idea of the verse-line's (and indeed the measure's) necessary completion by a blank:

Le vers composé d'une ligne et d'un blanc est cette action double, cette respiration par laquelle l'homme absorbe la vie et restitue une parole intelligible. (1963/ 1928: 64)

L'erreur la plus grossière de l'alexandrin qui devient insoutenable dès que l'oreille s'est formée à la règle que je viens d'énoncer plus haut, c'est qu'il fausse le principe essentiel de la phonétique française en attribuant à chaque syllabe une valeur égale tandis qu'une forte longue par exemple a besoin pour sa pleine résolution non seulement d'un grand blanc qui l'accueille, mais d'un nombre suffisant de brèves et de longues moindres qui la prépare. (1963/1928: 67–8)

---

[4] For further discussion of this kinship, see Guyard (1959).

But the blank, the pause, can only isolate or insulate for Claudel, as it could for Mallarmé before him; it is an essentially recuperative space, a space which is rich in repercussion, consolidation, divagation, but which is non-metrical. This condition of French pause relates to two inescapable prosodic facts. Because the tonic accent in French is a feature of the word-group or phrase rather than of the word, French verse can make no convenient distinction, as Patmore does, between grammatical stops and metrical stops; there is, as it were, no inherently metrical pause; and when Apollinaire removed punctuation from the proofs of *Alcools*—

Pour ce qui concerne la ponctuation je ne l'ai supprimée que parce qu'elle m'a paru inutile et elle l'est en effet, le rythme même et la coupe des vers voilà la véritable ponctuation et il n'en est point besoin d'une autre (letter to Henri Martineau, 19 July 1913, Décaudin 1966: 768)

—he was in one sense, only acknowledging an in-built redundancy. Secondly, because of the *isosyllabic principle of French versification, all French verse-lines are by definition acatalectic; that is to say, French metre resides exclusively in its syllables, in its textual presence, and it is for this reason that not only are the status of syllables and matters of pronunciation so crucially important, but also the lines drawn between different kinds of verse-line, as already discussed, are so categorical. But has this situation taken a new turn in free verse? Has the pause found a new lease of metrical life? Claudel may be right to dismiss the isochrony of French syllables—the justification for doing so has been demonstrated by experimental phonetics on many occasions—but can isochrony operate at the level of the measure, or the line?

Quite properly Claudel insists on the relativity not only of syllable, but of accentuation; accents themselves can create rhythmic configurations, by creating patterns of recurrence and variation both in their relative nature (accents of duration, pitch, intensity) and in their relative strength. Even the tetrametric alexandrine is, after all, a sequence, in its regular form, of two dipodes:

$$\underline{\quad (\prime) \quad \prime\prime \quad (\prime) \quad \prime\prime \quad}$$

in which the second accent of the pair is stronger than the first. But this basic pattern can be infinitely varied. And we have already had reason to mention Verluyten's argument for a 'rythme sous-jacent alternant' in French prosody. However much this last may owe to the proposals of the generativists Chomsky and Halle (1968) about the inherently alternating nature of English stress, a renewed interest in the accentual structure of

French has emerged with the emergence of free verse (1886) and is part of the shift in rhythmic perception that made free verse possible. Inasmuch as the constraints of French metre were identified as centring on a preoccupation with the syllable, any countervailing force was bound to reaffirm the claims of accentual thinking. The suggestion that French verse might be accent-timed rather than syllable-timed coincided, as we have seen, with the destabilization of syllabic values (*e atone*, diaeresis/synaeresis), which immediately facilitated a more 'improvised' approach to rhythm, by both poet and reader. At the same time, accent itself was more flexibly perceived, and not merely in the ways just mentioned; aside from the **accent tonique*, the word-group accent which segments the syntactic chain into rhythmic measures, free-verse theorists drew attention to intra-phrasal accents (which often ambiguate tonicity) and to supra-segmental accents or features of accent, those relating to stance, sustaining tone or speech-act, called variously the **accent d'impulsion* (Kahn 1897) or the **accent oratoire* (Souza 1892; Mockel 1962/1894). Accent is no longer bound to, and ensured by, a fixed number of syllables; the demands of accent govern length of measure, or are careless of it. Although for many poets, therefore, the line continued to be a central rhythmic *point de repère* (see Scott 1990), free verse tended to reinforce the view we have already canvassed, namely that the real locus of French rhythmic organization was not the line, but the stanza. With this difference, that the free-verse stanza affirms a rhythmic inimitability, which supersedes the line, while in regular verse the stanza affirms a metrical conformity and repeatability, which the line contributes to and is endorsed by.

I ended *Vers Libre: The Emergence of Free Verse in France 1886–1914* (1990) with this statement:

As we move from regular verse to free verse, rhythm ceases to be an affair of aesthetics, or of genre, or of linguistic convention; it ceases to be something objective, something which inheres in a linguistic configuration, something which is perceptible in language, and becomes the very relationship between subject and language, becomes, as it were, the experiential dimension of utterance. In this sense, the rhythm of *vers libre* is not quantitative but qualitative, is made not of homogeneous elements but of heterogeneous ones, is not susceptible to external chronometric measurement (the metronome) but is deeply implicated in the relativities of inner duration. (pp. 302–3)

To describe rhythm as a principle of repetition is to desemanticize and to displace it; rhythm is not to be dissociated from the particularity of its context (the verse-instance); it is part of the dynamic of perception and cognition, rather than an anterior or posterior hypostatization. The perception of rhythm is a psychological need, the means whereby phenomena are made sense of, and sensory stimuli are absorbed as subjective percepts. Rhythm compels the text to recover its status as enunciation (process), to resist being something that already exists, the enunciated (product).

Perhaps the most serious charge of all that can be brought against generative metrics is its erasure of rhythm; by setting out to formulate a set of correspondence rules which will anticipate all possible manifestations of a particular metre, the generativists effectively neutralize rhythm as a value, assuming it to be merely a feature of metrical complexity or of non-metricality. Linguistic variables are built into a predictive set of metrical options so that, in one important sense at least, novelty is preemptively denied to any new poem. Put another way, rhythm and metre, in generative terms, combine as surface structure and deep structure, with a clear privileging of metre, which determines what is possible within the rules of rhythmic transformation. Rhythm is thus assimilated to metre as a dimension of its complexity, rather than standing in tension against it, as a fundamentally different principle. If one argues that free verse cannot by definition be served by generative metrics, one might want to add that the modes of approach of generative metrics are peculiarly unsuited to French versification, since regular French verse's metricality, however strict, is minimal.

Plato described 'rhythm' as 'the name for order in movement' (*Laws* 2. 655a), and the kinetic element is crucial. Symmetry and proportion as spatial percepts can only become rhythm through the motions of the eye. Rhythm is thus not accessible in the text, but only in the linear reading of the text. It is to do with response, and with what activates and informs response, the transformations of choreography into dance. Many would argue not only that to place rhythm in the space between text and reader is to mystify it and remove it from investigation, but that it must be replaced in the text, and specifically in the patterns of structural differentia which derive from Saussurean linguistics. But outside metre, this project has been little pursued. And as long as rhythm is where prosodic analysis makes room for paralinguistic features (tempo, pausing, loudness, tone, intonation, etc.), and as long as rhythm is treated as a multilevel phenomenon, it must remain elusive to quantification and measurement.

In *Vers Libre* (1990) I tried to establish a point of departure for the scansion of free verse in the identification of three major types: a free verse of the measure, a free verse of the line, and cadence-accentual free verse. But I needed to emphasize that any scansion of free verse had to be undertaken with a constant awareness that a free-verse poem might not situate itself squarely in any one of these three types, but might occupy the ground between them, or combine the three in its rhythmic organization, or be susceptible of interpretation as any one of the three types. I emphasized, too, that the different kinds and degrees of rhythmicity constitute a seamless continuum, and that one of the essential freedoms of free verse is the freedom to dip into that continuum at any point at any time, according to the expressive needs of the moment and the ongoing fluctuations of the poet's psychophysiological life. This already complex set of variables is further complicated by the need, if one is to do justice to rhythm as just described, to incorporate paralinguistic features as far as possible, at least in some speculative form.

It is the enterprise initiated in *Vers Libre* which I wish to pursue in this set of studies. As in previous work, I will concentrate on particular poems, or particular collections of poems, and I will use these as instruments for the investigation of a series of free-verse features, while at the same time insisting, as previously, on the indissoluble link between scansion and interpretation, rhythm and meaning. The poems and poetic collections have been chosen to allow me to take into account an important factor in the determination of the function and shape of rhythm, namely the mental set, or perceptual ideology, of the poet. This, too, inevitably involves much speculation, but it is on such speculation that the reader develops his own mental set and receptive mechanisms. I have thus followed two thematic currents, the one connected with the kinetic aspect of rhythm: travel (Saint-John Perse, *Éloges* (1911); Cendrars, *Prose du Transsibérien* (1913); Supervielle, *Gravitations* (1925)); and the other with an ability to produce perceptual modifications: the visual arts (Apollinaire, *Calligrammes* (1918); Cendrars, *Dix-neuf poèmes élastiques* (1919) and *Documentaires* (1924); Reverdy, *Sources du vent* (1929)). As can be seen, the figure of Cendrars is both the bridge between the two currents and a substantial presence, partly because the time-span (1910–30) and the topics make it inevitable, and partly because his verse requires those constant adjustments of reading strategy which free verse should accustom us to, and which this book is about. And I have treated the works chronologically, so that the two strands are interwoven and so that any sense of the developing techniques and resources of free verse is not sacrificed to a more artificial thematic arrangement.

2

Saint-John Perse, Éloges *(1911)*
The Prosody of Boundary

IN the introduction, we mentioned that one of Derek Attridge's (1982: 34–55) fundamental objections to generative metrics is its minimization of the temporal dimension of reading. Attridge's concern with the temporal means that although he still operates with the generative notion of tension, it is a tension created by linear encounters with metrical variation, not by simultaneous awareness of a double structure (metre and prosody, or abstract pattern and verse-instance), and for this reason he rejects the term 'counterpoint'. Saint-John Perse has never left his readers in doubt that the temporal dimension, conceived of in Bergsonian terms of experiential duration, the movements of the subjective being, is at the source of his verse:

... alors que la poésie pour moi est avant tout movement—dans sa naissance, comme sa croissance et son élargissement final. La philosophie même du 'poète' me semble pouvoir se ramener, essentiellement, au vieux 'rhéisme' élémentaire de la pensée antique ... Et sa métrique aussi, qu'on lui impute à rhétorique, ne tend encore qu'au mouvement, dans toutes ses ressources vivantes, les plus imprévisibles. D'où l'importance en tout, pour le poète, de la mer. (1972: 563)

Part of Perse's espousal of Heraclitan flux ('rhéisme') is expressed in his fondness for italic script,[1] that script which still bears the mark of the handwritten, which resists the lapidary quality of upright roman by its forward inclination, by the calligraphic presence of the practising hand.[2] It is also evident perhaps, at least in the pre-World War II poems, in the

---

[1] In a letter to Valéry Larbaud of 20 Sept. 1923, Perse lays down as his conditions for the publication of *Anabase*: 'mon assentiment au choix de la revue; publication intégrale de l'ensemble; pseudonymat; impression en italique; et service d'épreuves' (1972: 803). Returning to this matter in another letter to Larbaud, of 13 Oct. 1923, Perse stipulates: 'Si Gallimard peut m'offrir une bonne édition de grand format, avec une belle et pleine italique, je lui réserverai cette publication en librairie' (1972: 805).

[2] Unfortunately the Pléiade edition of Perse's *Œuvres complètes* (1972) does not maintain the italic typeface to be found in the 'Poésie-Gallimard' edition (1960) and the two-volume *Œuvre poétique* (1962).

restriction of line-initial capitals to the beginnings of sentences; lower-case initial letters draw the voice on, deny the reader the opportunity of adopting a stance before the line, help, as we shall see, to soften inter-linear rhythmic contours. Finally, we might draw attention to remarks like those of Robichez (1977: 61–2), on the characteristic hesitancy of much of Perse's syntax, feeling its way forward towards revelation, resolution, seizure of reality or meaning: 'D'où, par exemple, un certain bégaiement, comme si l'idée, l'émotion, en quête de leur forme, allaient vers elle à tâtons' (p. 62).

It is considerations such as these which seem to me to make that scansion of Perse's verse which consists in the hunting out of regular units (alexandrines, decasyllables, octosyllables) mistaken. It would be difficult to deny that Perse's poetry is full of instances and traces of these units, a fact borne out by his own oft-quoted remark to Katherine Biddle (12 Dec. 1955):

Nous parlerons une autre fois de cette question de métrique interne, rigoureusement traitée dans la distribution générale et l'articulation de grandes masses prosodiques (où sont bloqués, par strophes ou laisses, dans une même et large contraction, avec la même fatalité, tous éléments particuliers traités comme vers réguliers—ce qu'ils sont en réalité). Il est facile, évidemment, au lecteur étranger de se méprendre sur cette économie générale d'une versification précise encore qu'inapparente, et qui n'a absolument rien de commun avec les conceptions courantes du 'vers libre', du 'poème en prose' ou de la grande 'prose poétique'. C'est même de tout le contraire qu'il s'agit là. (1972: 922)

Within this quotation would seem to lie ample justification for the kinds of prosodic analysis undertaken by, among others, Émilie Noulet (1965), Arthur Knodel (1966), Yves-Alain Favre (1977), and François Moreau (1987), all of whom, to a greater or lesser extent, subscribe to the view that Perse's verse is conspicuously metrical and can usefully be approached from traditional verse-lines. My objections to this procedure are fivefold. First, to suppose that Perse's rhythms are metrical in origin, that they assort themselves to ready-made exemplars from prosodic history's pattern-book, is to overlook two other passages from the same letter to Katherine Biddle, in which Perse refers not only to the poet's own 'input', in typically Bergsonian terms:

L'important, sous quelque déterminisme que ce soit et sous quelque dimension (la troisième ou la quatrième?), sera toujours le fait 'biologique' du poète en 'symbiose' (l'affreux mot!) avec la vie propre du poème. La justification première du poème sera toujours dans son élan vital . . . (1972: 922)

but also to the moulding presence of the subject itself, which comes to inform the linguistic configuration, or the poet himself, so that the poet's verse acts out the subject:

C'est que, dans la création poétique telle que je puis la concevoir, la fonction même du poète est d'intégrer la chose qu'il évoque ou de s'y intégrer, s'identifiant à cette chose jusqu'à la devenir lui-même et s'y confondre: la vivant, la mimant, l'incarnant, en un mot, ou se l'appropriant, toujours très *activement*, jusque dans son movement propre et sa substance propre. (1972: 921)

The discovery of pre-existent metres in Perse's verse constitutes the discovery of those metres, of their consecratedness, not of a poet, a subject, and a verse-form in tight, symbiotic relationship; it constitutes at best the discovery of an appropriateness, rather than of an appropriation; it can cast light on the subject only in the most general terms, as a feature of the ritual or the sacred.

Secondly, the pursuit of regular units within larger linguistic masses involves crucial decisions about segmentation and distribution, questions which cannot really be answered and which certainly should not be answered on the basis of what one needs to find (and the need to find bespeaks an unnerving lack of confidence in constructively improvised reading). Knodel (1966: 32) finds, in the final two verses of 'Éloges IX', 'two lines approximately the length of an alexandrine' plus 'two roughly decasyllabic lines'. Presumably if a line is 'approximately' or 'roughly' something, it is also approximately or roughly something else. Knodel's two decasyllables run:

> comme la présence d'une joue... O bouffées!
> Vraiment j'habite la gorge d'un dieu

so that, in fact it is more like a decasyllable preceded by an alexandrine or rather by a dodecasyllable, since the sixth syllable of the first line is an *e atone*. In fact, of course, Perse's line-division falls

> ... comme la présence d'une joue... O
> bouffées!... Vraiment j'habite la gorge d'un dieu.

So perhaps it is a decasyllable followed by an alexandrine (with a **césure enjambante*)? Or perhaps it is a measure of two syllables ('bouffées') sandwiched between two decasyllables? But is the 5 + 4 + 1 pattern of the first line really identifiable as a decasyllable? Why cannot it simply be left as it is, as 5 + 4 + 1?

The process of carving up the Persean **verset* to fit a variety of Procrustean beds of regular metres, whose combination remains apparently unrationalized or irrational, leads to my third objection, namely the preemptive attitude towards syllabic status that it necessitates. Confronted by this element from Perse's *Vents* (I. 4)

comme aux gisements des villes saintes de poterie blanche

Moreau (1987: 76) offers first an **alexandrin trimètre*, although this involves one standard and one non-standard instance of **apocope* (removal of word-terminal *e atone*) and two instances of **syncope* (removal of word-internal *e atone*), thus:

comme aux gis(e)ments | des villes saint(e)s | de pot(e)ri(e) blanche.   4 + 4 + 4

Moreau goes on:

Le lecteur qui trouverait cette prononciation trop heurtée pourra préférer un système à octosyllabe et décasyllabe emboîtés:

$$\overbrace{\text{comme aux gis(e)ments/des villes sain}}^{8}\text{/tes de poteri(e) blanche}$$
$$\underbrace{\phantom{\text{comme aux gis(e)ments/des villes sain/tes de poteri(e) blanche}}}_{10}$$

To offer the reader alternative readings is admirably open-minded, but under such constraints? What satisfaction is to be derived from hearing a sequence of three tetrasyllables (which, as if by magic, can then be called an *alexandrin trimètr*e, but on what contextual evidence?) only on condition that three syllables are first removed? Why cannot we hear a sequence of 5 + 4 + 6? And why is the **emboîtage* in the second line necessary? No metrical or interpretational justification is provided. Are the combinations octosyllable + 6, or 5 + decasyllable, some kind of rhythmic anathema? And how unconvincing this octosyllable and decasyllable are as octosyllable and decasyllable, in terms of structural coherence, of location of caesura and/or juncture. Saint-John Perse's verse, paradoxically, thanks to a method which seeks to establish his metrical credentials, turns out to be a ragbag of heterogeneous and inconsistent practices, stalked by decasyllabic and octosyllabic impostors.

This lack of contextual evidence for making metrical choices, which consequently can only seem arbitrary, a strangely neurotic end-in-itself, only underlines what has already been said in the introductory chapter: intertextual justifications for finding odd examples of regular verse-lines in alien contexts have only a limited validity; in the end, context alone bestows identity, coherence, and cohesion. To read Saint-John Perse without reference to the whole *verset*, yet alone to the whole stanza (strophe), is to set at nil all he has himself bothered to say about movement, *élan vital*, and the combinatory virtues of the stanza. To transform the Persean stanza into a patchwork of regular lines is to immobilize it, as a set of hermetically insulated rhythmic intervals which relate less to each other than to the pattern-book. Only by adopting the perspective of the stanza do we liberate ourselves from the need to construct temporary shelters along the way, shelters which then become unjustifiably obtrusive landmarks or *points de repère*. The virtue of the stanzaic perspective is that it does not compel us to formulate intermediate levels of combination; the *verset* or stanza can maintain its fundamental rhythmic units in their primary state (or almost, since some elementary combination, at the level of the phrase, is inevitable), and will thus not be embarrassed by the presence of, say, syllabic groups of five or seven. Rhythm in Perse is both in movement and expanding, not in the sense that its individual measures are getting larger, or combining in a sequence of larger units, but in the sense that more rhythm becomes available to the reader, more rhythmic duration, so that like a life inhabited by the mechanisms of Proustian memory, the poem, or stanza or *verset*, becomes richer in experiences of association, forgetting, focusing, and remembering.

My fifth and final objection relates to another kind of assumption, or set of assumptions, namely those about what constitutes metre. Is English metre as exclusively stress-orientated as the generative metrists would have us believe? Easthope for one (1983: 56–64) does not think so; he argues for the centrality of intonation as the determinant of syllabic prominence, and consequently for a relativized version of stress. Is syllabism the continuing source of metrical presence in French verse? Those analysts we have had cause to mention certainly think so. Or is it accent, and accentual variation, that the poets of free verse seek to exploit as the source of rhythmicity? There is undoubtedly much truth in this, as we have already pointed out. But it only requires a shift of optic to locate rhythmic presence elsewhere, or at least to diversify its presence. And it would be strange indeed if one of the express functions of the adoption of free verse had not been that of activating new rhythmic resources and new attitudes to rhythmicity. It seems to me to do little justice to the deeply exploratory nature of Perse's poetry to subject it to rhythmically foregone conclusions, or to use notions of rhythmic regularity to reassure the bewildered reader, the reader who has not yet learned to read Perse (for with each poet we undertake anew this autodidactic journey towards fruitfulness), that he means us no harm, that he is still playing the old tunes. With this kind of prejudicial forestalling, we shall learn nothing by reading.

It is this challenge that I wish to begin to take up in this chapter. Where (else) might rhythm be in Perse's poetry? What particular linguistic elements might contribute to the music which is peculiarly his? The material for this step-by-step investigation will be provided by *Éloges* (1911), and particularly by extracts from 'Écrit sur la porte', 'Pour fêter une enfance I' and 'Éloges IX'; in deference to the 1911 edition I omit consideration of 'Images à Crusoé', which, first published in 1909, were only to become part of the collection *Éloges* in the edition of 1925. It may seem an odd collection to choose in the light of my declared interest in free verse thematically imprinted by travel, since it is motivated by a nostalgic return to the Antillean cockpit, or, as Richard puts it (1964: 32) to the 'épaisseur d'un monde dont l'arrondi . . . lui fournit un merveilleux abri'. But the security of this child's universe is beset by the irritants of growth, the beckonings of space, the quest for an adequate language; the journey backwards must constitute a reimagining of the journey forwards, and the very tropical setting is itself constantly experienced as a provocation, both linguistic and spiritual, to transcend category and boundary, to transform *nomen* into *numen*.

The poem which finds itself as liminary in the 1925 edition is, not surprisingly, 'Écrit sur la porte'. This poem is originary inasmuch as it adopts the point of view of the father of the child, the point of view that the child will come to inhabit with a radically different awareness. It is about colonialism, or colonial attitudes, but cast more in the enlightened eighteenth-century mould of the chain of being than in the nineteenth-century Darwinian mode of a competitive order of species; the position of the planter-persona is a deistically central, but transcendent, one; indeed his return home operates as a religious consecration of the order, with his daughter acting as ministering priestess and celebrant. Rather than a colonialism of exploitation and subjugation, therefore, we see an individual whose work affirms an order of being which includes not only the proper distinctions between master and servant, human and animal, but also between the sexes (st. III). Or rather, the planter's return home from the coffee and cocoa plantations, after having symbolically 'tested' them for ripeness, is a ritual passage, daily repeated, from necessary exploitation to the purified ascesis of the steward of cosmic order; the planter is the more apt for the cleansing administered by his daughter, the dirtier and sweatier he has made himself in the pursuit of the fruitfulness of other people's earth. The poet allows us to see these ironies, partly through the way the planter uses the whiteness of his daughter (and indeed his house and clothing) to counteract his own inevitable assimilation to the climate and environment (v. 1), partly through a rather preciously abstract language:

En souriant, elle *m'acquitte de* ma face ruisselante . . .

(v. 7)

et *faisant grâce à* son cheval de l'étreinte des genoux . . .

(v. 13)

which may be intended as an ennobling, ritualizing transfiguration of simple acts, but which also disfigures simple acts, by aligning them with the exercise of colonial power in magnanimous gestures of liberation or forgiveness. Nor do we miss the note of unwarranted conceit in the final line:

que j'aperçois à la hauteur du toit de tôle sur la mer comme un ciel.

(v. 18)

In other contexts ('Je parle d'une haute condition . . .', 'dans la haute demeure', 'de hauts navires de musique' (FE I, IV, V)),[3] the terms 'haut' and 'hauteur' are particularly valorized, and the 'la tôle des toits' is suffused with solar splendour (E XVI). But here, the measuring of the conjunction of sea and sky against the height of the roof, with the implication that the roof is the instrument of that conjunction, and the setting of the 'toit de tôle' against the 'voiles des voiliers', without any sense of the incongruity of either number (singular against plural) or sound (/twa/ and /tol/ clumsily aping the sounds and near-perfect consonance of /vwalə/ and /vwalje/), reveal the self-aggrandizing delusions of the colonial, whose horizons do not stretch beyond the area of his own immediate authority.

The element in this poem's prosody which I wish to scrutinize first is rhythmic boundary, or rather the rhythm of boundary. The rhythmic potentialities of boundary have always been available and often exploited, but never systematically taken into rhythmic account. The regular tetrametric alexandrine, the third line of the first stanza of 'Le Lac' for example:

Ne pourrons-nous ⌐ jamais⌐ sur l'océan ⌐ des âges,⌐

---

[3] Here, as in ensuing pages, the following abbreviations are used: EP—'Écrit sur la porte'; FE—'Pour fêter une enfance'; E—'Éloges'.

will tend to produce a pattern in which the caesural and line-terminal boundaries will produce a break in enunciation (marked ˥), while the secondary accents within the hemistich will be characterized by an intonational fluctuation without a rupture in continuity (marked ⌢); it might be more accurate to mark the first of these secondary accents by – to indicate greater suspension at the boundary: 'ne pourrons-nous ⊤ jamais ˥'. But even the regular alexandrine will encompass many variations in this pattern, as for example in the first line, which looks more like:

Ainsi˥, toujours poussés‾vers de nouveaux⌢rivages˥.

And beyond questions of variation, there are equally questions of placement, created by ambiguities in the pattern of accentuation. Thus Baudelaire's line:

Vous me rendez l'azur du ciel immense et rond
('La Chevelure')

might be read as either:

Vous me rendez⌢l'azur˥du ciel immense‾et rond˥ 4 + 2 + 4 + 2

or as

Vous me rendez⌢l'azur‾du ciel˥immense et rond.˥ 4 + 2 + 2 + 4

This system of notation is crude and ever open to debate, as one would expect with any feature which reaches from the linguistic into the paralinguistic, which requires the reader to supplement the data of text with a dose of response. What is clear is that rhythmic boundary is the point at which prosodic punctuation may be non-coincident with grammatical punctuation. What is equally clear is that free verse, with its greater recourse to intra-phrasal accents and its absence of syllabic indicators, poses the question of placement more acutely, just as its ambiguous attitude to the status of the *e atone* diversifies the types of boundary connected with that particular phoneme. And we should, finally, be clear about the kinds of prosodic phenomena which are connected with boundary investigation; these are primarily factors of enunciation (pausing, voice suspension, inflection, intonation) which have consequences for, or indeed derive from, attitudes towards the connections between syntactic units. Inevitably involved also is the moulding of accentuation, and questions about its pitch, intensity, and duration.

But why does boundary seem the appropriate place to begin a prosodic exploration of Perse's poetry? Critics have not been slow in drawing our attention to it, whether it is called boundary, frontier, or threshold:

In all the multiple polarities considered above there is a frontier, a threshold. It lies between the known and the unknown, the known and the dreamed, loneliness and solitude, solitude and society, land and sea, land and sky, not having and having, not moving and moving, between, in fact, the negative pole of exile and the positive role of poetry. Every barrier must be converted into a frontier by action and movement . . . it is the symbol *par excellence* of separation and interpenetration. (Little 1973: 109)

And any cursory reading of *Éloges* will reveal the nagging insistence of terms such as 'règne', 'confins', 'limite', 'murs', 'maison', or more specific references to division:

> . . . et le nageur
> a une jambe en eau tiède mais l'autre pèse dans un courant frais; . . .
>
> (E XVI)

Underlying all this is the challenge posed by the *verset* itself, a unit which is a challenge to the respiration, to pacing, to segmentation, a piece of text in which orientation has still to be achieved, which often, by its length alone, demands to be put together as its unfolds, in a hesitant process of articulation.

The second stanza of 'Écrit sur la porte' runs:

Et d'abord je lui donne mon fouet, ma gourde et	3 + 3 + 3 + 2
mon chapeau.	+ 4
En souriant elle m'acquitte de ma face ruisselante;	4 + 4 + 4 + 4
et porte à son visage mes mains grasses d'avoir	+ 2 + 4 + 2 + 4
éprouvé l'amande de kako, la graine de café.	3 + 2 + 4 + 2 + 4
Et puis elle m'apporte un mouchoir de tête	2 + 4 + 5
bruissant; et ma robe de laine; de l'eau pure pour	+ 2 + 3 + 4' + 4'
rincer mes dents de silencieux:	+ 3 + 2 + 5
et l'eau de ma cuvette est là; et j'entends l'eau du	2 + 4 + 2 + 3
bassin dans la case-à-eau.	+ 4 + 5

Before proceeding any further, we should return to our remark that the ambiguous status of the *e atone* in free verse diversifies types of boundary. It is customary among analysts of free verse to find a fairly widespread adoption of the approach to the *e atone* canvassed by Gustave Kahn in his 'Préface sur le vers libre' (*Premiers poèmes*, 1897), namely that at the end of any accentual group, it should be treated like a line-terminal *e atone* in regular verse (not counted, but potentially phonated to a greater or lesser extent, or as he also puts it, regarded as a 'simple intervalle' (p. 31))), while within the rhythmic measure it should follow the rules of elision and retention that operate in regular verse. Thus Yves-Alain Favre, for example, feels confident in formulating the following principles for Perse's prosody:

- il convient tout d'abord de ne jamais pratiquer la syncope [compare this with François Moreau's attitude, see above p. 28]
- à la fin d'un groupe de mots (série cohérente qui comporte un accent de groupe), l'apocope est de rigueur.
- au contraire, l'*e* caduc doit être maintenu et l'apocope est exclue, au milieu d'un groupe de mots. (1977: 19)

But, of course, it is only necessary to frame 'rules' such as these if one cleaves to syllabicity as the first and underlying principle of French rhythmicity. I am sure that, as a rough guide, Favre's case for the application of the Kahnian model to Perse is justified—the major junctures between clauses and phrases in the *verset*, with their interruptions and falling intonations enjoin on the voice a muting of the 'e', which, if articulated in this exposed position, would sound quaintly archaic. But if exact numbers of syllables do not matter, if, that is, there is no benefit to be had from distinguishing between syllables that are metrical and 'syllables' that are extrametrical, then the treatment of group-terminal, and indeed line-terminal, 'e' can be more freely improvised. I have taken this line in the scansion above, so that even though there are instances of group-terminal 'e' erased by apocope ([E]), there are others treated more as the 'e' of a *coupe lyrique*, a final 'e', that is, which is articulated, but tucked back as it were into the immediately preceding accentuated syllable and followed by a break (←e). One of the advantages of a prosody of boundary is precisely that it restores interpretative freedom to choice about the value of syllables, whereas the scansion that is locked into the recuperation of syllabicity in free verse is likely to make unwarranted choices for purely metrical reasons, when those metrical reasons themselves are questionable. What I have proposed in my scansion, therefore, is a basic set of three types of boundary, namely ⅂, ⌢, and –; these types can be complicated by a variety of treatments of the non-elided *e atone*, to wit [E] (apocope), e→ (equivalent of *coupe enjambante*), and ←e (equivalent of *coupe lyrique*), although certain combinations are obviously impossible: e⅂→, ←⌢e; or less likely: ←⌢e.

These lines belong to the persona of the planter and it is not surprising to find a high incidence of the ⅂ boundary, which sets things apart from each other in time and space, or asserts a dominance and control over linguistic enunciation and the areas of experience it communicates. If there is something peremptory in the temporal and spatial placing—'Et d'abord', 'Et puis', 'est là', 'l'eau du bassin | dans la case-à-eau', l'amande de kako | la graine de café' (which reminds one of the passage in FE III which includes the lines 'A droite / on rentrait le café, à gauche le manioc')—if there is something briskly authoritative in the handing over of the whip or the testing of the crop, the activity of his daughter intro-duces a much greater dissolution of boundaries, or an ambiguation of those which look to maintain their definition. Thus it would do an injury to the way that meaning manifests itself in rhythm if one were to read '. . . mon fouet,⌐ ma gourde⌐ et mon chapeau⌐', where the stronger breaks would convey both a drilled enumeration and the bare gesture of a hand-ing over; but while the 'fouet' signifies actions and relationships unrelated to the daughter (subjection, the relationship with the horse, the beast of a potentially tumultuous outside), the 'gourde' relates to her both by the phoneme /u/, or rather the pair /uR/, about which we shall have more to say, and by the water it holds, the water of her ministrations, the water which is also shared by his '(chap)eau' which in its turn shares a white-ness ('couvert de toile blanche', v. 2) with his daughter. The /uR/ sound is taken up in 'souriant' whose participial form I have registered in the suspensive⁻, so that the simile suffuses the whole exchange; this is then followed by the two ê→ boundaries, which not only begin to undo categorial distinctions, distinctions both of language and sensory experience, but also set themselves, in anticipation, against the two ê→ of the following *verset* upon which they are an ironic comment: for these two ê→ of the following *verset* dissolve no distinction, but rather do the opposite, inas-much as they weld more closely together noun and noun complement, crop and fruit, in a world of severely localized connections safeguarded from other intrusions by a careful husbandry. In the second clause of the second *verset*, I have treated the boundary at 'visage' as [E]⌐ for two reasons: first because a *coupe enjambante* or *lyrique* would be syntactically inappropriate given that 'à son visage' operates as an *incise*, and secondly, despite the fact that both 'face' and 'visage' share the /a/ which punctuates the whole stanza, they are two different faces seen from different points of view: 'face' is the planter's face seen as the centre of a solicitous atten-tion, as the site too of a struggle between the liberating daughter and the clinging sweat of colonial labour; 'visage', on the other hand, the daughter's face, is a physical fact, seen from the exterior, the stage upon which is acted out the planter's absolution from the sordid greasiness of his land-owning obligations. In fact, the planter does not entirely see into himself, for the line-ending momentarily lifts 'avoir' to the status of noun, revealing an altogether more acquisitive motivation, and the testing of the fruit has a self-regarding satisfaction which not only obliterates the daughter's face, but revels in the decorative justifications of acoustic echoes: . . . /e/ . . . /ve/ . . . /la/. . . /də/. . . /dəka/. . . /la/ . . . /dəka/ . . . /fe/ (not forgetting that the /o/ of 'kako' links up with 'chapeau', 'peau', 'eau').

The pattern of doubled e→ in the second and third *versets* of this stanza find an echo of a related but different kind in the fourth: I have designated the boundaries at 'laine' and 'pure' as ←e⌐, that is to say, as breaks involving a back-directed *e atone,* as in a *coupe lyrique.* This *verset* continues in directions already adumbrated in the previous two: the reappropriation of his sovereignty by the planter after having momentarily ceded it to the necessary purgations and purifications of the daughter celebrant. Not surprisingly, therefore, the last two *versets* are conspicuous by the repeated presence of ⌐, and by the way that the 'face↔ ruisselante' pattern is once again denied in 'de tête[E]⌐ bruissant'. This, once again, is partly necessitated by syntax—the agreement of 'bruissant' with 'mouchoir' must be kept clear of the interference of the noun complement—but partly by the planter's ironically triumphant reassumption of the crown of dry noise (despite his own taciturnity) after the mask of unseemly transpiration ('ruisselante'). But the robes and insignia of this coronation still bear a 'withinness' which is something more than colonial retrenchment or the enfolding exclusiveness of the citadel-house: the softness and purity of wool and water do not offer the defensive, resistant inwardness of the planter's rough and unshaven cheek, nor the ill-adapted inwardness of his fever; they offer the inwardness of their own unresisting reality, they offer that transparency or penetrability which is their essence. And so for all the planter's return to complacent itemization, for all the growing insistence of the first-person possessive, the water and wool retain a certain acoustic autonomy, a yielding outline. Not surprisingly, after a rather arch reference to his silence, which deserves its suspensive boundary, given its slightly oxymoronic juxtaposition both with the act of rinsing the mouth and with the utterance of the poem, the planter's repeated invoking of water in the final *verset* of the stanza indicates no inhabitation of its being, but is rather a return to the classifying mode, as different kinds of water are assigned to their appropriate places in an order which is maintained by order.

This crude analysis has attempted to begin to show three things: that a prosody of boundaries can register, indeed embody, local meanings in a way that makes them a kind of subtext; that a prosody of boundaries can also help to project the larger, sustaining meanings of a whole poem or whole collection or, presumably, a whole *œuvre*. The boundaries here, for example, have not only shown a clash between insulation/isolation on the one hand, and categorial interpenetration on the other; but have also suggested a third impulse, in the ←e⌐ boundary, towards an inwardness which is not defensive or insulating, but which is autonomous and penetrative, an experience of the depth of self and other. This is certainly in keeping with the preoccupations of *Éloges* as a whole, the journey forwards that can only be taken on the condition of a journey backwards, to recover the sea and the light, the journey outwards, activated by the restive 'toiles'/'voiles', which must be doubled by an equal and opposite journey inwards:

A présent laissez-moi, je vais seul.

. . . .

Ou bien j'ai une alliance avec les pierres veinées-bleu: et vous me laissez également,
assis, dans l'amitié de mes genoux.

(E xviii)

The third point is that the system of boundaries is rhythmical in a very real sense, not merely as punctuation and juncture, not merely in its many variations between various kinds of momentary rupture and various kinds of supple liaison; but in the patterns it creates within the stanzaic unit; roughly speaking, in as far as our own particular stanza is concerned, we can propose that a sequence of break-boundaries, which render enunciation staccato, clipped, yield momentarily to boundaries which promote depth and liaison, before recovering their initial control, now, however, haunted both ironically and in good faith, by traces of the mentality embodied in the 'softer' boundaries. Where unelided *e atones* occur at break-boundaries they are either suppressed ([E]⌐) or internalized (←e⌐); where they occur group-internally they may constitute a threshold between different attitudes towards, or kinds of, experience which language is able to cross; or alternatively, they may merely confirm a relationship of appropriate belonging ('l'amande de kako', 'la graine de café'), which reinforces the status quo.

Reading the rhythm is a question of the prosodic resources you put at your disposal, and the freedom you allow yourself in the choice of prosodic priorities. We have made our first incision with boundaries, but in the course of the scansion have had cause to incorporate acoustic evidence. It is the relationship between boundary and acoustic considerations which

I now wish to investigate a little further, in the third stanza of 'Écrit sur la porte':

Un homme est dur, sa fille est douce. Qu'elle se	2 + 2 + 2 + 3
tienne toujours	+ 4 + 3
à son retour sur la plus haute marche de la maison	4 + 4 + 3′ + 4
blanche,	+ 2′
et faisant grâce à son cheval de l'étreinte des	4 + 4 + 3
genoux,	+ 4
il oubliera la fièvre qui tire toute la peau du visage	5 + 2 + 2 + 5 + 3
en dedans.	+ 3

[Note: Here, as elsewhere in Perse's work, I have presumed, where appropriate, to treat line-terminal 'e' as a 'full' syllable; 'blanche' (l. 2) echoes 'marche', with its /ʃə/, and more distantly 'douce', to express the daughter's tender inwardness.]

One might immediately say, since we have already referred to the connection between boundaries and local meaning, that the boundaries here have been moulded to the semantics of their immediate lexical environments; thus, for example, the suspensive boundaries at the end of the first *verset* are dictated by the daughter's (enforced) patience; the *coupe enjambante* at 'l'étreinte des genoux' is urged by the remorseless pressure of the knees in the horse's flanks; the break-boundaries after 'oubliera' and 'fièvre' are acts of imperious suppression which are however unable to prevent a vivid recollection of the physiological experience of fever, which takes relentless possession of the rest of the line (a sequence of ten syllables), until it disappears 'inside', in the *verset*'s **clausule*.

In this stanza, we shift from first person to third person as the planter reflects upon the proper demarcation line between the sexes. The broad structure of the stanza is thus fairly rigid: an initial, fundamental distinction, in the first sentence, is 'carried out' in the 2 (female) + 2 (male) pairings of the four lines, a division which is part reinforced, part muddied by an emergent set of *rimes croisées*, the assonant pair in /u/ crossing with the assonant pair in /ɑ̃/. The muddying of the medial division of the stanza is increased by the temporary ambiguity of the syntax of the third *verset*, which looks at first as though it might be a companion clause for the daughter: 'et faisant grâce à son cheval . . . , qu'elle . . .', and by the fact that the boundaries in this third line are non-obstructive, allow greater continuity than we have been used to in the planter's world.

As we have noted, the /u/ of 'douce' has already established itself as the phoneme of the daughter, particularly perhaps in the /uR/ combination ('toujours', 'retour'). And it would be partly true to say that the /y/ of 'dur' is the planter's phoneme, appearing elsewhere in 'mulet', 'rude', 'cuvette', 'suffisantes'—these last are the limited horizons that the planter finds best satisfy his vanity, particularly as he enjoys a superlativity within those limitations ('plus'): 'la plus haute marche', 'mon plus fin cheval' (st. IV). But it would not be entirely reliable to make this distinction: the planter, after all, has a skin 'couleur de tabac rouge', he has a hat 'couvert de toile blanche', he is 'boueux', it is his 'joue' which is 'rude'. Conversely, and most conspicuously, the water offered by the daughter is 'pure'; it is true that this differentiates itself from 'dur', as from its reverse 'rude', by the substitution of the unvoiced bilabial /p/ for the voiced (and where is the 'silencieux' now?) dental /d/, but the /y/ sticks, as does the *e atone*, at least with 'rude'. What I would suggest, therefore, is this: that the /u/ phoneme belongs to the daughter as desired quality and to the planter as despised quality, part of himself he would rather efface; and that the /y/ phoneme belongs to the planter as desired quality (of hardness, definition, but also of superiority), while the daughter tries to infiltrate this quality with other values.

There are, then, two ways in which 'dominant' phonemes relate to boundaries. First and obviously, boundaries project such phonemes; the important thing is that they explore and diversify them at the same time. If we extrapolate 'douce', 'toujours', and 'retour' from the first two *versets*, we find three different kinds of boundary, one suggesting inwardness, one duration and long-suffering, and one the certainty of the goal achieved. In the inexhaustible dispute about the relationship between sound and sense, we should be at pains to remember that this is by no means a dispute about a one-to-one relationship, whatever one decides; sounds may be identifying or structuring elements more than they are semantic ones, but this does not prevent particular sounds being 'modalized' by their prosodic environments, so that even though we cannot say that a particular phoneme means something, we can at least say that it assumes various expressive colourings from its linguistic context. Just as lexical items may be variously 'modalized' by their changing position in a regular structure like the alexandrine (see Scott 1986: ch. 1), so lexical items or particular phonemes may be expressively constituted and diversified by prosodic boundaries in free verse.

The second way in which a phoneme may relate to boundary is precisely a matter of relationship, that is to say of relative distance. At the boundary, the phoneme receives maximum accentuation, is the fully acknowledged, not to say celebrated, item, given its own particular aura as a prosodic destination. After 'douce', 'toujours', 'retour' comes 'genoux'; an odd term to valorize, it seems, as regards the planter, but not so as regards the daughter and her values, particularly inasmuch as she is representative of the child's view: we think once again of the final *verset* of 'Éloges':

> assis, dans l'amitié de mes genoux

or of the earlier *verset* (E II):

> . . . et j'ai pressé des lunes à ses flancs sous mes genoux d'enfant . . .

Here, then, it appears that values have been actually transferred from daughter to planter, or that the text has let the reader know that, although 'genoux' may not be of particular significance to either daughter or planter, it is of import to the text itself, or to the subtext of the collection as a whole. We may store this lexeme in our mental repositories for later application. But this notion of linguistic/prosodic sequencing as psychological implantation deserves further attention; and it might be suggested that the further a phoneme is from the point of accentuation, the less consciously it is enacted as a wish or undergone as a fear. The 'oubliera' of the last *verset* is perhaps a case in point; its /ub/ reverses the /bu/ of 'boueux', that despised quality which the daughter is called upon to remove. While the accentuated future ending looks forward to a point beyond discomfort and even shame, the phoneme that carries the stigma is recessed by distance and non-accentuation; indeed, even if we accept Verluyten's proposal of alternating strong and weak syllables in French, the second unit in the /i/lu/bli/ə/Ra/ sequence will be weak, since the sequence runs swsws. The phonetic constitution of 'oublier' is itself a forgetting, just as the following 'toute' hangs away from the boundary's accentuation, in an attempt to minimize itself; unfortunately the articulated 'e' of 'toute' gives it more lexical substance than it wants.

One further feature of boundary might be adverted to. If we accept Kahn's proposition that phrase-terminal non-elided 'e' in free verse can be treated in the same way as line-terminal 'e' in regular verse, should we similarly extend the currency of masculine and feminine endings? This admittedly is a question not about the enunciation of boundaries, but about their interpretation and potential structural function. Such a tactic is certainly at the reader's disposal and would certainly influence the placement of boundaries, if they seemed to provide a resource for embodying a poem's 'sexual' attitudes. I am not surprised to find, among those boundaries marked as group-terminal (ⁿ) in our scansion, two which are feminine in the second line, 'marche' and 'blanche' (furthermore affiliated by their common /ʃə/—is 'cheval', unexpectedly, a force of the feminine?); these are images of the place of the white feminine, both on the ladder of the chain of being, and in the life of the planter. What is more worrying, perhaps, given that in the pattern of 'end-rhymes' the femininity of 'blanche' is, not unexpectedly, superseded by masculinity, is the resurfacing of a feminine ending on 'fièvre' in the last *verset* (I am assuming that the 'e' of 'visage' is strictly speaking elided and therefore *hors de cause*). This has links, I think, with what has already been implied about the duplicity of the /u/ phoneme: the daughter has, as positive attributes, qualities which the planter may despise in himself. But here this is given a more sinister sexual turn; the planter lives for his return to the church-citadel of the white house, to a ritual of purification administered by his daughter, to an inwardness which is an ethnic centredness, an unmaskable racial identity; viewed sexually, however, this inwardness is also a symptom of a malady, a malady which is imputed to the feminine. It is difficult to tell, and perhaps need not be decided, whether it is the feminine as opposite sex or the feminine as sexuality which is adumbrated here; and certainly it is not entirely clear, in relation to the rest of *Éloges*, whether the feminine is a threatening stability or stagnancy in its maternal aspect, or in its eroticism, or both; for though eroticism may seem to herald an awakening, a need to relate elsewhere, a curiosity, it is equally connected with images of warmth, fermentation, and yielding: 'Ces rives gonflent, s'écroulent sous des couches d'insectes aux noces saugrenues' (E IV).

Part of the reason for our investigation of boundaries as one possible source of rhythmic organization in free verse (and in the *verset,* in particular) was scepticism about those scansions which seek to identify recurrent, regular syllabic groupings, especially of a superordinate kind (alexandrine, decasyllable, octosyllable, etc.). One of the objectives of such a scansion is characterization of the superordinate groups involved, either in very broad terms (ritualization, the hallowed difference between *pair* and *impair* lines), or in more precise classifications of the kind offered by Morier in his *Le Rythme du vers libre symboliste* (1943–4): in his study of Henri de Régnier's use of the hendecasyllable, for example, he develops a taxonomy which includes 'le 11 dynamique', 'le 11 majeur', 'le 11 énergétique', 'le 11 emphatique', 'le 11 défaillant', 'le 11 apparent (ou décasyllable à sourdine)', 'le 11 polaire'. Studies like this can be extremely rewarding; but the investigator must be confident about his syllabic data and methods of combination and segmentation; because a difference of one syllable is, in traditional French versification, *all* the difference, syllabic assessment becomes absolutely critical in the very context—free verse—in which it is most beset with uncertainties. Besides, what if one of the objectives of free verse is, after all, to create more proximate or multiple attitudes to the syllable? If this approach is to be espoused, then it seems more advisable to focus on primary units, treated with some margin of tolerance, rather than on starkly defined superordinate groups, on whose definition a whole system of reading either stands or falls. Besides, as we have already argued, scansion by metric group makes a rhythm into a sequence of juxtaposed, fixed intervals, existing in and for themselves, so that ultimately free verse has to surrender its Bergsonian notions of a rhythm which is movement, which is heterogeneous, qualitative, and continuous, and revert to an essentially spatialized view of rhythm, which makes it quantitative, discontinuous, and more or less homogeneous. Without the dynamic of unfolding heterogeneous units, without the dynamic of heterogeneity indeed, the rhythmic perspective of the stanza is lost, because the stanza no longer has the function of synthesizing, justifying, patterning the particular rhythmic choices made.

One way of validating an approach to Perse's verse which focuses on measures not as self-sustaining or essentially prefabricated units, but as modified versions of each other, developing in relationships of expansion and contraction, is to refer back to Perse's enthusiasm for Pindar, expressed in letters to Gabriel Frizeau, 23 March 1908 and 30 April 1911:

... mais il y a dans son ivresse lucide, dans son ivresse à froid, un grand sens unitaire imposant la retenue du souffle—le mouvement même, chez lui, l'indispensable mouvement, s'attachant au seul rythme d'une modulation préassignée. (1972: 734)

Car chez Pindare (le plus délibérément musicien de tous les poètes) le vers est envahi, et toute la strophe (. . . '*invahi*' serait mieux), d'incidences qui font que la ligne mélodique ondule parmi toutes les surprises d'une danse. (1972: 753)

Out of this has grown that 'school' of scansion which makes use of classical concepts and classical feet to trace modulation in Perse's verse. Yves-Alain Favre (1977), for example, for all his flirtation with standard syllabic modes of analysis, concludes:

Plus important que le compte des syllabes, la répartition des voyelles longues et des voyelles brèves, autrement dit des syllabes accentuées et des syllabes dépourvues d'accent. Le rythme devient plus subtil, plus discret, plus secret et charme d'autant mieux. (pp. 25–6)

This leads him to scan by short classical foot-units: iamb ($\times$ ʹ), anapaest ($\times \times$ ʹ), and fourth paeon ($\times \times \times$ ʹ). This is roughly speaking the method also used by Jacqueline Bateman (1976), who traces in particular the privileged interplay between iamb and fourth paeon, emphatically asserts the predominance of tonicity over syllabicity in Perse, and summarizes her findings with these words: 'Voilà illustré le paradoxe de la métrique persienne qui à la fois déborde toute étroite computation et repose sur des mesures syllabiques non pas uniformes mais régulières, avec des rappels et une périodicité sensibles' (p. 49). Nor should the contribution of Pierre van Rutten (1975) be overlooked, for although he sets out from kymograph data (i.e. micro-data derived from the analysis of recorded readings) and thus from beyond the 'common' reader's powers of rhythmic perception, he challengingly introduces intonation, pause, and relative duration among his coordinates of scansion, explores 'les rythmes croissants et décroissants', and suggests that lurking behind the arras of Perse's verse is the Latin hexameter, a syllabically loose structure which allows variation because of its countervailing principle of isochrony:

L'hexamètre, de quantité toujours égale, compte de 13 à 17 syllabes. Perse n'adopte-t-il pas le principe de l'équilibre en durée sans trop tenir compte des syllabes? La tendance naturelle est d'ailleurs d'équilibrer les membres de phrases en accélérant ou ralentissant le débit selon le nombre différent de syllabes pour obtenir des éléments phoniques égaux. (p. 28 n. 19)

The question of isochrony is one to which we shall return later; what is important to note here is simply that syllable-timing is giving way to accent-timing; one no longer needs to keep the number of syllables equal if one wants equal timing, on the assumption that all syllables are of equal duration; instead accentual interval is what is equal, and this depends not so much on the exact number of syllables, but on a rough parity of syllables equalized by features such as pausing and tempo. Further on, van Rutten admits that 'alexandrin allongé' might be a more appropriate name than 'hexameter', since the unit he finds characteristic usually has four accents rather than six, and has a caesura determined by syntax rather than by arbitrary convention. While van Rutten seems to me mistaken in worrying overmuch about superordinate units, for reasons already adduced, and while concern about the caesura is a red herring, unless he *is* talking purely about a type of syntactical juncture rather than about something to which he wishes to attribute a definite metrical status, he none the less does strengthen the argument for an approach to Perse which works with the proximate, the variable, and the relative.

Let us proceed to an analysis of the first poem of 'Pour fêter une enfance', using some of the attitudes outlined above. Attention will now be focused on the lengths of measures; but boundaries will continue to be marked, on the model expounded in the previous analysis:

Palmes… !	2′
Alors on te baignait dans l'eau-de-feuilles-vertes;	2 + 4 + (2 + 4)
et l'eau encore était du soleil vert; et les servantes de	+ 4 + (2 + 4) + 4
ta mère, grandes filles luisantes, remuaient leurs	+ 4 + 3 + 4′ + 3
jambes chaudes près de toi qui tremblais…	+ 2 + 3′ + 3 + 3
(Je parle d'une haute condition, alors, entre les	2 + 4 + 5 + 2
robes, au règne de tournantes clartés.)	+ 4 + 2 + 4 + 3

It should be said immediately that this scansion does not entirely correspond with that offered by Bateman (1976: 33) which runs:

′	1
.′…′.….′…′	2 + 4 + 6 + 4
..…′..…′…′..′..′	6 + 4 + 4 + 3 + 3
..′…′..′..′	3 + 4 + 3 + 3
.′..…….′.′…′.′	2 + 8 + 2 + 4 + 2
…′..′	4 + 3

But the differences are relatively insignificant. I have chosen a dissyllabic 'Palmes', with a *coupe lyrique*, not only to 'express' the *points de suspension* by which it is followed, but also to create a tension with the following 'Alors', a tension which, I think, permeates the whole stanza. While 'Palmes' is a dissyllable with the accent on its first syllable, a falling, fading dissyllable, the dissyllable of affective, involuntary memory, a dissyllable made of embodied geographical distance, 'Alors' is a rising dissyllable of voluntary memory, of temporal fact, of brisk location, however unspecified. These characteristics are reinforced at its second appearance in the last *verset*, where it operates as a curt *incise*, multiplying the break-boundaries in the *verset* as a whole.

Here I must briefly digress to make two general but important points. We are, through this analysis, examining syllabic variation as a manifestation of a single rhythmic phenomenon or principle, as processes of expansion or contraction around a central rhythmic core. It is extremely easy, faced, say, with a sequence of tetrasyllables, for the commentator to conclude that the poet has established a rhythmic regularity, is using the resource of a repeated measure. But we should remember that while regular verse may be said, indeed, to regularize the regular, to imply a uniformity where it can, one of the precious freedoms of free verse is to deregularize or irregularize the regular, so that even a sequence of tetrasyllables may seem to the ear a sequence of heterogeneous or conflicting measures. All the dissyllabic (as indeed all the tetrasyllabic) measures in the stanza may provide both some sense of common purpose (expressing, for example, directness, urgency, focus) and a dynamic sense of variation, incomparability, self-differentiation. This variation is provided partly, as we have seen, by variation in boundary, partly as variation of location and prominence in the syntactic chain, partly by variation in syllabic and accentual quality—it is quite clear, for example, that the rise in pitch on the first syllable of 'Palmes' is much more abrupt and steep than it is on the second syllable of 'Alors'.

The second and related point is that a principal contributor to variation in syllabic quality is the *e atone*. While regular verse, having ordained that the non-elided 'e' within the line has syllabic status and thus must be treated on a par with other syllables (regular French verse *is* isosyllabic metrically even if those syllables are far from isochronous), has little further interest in it (apart from the question of *coupes enjambantes* and *coupes lyriques*), free verse is free to exploit its syllabic reality; by 'syllabic reality', I mean the fact that the *e atone* can be phonated at a whole variety of different levels, but that these levels are all lower than those of 'full' vowels, so that the *e atone* seems to have more a reinforcing or liaisory function that an independent syllabic identity. The group of four in the second *verset* of our stanza, constituted by '-es luisantes', for example, presents two 'full' vowels, a lexeme, enveloped in the acoustic soft-focus of articulated 'e's which are themselves manifestations of the servant girls' glisteningness: the preceding 'e' ties their glow to a certain suppleness, underlining as it does the undulating crests and troughs of 'grandes filles luis-' (indeed, as we can see, it lifts the first syllable of 'luisantes', in such a way that the second syllable must positively outleap it); the following 'e' then catches the reflections and refractions of this epidermic light. Compare this particular tetrasyllabic pattern ($/ə \ldots \text{ɥi} \ldots \tilde{a} \ldots ə/$) with the pattern of 'rè | gne de tournan | tes' ($/ə \ldots ə \ldots u \ldots \tilde{a}/$) in the final *verset*; in the latter instance, the participial ending is given greater duration by the fact that its following e creates a *coupe enjambante* rather than a *coupe lyrique*, so that the light turns or spirals with a certain langour; and the two preceding schwas are a moment of non-semantic vertigo as the reader looks for resolution in 'tournantes clartés'.

My second disagreement with Bateman concerns my (2 + 4) treatment (where the bracket indicates that the accent on the first of the two measures is only slight) of elements treated by her as hexasyllabic: 'dans l'eau-de-feuilles-vertes' and 'était du soleil vert'. It is easy to understand and consent to Bateman's point of view: she presumably wishes to install a process of expansion as the experience of bathing in the leaf-green, sun-green water is ever more intensely recollected; thus the syllabic sequence 2 + 4 + 6 + 4 + 6 presents expansion on a double respiration, before a marginal contraction, connected with close-up and some withdrawal on the poet's part, comes to occupy the remainder of the *verset.* My reading derives from two considerations: first, I wish to set the stanza's area of rhythmic operation between the dissyllable, which is the stanza's opening invocation, and the pentasyllable of 'hau | *te condition* |' which is the centre of the stanza's albeit bracketed refrain, the word that synthesizes and generalizes the whole of the experience; secondly, I wish to install hesitancy, or difficulty of recovery, as the underlying modality of the stanza: the poet's journey backwards is a sensory and spiritual education, a reinhabitation of the past which is not merely remembering, recalling, but reliving in order to emerge differently—the journey back which is a journey out; I read 'toi qui tremblais' not so much as nascent sexuality or simple coldness, but as an existential posture in front of a reality which holds a key to the future. Metaphorically, therefore, the poet is testing the water, re-entering it in the hopes of a new knowledge; though the hyphens make a compound of macerated or reflected leaves and water, the water itself is the element of transformation.

Equally, in the second instance ('était du soleil vert'), one of those inversions of space which are part of the child's desire, and which are made more dramatic by his polarization of far and near, comes into being with a gradualness which bespeaks a wonder as much as the doubts of the creator or the relished exercise of a power. In addition, the 2 + 4 reading prefigures the defeat which will be admitted in the poem's final line:

(J'ai fait ce songe, il nous a consumés sans reliques.)

By suggesting a suspensive boundary at 'encore', I have tried to supplement its 'also' meaning with the notion of desired temporal persistence, a persistence which, poignantly, the following imperfect both affirms (imperfective) and denies (past tense). All in all, there is something to be said for maintaining as much gravity and slowness as the unfolding of meaning allows:

Alors, les hommes avaient
une bouche plus grave, les femmes avaient des bras plus lents.

This last consideration applies equally to my choice of 4 + 5 for the final *verset*'s '| e d'une hau | te condition |', rather than Bateman's superordinate 8. Her reading also involves a three-syllable 'condition' (/kɔ̃disjɔ̃/) rather than the etymologically more 'correct' four-syllable version (/kɔ̃disiɔ̃/).[4] But, as previously stated, I feel this last *verset* should not only set the outer limits of the stanza's rhythmic structure, 2 and 5, but also recapitulate the modules in between. More importantly, perhaps, we should also feel this last line as an assault on a central value which discovers that it has to give ground, to suffer erosion; the gradual expansion of the first three rhythmic modules 2 + 4 + 5, with their continuity-creating *coupes enjambantes*, is unceremoniously cut short by the temporal reminder 'alors', isolating the past between its break-boundaries; the subsequent attempt to retrieve the experience—4 + 2 + 4 + 3—is not so much a rocking motion between fours and lesser denominations, as 4 | 2 + 4 + 3, that is to say a fragmentary 4 followed by a sequence which both by its tripartiteness and by its activation of *coupes enjambantes* imitates the opening sequence of the *verset*—2 + 4 + 5—without however being able to match its climbing numbers.

My final disagreement with Bateman concerns *coupes lyriques*: she counts neither the 'e' of 'luisantes' nor that of 'chaudes'. In general, the use of the *coupe lyrique* in the scansion of Perse's verse is to be defended on the grounds already outlined: it enacts a recuperative movement in which the reader is drawn back into the accentuated lexeme, is invited to an exploratory inwardness, a dwelling on phenomena which is also a participation in their mysteries (in a religious sense). We have already spoken of the effect of the schwa-flanked 'luisantes'; a similar effect is to be sought in '-es chaudes', where the *e atones* quite literally envelop, enwrap the lexeme, generate its warmth; what is then produced is a sequence with a full vowel at the centre /ə od ə/ followed by the sequence of the poet ('près de toi') which is the opposite, a schwa flanked by full vowels /ɛ də a/, an emptiness at the heart of full existence. It is worth adding that '-es chaudes' is an important element in translinear acoustic connections: it harks back to the second *verset*'s 'l'eau-de-feuilles-vertes' (/lodə/) and anticipates the final *verset*'s 'Je parle d'une haute condition' (/əotə/).

This analysis shows the ways in which measures mean, not by

---

[4] Strictly speaking 'condition' derives from Latin 'condicio', frequently written in the erroneous form 'conditio'; Robert gives 'conditio' as its Low Latin derivation. Is this an orthographic matter or an etymological one? At all events a false etymology is the outcome, and one perhaps that Perse would wish us to be aware of, since the Latin 'conditio' means 'a spicing, a seasoning, a flavouring', i.e. a 'condition' which is peculiarly Antillean.

reference to some static norm which they imitate and which draws its justification from elsewhere, outside the poem, from the world of metrical numbers, but by reference to their own acoustic and syntactic constitutions, and to the way they interact with adjacent measures in the sequence of reading. In a stanza whose bottom line and whose basic constituents are marked by 2 (leaves: 'Palmes', water: 'dans l'eau', physical closeness of servants: 'leurs jambes', time past: 'alors', present poet: 'je parle'), a tension is set up between this measure and its doubled, liberated form 4 (cf. Bateman's comment about Perse's privileging the combination of iamb and fourth paeon); 4 enjoys a temporary advantage but yields to a less confident, contracted form of itself, 3. In the final *verset*, the 4 attempts to re-establish itself, reaches a pinnacle in 5, but then undergoes some erosion. This analysis has arisen from the argument that the smaller the rhythmic measures, the more reliable they are as sources of rhythmic information. But this question needs some further investigation, particularly where issues such as expansion and contraction are concerned, and where the sense of varying length of measure as variation on a rhythmic norm is not easy to demonstrate.

The third stanza of 'Pour fêter une enfance I' is the companion of the first, since the bracketed stanza-terminal refrains set up an alternating pattern. Like the fourth stanza, the third is made up of five *versets*, an expansion on the first two stanzas which have three and four *versets* respectively:

Et les hautes	4
racines courbes célébraient	4 + 3
l'en allée des voies prodigieuses, l'invention des	3 + 6 + 4
voûtes et des nefs	+ 2 + 4
et la lumière alors, en de plus purs exploits	4 + 2 + 6
féconde, inaugurait le blanc royaume où j'ai mené	+ 2 + 4 + 4
peut-être un corps sans ombre...	+ 6 + 5
(Je parle d'une haute condition, jadis, entre des	2 + 4 + 5 + 2
hommes et leurs filles, et qui mâchaient de telle	+ 4 + 3 + 4
feuille.)	+ 4

It would be easy to argue that nothing here makes the hexasyllabic measures mandatory, nothing prevents them being read as (2 + 4) or (4 + 2), just as conversely, one might add, nothing is to prevent the 4 + 2s of 'l'invention des voûtes' or 'et la lumière alors' being read as hexayllables:

while unaccentuated syllables cannot easily be promoted to accent, accentuated syllables can be relatively demoted by the removal of intonational and durational support. There is quite simply a point beyond which one cannot go in the determination of the prosodic, and each reader, at each reading, will have certain personal and inescapable questions to answer. However, certain fundamental principles can be assented to, to wit here, that each stanza can to a greater or lesser extent define its own rhythmic priorities and parameters, and that the rhythmic norm may correspondingly be adjusted from stanza to stanza, in relation to structure or to the median measure. If with the first stanza we used the stanza-initial, minimal measure (dissyllable) as the 'norm', as the rhythmic perspective out of which other 'views' emerged, then it was largely because this stanza *was* the originary one. In this third stanza, again because it occurs as the stanza-initial measure, but also because it is the median measure between 2 and 6, we would choose the tetrasyllable as our rhythmic *point de repère*; this is made the more apt in that our hexasyllables are potentially 2 + 4 or 4 + 2 combinations, allowing the 2 to operate easily as a supplement.

In this stanza the poet works forward from a remarkable tetrasyllable— 'Et les hautes'—which has only one syllable of import /ot/, the rest of it being filled with phonated air; the *coupe lyrique* acts to draw us into altitude, and we move among the high curved roots which are either literally high (the banyan tree) or an inverted image of the topmost branches (the 'pacte inextricable' referred to in the previous stanza). This measure is then drawn in a little, in the first main verb and its object, as if to act as a spring for 'des voies prodigieuses', covering expanses of space in a moment of time, ramifying in all directions, impatient to reach the far destination of the next boundary. 'L'invention des voûtes et des nefs' implies a more careful tracing and discovering, but the enclosing capacity of the 'voûtes' is opened again in the ambiguity of 'nefs' (nave, ship). The fourth *verset* also begins with a movement of contraction, the better to achieve a release; but the contraction here is more accelerated and the achievement even less defined. Strangely, the *verset* seems to end on a rather non-committal note, a drifting away from purpose—the final measures, although long, do not have the kind of sturdy result promised by 'féconde, inaugurait', and their ambiguity (his own or someone else's virginal body?) and expressed doubt ('peut-être') make the standing outside of self far from ecstatic; rather than the light of illumination the poet seems to encounter a light strong enough to erase him. The stanza ends with the refrain in which 'alors' is replaced by the more definitively past and out-of-reach 'jadis', and a modification of the final phrases which can

only manage to be arbitrarily circumstantial. The chewed leaf is an altogether more banal and down-to-earth function for foliage that has been
part of vaulting cathedrals, and the relationship between fathers and
daughters is, if 'Écrit sur la porte' is anything to go by, a mixed blessing
(hence my reading by break-boundaries). The final 4s are but pale reflections of those with which the stanza started out.

We use scansion to embody a subject as we use the interpretation
of, and intuitions about, the subject to help us towards a scansion. The
choice of boundary, the treatment of accents as either intra-phrasal or
phrase-terminal, gives us certain itinerary through the poem, a certain
structure by means of which we form interpretation. The danger of non-
primary measures, of superordinates, is both that they interfere with the
dialogue between measure and stanza, by introducing an intervening unit,
the pseudo-line or pseudo-hemistich, and that they transform particular
measures, in a particular structure of meaning in a particular poem, into
something else, the predictable fraction of a conventionally ordained
metrical unit which has meaning only in another context, that of regular
verse, with others of its kind.

For my final analysis in this chapter, I would like to consider extracts
from 'Eloges IX', for which I none the less provide a complete scansion.
My purpose in this analysis is to return to the point raised earlier, and
returned to in the quotation from van Rutten (see above, p. 43), namely
isochrony. How far is our reading of rhythmic modulation, of processes
of expansion and contraction, counteracted by our desire to equalize
measures, either by means of tempo regulation or pausing?

1.	... Oh finissez! Si vous parlez encore	4 + 6
2.	d'atterrir, j'aime mieux vous le dire,	3 + 3 + 3
3.	je me jetterai là sous vos yeux.	6 + 3
4.	La voile dit un mot sec, et retombe. Que faire?	2 + 4 + 3 + 2
5.	Le chien se jette à l'eau et fait le tour de l'Arche.	2 + 4 + 4 + 2
6.	Céder! comme l'écoute.	2 + 4
7.	... Détachez la chaloupe	3 + 3
8.	ou ne le faites pas, ou décidez encore	6 + 6
9.	qu'on se baigne... Cela me va aussi.	4' + 6
10.	... Tout l'intime de l'eau se resonge en silence	3 + 3 + 3 + 3
	aux contrées de la toile.	+ 3 + 3

11. Allez, c'est une belle histoire qui s'organise là   2 + 6 + 6

12. — ô spondée du silence étiré sur ses longues!   3 + 3 + 3 + 3

13. ... Et moi qui vous parlais, je ne sais rien, ni   2 + 4 + 4

     d'aussi fort, ni d'aussi nu   + 4 + 4

14. qu'en travers du bateau, ciliée de ris et nous   3 + 3 + 5

     longeant, notre limite,   + 4 + 4

15. la grand'voile irritable couleur de cerveau.   3 + 4' + 5

16. ... Actes, fêtes du front, et fêtes de la nuque!   2' + 1 + 3 + 2 + 4

17. et ces clameurs, et ces silences! et ces   4 + 4

     nouvelles en voyage, et ces messages par marées,   + 4 + 4 + 4 + 4

     ô libations du jour!... et la présence de la voile,   + 5 + 2 + 4 + 5'

     grande âme malaisée, la voile étrange, là, et   + 2 + 4 + 4 + 1

     chaleureuse révélée, comme la présence d'une   + 4 + 4 + 5

     joue... ô   + 4 + 1

18. bouffées!... Vraiment j'habite la gorge d'un dieu.   2 + 4 + 3 + 3

Prosodic commentators have not been slow to draw attention to Perse's exploitation of silence:

> Saint-John Perse utilise aussi avec beaucoup de bonheur les silences; son art devient semblable à celui du musicien qui, par des pauses, des demi-pauses et des soupirs, rompt la ligne mélodique plus ou moins longuement. Le vers régulier ne permet guère cela: mis à part les arrêts syntaxiques marqués par les signes de ponctuation, mais qui ne lui sont pas propres, la seule pause métrique se situe à la fin du vers; rejets et contre-rejets permettent un certain jeu et de légers décalages entre structures métriques et structures syntaxiques. Les effets restent néanmoins très limités. En revanche, le verset laisse au poète une très grande liberté, et Saint-John Perse sait en profiter. (Favre 1977: 28)

Favre is quite right to point out, as we have already done, that regular French verse is by nature acatalectic; all its syllabic positions are by definition 'filled', where 'by definition' means 'by the fact that French regular verse is isosyllabic'. Pause, therefore, can only operate (1) line-terminally; (2) at metrical or syntactic junctures (which in fact coincide), i.e. measure-terminally. As Favre also points out, regular verse has at its disposal various resources which allow it to vary interlinear pause, resources which boil down to variations in interlinear syntactic junctures. But if the truth be known, in Favre's account at least, Perse hardly draws on any additional resources; it is true that he can use variations in length of *verset* to affect pause; but this does not make the pausing any less interlinear or any more metrical; and he may exploit more systematically a wider range of punctuation, but these punctuation points still occur measure-terminally (apart from those *points de suspension* that Perse uses measure-initially, as on several occasions in our text here) and they are certainly not unknown to the poets of regular verse.

Van Rutten, for his part, can analyse in detail his own experimental findings about the way pause functions in Perse, but the conclusions he can come to do not differ from Favre's and certainly do not envisage a metricity of pause:

D'après nos calculs la durée des pauses est de 25% à 35% celle de la lecture du texte: l'effet et l'impression de ralentissement produits sont importants.

Si nous avons signalé quelques procédés, surtout syntaxiques, de ralentissement, nous ne devons pas négliger l'importance de la disposition graphique des versets plus ou moins longs et surtout l'abondante ponctuation très contrôlée. La fréquence inhabituelle des points de suspension, des points d'exclamation, des tirets impose des arrêts au lecteur et prolonge l'impression des mots. Les pauses sont des instants de méditation. (1975: 36–7)

But pausing is only part of our problem. We have examined 'Pour fêter une enfance I' in pursuit of the argument that measures in free verse are not a series of discontinuous units deriving from different kinds of known metre, but that they are different manifestations of a single underlying measure, which they either repeat, with different configurations of syllabic quality, or expand, or contract; in other words a free-verse poem, or free-verse stanza, is about the dynamic, the psychic life, the aspirations and fears, of a particular rhythmic nucleus. It is the related but converse view which we are at present exploring: that apparent syllabic variations in the measures of a free-verse poem are only apparent, and that the process of reading irons out these variations and equalizes the measures, by constant reference to an in-built and intuitive mechanism of isochrony; the means by which the reading mentality compensates for inequalities are: if a measure is over-syllabic (has more syllables than the norm) an increase of pace and lighter intra-phrasal accentuation is resorted to; if a measure is under-syllabic (has fewer syllables than the norm) then pausing and pro-traction of duration (slowness of reading, longer accents) are resorted to.

The difference between these two views is, of course, fundamental and crucial. The first presupposes the life of the text, or the life of the poet in the text, or the life of the subject in the text; the eventfulness of the text lies fairly and squarely in the linguistic data of the text, and its rhythmic fluctuations are evidence of the psychophysiological, organic presence which invests the text. The second presupposes a text informed by the life of the reader, with its rhythmic dynamic directly dependent on the eventfulness of the reader's response, on the activation of those features which are in large part paralinguistic—tone, intonation, loudness, tempo, pausing, enunciation. I say 'in large part' because there are obvious ways in which a text can linguistically influence paralinguistic features: if we read the first stanza of Gray's 'Elegy' with a melancholy tone, with a laboured slowness, and quietly, it is because we are conditioned to by 'Elegy', 'curfew', 'toll', 'knell', 'parting', 'winds slowly', 'plods', 'weary', 'darkness'. In terms of the features we are inspecting here, we might say that while pause can be metrified, made linguistic, in English (the generative metrists' neglect of it is hard to understand), it cannot in French; and that tempo/duration may have a variable linguistic : paralinguistic ratio in both languages; unless, that is, we are prepared to be convinced that free verse can change this, can install new forms of prosodic thinking which encourage the reader to believe that the text is fundamentally informed, is rhythmically constituted, by readerly input, including the paralinguistic features of recitation, silent or otherwise.

The analysis which follows, therefore, is highly speculative, claiming no validity for itself; but it ought at least to be envisaged *as a mode of reading*. Many readers will want to make different choices, many will find the moves arbitrary, many will remain unpersuaded. But whatever one's attitude, this set of principles needs to be confronted.

The ninth of the 'Éloges' is the last of the short 'inner cycle' (V to IX) which is set on or near the sea, and is indeed the climax of this series; one might argue that it is structurally the most evidently purposive, moving though its sequence of 'tercets' to a penultimate *verset* of some sixty-nine syllables, after a syllabic variation of between only six and nineteen syllables. The poem is consummated in the enjambing 'ô / bouffées', the inhalation of the child-god and the exhalation of the god-poet, before subsiding into the confident expression of a new truth, with its peculiarly biblical ring: 'Vraiment j'habite la gorge d'un dieu.' This transfiguration is achieved only after some spiritual turmoil: the first two 'tercets' are full of the staccato, as the mood oscillates between exasperated impatience and indifference; what is emphasized here is the domestication of the boat, its attachment to the earth, its becalmedness, its paralysis in the spiritual doldrums. It is no longer feeding the sea with the 'contrées de la toile'. The sea as the synthesis of all journeys, all questing, however, begins to reinhabit a silence of anticipation, the silence which is the beginning of a respiration, a rhythm ('— ô spondée du silence étiré sur ses longues!'); and equally the poet feels the pull of all those journeys of which the sea is the palimpsest. The wind rises, teasing the sail ('la grand' voile irritable'), swinging it across the boat as it reorientates itself as a new horizon for the poet ('notre limite'). Finally the boat is caught up in the activity of its sailing and deciphering ('ces nouvelles en voyage et ces messages par marées'), while the child, in the sail, finds wind, sea, and warm humanity conjoined.

Because I want to maintain tireless, excited pressure in the sixty-nine-syllable *verset* and since the dominant measure in this *verset* is tetrasyllabic, I am setting my 'standard discourse' unit at 3, the trisyllable. This would mean, then, that the poem opens on increasing speeds, with an outburst of frustrated anger, which momentarily collects itself, only to be once again discharged in the first measure of the third *verset*. This same mood is to be found, now nuanced with carelessness, in the second and third *versets* of the third 'tercet'. We can imagine these precipitate words, these words delivered *d'un seul jet*, as addressed to a third person; this public, outward speech, restive, unthinking, occurs again at *verset* 11, where the 'Allez' needs to be brought up to a power of 3 by drawl: 'Allez'. This *verset* is flanked by a very different discourse, of self with self, measuring self in meditation, where the trisyllable is connected with a recovered equanimity.

On other 'short' measures, the following decisions might be made: 'Que faire' (v. 4) lengthened to 3 by suspensive boundary; 'Actes' (v. 16) brought up to three by preceding pause, positively experienced as momentarily withheld exclamation; first 'fêt | es' treated in the same way as 'Actes', with lengthening of accent by following articulated 'e'; 'là' (v. 17) expanded to three by preceding and succeeding pause '∧ là ∧'—this 'filled', inflated, or hovering 'là', the sail bearing the impress of wind and space, should be compared with the peremptory and dismissively hurried 'là' of *verset* 3; 'ô' (v. 17) lengthened by suspensive boundary and preceded by the pause of syncopated explosion common to 'Actes' and 'fêtes'; finally 'bouffées' given substance by an *accent d'intensité* or *accent oratoire* (expressive, imitative accent) on its first syllable, so that this word, and especially this word, becomes a 'spondée . . . étiré sur ses longues'.

It will be noticed that in dealing with these shorter measures I have omitted all instances of 2 attached to 4. This is largely because two strategies are available with this configuration: either one might argue that they are reciprocally compensating, or that they should indeed be treated as separate measures and the necessary adjustments accordingly made in each. This dilemma should, I think, be resolved by reference to boundary. Any 2 + 4 or 4 + 2 combination joined by a ⌢ or − boundary can be treated as a self-rectifying pairing, while those separated by a break-boundary, ꟷ, should be available to the kinds of compensation already outlined. Thus 'La voile dit un mot sec' (v. 4), for example, might be read 'La voile ^[E] ∧ dit un mot sec', that is, in such a way that the sail seems to be looked to expectantly, an expectation disappointed by a terse reply, in which the more or less redundant 'un mot' is slurred. Similarly 'Et moi qui vous parlais' (v. 13) demands a dissociation between its parts, so that the 'moi' can detach itself from the past tense of 'parlais', can detach itself from the very process of speaking, inasmuch as that speaking has been associated in previous lines with a waste of words, with an expenditure of fruitless energies; the 'moi' needs to evacuate the mode of speaking to inhabit the mode of knowing, for it is only through the inhalation of the wind-filled sail that the poet can achieve that exhalation which fills the sails, can become the throat of a god; thus 'Et moi ∧' or indeed '∧ Et moi', followed by a slightingly hastened 'qui vous parlais'. Finally, one might suggest that, in those instances in which *points de suspension* precede text (i.e. beginning of 'tercets' 1, 3, 4, 5, 6), they will constitute either the silent part of the measure with which the 'tercet' begins (as in 5(?) and 6), positively generating the accent, or as a complete (trisyllabic) measure, with a silent accent, which 'engages' the reader, which produces the first words of the 'tercet' not out of a featureless silence, but out of a silence already mentally occupied, rhythmically expectant, on the alert. It is only if arguments like this can manage to persuade, that we can begin to envisage a specifically rhythmic, rather than merely expressive, function for pause in French.

All the foregoing remarks must by their nature remain contentious. But this should not be allowed to detract from the underlying argument, that the reading of free verse entails the freedom freely to draw upon the whole range of metrical and prosodic features, and to apply them in whatever dosages, and in whatever order of priority, best correspond to the reader's perception of the poem's, or stanza's, metabolism. Prosodic and metrical features reveal the text and are revealed in the text by the reader, and this involves the kind of prosodic negotiation between interested parties (poet, subject, reader) which we have been investigating in our treatment of the rhythmic measure in Perse. What must at all costs be emphasized is this: rhythm, in free verse, is not something read *out of* a text, as if it already existed in the text, in the form in which reading should retrieve it; on the contrary, rhythm is something to be read *into* the text, by the reader, as an integral part of the cognitive and hermeneutic processes of reading; the prosodic and metrical features of a text are inert and inchoate and unorganized, until activated and co-ordinated and articulated by the reading mind.

Blaise Cendrars, Prose du Transsibérien et de la petite Jeanne de France *(1913)*
The Prosody of Locomotion

THE journey depicted in Cendrars's *Prose du Transsibérien* is not, like Perse's, a journey backwards to reinvent a journey forwards, but a journey forwards which necessitates, or is haunted by, a journey backwards. Like the Baudelaire of 'Le Voyage', the poet of *Prose* encounters on the journey, in the compartment and through its windows, a microcosm of humanity, unregenerate and dispiritingly predictable; even the journey within the journey, the poet's three-stanza *invitation au voyage* to Jeanne, reminiscent of Ax'ël's to Sara, is already pre-emptively entropic:

> L'amour pâme les couples dans l'herbe haute et la chaude
> syphilis rôde sous les bananiers
>
> (l. 249)
>
> Et nous nous aimerons bien bourgeoisement près du pôle.
>
> (l. 278)

This is a *Liebestod* which, immediately followed by the poet's lullaby (ll. 280–90), is no consummation, but an ironic comment on the journey as itself sexual stimulant or necessary theatre for romance, leaving the poet glad of his solitude. But if Cendrars's journey shares with Baudelaire's a certain moral purposefulness, a certain apocalyptic persuasion, envisaging death as the ultimate and imperative challenge:

> La mort en Mandchourie
> Est notre débarcadère est notre dernier repaire
>
> (ll. 206–7)

Cendrars's poet, like the poet of Rimbaud's 'Le Bateau ivre', is unable to live out the consequences of his gesture of radical liberation; vision becomes traumatism, and the Paris to which the *Prose* returns looks something like the equivalent of Rimbaud's 'Europe aux anciens parapets', a refuge deeply permeated with a reassuring old-world culture; Cendrars's

'J'ai vu' stanza (ll. 369–84) recalls the same motif in stanzas 9, 13, and 22 of 'Le Bateau ivre', but, like Rimbaud, the poet has been unable to live himself out, to go 'jusqu'au bout', and withdraws to the 'Lapin agile' with more Verlainian ambitions: 'me ressouvenir de ma jeunesse perdue / Et boire des petits verres' (ll. 442–3). It is Jean Cocteau who first pointed out the kinship between 'Le Bateau ivre' and *Prose*, which he described as 'un véritable train saoul après le "Bateau ivre"' (1920: 105); like Rimbaud's boat, Cendrars's train is an *entraînement*, a motive force buried in his physiology:

Et si j'écris, c'est peut-être par besoin, par hygiène, comme on mange, comme on respire, comme on chante. C'est peut-être par instinct; peut-être par spiritualité . . . c'est peut-être aussi pour m'entraîner, pour m'exciter—pour m'exciter à vivre, mieux, tant et plus! (1987: 195)

But while both Rimbaud's and Perse's boats are susceptible to anthropomorphism, are already culturally and organically integrated, Cendrars's machine reality is a new book in which the 'caractères cunéiformes' of the culturally consecrated texts he was deciphering at line 18 are replaced by the new and variegated sound world of the wheels of the locomotives, which equally must be deciphered:

> J'ai déchiffré tous les textes confus des roues et j'ai
>   rassemblé les éléments épars d'une violente beauté
> Que je possède
> Et qui me force.
>
> (ll. 405–7)

If Cendrars's journey belongs to a tradition which passes back through Rimbaud to Baudelaire, it also belongs with the kind of journey already created by himself and Apollinaire in 'Pâques à New York' and 'Zone'. The debate about which of these two poets is indebted to the other, and for what, continues unabated; but many critics have come to feel that the debate is fruitless, partly because there is no way of bringing it to a reliable resolution, partly because it is an irrelevant concern where exchange, quotation, collage, plagiarism are the foundation of a new view of originality, a view of originality which privileges immediacy over authenticity, or where authenticity lies in intensity rather than sincerity. Cendrars quotes lines from Apollinaire's 'Les Fiançailles' at lines 347–9, but, more important perhaps, the modality of the final section on Paris is that of the urban un-pilgrimages, or pilgrimages *manqués*, that 'Pâques à New York' and 'Zone' are, a sense of entropy, of pointless sentimental adventures which have become sordid in memory, of a modernism which cannot mask a spiritual medievalism. One might compare the burlesque of pastoralism in the two poets:

> Des troupeaux d'autobus mugissants près de toi roulent
>
> > (Apollinaire, 'Zone', l. 72)
>
> Les moteurs beuglent comme les taureaux d'or
> Les vaches du crépuscule broutent le Sacré-Cœur
>
> > (Cendrars, ll. 418–19)

the common props of poster, brochure, siren, the solitary return home; and more generally one might point to the shared preoccupation with images of fire and blood, with the project of consuming the universe:

> Je suis ivre d'avoir bu tout l'univers
> > (Apollinaire, 'Véndémiaire', l. 167)
>
> Car l'univers me déborde
>
> > (Cendrars, l. 339)

the shared mixture of disgust and pity for prostitute companions:

> J'ai une pitié immense pour les coutures de son ventre
> > (Apollinaire, 'Zone', l. 142)
>
> Ton ventre est aigre et tu as la chaude-pisse
> C'est tout ce que Paris a mis dans ton giron
> C'est aussi un peu d'âme... car tu es malheureuse
> J'ai pitié j'ai pitié viens vers moi sur mon cœur
>
> > (Cendrars, ll. 224–7)

the shared reference to the clock in the Jewish quarter in Prague whose hands move anti-clockwise, even perhaps the shared loss of buttons (Apollinaire, 'Annie', l. 12; Cendrars, l. 70).[1] But underlying these kinships of image and theme is a marked difference in their appraisal of the poet's role and stance; for if Apollinaire is convinced of his Orphic destiny, of his solar nature, Cendrars wants to make no claims for poetry, either against life or against any other kind of writing. In explaining the

---

[1] One might add to this list the parallel between Apollinaire's: 'La nuit s'éloigne ainsi qu'une belle Métive / C'est Ferdine la fausse ou Léa l'attentive' ('Zone', ll. 146–7), and Cendrars's: 'Toutes les femmes que j'ai rencontrées se dressent aux horizons / Avec les gestes piteux et les regards tristes des sémaphores sous la pluie / Bella, Agnès, Catherine et la mère de mon fils en Italie' (ll. 428–30).

title of his poem in a letter to Victor Smirnoff (23 Dec. 1913), Cendrars declares: 'Pour le mot Prose, je l'ai employé dans le *Transsibérien* dans le sens bas-latin *prosa, dictu*. Poème me semblait trop prétentieux, trop fermé. Prose est plus ouvert, populaire' (1987: 196).[2] Cendrars, like his locomotive, wants a text which moves straight forward, or rather straightforwardly, a text which has direction but no predetermined shape, a text of easy access, making no claims. Not surprisingly, Cendrars's free-verse prosody is not like Apollinaire's; while Apollinaire's prosody is balanced between a free verse of the measure and a free verse of the line (see Scott 1990: 269–94), that is to say, is a prosody in which the syllable and syllabic number are matters of crucial sensitivity, a sensitivity Apollinaire uses to activate multiple prosodies and thus multiple versions of the text (see Bobillot 1990), Cendrars's attitude to the syllable is much more cavalier; he favours the cadence-accentual mode, that prosodic mode which centres the measure on its accent rather than on its syllabic count, and the line on the number of measures rather than on the number of syllables.

Before embarking on an investigation of this prosody, we should make clear that our subject of study will be the pseudo-*Prose*, that is to say not the two-metre-long unfolding poem (the height of the Eiffel Tower when its limited edition of 150 copies are put end to end), with its prefatory map of the Trans-Siberian Railway (begun in 1891 and completed in 1916), its Orphist accompaniment by Sonia Delaunay (itself culminating in a final image of the Eiffel Tower), and its radically visual layout: ten different typefaces, multiple margins, and areas of colour encroaching from Delaunay's design; but rather the 'second edition', with uniform typeface and margin, the pure text, whose validity, however, Cendrars himself was willing to concede. Although we shall have cause to refer to the *Urtext*, the 'édition unique, dite du *Premier livre simultané*' (subtitle), the reader should consult Pierre Caizergues (1983: 57–74) for further details.

In *Vers Libre* (1990: 98–110) I briefly traced the possible prosodic debt which French free verse owed to the poetry of Walt Whitman, through the translations of, among others, Laforgue and Francis Vielé-Griffin. This debt seemed to relate particularly to the emergence of cadence-

---

[2] Caizergues's observations on the ambiguity of the title should also be noted: 'La première partie du titre appelle, à elle seule, plusieurs possibilités de lecture: prose écrite sinon dans le Transsibérien, du moins à partir des souvenirs que Cendrars feint d'avoir conservé de ce voyage, mais prose écrite par le train lui-même qui fournit au texte son rythme particulier . . .' (1983: 57).

accentual free verse, in which the line continues to be the rhythmic unit (rather than the stanza, as is the case with Perse's prosody), determined by a consistently recurring number of measures and sense-accents. By 'sense-accents', two aspects of a single phenomenon are meant: first, because there are no syllabic determinants in cadence-accentual free verse, so there is no metrical accent; tonic accent, the linguistic accent at the end of each phonosyntactical unit, still remains available, but using it as part of a predetermined metrical pattern is no longer obligatory; as a result more freedom in the placement of accent, and more freedom in the degree of accentuation applied, can be enjoyed by the reader. And this has the second aspect as its consequence: the freedom to place accent, and the freedom to assess its degree, are freedoms to motivate meaning and to participate emotionally in the message. What is remarkable in generative metrics is the way in which the Trager–Smith classification (1951) of four degrees of stress is constantly being collapsed into a binary on/off, strong/ weak distinction, as stress is constantly reduced to a purely metrical role, where expression is less needed than a binary pattern. And even in Verluyten's principle of the alternation of relatively prominent and relatively non-prominent syllables in French, the notion of relativity soon becomes only a nod in the direction of expressive variability. In the placing and degree of accent, the reader is able to make up his mind what kind of speech-act he is dealing with, where lexical loading should fall, according to his own perceptions, and what kind of modality or affective charge that loading should have.

If Whitman is an important source for Cendrars's prosody, then he is no less so for the vehicle chosen to enact and embody that prosody, the steam locomotive. Cendrars, by virtue of listening to the diverse musics of different trains, has come into possession of a violent beauty which he controls but is no less coerced by (ll. 405–7). These lines are reminiscent of

> Fierce-throated beauty!
> Roll through my chant with all thy lawless music, . . .

of Whitman's 'To a Locomotive in Winter', which appeared in the sixth edition of *Leaves of Grass* (1876). It is with this poem that I would like to begin my enquiry into Cendrars's verse-art, using it as a way to restate the founding principles of cadence-accentual prosody, and as a way of giving some shape to the analysis which follows. Shape is the more necessary in any investigation of Cendrars because the body of critical writing devoted to his *œuvre* is singularly lacking in any sustained study of his versification; remarks that are made on this subject tend to be of a summary and inclusive kind:

La même étonnante variété se décèle au niveau métrique, avec l'alternance de mètres réguliers parfois regroupés en strophes, la présence ou l'absence de rimes, et, le plus souvent, le triomphe du vers libre de toute entrave excepté celle du sens, du vers où l'image donne à elle seule la mesure. Ici rythme saccadé, rapide, là, lentes et sinueuses périodes; syntaxe régulière ou juxtaposition. (Caizergues 1983: 69)

Caizergues's remarks are summary largely because the subject of his article is elsewhere. But they do evince a set of attitudes which perhaps explain why Cendrars's verse has been assumed to be prosodically uninteresting. To affirm that his verse is 'libre de toute entrave excepté celle du sens' is half to imply that meaning has no rhythm and rhythm no meaning, or that the production of meaning is not a verse discipline. Of course, if one values visceral, non-cultural contacts with language, of the kind that Barthes celebrates in *jouissance* (as opposed to 'pleasure'), then questions about the hermeneutics of rhythm will be beside the point. And there can be no doubt, as we shall see, that a zero degree of rhythm is an important rhythmic resource in Cendrars's poetic. But such considerations aside, one might venture to suggest that rhythm has at the very least a phatic function, in establishing a channel of communication, that it facilitates the emergence of meaning and guarantees intelligibility—nonsense poetry can be uttered with all the paralinguistic evidence of apparent meaningfulness because of the rhythm which subtends it. Moreover the idea that 'l'image donne à elle seule la mesure' opens on to a mystery as opaque as the length of a piece of string, as though length itself had nothing to do with function or linguistic context or the models of the poet's utterance. Peculiarly, with Cendrars, the identification of his verse as free seems to be the adequate terminus.

The rhythmic secret of Whitman's 'To a Locomotive in Winter' might be reckoned to lie in its third line:

Thee in thy panoply, ‖ thy measured dual throbbing ‖ and thy beat convulsive.

As in my previous scansions of Whitman (1990: 102–4), I treat the sense-stress (s) in the phrase as a nuclear stress, that is, as the principal stress of the phrase, acting as a gravitational centre, or the point of focus, for other stressed material within the phrase. Normally one would expect the sense-stress, as coincident with the primary stress, to fall on the last word or syllable capable of bearing stress, in accordance with the underlying principle in English, whereby sound units tend to follow a curve of increasing prominence. But there may be reasons for reversals of this sequence; Gates (1985), for example, mentions mechanisms of contrast and co-ordination; but there are many kinds of markedness that might warrant special attention: in our example, the fact that 'Thee' aspires to the status of apostrophe, rather than mere vocative, justifies its promotion, and the consequent demotion of 'panoply'.

The rhythmic secret buried in this line is in the tension between the three phonosyntactic units and the reference to a '*dual* throbbing'. Which does the poem opt for, the bipartite line or the tripartite? Lines 9–12 would seem to argue for the latter, despite line 9:

> The dense and murky clouds | out-belching from thy smoke stack,
> Thy knitted frame, | thy spring and valves, | the tremulous
>   twinkle of thy wheels,
> Thy train of cars, | behind, obedient, | merrily following,
> Through gale or calm, | now swift, now slack, | yet steadily
>   careering.

I have reversed the order of prominence in the second half of line 9 to catch the semantic charge, as again in the first two units of line 12, where the first element of each pair is the active, dynamic one; the reversal in the final element of lines 10 and 11 is necessitated by the shift of emphasis from structural features of the train to the sensation connected with them. These lines seem to consolidate the three-measure line, and in so doing allow a further principle to emerge, namely that the measures of a two-measure line have three stresses per measure, while the measures in a three-measure line have two; this then adds a further possible source of variation. The poem's final lines seem to capture some of the possible ambiguities and permutations of this design:

> (No sweetness debonair | of tearful harp | or glib piano thine,)
> Thy trills of shrieks | by rock and hills return'd,
> Launch'd o'er the prairies wide, | across the lakes,
> To the free skies unpent | and glad | and strong.

> (ll. 22–5)

The bipartite lines 23–4 seem, with their two-stress units, to aspire to a tripartite structure, while the final line might collapse into a two-part line if not sustained by stress-intensification and supplemented by silent off-beats. Once again we see how an individual poem creates its own rhythmic parameters, with which it can then play in order to achieve particular expressive effects.

Among other resources typical of the rhythmics of cadence-accentual free verse are: (1) varying length of phrase; (2) changing position of secondary stresses within the line, and their relative proximity to, or distance from, the sense-stress; (3) variation in the part of speech upon which the sense-stress falls. This last effect is particularly apparent in the lines analysed above: the first element of line 22 disappoints by anticipation the adjective + musical instrument of its last two measures, but at least the stress on the last syllable of the postposed adjective pushes into prominence a syllable, '-air', with musical overtones; line 23 foregrounds harsh sounds and their echo, while playing down those natural elements which will become the emphasized features of the line following, though the sense-stress on 'returned' encourages perhaps a similar stress on the adjacent verb and a triphrasal reading of line 24:

$$\text{Launch'd} \mid \text{o'er the prairies wide,} \mid \text{across the lakes.}$$

After a final highlighting of a natural element, 'skies', primary stressing shifts to adjectives, adumbrated in the relatively recessed phrase-terminal 'unpent'. This is, after all, a complex and varied music.

If anything, French verse will have an even stronger tendency to normalize the contour of increasing accentual prominence towards the phrasal boundary. But the location of the phrasal boundary may itself be put in doubt. Besides, regular verse has already accustomed us to the notion that so-called 'secondary' accents may be promoted by syntactical and semantic considerations, and outweigh accents falling at conventional metrical junctures. And it is even conceivable that purely expressive, non-tonic, paralinguistic accents (*accent oratoire* or *accent d'intensité*), the kinds of accent that generally affect the syllable succeeding the first consonant in polysyllabic words, can appropriate the primary sense-accent, as I have tried to demonstrate elsewhere (1990: 106). These are the possibilities which we should be aware of as we confront the *Prose*, which takes up the locomotive/Whitman/cadence-accentual prosody constellation from Valéry Larbaud's 'Ode' (*Les Poésies d' A. O. Barnabooth*, 1908).[3]

[3] Betsy Erkkila (1980: 187–99) deals with Whitman's influence on Cendrars's verse more fully, as indeed with Whitman's influence on Larbaud (pp. 178–87). Suggestions for Cendrars's possible debts to, and kinships with, Whitman's work are also to be found scattered through the pages of Jay Bochner's *Blaise Cendrars: Discovery and Re-creation* (1978).

The first specimen of Cendrars's verse I would like to inspect is the long line 31:

> Et toutes les roues des fiacres qui tournaient en tourbillon
>   sur les mauvais pavés.

And the first assumption we seem justified in making, given the poem's title and Cendrars's professed wish to create a poetry which is 'plus ouvert, populaire', is that *e atones*, where not elided, should remain silent, as in the spoken language. We might further suppose that Cendrars's verse, where possible, will reduce diaereses to synaereses, again in line with the natural 'laziness' of the spoken language. If then we practise apocopes on 'tout(es)' and 'fiacr(es)', and if we treat 'fiacre' as /fjakR/, we discover that we have an eighteen-syllable line which falls conveniently into three hexasyllabic units:

> Et toutes les roues des fiacres | qui tournaient en   4 + 2 | 3 + 3 | (1)
>   tourbillon | sur les mauvais pavés.   4 + 2

This is a satisfying symmetrical structure in which two 'hemistichs' of 4 + 2 imitatively rotate or pivot around the central energy source, the evenly distributed 3 + 3. We might go as far as suggesting that this line of eighteen syllables is in fact a pair of alexandrines 'emboîtés'; that, in other words, the central 3 + 3 is the second hemistich of the first alexandrine and the first hemistich of the second. This reading, attractive, persuasive even, though it may be for this line, is something of an illusion. It asks no questions about the structural pressures that contextual lines might bring to bear on this one, nor does it ask about the most appropriate pattern of accentuation in terms of prominence, nor is it able to admit that the hexasyllabic structures are anything other than prosodic achievements, affirmations of, or allusions to, a certain metrical tradition—but perhaps these elements were just as likely to be pentasyllables or heptasyllables, or perhaps they are not all as classically biaccentual as they look.

In order to cast doubt on easy assumptions, I need first to reconstruct the obvious but important acoustic/lexical underpinning of the poem, whose central phoneme is /u/. Out of this central phoneme grow two strands, the one on a /uR/ combination, whose origin and destination is the 'Tour', the other on a /Ru/ combination, whose presiding spirit is the 'Roue':

> Paris
> Ville de la Tour unique du grand Gibet et de la Roue.

These Parisian landmarks, which belong in adulterated, or only half-remembered, form in Moscow ('mille et trois tours', 'Place Rouge') are the very dynamism of the locomotive, of the poet's imagination, and indeed of the Orphist painting of Robert Delaunay (Eiffel Tower series 1909–11, *Formes circulaires*, Apr. 1912–13). Each of these landmarks projects an itinerary: 'roue > rouge (rougeoyer) > route > rouler > rouiller'; 'tour (in all senses and including "tour à tour") > tourner > tournoyer > tourbillon', and the related 'courir', 'à rebours', 'jour', 'toujours', 'journal', 'carrefour'; and they are joined to each other by the inclusive 'tout', in both its adjectival and adverbial forms. If the cyclical journey is failure or chimera, if the cyclical journey is at best entropic advance and at worst regression, then it is because the poet has not the stomach for the linear, the impulse that ruptures the charmed circle and flies off 'jusqu'au *bout*'. These tracings, of course, are only the framework, the principal 'escales', or stations, of the poem's phonological structure. But through the length and breadth of the poem, the /u/ perpetrates all kinds of hauntings and focuses all kinds of obsession: 'fou', 'j'aurais voulu', 'Moscou', 'souvenirs', 'douce', 'coucou', 'chouchou', 'poupoule', 'toucan', and so on. Line 31, therefore, is already likely to amplify these sounds, or fixate on them, so that the real pairing is not the first hexasyllable with the last, but the first with the second, and the real system of accentuation runs through the associating pairs rather than through the tonic accents, thus

$$\text{Et toutes les roues des fiacres } | \text{ qui tournaient en} \qquad (2)$$
$$\text{tourbillon } | \text{ sur les mauvais pavés.}$$

This choice of an expressive accent as the dominant accentuation of the second hexasyllable, on both 'tournaient' and 'tourbillon', may strike the reader as excessive, melodramatic. But the pressure of the assonance is undeniable, so that at least the second, climactic item, 'tourbillon', should, I think, take an *accent oratoire*: 'qui tournaient en tourbillon.'

In the third phrase, I have placed the principal accent on 'mauvais', for two reasons: ostensibly this line derives from a 'real scene' of cabs in Moscow; in fact it is an hallucinatory Futurist image in the manner perhaps of Boccioni's *The Forces of the Street* (1911), in which a street, through its passers-by and vehicles, releases lines of force which are themselves experienced as psychic and emotional impulses, in both the collective and individual consciousness. The perceiving mind moves elastically through space, reversing natural proportions and varying proximity, and at the same operating a process of abstraction whereby we experience not so much the dynamism of an object as the dynamism of dynamism itself. In line 31 the cabs and cobblestones are but the accidental and contingent origins of a psychic event which far surpasses them. Secondly, this line contains the second occurrence of 'mauvais' in the stanza; the word first appears in this stanza in its first line (echoing an earlier instance at l. 10):

> Pourtant, j'étais fort mauvais poète.
> Je ne savais pas aller jusqu'au bout.
>   (ll. 24–5)

Inasmuch as the poet is himself tower/turn and wheel, inasmuch as it is his own shortcomings which prevent his realization of the potentialities of the dynamic principle which he is, so line 31 becomes a kind of objective correlative of this situation, an image of movement impeded, of movement across a surface not ready for it, a surface both archaic and in disrepair.

Before I continue with this analysis, one emerging and absolutely fundamental point must be insisted upon. If I am able to read line 31 as a Futurist line, it is only by virtue of the rhythmic 'distortions' and the particular distribution of accent that I practise on it. Line 31 is not of itself a Futurist line; indeed, if I persisted with the reading first envisaged, I would create an 'unmarked' image, significant for the Highways Department of the Moscow Council perhaps, and for the Ministry of Transport, but in no senses a psychological event. Texts become representative of certain modes of vision by the ways in which they engage the reader as much as, if not more than, by virtue of what they are linguistically. It is rhythmic choices of the kind I am describing which determine the modality and mode of operation of the image. One of the yawning gaps in our assessment of the relationship between the visual and literary arts is our inability to provide an equivalent, in reading, of the process of perceiving a visual image, an equivalent of the movements of the eye, of responses to colour and so on. If we distinguish between a disinterested, or culturally interested, 'looking at' a picture (Barthes's notion of *studium* in photography), and an involved, participating, illuminated 'seeing' of a picture (Barthes's experience of *punctum* in photography), could we make the same distinction in reading? Are the two readings of line 31 I have just presented something approaching that distinction?

The final question that might be asked about line 31's rhythmic disposition is whether our identification of an essentially triphrasal structure is correct. If the underlying acoustic pattern is one that parallels the pair 'toutes'/'roues' with the pair 'tournaient'/'tourbillon', then perhaps we should envisage:

> Et toutes les roues des fiacres | qui tournaient en tourbillon   (3)
>   sur les mauvais pavés

or to improve the balance, and by recessing the initial elements in all syntactic units:

> Et toutes les roues des fiacres | qui tournaient en tourbillon   (4)
>   sur les mauvais pavés.

This radical flattening out of intonation, and the more accelerated reading which that would imply, would suggest an increasing loss of engagement or response coupled with an increasing prolixity. The only way we can attempt to solve this problem is by replacing the line in its immediate context (ll. 29–32):

> Et toutes les vitrines et toutes les rues
> Et toutes les maisons et toutes les vies
> Et toutes les roues des fiacres qui tournaient en
>   tourbillon sur les mauvais pavés
> J'aurais voulu les plonger dans une fournaise de glaives.

It is clear that lines 29–30 have a binary structure with a probable two accents per phrase (both lines follow the same syntactic conformation and shift from dissyllabic to monosyllabic nouns, to give a 5 + 4 pattern). Line 32 also looks to have a tetrametric structure within a binary framework:

> J'aurais voulu les plonger | dans une fournaise de glaives.   7 + 6

This would seem to argue for the adoption of (4). But we might wish for the moment, too, to keep in tension, as in Whitman's 'To a Locomotive in Winter', a pattern ⁄ ⁄ | ⁄ ⁄, and a pattern ⁄ | ⁄ | ⁄ with variable number of supplementary accents.

If we look slightly further afield, to the section which precedes lines 29–30, namely lines 27–8:

> Et tous les jours et toutes les femmes dans les cafés
>   et tous les verres
> J'aurais voulu les boire et les casser

our sense of tension will become more acute since, while both lines are susceptible of a triphrasal reading:

Et tous les jours | et toutes les femmes dans les cafés
| et tous les verres
J'aurais voulu | les boire | et les casser,

line 28 also tolerates a biphrasal one:

J'aurais voulu les boire | et les casser

the 'absent' second accent in the second phrase being compensated for perhaps by a 'filled' pause immediately after the *coupe*.

The lines immediately following lines 29–32, namely lines 33–5:

Et j'aurais voulu broyer tous les os
Et arracher toutes les langues
Et liquéfier tous ces grands corps étranges et nus sous
les vêtements qui m'affolent. . .

present the same kind of oscillations: line 33 is unmistakably binary and tetrametric:

Et j'aurais voulu broyer | tous les os

but, like our second version of line 28, line 34 is biphrasal and triaccentual:

Et arracher | toutes les langues

As for the nineteen-syllable line 35 (practising apocope on 'étrang(es)' and syncope on 'vêt(e)ments'), we can here choose a biphrasal reading, which will involve the recessing of several of the accents:

Et liquéfier tous ces grands corps | étranges et nus sous les   (5)
vêtements qui m'affolent . . .

or a triphrasal one which will allow us freer play with accentuation:

Et liquéfier tous ces grands corps | étranges et nus | sous   (6)
les vêtements qui m'affolent. . .

About this choice, characteristic of the longer line, two things should be said: first, it polarizes the reading experience itself, taking the reader, on the one hand, through the minimization of accentuation, towards a reading across the surface, towards the consistent attention (or inattention) of the globetrotter, meeting each experience with a certain equanimity, and, on the other, in the triphrasal and free-accentual alternative, towards a reading into the text, towards a much more complex involvement with the text, in which language is shaped and reshaped to produce images of psychophysiological sensation; if the first of these kinds of reading is the reading of the 'professional' traveller for whom all reality is a sequence of images projected on a screen, then the second is the Futurist/Orphist reading, a fundamental revising of consciousness, a way of discovering and releasing dimensions of being hitherto unsuspected; as the poet himself says:

La voie ferrée est une nouvelle géométrie $2 + 2 + 4 + 4$

(l. 324)[4]

which, after the mention of 'Paraboles' in the previous line, presumably refers to both the curved spaces of non-Euclidean geometry and the complicated superimposition of spatial grids in four-dimensional or n-dimensional geometry. About this polarization and its implications for meaning we shall have more to say later.

Secondly, and relatedly, the long line *is* traversal, *is* horizontal motion, is trajectory, is itinerary, a full acceptance of linearity. Sequences of short lines tend to be enumerative, that is to say hypertrophies of paratactic syntax, accumulations, juxtapositions, superimpositions, itemizations, and mixtures of these various modes, refrains too, but all kinds of journeying without moving. The long line on the other hand begins to unravel hypotactic structures, becomes chains of sequence, consequence, and circumstantial pressure. It is no accident perhaps that it is in a long line that the poet acknowledges:

Autant d'images-associations que je ne peux pas développer dans
mes vers

(l. 337)

because he is a bad poet, because he is not capable of going 'jusqu'au bout'. And this very line of admission seems to hang back from triphrasality, or enter it only tentatively; if one reads:

Autant d'images-associations | que je ne peux pas développer

dans mes vers

then the third element easily becomes a *sotto voce* appendix. If we are to make this line into an acknowledgement of a condition, rather than a

---

[4] Compare this line with a passage from 'Le Principe de l'utilité' (1924): 'Les routes, les canaux, les voies ferrées, les ports, les fortifications, les lignes électriques à haute tension, les conduites d'eau, les ponts, les tunnels, toutes ces lignes droites et ces courbes qui dominent le paysage contemporain, lui imposent leur géométrie grandiose' (1987: 43).

statement of regretful fact, then we have to dig deeper into its accentual structure:

$$\overset{s}{\text{Autant d'images-associations}} \mid \text{que je ne peux pas} \mid \text{développer}$$

dans mes vers.

In short, then, triphrasality crosses a crucial boundary, explores a further dimension, commits the poet to risk, discovery, the threat of reality. Biphrasality maintains the poet in the enumerative paratactic mode, where phenomena can be multiplied rather than developed, passed over, are never more than possibilities. Put more fundamentally, biphrasality and triphrasality are the point at which train and journey part company: biphrasality is the train as train, as mechanism, as rhythm of reproduction and association, while triphrasality is the train as travelling, almost against the poet's will, towards the realities of the Russo-Japanese war (1904–5) in Manchuria; biphrasality is the train as rhythmic automatism, triphrasality is the train as the psycho-rhythm, the consciousness of the poet ('Le lyrisme plonge par ses racines dans les profondeurs de la conscience individuelle', 1987: 91).

For line 35 then, and taking full account of the line-terminal *points de suspension*, we must allow the poet to make his journey towards the madness which will become a leitmotiv for the whole poem:

$$\overset{s}{\text{Et liquéfier tous ces grands corps}} \mid \text{étranges et nus} \mid \text{sous}$$

les vêtements qui m'affolent. . .

This is the climax of the poet's destructive, apocalyptic intoxication; and in this line we intuit motives for the destruction, motives of exasperation, feelings of inferiority or arousal; the poet is not just a cleansing power, but an avenger with personal interests. His attention has shifted from the inclusive 'tous'/'toutes', which in previous parts of the enumeration had absolved him from saying anything further about his targets, to circumstantial factors which begin to form an autobiography. The structure of enumeration has changed too: in lines 27–8, and 29–32, the noun-objects precede the verb, where they are taken up by an object pronoun:

Et toutes les . . .
J'aurais voulu les + infin.

The final enumerative section, lines 33–5, reverses this order, separates out the different targets, and applies to each a different infinitive:

Et j'aurais voulu infin. + noun
Infin. + noun
Infin. + noun.

Concomitantly the long line shifts its position in the sequence of events:
in lines 27–8 it is initial and itself enumerative; in lines 29–32 it is
penultimate and syntactically extensive, a journey into consciousness; in
lines 33–5 it is equally a journey into consciousness, but now it is section-
terminal; accordingly, where line 31's final phrase 'sur les mauvais pavés'
is perhaps of secondary significance in the line, the final phrase of line
35, 'qui m'affolent', is a semantic terminus, a 'main' clause concealed in
a relative clause, and its accent is as much expressive, an *accent oratoire*,
as it is a tonic accent. This tells us that not only is the triphrasal line a
journey in itself, it is also an element in the journey undertaken by the
structure of a stanza, or of sections within the stanza. In our three sections, the long line begins as section-initial and ends as section-terminal,
taking on an ever-profounder colouring as it moves towards that destination. Not surprisingly then, line 35 leads immediately into another triphrasal
long line, likewise rounded off by *points de suspension*:

> Je pressentais la venue | du grand Christ rouge | de la
> révolution russe. . .
>
> (l .36)

As himself an agent of the coming revolution (1905), the poet is the red
Christ, the force of revolution by the wheel. But the Christ-revolutionary
of Moscow and St Petersburg, after he has undertaken his journey from
West to East, becomes the familiar Christ-victim, bathed in his own
blood in Harbin:

> Je débarquai à Kharbine | comme on venait de mettre le feu |
> aux bureaux de la Croix-Rouge.
>
> (l. 411)

The poet arrives just in time for his own crucifixion, out of which grows,
as a phoenix, a resurrected Paris (ll. 412–46), or a Paris which absolves
him from taking the journey he has just taken.

As a final comment on the stanza which has so far been our principal
preoccupation (ll. 24–38), I would merely say that it shares with the poem
as a whole a combination of linear and cyclical structures. We have
already seen in what sense the stanza is a progression, and part of that
progression is a movement towards a showdown with the triphrasal line.

Line 36 reminds us of the cyclical: the last three lines of the stanza take up the imperfect tense of the first three, coming back to the autobiography of a life; sandwiched in between are the conditional tenses of the autobiography of a consciousness. And the endings of both imperfect and conditional /ɛ/ are part of an acoustic leitmotiv ('poète', 'verres', 'maisons', 'fournaise', 'glaives', 'vêtements', 'plaie'), which itself becomes cyclic in the refrain 'mauvais(e)' which punctuates the stanza at lines 24, 31, and 37.

Conversely, one might add that though the poem's principal refrain 'Dis, Blaise, sommes-nous bien loin de Montmartre?' is cyclic, not only by virtue of its return, but also because the first and last of its six occurrences (ll. 162 and 241) invert the first two words, thus 'Blaise, dis, sommes-nous . . .', it is also intended as linear; the fact that the *Urtext* uses a different typeface for each of its appearances suggests that on each occasion the reader should be animating the line with different linguistic and paralinguistic resources; it is also, of course, a triphrasal line, that is, it both invites to a journey and offers itself as journey:

⟨⟨Dis, Blaise, | sommes-nous bien loin | de Montmartre?⟩⟩

The poet's changing responses to Jeanne—affection, reassurance, irritation, impatience, contempt, pity—are as much changing responses to the changing modalities and modulations of the refrain as they are changing responses to a woman; compare, for example:

⟨⟨Dis, Blaíse, | sommes-nous bien loín | de Montmártre?⟩⟩

with:

⟨⟨Bláise, dĭs, | sommes-nous bĭen loín | de Montmártre?⟩⟩

And if Cendrars fails to resolve these tensions between the cyclic and the linear, the train and the journey, the journey over and the journey into, one indication of that failure is the arch ambiguity of the final line of the poem:

Ville de la Tour unique du grand Gibet et de la Roue.

This line has all the look of triphrasality, of a journey undertaken and a destruction arrived at—note the progressive focusing in the sequence: monosyllabic noun and dissyllabic adjective ('Tour unique') > monosyllabic adjective and dissyllabic noun ('grand Gibet') > monosyllabic noun ('Roue'). But to read the line as

Ville de la Tour unique | du grand Gibet | et de la Roue

would be to risk identifying as three elements what only adds up to two: 'du grand Gibet' stands in apposition to 'de la Tour unique', so that the duality which is inherent in 'Roue' (Ferris wheel erected for 1889 Exhibition and dismantled in World War I; form of punishment) can be expressed in relation to the Eiffel Tower. A truer semantic representation of the line would be:

Ville de la Tour unique (du grand Gibet) | et de la Roue.

But about these tensions we shall have more to say in a moment.

If the long line has undoubted interpretational implications for the poem as a whole, it has also, as we have already seen, a structural function: it acts as a **palier* in a sequence of lines, that is to say, as a landing between, or at the summit of, flights of steps, a moment of horizontality between two declivities, a stabilizing stage between two unstable movements. In the 'J'ai vu' stanza (ll. 369–84), for example, in which the poet itemizes some of the disasters of the Russo-Japanese war and in which trains are now columns of soldiers, now funeral processions, now forces of chaos and dispersal, now the agents of hallucination, long lines initiate the three sections headed by 'J'ai vu / J'ai vu . . .' or 'J'ai vu . . .': thus lines 369–70:

J'ai vu

J'ai vu les trains silencieux les trains noirs | qui revenaient
    de l'Extrême-Orient | et qui passaient en fantômes

line 375:

J'ai vu dans les lazarets | des plaies béantes des blessures |
    qui saignaient à pleines orgues

and lines 381–2:

Et j'ai vu

J'ai vu des trains des 60 locomotives qui s'enfuyaient à toute
    vapeur | pourchassées par les horizons en rut | et des bandes de
    corbeaux qui s'envolaient désespérément après.

What again is remarkable about these lines is the way in which the primary sense-accents produce a kaleidoscopic mingling of sensations; sometimes these sensations have a continuity, a semantic consistency, as in line 370 ('noirs' > 'extrême' > 'fantômes'), sometimes they throw the reader jarringly across categories, across different perspectives ('lazarets' > 'béantes' > 'orgues'; 's'enfuyaient' > 'en rut' > 'désespérément'). What traces of buried anxiety or fantasy do we find in these Futuristic whirls of phenomena?

Similarly, in the three 'invitation au voyage' stanzas (ll. 247–79), each stanza is constructed around *palier* lines which themselves enact a progression. In the first of these stanzas the poet invites Jeanne to the Pacific, and first of all to Fiji where they are spectators of a love threatened by the diseases of encroaching civilization:

> L'amóur pâme les coúples dans l'herbe haúte | et la chaude
> syphilis | rôde sous les bananiers.

> (l. 249)

This line might almost appear binary, its parts co-ordinated around the central 'et'; indeed, Cendrars perhaps wished the reader to be momentarily deluded. If the rhythm was binary, then we would be in danger of perpetuating the paradisal ease of the first element. Only by insisting on the triphrasal structure can we release the predatory wild beast of syphilis with an appropriate syncopation of primary accentuation.

If, in the Fiji stanza, Jeanne and the poet are observers of a primitive, if poisoned, paradise, they become in the Mexico stanza participants in an idyll sanctified by civilization, but a civilization old and mysterious; Douanier Rousseau has been their pathfinder in this landscape. Here the *palier* lines double, with one devoted to those constructions which mark civilization's presence and the lovemaking of the couple:

> Nous nous aimeróns | dans les ruínes majestueúses | d'un témple
> aztèque

> (l. 267)

and the other to Jeanne's transformation by the exotic environment:

> Une idóle bariolée enfantíne | un peu laíde | et bizarrement
> étrange.

> (l. 269)

Finally, the scene moves to Finland ('le pays des mille lacs') and to the present (an aeroplane is the offered transport). The two long lines which relate to those of the previous stanza are:

>   s   s
> Et je construirai un hangar | pour mon avion | avec les os
>   s
> fossiles de mammouth

> (l. 275)

and:

>   s   s   s
> Et nous nous aimerons | bien bourgeoisement | près du pôle.

> (l. 278)

There are two principal areas of difference between these pairs. First, the elements are differently arranged: where lines 267 and 269 present 'Love-making couple + construction (ruins, but majestic)' and 'Jeanne as troubling idol' respectively, lines 275 and 278 combine the ingredients as follows: 'Poet as engineer + construction (a new application of old materials in a utilitarian spirit)' and 'Lovemaking couple (also in utilitarian style)'; secondly the rhythmic activity is much less in lines 275 and 278, and there are no instances of rhythmic distortion (displacement of primary sense-accent). But what is also noticeable is the relative increase in relatively longer lines; there is a sobering of language consonant with the monocultural directions which the stanza moves in. Once again we encounter the curious interweaving of a definite linear progression with a cyclical structure (the opening and closing of the sequence with 'Oh viens!' and the intermittent punctuation of the intervening lines by 'Viens' or 'Oh viens!').

These stanzas directly precede the lullaby-stanza to Jeanne, which puts a different complexion on the view of her that criticism has tended to favour. Jeanne the homesick prostitute from Montmartre joins the train at line 92 ('L'épatante présence de Jeanne') and seems out of place with the other camp followers and travelling 'businesswomen':

> Puis il y avait beaucoup de femmes
> Des femmes des entre-jambes à louer qui pouvaient aussi servir
> Des cercueils

> (ll. 58–60)

only by virtue of her peculiar focusing of abjectness and mythic potential. She is France, Jeanne d'Arc the degraded religious icon, the icon of a degraded religion, the image of a spiritual exile, the mirage of love which needs to be erased in sleep. And in as far as the journey of the Trans-Siberian Express is a journey into writing, she is what survives of a courtly, symbolist tradition: 'L'idéal symboliste est progressivement

désacralisé au cours du poème en la personne de la petite Jehanne de
France. Les premiers vers qui lui sont consacrés [ll. 115–34] . . . relèvent
à dessein de l'écriture symboliste' (Bozon-Scalzitti 1972: 47–8). And it is
because she is out of tune with the music of the rest of the poem, Bozon-
Scalzitti's argument continues, that she loses her original grace and has to
undergo the disparaging remarks of lines 222–5. She represents the past
(medieval orthography of her name, l. 158) and fixity (in the recovered
singularity of the station, Tower, and Wheel in Paris, compared with
their plurality in Moscow and on the train journey). Thus she remains
obstinately outside the experience of the journey, a fact confirmed by her
sleep, a sleep denied to the poet (l. 399):

> Elle dort
> Et de toutes les heures du monde elle n'en a pas gobé une seule.

> (ll. 291–2)

There is much truth in all this. The five quatrains of the tributary
poem (ll. 115–34) are like a pastiche of *vers libéré*, clearly binary in
structure, but with hemistichs varying between four and eight syllables,
and with the occasional statutory *trimètre*:

> Elle fait un pas, puis ferme les yeux — et fait un pas.   4 + 4 + 4
> Elle est toute nue, n'a pas de corps — elle est trop pauvre.   4 + 4 + 4

Presumably one would feel justified in reintroducing into this sequence
some articulation of the *e atone*, to catch the plaintive, melancholic self-
indulgence of it all. But there seem to be good reasons for arguing that far
from being left behind, or ousted, by the music of a new poetry, Jeanne
is the poet's muse and companion on this journey into revolutionized
language. The tributary quatrains, it is true, represent a linguistic point
of departure, a point of departure that the poet himself is happy to see
immediately superseded; the lines immediately following them brand
them as cliché, as the romantic diversion of the travelling masses:

> Et cette nuit est pareille à cent mille autres quand un train
>   file dans la nuit
> — Les comètes tombent —
> Et que l'homme et la femme, même jeunes, s'amusent à faire
>   l'amour.

> (ll. 135–7)

And the dashes in line 136, and the commas in line 137, remind us that
although the tributary quatrains are not the only surviving site of an

outdated, too strictly chronometric, and over-rational punctuation, they *are* characterized by punctuational saturation. But we must remember that Jeanne is the poet's exclusive companion and addressee in the 'invitation au voyage' stanzas, and, even further down the road of linguistic novelty and experimentation, she is the subject of the lullaby (ll. 280–90).

It is difficult to grasp the full novelty of this lullaby without referring oneself to the *Urtext*, where it appears with seven different typefaces and is articulated around a central axis rather than aligned with a margin, thus:

> Jeanne Jeannette Ninette nini ninon nichon
> Mimi mamour ma poupoule mon Pérou
> Dodo dondon etc.

The train, one might propose, is the emblem of that monoculturism of which America is the shining example, and which Cendrars celebrates in 'Le Principe de l'utilité':

La loi de l'utilité a été formulée par les ingénieurs. Par elle toute la complexité apparente de la vie contemporaine s'ordonne et se précise. Par elle l'industrialisation à outrance se justifie et par elle les aspects les plus nouveaux, les plus surprenants, les plus inattendus de notre civilisation rejoignent les plus hauts sommets atteints par les plus grandes civilisations de tous les temps. (1987: 44)

At the end of his essay Cendrars provides a description of the new language which characterizes internationalism, the constant formation of new geographical equations, the constant movement of the most exotic and commonplace goods:

la langue se refait et prend corps, la langue qui est le reflet de la conscience humaine, la poésie qui fait connaître l'image de l'esprit qui la conçoit, le lyrisme qui est une façon d'être et de sentir, l'écriture démotique, animée du cinéma qui s'adresse à la foule impatiente des illettrés, les journaux qui ignorent la grammaire et la syntaxe pour mieux frapper l'œil avec les placards typographiques des annonces, les prix pleins de sensibilité sous une cravate dans une vitrine, les affiches multicolores et les lettres gigantesques qui étayent les architectures hybrides des villes et qui enjambent les rues. (1987: 52)

Nobody reading this passage can avoid being struck, I think, by the profound discrepancy in the concept of linguistic function which exists between the first lines of this passage (up to 'façon d'être et de sentir') and what follows (from `l'écriture démotique'), between a language serving the vitalism of the self, springing from an unmistakably single psyche, a manifestation of a particular creativity, and the 'unanimous' language which belongs to everyone and no one, exists not as utterance but as something indistinguishable from the consumer products it supports or replaces, which is part of urban event, part of the city's indefatigable assault on the senses, a language ceasing almost to be language and becoming part of a multi-media environment. There is no reason why these two very different visions of language should not coexist. The question is: can the one afford to yield to the other? How far can the Bergsonian surrender to, or incorporate, the mechanistic?

If we wish to reformulate this division in musical terms, terms that may be helpful to our understanding of its rhythmic implications, then we should turn to Futurist music, and its project of extending the range of music to include that hitherto unexploited, but densely rich, source of acoustic experience, the noises of the modern world. As Russolo puts it in *The Art of Noises* (1913):

This MUSICAL EVOLUTION IS PARALLELED BY THE MULTIPLICATION OF MACHINES, which collaborate with man on every front, not only in the roaring atmosphere of major cities, but in the country too, which until yesterday was normally silent, the machine today has created such a variety and rivalry of noises that pure sound, in its exiguity and monotony, no longer arouses any feeling . . .

THIS LIMITED CIRCLE OF PURE SOUNDS MUST BE BROKEN, AND THE INFINITE VARIETY OF 'NOISE-SOUND' CONQUERED . . . For many years Beethoven and Wagner shook our nerves and hearts. Now we are satiated and WE FIND FAR MORE ENJOYMENT IN THE COMBINATION OF THE NOISES OF TRAMS, BACKFIRING MOTORS, CARRIAGES AND BAWLING CROWDS THAN IN REHEARSING, for example, THE 'EROICA' OR THE 'PASTORAL'. (Apollonio 1973: 75–6)

For Marinetti, on the literary front, this transition from pure sound to noise sound, from a limited aesthetic of harmony to an inclusive lived experience of harmony and discord, involved a transition from free verse, which 'artificially channels the flow of lyric emotion between the high walls of syntax and the weirs of grammar' (Apollonio 1973: 99), to 'words-in-freedom', with their semaphoric/lighthouse/atmosphere adjectives, infinitive verbs, onomatopoeic effects, typographical revolution, multilinear lyricism, and free expressive orthography.

We may assume that Cendrars did not want to follow a Marinetti-type programme 'jusqu'au bout'. He is a *verslibriste* by temperament, and his three 'Sonnets dénaturés' of 1916 are a limit he rarely visited. While Marinetti concerns himself with releasing and intensifying expressive force, Cendrars is preoccupied with a lexical 'profondeur', which can only be attained through the play of the lexeme in a linguistic environment, an environment which will produce specific colorations, connotations, modalities. Words are not sledge-hammers but repositories, or multi-dimensional objects, which can be seduced into many kinds of life. It is for this reason that he rejects Marinetti's verbal showmanship:

Chaque mot est variable, multiple, coloré. Et suivant l'inspiration, il obtient une profondeur sensuelle qui le rend inédit, qui l'enrichit. Il faut être riche. Il ne s'agit pas de compter la menue monnaie des syllabes sur ses doigts. Il ne s'agit pas d'acrobatie, ni de mots en liberté. (1987: 193)

But he was bound to travel some way down the road to the mechanized words-in-freedom, and this is part of the drama that is played out with Jeanne.

Earlier in this chapter, we made a distinction, in relation to the longer line, between, on the one hand, a reading which minimizes accentuation and thus gives itself up to an unimpeded touristic mentality, experiencing travel as psychological ease and spectacle, and on the other the kind of triphrasal reading which is an investigation and revision of consciousness, a discovery of new modes of being. We further set the triphrasal long line, as a hypotactic journey of discovery, a chain of consequence which one follows at a certain psychological risk, against short lines (which are in fact predominantly biphrasal) whose paratactic structures accumulate, itemize, superimpose, without any real psychological movement, any progression. The gap between the hypotactic long line and the paratactic short line is the gap between the train as journey and the train as train, as principle of mechanical dynamism which may not in fact be going anywhere (i.e. the journey as train). There are, therefore, two senses in which the 'mauvais poète' was incapable of going 'jusqu'au bout': the first of these concerns the triphrasal long line alone, that line which constantly takes the poet to a threshold of experience or consciousness that he cannot, existentially, afford to cross, or introduces him into kinds of perception which are close to hallucination; the second concerns the crossing over from the kind of discourse embodied in the long line, a discourse of consequence and circumstance, which presupposes a unifying consciousness, an 'author', a psychic autobiography ('l'image de l'esprit qui la conçoit'), to the staccato, free-floating word or image, unattached to a subjectivity, produced by the train and totally without syntactic itinerary ('les journaux qui ignorent la grammaire et la syntaxe pour mieux frapper l'œil [l'oreille] avec les placards typographiques des annonces'). It is this second failure to go 'jusqu'au bout' that I want to explore through the Jeanne lullaby.

The Jeanne lullaby, the clickety-click of the train's wheels fleshed out in language, transforms language in two closely related ways. First and most obviously it onomatopoeicizes language, transforming the symbolic into the imitative, transforming a train of sememes into a train of phonemes, a concept into a percept. Onomatopoeia is an important item on the Futurist agenda, in their attempt to make language an event, in action, lived rather than read:

I proposed instead a swift, brutal, and immediate lyricism, a lyricism that must seem anti-poetic to all our predecessors, a telegraphic lyricism with no taste of the book about it but, rather, as much as possible of the taste of life. Beyond that the bold introduction of onomatopoetic harmonies to all the sounds and noises of modern life, even the most cacophonic. (Marinetti, in Apollonio 1973: 104)

Certain statements made by Cendrars seem to coincide very much with the position outlined by Marinetti, for example 'Je prends un mot et je le brutalise' (1987: 193) or 'La littérature fait partie de la vie. Ce n'est pas quelque chose "à part"' (1987: 195). But what is noticeable is that Cendrars explores onomatopoeia not simply for its own sake, but, as we have said, as a certain kind of *transformation* of language; even the most unequivocally onomatopoeic notation in the poem, at line 189:

Le *broun — roun — roun* des roues

reveals an inverted version of the sequence 'roue > roun > broun'; the wheel as image of modern technology (Ferris wheel, locomotive wheel), as radiant node (sun), as colour disc, as image of integrity, eternity, and so on, becomes a sound in the mouth, imitating the noise of its own motion.

The evidence is that Cendrars regards this transformation with profound scepticism, if not horror. In the Jeanne lullaby the transformation of words into sounds by the coercions of a rhythm is doubled, parodically perhaps, by another transformation, that of a terminology of abuse, or condescension or disrespect, into a terminology of endearment. This transformation, too, is produced by a set of mechanisms, applicable indiscriminately to any substantive: the use of the first-person possessive adjective, of diminutive forms, of repetition of syllables (cf. l. 189 above); thus sexual slang ('nichon', 'mimi'), where it conforms to the mechanism, can be appropriated into an altogether more benign language, and more direct insults ('crotte', 'con') can be given the treatment ('ma crotte', 'concon') and become inoffensive pledges of affection. Or can they? Is it only that contempt becomes veiled contempt, that this linguistic mechanism allows one to be offensive with impunity? In the end, one is led to

conclude that these lullaby lines are the 'contemporary' equivalent of the
tributary quatrains, that they potentially act as a parody of the dowdy,
pretentious, soulful language of the quatrains. But in fact they are as
much self-parodying as parodying, and provide no persuasive modern
alternative. If the poet takes Jeanne with him to all stations on his journey
through language, it is perhaps in an attempt to find the language that
does justice to their love for each other. And has he, in this lullaby,
journeyed too far, has he made it impossible for himself to recover the
language of his feelings? Has he journeyed into that world of linguistic
ready-mades which no longer knows how to value its inhabitants:

> Je voudrais
> Je voudrais n'avoir jamais fait mes voyages
> Ce soir un grand amour me tourmente
> Et malgré moi je pense à la petite Jehanne de France
> C'est par un soir de tristesse que j'ai écrit ce poème en son honneur
> Jeanne.

(ll. 434–9)

The poet must return to his point of departure (at least as far as his
writing goes), Paris, in order to recover the true measure of his love for
Jeanne.

But he must also turn to Paris for another reason connected with the
lullaby. It is fitting that among the terms of endearment showered on
Jeanne should be a place, 'mon Pérou', well attested in colloquial and
slang language as the land of treasure and wealth. Peru is fortunate in this
destiny, in this semanticization; Patagonia is not so fortunate: the line
after the significant confession 'Et j'ai perdu tous mes paris' (l. 154) runs:

> Il n'y a plus que la Patagonie, la Patagonie, qui convienne à
>   mon immense tristesse, la Patagonie, et un voyage dans les mers du
>   Sud.

(l. 155)

Paris is both brought into existence and removed from it by the pun.
Likewise Patagonia is briefly glimpsed as a meaning and then removed
from meaning as it becomes merely the rhythm of the train: patagonie,
patagonie, patagonie. This onomatopoeicization of Patagonia is clearer
in the *Urtext*, where the name is provided with a different typeface and
printed in capitals on its third appearance. The train transforms words
into its own noise, the symbolic into the imitative; even in this process,
most common nouns will hang on to some of their original meaning,

however far into the perceptual background this may fall. But proper nouns whose only inherent meaning is deixis or identification, which exist in literature expressly for the purpose of being semanticized, of utilizing their cultural accretions and associations, are peculiarly vulnerable when it comes to the 'new language'. With proper nouns, meaning can disappear completely. Fear of loss of meaning haunts Cendrars's otherwise positive attitudes to modern linguistic techniques: 'Le mot, par sa valeur représentative, communicable, offre les mêmes commodités que le papier-monnaie, mais il est également dangereux dans la mesure où il peut être vide de réalité, devenir un *flatus vocis,* une imagination vaine' (1987: 95). Cendrars's fears have much in common with Mallarmé's before him, with the crucial difference that while Mallarmé would wish to speak of meaning as the word's self, as its inalienable fiction, for Cendrars meaning is a word's ability to engage with reality, an ability threatened by fictionalizing processes, of which onomatopoeic transformation is one. The Trans-Siberian journey, and all other imaginable journeys, are journeys across a map whose names are constantly threatened by erasure, not just through historical circumstances like the Russo-Japanese war:

> Nous ne pouvons pas aller au Japon
>
> (l. 254)

but because names are in constant danger of evacuation, of becoming pure 'fillers' of space or counters for the train's motion. The last word of line 204, 'Tomsk', appears as the first word of the following line in the *Urtext,* a line which is isolated from its immediate textual environment by its change of typeface, and adoption of italic rather than roman:

> Tomsk Tchéliabinsk Kainsk Obi Taïchet Verkné Oudinsk Kourgane
> Samara Pensa-Touloune.

What undecipherable text is this, tapped out by the wheels of the loco-motive? For the traveller, names and their places are the journey. What point is there in travelling if these names have no places, or, worse still, if names are not so much names as strings of phonemes designed to fuel the train's motion? In the end, as we have already suspected, train and journey become antagonistic forces, and the journey as an image of writing equally finds the train a hostile destination.

It is no wonder then that the poet should need to leave the train and get back to Paris, to the name that can be repossessed in its fullness. This fullness is borne witness to in the apostrophe it twice attracts (ll. 412, 421); Paris can be invoked as reality and meaning; it is home ('Grand

foyer chaleureux . . .', l. 413); it is light and colour; it is the origin not
only of Cendrars's poem but of all writing:

> Jaune la fière couleur des romans de la France à
> l'étranger.

> (l. 416)

Viewed from this angle, Jeanne's repeated, anxious question:

> 《Dis, Blaise, sommes-nous bien loin de Montmartre?》

is not a tiresome nervous tic, nor a characteristic indication of her lack of
any sense of time or place. It is a series of urgent attempts to bring Blaise
to an awareness of what he is putting at stake, the name of his own
singularity as a writer. And the pressure that Jeanne applies with her
questions is a pressure that ultimately the text itself applies. If one exam-
ines the *Urtext*, one sees that some time after Jeanne has fallen asleep,
from line 343 to be exact:

> J'ai peur
> Je ne sais pas aller jusqu'au bout
> Comme mon ami Chagall . . .

> (ll. 343-5)

sections of the text moving 'leftwards' from a right-hand margin begin to
alternate with sections moving from the left-hand margin, until these two
inward-acting pressures produce a final

> Paris
> Ville de la Tour unique du grand Gibet et de la Roue

centre-page. If the lines across the page encode the movement from West
to East along the Trans-Siberian Railway, then we may say that the end
of the line in Manchuria, the 'jusqu'au bout' of violent experience and
locomotive-writing, itself persuades Cendrars back to a centre, to a

> Gare centrale | débarcadère des volontés | carrefour des inquiétudes

back to a centre which has escaped the train, but is still the locus of a
triphrasal journey. This return to Paris is, as we mentioned earlier in the
chapter, beset by a vague despondency, solitude, a sense of failure; after
all, Cendrars has failed to see modernity through, has refused the linguistic implications of the monoculture, has been unable to reconcile the
two linguistic directions his own verse has explored.

In rhythmic terms, Cendrars's refusal is not really surprising. In his essay on 'Henri Rousseau, le Douanier', dated January 1913, he declares: 'En poésie, la technique est enfin personnelle, elle a conquis tous ses droits. Aujourd'hui, chaque poète fabrique lui-même son instrument' (1987: 177). It is in the freeing of rhythm and the diversification of its resources that poetic technique has won its right to be the instrument of a subjectivity. It was hardly likely that Cendrars would be prepared to surrender those rights. But in those passages in which the train breaks free from the journey to become its own self-sustaining principle—and we should add the passage at lines 320–35 as another example—rhythm becomes a puppet-master on whose strings language dances; rhythm is no longer created by and through language, it is that to which language is made subject; this is rhythm which comes from no subjectivity, no discourse, but from a mechanical principle; it is a predatory form of rhythm, in search of a language which can sustain it; it produces a profoundly unsettling schism in poetry, a hypertrophy of rhythm and an atrophy of language. In a sequence such as

> Carótte ma crótte
>
> Chouchóu p'tit cœur
>
> Cocótte
>
> Chérié p'tite chèvre
>
> Mon p'tit-peché mignón . . .
>
> (ll. 283–7)

the recurrent dissyllabic units hustle the language along, deny it any room for expressivity. It is a rhythm that has no necessary relation to that language; it compels syncopes on 'petit(e)' whether they are desirable or not. Just as the mechanisms of terms of endearment turn any lexical item, even offensive ones, into the benignly condescending, so the rhythm of the train in its turn empties these same terms of endearment of any affection they might have been intended to convey, and appropriates to itself the role of soporific. The train prevents the poet from establishing or consolidating a relationship with Jeanne because it constantly alienates him from his own language; for this reason, and in fear of the 'jusqu'au bout', he must quit the train and recentre himself in Paris. Through rhythm the writer possesses his language and himself; this is the crucial sense in which rhythm is meaningful, it makes manifest the coherence of a psyche. Deprive the writer of rhythm and what we are left with is that rather frightening paradox: an excess of rhythm which is also a rhythm degree zero, a rhythm unattached to utterance.

It has not been the purpose of this chapter to examine the relationship between the *Prose* and contemporary trends in the visual arts; it has been concerned with the train journey as an exploration and enactment of rhythmic possibilities, and of their limits, in free verse. But it has not been possible, nor indeed desirable, to exclude all consideration of Cendrars's position on the map of contemporary directions in the arts. It certainly does not seem appropriate to attribute Cubist interests to Cendrars's work, as, for example, Erkkila (1980: 191–9) has done. Cendrars's two essays on Cubism—'Quand les cubistes . . .' (1913) and 'Pourquoi le "cube" s'effrite?' (1919)—make clear what he considered its shortcomings: its multiplication of space by time and, concomitantly and consequently, its underlying and short-sighted fixation on the reality of the object at the expense of any exploration of the reality of reality itself (which Cendrars calls 'profondeur'). Cendrars is much closer to the Futurists in the 'manière de voir vitalistique' which he celebrates, in his essay on 'La Perspective' (1912), against the 'manière mécanique' and immobilism of Renaissance perspective:

Pour la compréhension de la peinture moderne, le côté psychologique est encore plus important. Dans cet état de conscience, si la vie intérieure s'impose, la discipline perspective spatiale est complètement anéantie. Je marche dans la rue. Tout meut autour de moi. Les maisons s'évident ou s'arc-boutent. Parfois passe une figure dans une fenêtre oblique, des lumières dansent, passent. Les murs s'inclinent très loin au-dessus de la rue. (1987: 180)

But we would not be justified in calling *Prose du Transsibérien* Futurist. Rather we should call it Futuro-Orphist, not merely because of Cendrars's collaboration with Sonia Delaunay, nor because Orphism supplied Cendrars with the answer to the problem of expressing 'profondeur'—though these are of vital significance and will be addressed in a later chapter—but more because, as we have seen, Futurism was the 'jusqu'au bout' that Cendrars baulked at; and the Futurist 'jusqu'au bout' was a kind of unholy alliance between 'words-in-freedom' and the mechanical spirit of the train, an alliance which involved the sacrifice of rhythm (the gradations and modulations of matter) to dynamism (movement of the object through space), the sacrifice of 'chimisme' (the play of impulse, reaction, inner structures, metabolism) to mechanism; these distinctions are made in a footnote in Cendrars's essay 'Pourquoi le "cube" s'effrite?':

Les futuristes, eux, divisèrent l'espace par le temps et n'étudièrent jamais que le *dynamisme* (de l'objet) et non pas la *rythmique* (de la matière), c'est-à-dire la *progression sur un plan* et non pas la *progression dans l'espace*; la *mécanique* et non pas le *chimisme* dont certains cubistes se sont tout de même doutés. (1987: 64)

Cendrars's opposition to the mechanical, in vision or as motive force, seems to have been remarkably consistent; or rather his resistance to the mechanical which overmasters the inner. In *Prose du Transsibérien* the poet leaves the train at Harbin:

> Je ne vais pas plus loin
> C'est la dernière station
>
> (ll. 409–10)

and returns to Paris. If he has not been able to go 'jusqu'au bout', it is perhaps more because he has failed to find the formula than because the train in itself is a rhythmically destructive force. Cendrars's abandonment of the journey is only temporary; he is the first to admit its incompleteness:

> J'ai déchiffré tous les textes confus des roues et
>   j'ai rassemblé les éléments épars d'une violente beauté
> Que je possède
> Et qui me force.
>
> (ll. 405–7)

How are the 'éléments épars' to be welded together, how is the contradiction of lines 406–7 to be resolved? These are problems that Cendrars will return to in the *Dix-neuf poèmes élastiques* (1919), and to which we shall return in Chapter 5.

4

Guillaume Apollinaire, Calligrammes
(1918)
The Prosody of the Visual

THE years immediately preceding the war were thus years of crisis for free verse. As we have seen, Marinetti's 'words-in-freedom' already threatened to mark free verse's supersession ('Free verse artificially channels the flow of lyric emotion between the high walls of syntax and the weirs of grammar', in Apollonio 1973: 99). What was at stake? Briefly, one of the fundamental purposes for which free verse had been created in the first place:

> L'importance de cette technique nouvelle, en dehors de la mise en valeur d'harmonies forcément néligées, sera de permettre à tout poète de concevoir en lui son vers ou plutôt sa strophe originale, et d'écrire son rythme propre et individuel au lieu d'endosser un uniforme taillé d'avance et qui le réduit à n'être que l'élève de tel glorieux prédécesseur. (Kahn 1897: 28)

If Cendrars could not contemplate going 'jusqu'au bout' in *Prose du Transsibérien*, it was because to do so would have alienated him from himself, it would have been to 'plaquer du mécanique sur du vivant', to yield to an appropriation of self by other, equivalent to that deviation from normality that Bergson identifies as comic: 'Les attitudes, gestes et mouvements du corps humain sont risibles dans l'exacte mesure où ce corps nous fait penser à une simple mécanique' (1983/1900: 22–3).

There are two particular ways in which this surrender to appropriation might manifest itself. The first is a typographic one: the lullaby to Jeanne (ll. 280–90) has, in the *Urtext*, a medial axis; the other passage of syntactic minimalism and variety of typeface in the *Urtext* (ll. 320–35) almost has a medial axis, though it would be more accurately described as a constantly changing margin (there are nine margins in the space of the sixteen lines). In free verse, a maintained left-hand margin is the guarantee of a presiding consciousness; the act of going *à la marge* is an act whereby consciousness reorientates itself, reaffirms its will to utter, to create a continuity and a pattern; and frequently, of course, the return to the margin coincides with syntactic decisions. The medial axis is a principle of organization that belongs apparently to the text, which minimizes line-endings and line-beginnings, the traditional *loci* of structuration (anaphora, epiphora, rhyme), in favour of a purely visual or decorative imperative, symmetry. The dissolution of margin is of a psychological and aesthetic significance not to be underrated; and it is perhaps no accident that the 'second edition' of *Prose* takes the opportunity to reinstate the poem unequivocally as free verse, around a single 'autobiographical' left-hand margin.

The second surrender to appropriation is the reduction of secondary rhythm to primary rhythm. The terms belong to Chatman (1965), as does the following explanation:

Primary (cardiac) rhythm is the simple periodic return of a given stimulus. It can be represented graphically by a sequence of asterisks separated by equal spaces: * * * * * *. These represent the regular recurrence of events precisely equal in weight or emphasis. Secondary rhythm, on the other hand, is recurrence which groups the elements into a secondary pattern: * * * * * * * * * * * *. There is not only regular return of sensory stimuli but also periodic differentiation of these stimuli. Secondary rhythm has a kind of internal structure that does not exist in primary rhythm. (p. 20)

The manner by which we assimilate what is mechanical, unpurposeful, and unconcerted in primary rhythm is precisely to introduce differential phenomena of grouping and highlighting (by relativized prominence): thus tick-tick-tick-tick becomes tick-tock-tick-tock; thus, in *Prose*, the pattern - ´ - ´ . . . becomes the acoustically modulating 'Ninette nini ninon nichon'. Primary rhythm is not meaningfully rhythmic, only secondary rhythm is, because secondary rhythm alone is part of the dynamic of perception and cognition, is a perceptual experience not to be dissociated from the particularity of its context, as we have already noted. But the poet or the poem can be dispossessed of the faculty of secondary rhythm, in which case it regresses to a mechanism exterior, and probably anterior, to utterance, or it steps outside recognized rhythmic configuration altogether, becomes no more than incipient. We have seen how Cendrars has to resist the rhythmic erosions of the train; at the end of 'Automne malade' (*Alcools*), Apollinaire finds himself in a rather similar position:

> Les feuilles
> Qu'on foule
> Un train
> Qui roule
> La vie
> S'écoule.

Despite the articulatory function of the rhyme, and despite the fact that a process of *remontage* might be practised on these lines, to produce a trimetric alexandrine echoing that of line 17 of the same poem (see Scott 1990: 293), we must still agree with Mathews that 'the final lines of Apollinaire's poem, in relation to the poem as a whole, fragment reference definitively and the language itself undermines the possibility of dominating experience' (1987: 87).

The intrusions of the train threaten Cendrars more than Apollinaire perhaps, simply because Cendrars's cadence-accentual verse is diametrically opposed to the short, insistent, carefully numerical patter of the train. For Apollinaire, on the other hand, a free-verse poet of the measure (i.e. a poet whose verse draws its rhythmicity from the interplay of measures, syllabically defined and usually dominated by a leitmotivic *constante rythmique*, rather than from the line), there is greater complicity with the phenomena of modernity and with their assault on subjectivity; there is, that is to say, more of Futurism in Apollinaire's prosody, if not in his imagery. Indeed his description of his *Calligrammes*, in a letter to André Billy of 29 July 1918, looks beyond *verslibrisme* as Marinetti does, while none the less affirming a last commitment to it: 'Quant aux *Calligrammes*, ils sont une idéalisation de la poésie vers-libriste et une précision typographique à l'époque où la typographie termine brillamment sa carrière, à l'aurore des moyens nouveaux de reproduction que sont le cinéma et le phonographe.' What Apollinaire means by 'idéalisation' we shall probably have to discover *ex post facto*, but it is quite clear that he is happy to visit the limits of free verse. What we should bear in mind is that however much Apollinaire may concede an expressive function to typographic resources, that expressive function is limited by the limitations of available typefaces. Even in the midst of his calligrams, Apollinaire cleaves to the handwritten, to poems permeated by the stylistic consistency of his own handwriting. While gladly yielding to the publicly owned languages of a consumer culture, Apollinaire cheekily harnesses the powers of technology (in this case photographic printing) to serve unextinguishable idiosyncrasy. If the scansionalist finds it increasingly difficult to unearth the true poet from a poetry which is not rhythmically generated, then at least the graphologist may take his place.

In the following study of some of Apollinaire's calligrams, I shall be making reference to some of the devices and effects to be found in the contemporary visual arts, and in Cubism in particular. About this flirtation, three things should be said. As an impresario of the 'nouveau', Apollinaire was the promoter of almost anything that led in new directions.

To affiliate him aesthetically with, or lock him temperamentally into, any of the ongoing art movements would be mistaken. A glance through his critical writings shows the incorporative nature of his critical ambitions. *Les Peintres cubistes: Méditations esthétiques* (1913), for example, is a patchwork of criticism, Apollinaire's collected thoughts on Cubism, and art more generally, between 1905 and 1912; and in the seventh section, the account of Cubism's development, Apollinaire uses the taxonomic tactic, multiplies the categories of Cubism—scientific Cubism, physical Cubism, Orphic Cubism, instinctive Cubism—to find a place for anyone who seems worthy of attention. Mark Roskill (1985: 28) gives a taste of Apollinaire's adaptability, or policy of tireless progressivism:

By early 1912 he had taken up on Futurism; he began to look for a more definitive development that could be seen as emergent from the 'researches' of the Cubists, and by the end of the year he had shifted both his terminology and his basic point of view in order to make acknowledgement of Orphism, and especially the 'pure painting' of Delaunay.

But if it would be foolhardy to try to assess Apollinaire's precise debt to, say, Picasso or Braque, and not only foolhardy but misleading, contrary to his habit of 'making free' with the art of his contemporaries, it must none the less be emphasized, as it has been by Durry (1964: 177–219) and Debon (1982), that Apollinaire's verse is unthinkable without this input, without the pressure put upon him, by activity in the sister arts, to situate himself and his writing, to adopt a terminology, to test his own perceptions. And besides, as Mathews points out (1988: 293), Apollinaire needed the help of Cubism in adapting his perceptual mechanisms to the twentieth century:

It is to a point such as this that cubist art leads us. We are left with the awareness that as we move out from under old forms, the pursuit of the modern is a process as estranging as it is liberating. We are not freed from the world as we find it or from the structuring in history and in memory of the ways we perceive. Objects and figures are made ever more complex in the effort to unearth the ways in which we build them up in our own perception.

This quotation serves to introduce our second point. As readers of Apollinaire's verse we too need help, need help in discovering the kind of perceptual mode which will enable us to maximize the productivity of the poem before us. It is as foolish to assume that every poem can be approached with the same mental set as it is to assume that it is not each poem's express purpose to transform the reading mentality.

Incomprehension is as likely to be the inability to read appropriately as it is to be a failure of understanding, or a feature inherent to poetry. To read Apollinaire in the light of Cubism, Futurism, or Orphism, therefore, is not a question of tracking down the exact dose of these movements in particular poems—since the adequate interpretation of Cubism or Futurism or Orphism is as beset with impossibility as the adequate interpretation of a poem by Apollinaire—but to use these movements as perceptual coordinates, as models of diagnosis, whose applicability is from the outset accepted as metaphorical, approximate; in short these movements—and Cubism in particular—will be agents in the development of new reading habits, rather than interested parties in a controversy about influence.

Finally, this exploration of a sample of calligrams will be as much devoted to a consideration of the visual as of the visual arts. Our concern is the nature and function of rhythm in free verse, and the rhythmicity of the calligram is more dependent on its visual nature than on any debt it may owe to Cubism. If Apollinaire was clear about the Futurist's central place in the ancestry of his own calligrams:

Libre à lui [Barzun] de faire des poèmes peints, de s'essayer désormais non plus dans le simultanisme dramatique, mais dans le simultanisme impressif, toutefois qu'il ne dise pas ensuite qu'il l'a inventé, car il a été précédé là-dedans par les nouveautés typographiques de Marinetti et des futuristes qui même sans couleurs firent ainsi faire un pas à la couleur et inaugurèrent la simultanéité typographique entrevue par Villiers, par Mallarmé, et non encore entièrement explorée. (Décaudin 1966: 891–2)

he was equally clear what their 'words-in-freedom' put at risk, namely rhythmicity itself. In his article entitled 'Nos amis les futuristes' for *Les Soirées de Paris* (15 Feb. 1914), he celebrates the Futurist's contribution to the linguistic revolution, but qualifies his praise with the observation that Futurist language is best suited to the descriptive, didactic, and anti-lyric:

Certes, on s'en servira pour tout ce qui est didactique et descriptif, afin de peindre fortement et plus complètement qu'autrefois. Et ainsi, s'ils apportent une liberté que le vers libre n'a pas donnée, ils ne remplacent pas la phrase, ni surtout le vers: rythmique ou cadencé, pair ou impair, pour l'expression directe. (Décaudin 1966: 884)

This begins to make Apollinaire's 'idéalisation de la poésie vers-libriste' sound like a verse that incorporates Futuristic innovation without sacrificing *verslibrisme*'s contact with lyric discourse. Certainly these remarks are consonant with Arbouin's response to the publication of 'Lettre-

Océan' in *Les Soirées de Paris* (June 1914), when he warned against the sacrifice of rhythm, that channel of affective communication, to typography; Lockerbie (Lockerbie and Greet 1980: 11) suggests that Arbouin's misgivings led Apollinaire to make typography subservient to pictorial shape, though it is difficult to see how this is 'more compatible with the rhythmic expression of feeling'.

The first poem I would like to consider is 'Il pleut', the final poem of 'Ondes', the first section of *Calligrammes.* Lockerbie and Greet (1980: 402) for a moment entertain the idea that Apollinaire may have based his slanting lines of rain on Boccioni's Futurist paintings of 1911, *States of Mind II: Those Who Go* and *States of Mind III: Those Who Stay,* 'in which diagonal and downward moving lines are associated, respectively, with speed and sadness', before dismissing the possibility on the grounds of unlikeness of tone and subject-matter. But in fact the wavering, meditative movement of the rain in 'Il pleut' has much in common with the slow ghostliness of the latter picture, in which disconsolate figures are erased by the curtain of rain they slip behind. Apollinaire's poet gazes at the window down which the rain trickles in a process of disaggregation. But if Boccioni is here, it is in the second version of his triptych, the one painted after his return from Paris, in late autumn 1911, when he had absorbed Cubism and its new forms of spatial organization. And if Boccioni is here, so of course is Verlaine:

> Il pleure dans mon cœur
> Comme il pleut sur la ville
>
> ('Ariettes oubliées III')

These lines lie behind Apollinaire's association of 'pleuvoir' and 'pleurer', and also perhaps behind the cryptic 'villes auriculaires'.

What we should insist on first, then, is the consistency of a certain lyric tonality. If Boccioni's second version of *Those Who Stay* bears witness to Cubist influence, it is Cubist influence acting on the Impressionist/ Symbolist paint-lickings of the first version. The same might be said of Apollinaire's poem, where the very uniformity of the typeface (now a positively expressive factor rather than a neutral one) bespeaks a lyric homogeneity. If these lines of rain are also the strings of an instrument then they are in need of tuning; or the Verlainian mandolin has been converted into a Cubist one.

The rain as stringed instrument is a necessary connection, given the emphasis on the rain as auditory experience, and the reference 'pleurent

Il pleut

Il pleut des voix de femmes comme si elles étaient mortes même dans le souvenir

c'est vous aussi qu'il pleut merveilleuses rencontres de ma vie ô gouttelettes

et ces nuages cabrés se prennent à hennir tout un univers de villes auriculaires

écoute s'il pleut tandis que le regret et le dédain pleurent une ancienne musique

écoute tomber les liens qui te retiennent en haut et en bas

une ancienne musique'. And this auditory emphasis is perhaps the first
cause of difficulty in the poem: the page compels us to see the rain as
trickling across a window pane, while the words urge us to hear, so that
the rain as it is read is superseded as a mute visual image, undoing itself,
stopping, by the rain beyond the window, or as it initially strikes the
window. In other words, the process of reading which ties us to the visual
image, because of the difficulty of decipherment, dragging us down the
window, towards the earth or extinction, equally invites us out of the text
into a world beyond, which we can only make contact with through an
unreliable auditory experience. I call the auditory experience 'unreliable'
because it is not clear whether the poem is urging us to apprehend
metaphorical sounds or literal ones: we move through a sequence of
syntactic structures of increasing doubt ('Il pleut . . .' > 'c'est vous . . . qu'il
pleut' > 'écoute s'il pleut') just as we move through an equal and opposite
sequence of potentially increasing literalness—it is only in the fourth line,
'écoute s'il pleut', that we begin to feel that 'il pleut' refers to falling rain
rather than, say, a process of remembering, or to purely evocative sounds,
for which 'il pleut' is a metaphor. But one of the consequences of this particular conflict of sensory experiences is an interpretation of the poem's
'final line':

> écoute tomber les liens qui te retiennent en haut et en bas.

The 'liens' which constrain us here 'en haut' and 'en bas' are the lines of
verse, difficult to read, and binding us to the visual and to the page; if we
can hear beyond the poem, then at the same moment we shall hear the
'liens' fall away; if, on the other hand, we cannot, then we shall hear only
the falling of this language which ties us to the page, top and bottom.
There are, of course, other possible interpretations of this line, to which
we shall shortly return.

We might think of all these factors as acting together in a play of
achieved simultaneity, of ideogrammatic synthesis, of the kind described
by Apollinaire in his reply to Félicien Fagus (*Paris-Midi*, 22 July 1914):
'Les figures uniques de Rabelais et de Panard sont inexpressives comme
les autres dessins typographiques, tandis que les rapports qu'il y a entre
les figures juxtaposées d'un de mes poèmes sont tout aussi expressifs que
les mots qui le composent.' But what should be underlined here is the
adversative implication in 'tout aussi expressifs'. As much as the calligram
conjoins the verbal and the visual in a single interactive experience, by so
much does it also polarize them. Or, more accurately, the degree to which

the verbal and visual conjoin in a composite experience is proportional to the degree of their polarization. Simultaneity is much more to be found in the tensions of oppositions that in the suspensive accumulation of like with like (where the metonymic can submerge the metaphoric) or of purely heterogeneous elements. The simultaneity to be sought in the calligram will be found as much in the Orphist principle of the simultaneous contrast of colours as in the principles of overlap and transition, or embedding, to be found in Cubism or Futurism.

How does this process of polarization work? The calligram provides the poet with the licence to use typography as flexibly as necessary, both to feed into it more paralinguistic information, more instruction to the voice, and also to create purely graphic configurations which cannot be uttered. Merely by removing the lines of 'Il pleut' from the horizontal, Apollinaire makes them graphically expressive; the conventionality of the horizontal spells graphic inertia. This immediately casts the title 'Il pleut' into outer darkness, attributes it to another, unreliable order of meaning which does not go beneath the surface; in fact the title attempts to make the poem self-evident, the typography purely imitative, the design rhopalic; the conclusion looks foregone. The status of 'Il pleut' as title removes it from speech, from speech as manifestation of an interiority, as tonality and inflexion; as a title it is totally transferable. Not surprisingly Apollinaire's signature (printed), which appeared with the poem's first publication in *SIC*, December 1916, but not thereafter (see Sacks-Galey 1988: 28), is also in the vertical axis, the axis of expressivity, himself as the semantics of rain. So we begin to read, to decipher, and for the first time, perhaps, reading as a hermeneutic problem coincides with reading as a physical problem, the problem of spelling out. The graphic dimension compels upon the voice that hesitancy, that groping forward, which is the whole mechanism of understanding. And the differential intonation of a (horizontal) stanzaic structure is missing; there are five lines (or $1 + 4$) it is true, and roughly of the same length, a spectral survival of Apollinaire's favoured *ababa* stanza perhaps, but their verticality destroys all previous readerly suppositions. We are, it seems, urged to read all these lines with the same careful, halting enunciation, and the same intonational shape, monotonously falling, but with slight pauses and changes of tempo, as wonderfully befits the subject. A further paralinguistic consequence of this verticality is the lack of confidence the voice has in the mechanisms of syntactic cohesion, which cannot graft themselves on to a ready-made discourse structure. Thus though we detect a minimal linkage between the lines, a linkage which is essentially paratactic:

1. Il pleut des voix de femmes comme si elles étaient mortes même dans le souvenir
2. C'est vous *aussi* qu'*il pleut* merveilleuses rencontres de ma vie ô gouttelettes
3. *et ces* nuages cabrés se prennent à hennir tout un univers de villes auriculaires
4. écoute s'*il pleut* tandis que le regret et le dédain pleurent une ancienne musique
5. *écoute* tomber les liens qui te retiennent en haut et en bas

we encounter these cohesive elements as peculiarly arbitrary; cohesion is not a device of reassurance, but of challenge; we cannot understand its motivations, and thus it is here, as much as anywhere, that the reading voice will register its disquiet.

But if the voice learns from these graphic implications, learns how to speak the poem, it also learns to a greater or lesser extent the impossibility of speaking the poem. Actually it is impossible to speak rain. Actually it is impossible to read and see rain. And inasmuch as the poem is about the processes of disaggregation and crystallization that the formation of droplets on the windowpane enacts, it is impossible for the voice to capture the visual experience. It is true that meaning and syntax can do something to convey this: for example, in the first line, in which remembered sound is disaggregated until it can no longer be remembered, we progress from noun phrase ('des voix de femmes') to pronoun ('elles'), to the extinction of pronoun ('mortes'), to qualification of that extinction ('même dans . . .'); in the second line, we move in the opposite direction, towards experience which is multiplying and self-enriching: the object pronoun 'vous' becomes a fully circumstantial noun phrase, 'merveilleuses rencontres de ma vie', which in turn becomes an irrepressible apostrophe, 'ô gouttelettes'. Equally we might say that a phonemic chain can imitate the process of disaggregation: it is of crucial structural significance to the poem as a whole that line 5 ends with the sequence:

en haut et en bas: /ɑ̃ o e ɑ̃ bɑ/

where /b/ is as it were the last vestige of lexemic wholeness, where the line itself is about disaggregation—'tomber les liens'—and where these 'liens' may indeed be a language: 'les liens qui te retiennent', with its repeated semi-consonant /j/ (/ljɛ̃/, /rətjɛn/), significantly echoes 'ancienne (/ɑ̃sjɛn/) musique' of the previous line. But despite these factors, and despite the fact that 'Il pleut' is far from being an extreme example of the polarization of the verbal and the visual, there remains an unextirpatable sense in which it cannot be uttered; for one thing, as we shall see, to read the words with rhythm is to refuse to read them as rain.

If polarization is the key to simultaneity in the sense that it stimulates processes of vibration and oscillation rather than those of sequential accretion, and in the sense that it superimposes after-image on image and positively thwarts linearity, and if this conception of simultaneity belongs more with the Orphists than with the Cubists or Futurists, is there any sense in which the Apollinairean calligram is Cubist? The answer is very much 'yes'.

We think of Apollinaire's poet as one of those who stay, immobilized behind the window, unable to prevent the lessons of the rain writing themselves on the glass pane, pursuing their destiny through the rain's various displacements. If we look through the typical works of Picasso and Braque in the high-analytic, or hermetic, period of Cubism (1910–12), works like Picasso's *Man with a Pipe* (1911), *Man with a Mandolin* (1911), *The Aficionado* (1912), or Braque's *Le Portugais* (1911), *Woman Reading* (1911), then we must be struck by their transfixative quality. If Cubism espoused the dynamism of modern life in its multiplication of perspectives, then we need to qualify that remark by adding: Cubism centres this perspectival dynamism in the object and, paradoxically, in the still life and portrait; the dynamism of the object is not intensified by the dynamism of a spectator at the centre of the picture (as was Futurism's aim), for with Cubism the spectator is outside a picture which can only achieve pictorial autonomy by this exclusion. The dynamism of the spectator has thus been pre-emptively dealt with by the picture/object; that is to say that the object bears the traces of shifting perspective, is the record of a spectator's dynamism, but not an enactment of it. The Cubist picture is a picture, and it is its surface with which the spectatorial eye (rather than body) has a dynamic relationship, not the object depicted. There is still an ocular dynamic, but the dynamic of the body has been yielded to the object. But in addition, since Cubism is still essentially perspectival—to undo perspective it depends on an arrangement of perspectival data perspectivally interpreted:

Ainsi le cubisme croyant apporter un nouveau langage—expressif—ne faisait qu'apporter une modification extérieure dans un système qu'il n'abolissait pas—mais qu'il soutenait: l'introduction de plusieurs points de vue d'un objet sur la toile ressortissait de la même vision sinon complétée (Delaunay 1957: 57)

—since it still uses shading to embody planar recession, and remains planar in fundamental construction, it still tends to immobilize the spectator. And, if anything, this immobilization is intensified by the Cubist picture's tendency to withdraw towards its centre. There is certainly no invitation into a 'blind field' in Cubist painting; in fact, if anything, the opposite occurs: the motif, having been alienated from an originary environment in a traditionally perceived world, undergoes a series of metamorphoses (conceptualizations) which involve it with its own structural rationale, and beyond that with structural essentialism. To propose this is to propose that the non-Euclidean and *n*-dimensional (fourth-dimensional) geometry of the Cubists is principally to do with complex configurations within 'empty' conventional space, rather than constituting a reinvention of space itself, either by a revision of the concept of plane (curved space, soft space), or by the multiplication of *kinds* of space (parallel realities, inner space, etc.). It is within this perceptual frame that I think 'Il pleut' is set. And there are two particular dimensions of this perceptual frame that I wish to pursue: transition/displacement and memory/creation.

Speaking of the 1909–12 period of Cubism, Mark Roskill characterizes it thus:

More recent interpretation of this phase of Cubism, stressing fluctuation and oscillation, or ambiguity and playfulness, or the basic tensions set up between surface and depth, or *passage* as a device of linkage between disparate planes, is truer, therefore, to the character of the paintings themselves, than is the traditional interpretation based upon the theory of the time. (1985: 51–2)

As an art of linkage, of transition, Cubism activates the spectatorial eye, inviting it to lose and recuperate the depicted subject, to pass through a spatial continuum which is spatially problematic, an open space which turns out to be a maze. The eye constantly adjusts itself to the tireless disorientations, mapping out not so much the contours of an object as its own exploration, testing proximities and distances, projections and recessions: 'To look at such a picture is to become involved in seeking out fixity where there is none, in striving to establish stable relations where all relation is mobile' (Mathews 1988: 187). To be in passage, to travel through transitions and displacements may be, initially, to be in pursuit of the heart of the matter, a possible destination; but the journey to a unicursal centre quickly reverses into a journey out of, or along, or across, a multicursal or multidimensional figure which can only be apprehended by displacement and transition. We have already had cause to assert that the elements of cohesion in 'Il pleut' bind by dislocation, or dislocate as much as bind. We have watched the first two lines move syntactically in

T ABLE I

Line	Address	Plurality	Sub. clause	Pleuvoir	Spacing	Length	Auditory
1	$a - ?$	+	+	+	−	+	+
2	$b + $ pl.	+	+	+	+	−	−
3	$a - ?$	+	−	−	+	+	+
4	$c + $ s.	−	+	+	+	+	+
5	$c + $ s.	+	+	−	+	−	+

Note: This selection of categories must of course, have something arbitrary about it, but it does cover many of the dominant features, both visual and verbal. Under 'Address', I am assuming that lines 1 and 3 are 'minimally' addressed, and to the same interlocutor(s), though there is no way of being sure; signs of address are in the explanatory 'comme si' clause and in the deixis of 'ces'. Under 'plurality', the − of line 4 registers neither that the singular nouns are abstract nor that they are personified. 'Spacing' merely indicates the unusual isolation of the first line. 'Length' indicates that lines 2 and 5 do not reach a putative ground. Under 'Auditory' I have entered a − for line 2, because although 'il pleut' appears, there is no other intimation of auditory experience.

opposite directions, the one towards substantival disaggregation, the other towards substantival crystallization. Following up this latter indication, we might further propose that the five lines are not 1 + 4 (registering the spatial separation of the first line) but 4 + 1, an enclosed quatrain followed by a line of summary. While the two outer lines of the quatrain are haunted by an evanescent and regretted past, the two inner lines are celebrations of regenerative encounters and an aggressive encompassment of humanity. In order to follow up the constantly changing patterns of affiliation and exclusion, and to map the transitions between different structural perceptions of the poem, so that its own multidimensional, multiperspectival nature becomes visible, I present in Table 1 a componential analysis based on simple ± differentia. This table reveals the great variety of patterns of inclusion and exclusion, the constantly changing groupings. Surprisingly, perhaps, line 3, which looks so different in syntactic structure, which has the paired 'il pleut' lines on one side and the paired 'écoute' on the other (the first of which also contains 'il pleut'), turns out in the table to merit no privileged status.

Beyond this are the complications of the rhythmic structure, a version of which I give without further ado:

1. Il pleut des voix de femmes | comme si elles étaient   6 + 6 + 6
   mortes | même dans le souvenir

2. c'est vous aussi qu'il pleut | merveilleuses rencontres   6 + 8 + 4
   de ma vie | ô gouttelettes

3. et ces nuages cabrés | se prennent à hennir | tout un   6 + 5 + 5 + 6
   univers | de villes auriculaires

4. écoute s'il pleut | tandis que le regret | et le dédain   4 + 6 + 4 + 6
   pleurent une ancienne musique

5. écoute tomber les liens | qui te retiennent | en haut   6 + 4 + 5
   et en bas

This scansion is an approximate one; I have taken my cue from the visual image in muting or muffling enunciation by suppressing word-terminal *e atones*; I have however maintained a certain measuredness in articulation by avoiding syncope (suppression of word-internal *e atones*): thus /suvənir/, /gutələt/. The rhythmic notation shows that lines 3 and 4 are exceptional in having a tetraphrasal structure, although in line 3 the measures create an enclosed pattern, while in line 4 they are alternating. It also shows that the hexasyllabic measure is the dominant. Here I would take the same view as I took with the tetrasyllable in 'Automne malade' (1990: 290–1):

Thus even though the tetrasyllable may enjoy some structural prestige as a point of reference, it does not set itself against other measures so much as become them. In other words, the poem is not the dramatic arrangement of fixed-value measures so much as a rhythmic progress in which measures are constantly relativized and adapted by their immediate rhythmic environment . . .

or as was broached in the treatment of measures in Saint-John Perse's *versets*: that changing measures are expansions or contractions of a given rhythmic norm. Philippe Renaud (1969: 277) is certainly wrong, I think, to maintain that 'dans *Il pleut*, la seule "musique" de ce poème dénué de rimes et de rythmes est celle, très subtile et pénétrante, que crée un phénomène extérieur et présent'.

Once again, as we approach these lines, and identify the hexasyllable as the norm, as the *constante rythmique*, we need to remind ourselves that to call the six-syllable string a hexasyllable is in no way prejudicial, does not imply the concept 'hemistich' or, beyond that, the concept 'alexandrine'; it is quite simply a syllabic segment in discourse which is of rhythmic interest because it defines a certain range of possible rhythmic effects. In the first line, for instance, the shifting configurations of the hexasyllable—

2 + 4, 6, 1 + 5—help to underline the elusiveness of remembered voices, and indeed the absence of a secondary accent in the second measure encodes with wonderful aptness the lack of resistance to slippage, to effacement, and the acceleration of loss, while the braking effect of the accentuated 'même' immediately following 'mortes', the determination to re-establish consciousness, does not recover the voices, but merely underlines the completeness of their loss. The consistency of the hexasyllabic segmentation serves to convey the relentless gradualness of the process of extinction. As already mentioned, the second line moves in the opposite direction, and, not surprisingly, it is rhythmically more eventful; against the process of uniform etiolation, we have a movement of expansion (6→8) followed by a moment of apostrophic crystallization (4). Not surprisingly, too, its first hexasyllable foregrounds the rain, by giving it a measure-terminal position, whereas it is recessed in the first measure of the first line; while in the first line the rain is the indistinct undertone of voice, in the second line it is the agent of triumphant memory, the worker of wonders, the encapsulator of rich experience.

One might then go on to argue that lines 3 and 4 are also set against each other. Here, for example, a foregrounded 'hennir' (and 'pleut' in l. 4) is set against a recessed 'pleurent', as rebellious affirmation against eroding regret, while the sharp focus of the metaphor 'nuages cabrés', the two words each accentuated, and juxtaposed in the same measure, gives way to the more discursive personification of 'regret' and 'dédain', carefully distinguishing themselves from each other, each rather sanctimoniously perhaps occupying its own measure. The final hexasyllables confront the 'villes auriculaires' with the 'ancienne musique', confront a music which is in the capacity to hear, to absorb sound (and the sounds of modern life), with a music which is in a score or an emotion, which follows recognizable forms (hence the indefinite article); the 'villes auriculaires' are places where regret and disdain are no longer part of the population. Part of the novelty of line 3 lies in its imagery, its difficulty, its ambiguous syntax (is 'tout un univers' in apposition to 'nuages cabrés' or is it the object of the usually intransitive 'hennir'?); part of the old-fashionedness of line 4 lies in its abstract nouns, in its careful hypotaxis, in its syntactic transparency. But this contrast is also to be found in the disposition of the measures of these two lines: line 3 presents a self-completing chiastic structure and thereby affirms the autonomy of its imagining; line 4 presents an alternating structure which we associate with narrative or continuing discourse, and where the regular movement of expansion and contraction is rhetorical periodization; line 3 blurs the line between contracted (5) and full (6) measures, by minimizing differentiation so that slight rhythmic doubt and disorientation accompanies the semantic disorientations produced by the line; in line 4, on the contrary, the differentiation between 4 and 6 is clear, and is made clearer still by the pattern of alternation, so that, rhythmically speaking, we know where we are.

Finally, line 5 comes to maintain the tension we have just described. It is a mixture of the interested rhythmic parties from lines 3 and 4, and this ambiguity is intensified by its own apparently unpurposeful development. It returns to the triphrasality of the first two lines, thus drawing them into its theatre of concern, but the 6 + 4 + 5 sequence gives no hints about intention or destination or organization.

What this brief analysis has attempted to show is the ways in which fluctuating rhythm in free verse registers the movements of mind and the uneven life of the sensibility, and the senses in which rhythm is meaning (signification), or at least the meaning (illocutionary act) of the speaker (poet or reader). But for rhythm to emerge at all the reader must have access to a rhythmical reading of the text; the rhythmic structure of 'Il pleut', as we have just described it, belongs to the kind of continuous, intonationally modulated (let us not forget that pitch is a constitutive ingredient of accent) discourse that the typographic layout of 'Il pleut' in fact makes unavailable. The problems of decipherment in 'Il pleut' are only mild compared with those to be encountered in other calligrams; but even here, after a first reading, we may find it easier to read by memory than to track the letters down the page in a repeated process of reconstitution. In the disaggregated form of raindrops this poem has no rhythm; it has rhythm only in the continuity supplied by memory. This gap between the essentially non-rhythmic, or pre-rhythmic, or post-rhythmic, and the rhythmic is the gap between 'Il *pleut*' and 'le regret et le dédain *pleurent* une ancienne musique', between an impersonal, 'primary' rhythmic, natural phenomenon and a personalized, 'secondary' rhythmic, cultural one. Nor is it surely any accident that the gap between these two modes is occupied by 'tandis que', the conjunction which at once expresses simultaneity and opposition, or, to revert to our earlier argument, simultaneity through opposition, for here once again, the opposition is polarized.

Cubism starts from an acquired knowledge of the real world and, by a process of conceptualization, makes that acquired knowledge the source of perceptual discovery; this transformation of seeing into imagining, of knowing into discovery, of memory into creation, involves the transformation of painting as image of a percept into painting as reality of perception. Part of this drama is expressed by Mathews (1987: 109–10) as follows:

> The Cubist approach emphasized the artistic object as a conceptual object—an object that inaugurates experience (that *is* experience), as well as a critical self-consciousness in experience. Cubism produces artistic objects that continually represent the struggle to establish self-consciousness, to distinguish it in the seamless transition from object to memory that, for the Cubist practitioner, constitutes experience.

To keep rhythm alive, to ensure the legibility of the calligram, we allow memory to anticipate the problems of decipherment. If we give ourselves up to decipherment, we may well learn a new language, a new way of reading, but it will be at the expense of memory and at the expense of rhythm as guarantor of coherence, of the organic implantation of subjectivity in experience, of possession, of continuity. But Apollinaire does not have to return to Paris to avoid the 'jusqu'au bout' as Cendrars does; in the calligram of 'Il pleut' he has the poetic machine by which he can stretch sensibility between rhythmic reading and decipherment, and in the very stretch itself inhabit both extremities simultaneously. This is why the final 'line':

écoute tomber les liens qui te retiennent en haut et en bas

is genuinely ambiguous, not with ambiguity of an either/or, an optional polysemy, but with the ambiguity of simultaneous double meaning—the 'liens' of 'ancienne musique' 'qui te retiennent' (in the obstructive sense) do fall away and allow the new music of the rain and the whinnying cloud-horses to fall on the modern cities straining their ears to catch the 'noise-sounds' of Futurist *Intonarumori* (a visual equivalent of this reading is the rain as disaggregating puppet strings releasing the poet from the automatic transposition of 'pleuvoir' to 'pleurer'); simultaneously those same 'liens' sustain the poet, prevent the process of disaggregation even as it occurs, return the rain to its job as stimulus of memory, and musician of nostalgia and regret.

If 'Il pleut' polarizes within narrow limits and envisages disaggregation only to counter it with crystallization and the stringing together of the self-unstringing, then 'Voyage', also from 'Ondes', radically widens the polarization, and counters disaggregation with constellation.

One of the factors which intensifies the polarization of verbal and visual in 'Voyage' is the presence of the exclusively graphic telegraph pole. For Morier this image is redundant 'car elle intersecte une partie du

VOYAGE.

A DIEU AMOUR NUAGE QUI
FUIS REFAIS LE VOYAGE DE DANTE
ET N'A PAS CHU PLUIE FÉCON

TÉLÉGRAPHE
OISEAU QUI TOMBER
LAISSE
SES AILES PARTOUT

? E L A P

OU VA DONC CE TRAIN QUI MEURT AU LOIN TENDRE ÉTÉ SI P
DANS LES VALS ET LES BEAUX BOIS FRAIS DU

LA DOUCE NUIT LUNAIRE ET

ÉTOILES

LA PLEINE

NE

J E

C' EST TON SA VI GE

VOIS

PLU
S

QUE

sens' (1975: 913); but in fact it serves two important purposes: it precisely marks the outer limit not only of the visual, but of the literal and iconic; in this way it offers the reader the lure of a landscape, an autobiographical realism behind the images against which the figurative and absent can pull in another experience of simultaneous contrast. Secondly and relatedly, it acts out, with the figure of the 'télégraphe-oiseau' next to it, the transformation which the poem is about: an immobile image of communication becomes a dynamic one, because the telegraph-bird is not only the telegraph pole distorted and set in dizzying motion by speed, in true Futurist style and as already noted by Verlaine:

> et des plaines entières
>
> .   .   .   .
>
> Vont s'engouffrant parmi le tourbillon cruel
> Où tombent les poteaux minces du télégraphe
> Dont les fils ont l'allure étrange d'un paraphe.
>
> ('Le paysage dans le cadre des portières')[1]

but the telegraph becoming the communication it sends along its wires: the bird lets its wings drop everywhere, like so many messages tumbling on to a waiting world. At the visual extreme also are the shapes and directions of the letters and words that it is impossible for the voice to convey, although it should be said, at the other extreme, that the constellated sky is a series of intonational instructions to the voice, a map of pitch change, a score of the aspirations, affectionate roundnesses, dispirited fallings, or level equanimities of utterance. In similar fashion the small-capitalized, spaced-out monosyllables (all, except 'été') enjoin upon the would-be reciter the staccato puffing of the train, a puffing which resists the voice's attempts to impose a 'secondary' rhythm on the primary

— — — — — — — — — etc.

But the voice which is after all not the train, but a distant observer of it, will also manage to find its interiority, the periods of its interrogation:

---

[1] These images also look forward to Valéry's delightful description, in 'Le Retour de Hollande' (1926), of the effects of the speed of the train on the perception of landscape, a description which reminds us that the train is very much Time personified: 'Je quitte la Hollande . . . Tout à coup, il me semble que le Temps commence; le Temps se met en train; le train se fait modèle du Temps, dont il prend la rigueur et assume les pouvoirs. Il dévore toutes choses visibles, agite toutes choses mentales, attaque brutalement de sa masse la figure du monde, envoie au diable buissons, maisons, provinces; couche les arbres, perce les arches, expédie les poteaux, rabat rudement après soi toutes les lignes qu'il traverse, canaux, sillons, chemins; il change les ponts en tonnerres, les vaches en projectiles et la structure caillouteuse de sa voie en un tapis de trajectoires . . .' (1957: 844).

OÙ VA DONC CE TRAIN | QUI MEURT AU LOIN   5 + 4

DANS LES VALS | ET LES BEAUX BOIS FRAIS | DU TENDRE ÉTÉ   3 + 5 + 6

SI PÂLE?

From the visual, from the present of the train, we receive one message about reading; from reflection, imagination, memory we hear another. And the sub-rhythm, or suppressed rhythm, I have tabulated here is wonderfully nuanced and sensitized. We notice the slight syllabic diminution in the second measure of the first line as the train recedes; we notice an increased and corresponding expansion of measure in the second line as the failing, fading summer is ever more broadly and affectively reinhabited; we notice, too, how this expansion is accompanied by first one accent, ('vals'), then two immediately adjacent ('bois frais'), and then two separated by a syllable, and we notice that the syllable framed by these last accents is precisely an adverb of affect, of subjective response. But this insertion of response and desire into the neutral, public, printed, primary puffing of the train has already occurred in the first line, where the pairs of accents also sandwich an unaccented syllable, unaccented syllables (the demonstrative adjective and preposition) which also are moments of involvement for the speaker. And if 'pâle' and its question mark form the locomotive's funnel and a wisp of smoke, they equally urge the voice to rise, so that summer's pallor is as yearned for as it is evanescent.

In rather similar fashion, while there are many senses in which we cannot read the figures which make up the 'télégraphe-oiseau', we can use the visual instructions it gives in order to counter its verbal message: 'télégraphe' may fall, but 'tomber' holds level steady, so that the wings beneath it can fly up again. Obviously the reversibility of downwards and upwards movement, but particularly of downwards movement, is crucial for the meaning of the poem as a whole. But how are we to compose these words rhythmically? As a set of pentasyllables which make telegraph and bird a compound noun?

> Télégraphe oiseau
> qui laisse tomber
> ses ailes partout

This reading also necessitates the articulation of the *e atones* on 'laisse' and 'ailes', but after all the swooping, rocking flight of bird and message, or of telegraph wires as they pass the train windows, justifies this lilt-factor. Alternatively, one might argue that the function of imagery in modern poetry is precisely to undo discourse, to explode comfortable continuities, and that the image precisely should dictate verbal distribution:

> Télégraphe
> Oiseau qui laisse
> tomber
> ses ailes partout

This particular issue, of the relationship between rhythm and image in modern poetry, is one that will be confronted in greater depth in the next chapter. What should be noted here is the frequency with which Apollinaire develops his images through relative clauses:

> Amour nuage qui fuis et n'a pas chu . . .
> Télégraphe oiseau qui laisse tomber . . .
> ce train qui meurt au loin . . .
> ton visage que je ne vois plus . . .

This in itself bespeaks a desire to project the image as instantiated subjectivity or objective correlative, for while it is true that relative clauses like these are unrestricted (*explicatives*), the relative pronoun indicates that 'personal interest', that act of possession so vital if images are to be kept within the umbrella of a presiding discourse.

The copresence of two typefaces in the cloud figuration would indicate two voices, two tones, two kinds of emotional colouring. This duality expresses, too, the duality of the voyage. The command 'Refais le voyage de Dante', given its larger type, seems to be the informing task for the whole poem. This is surely not Dante's voyage into exile, but the spiritual journey of the *Divine Comedy*, a journey downwards into the hell of a departing train in order that an ascension to the heaven of Beatrice recovered (the constellated sky) shall be achieved. One may argue that this goal is not attained, that the train leaves the landscape, removes Beatrice/Marie,[2] who will never be seen again ('C'est ton visage que je ne vois plus'). But of course the night sky cannot rid itself of its crescent moon and all its stars; the poet must just give himself time to learn the hard lesson of transfiguration, or sublimation. If the 'voyage de Dante' is the journey as spiritual task, the cloud is the journey as unmitigated physical loss. It is often argued that Apollinaire radically foreshortens his landscape here: his cloud occurs at the same level as the telegraph wires. But

---

[2] It is generally assumed that if 'Voyage' has a basis in biography, then it concerns the definitive loss of Marie Laurencin, who had married a German painter on 21 June 1914 and departed by train on her *voyage de noces*.

surely this is a cloud of smoke from the locomotive, for two reasons apart from its position relative to the telegraph. First, it is given shape by the 'rhythm' of the train, a rhythm with which Cendrars has made us only too familiar:

Adieu	2
Amour	2
Nuage	2
Qui fuis	2

Secondly, it is not a rain cloud, and if it has anything to 'drop', it is 'suie noircissante' rather than 'pluie fécondante'. As the train exits page right, the smoke cloud, telegraph pole, and telegraph-bird will exit page left, blown back (hence backward-sloping bird's wings) and left behind by the steaming locomotive. Only the constellated sky is impervious to this kind of centrifugal movement; indeed for all the dispersal it seems to denote, all the lack of pattern, it none the less is clearly centripetal, the bold capital C acting as the pivot and magnetic centre of the sky. But it is important that we should come to understand that the dual image of the journey contained in the cloud is in fact one: we should opt for 'dante' as the ending of 'fécon', rather than the 'de' immediately above it, for it is Dante who leads us out of the cloud, Dante who turns the departing train to good account in a process of transfiguration, and it is Dante, therefore, who releases the fecundating rain, who turns the smoke cloud of the machine into the vapour cloud of nature; and if we had any doubt that the constellated sky is also an image of falling and fallen rain, we should look to the 'last' word of the text, 'plu'.

The final sense in which the visual in this poem pulls particularly hard against the verbal is the way in which space is figured by text. Lockerbie and Greet (1980: 395) draw particular attention to this feature: 'Rather than a "picture", therefore, what is built up is a mental construction of space which, though closely tied to the graphic form, still creates an evocative impression of distance and spatial perspectives.' There are two basic modes of spatial figuration. The first concerns the creation of three-dimensional space by distance and proximity. While the size of typefaces may indicate to the voice what to foreground and what to recess, what to isolate and emphasize, and what to slur, the voice cannot easily translate spatial effects by acoustic variation, particularly variation in loudness. It does not really matter that the constellated sky seems, on a two-dimensional plane, to be below the train, it is so much further away in three-dimensional space that it all but envelops the train. The heavy type of 'tendre été si pâle' may differentiate the locomotive from the train, may tell the voice to intensify utterance at this point, to throw the phrase into relief, but it may also indicate that the train is actually coming towards us, on rails curving round from the left. The final 'S' of the text depicts a star which is either larger than the rest, or closer, or both.

Against this mode, the mode of dimension, is the mode of point of view. Do letters on the page stand up or are they lying flat? Do we see them along a horizontal line or down a perpendicular one? And if we see them *down* a perpendicular line, do we see them *up* a perpendicular line at the same time (this would certainly be one way of getting the constellated sky up in the air!). What the calligram does through its figures is precisely to make language available to these different points of view. We shall treat the cloud and train as horizontal views, though the train might be an aerial view, with the smoke blown at right angles to it. The telegraph-bird could well be a deconstructed aerial view (the 'oiseau qui laisse' providing a cross-section through the pole from which the wires have been sucked by the speed of the train). And presumably the constellated sky is a vertical view from below, unless we as readers are afloat in the empyrean. In what senses, however, do these shifts of point of view affect the way we read? As in the viewing of photographs or paintings, they affect posture, posture towards the uttered, as well as posture towards the image. The aerial view introduces us to the unfamiliar aspect of things, the unseen (as Cubist painting does); it produces strange effects of foreshortening; at the same time it allows the viewer to dominate the scene, to view reality with more detachment and a broader perspective, to view reality *sub specie aeternitatis*; at the same time the viewer is given a floating position, gravity disappears, distance and size become difficult to gauge, all largely because there is no horizon:

In a downward-looking view, the familiar landscape-format distribution of visual 'weight'—that set heavy, earthward things low on the canvas, and made forms closer to the viewer bigger—was negated. The elements of the scene could thus be dispersed without regard for gravity or recession. (Varnedoe 1989: 221)

Thus it is that the calligram can produce an estrangement from language; linguistic forms are no longer anchored in syntax, no longer ballasted and constructed by known morphological units. It is in this sense that, through a revision of readerly posture, the calligram can produce the appropriate mental set to cope with linguistic disaggregation, as we shall see in a moment. One final point should be made about the aerial or vertical point of view. In tracing his development of an abstract art, El Lissitzky reported: 'The picture's one perpendicular axis (vis-à-vis the horizon) turns out to have been destroyed. We have made the canvas rotate. And as we rotated it, we saw that we were putting ourselves in space' (quoted Varnedoe 1989: 254). Now we see how the capital C of the crescent moon can become the magnetic pivot of the constellated sky, endlessly revolving around it. Now we see, too, how the exclusion undergone by the poet in 'Il pleut', looking into reality from the other side of the windowpane, has been reversed and how the transfixative force of the image has been undone. The poet, afraid of having to witness the departure of yet another train, without him, can now throw off his impotent immobility, move freely through landscape and skyscape to regain his kingdom, his ability to see the other side of things, and thus fulfil the wish of the Futurists:

The construction of pictures has hitherto been foolishly traditional. Painters have shown us the objects and the people placed before us. We shall henceforward put the spectator in the centre of the picture. (*Futurist Painting: Technical Manifesto 1910*, in Apollonio 1973: 28)

I hope there is sufficient evidence in the analysis so far to refute Renaud's conclusions about 'Voyage':

Cela revient à dire que l'on peut lire ses parties indépendamment les unes des autres—ni plus ni moins qu'on peut le faire des strophes d'un poème aux rapports assez lâches: cela n'a guère de ressemblance avec les schémas de *Lettre-Océan*; ce n'est pas faire œuvre 'simultaniste' que de montrer dans un poème les divers éléments d'un paysage. (1969: 373)

If there is not, then perhaps the poem's concerted effort to produce a new apprehension of language and of rhythm will finally be persuasive. Like 'Il pleut', 'Voyage' concerns itself with a process of linguistic disaggregation, but it does so more radically and more constructively. The sense in which the journey through the poem, along the well-trodden coordinates of left to right and top to bottom, is a journey upwards as much as it is a journey downwards, lies in the fact that it traces a process of increasing disaggregation, which, far from destroying the poet's existential and poetic identity, allows it to reformulate itself in a more permanent and inclusive set of constellations.

The 'facts' of this disaggregation are not difficult to summarize. From a cloud and telegraph-bird of normal lexical fullness (polysyllabicity), we descend to a train made up exclusively of monosyllables (apart from 'été'). Many of these monosyllables already look extremely tenuous as words (e.g. 'où', 'ce', 'au') and indeed are no more than isolated phonemes.

Another step down takes us to the floating linguistic particles and deconstructed lexical entities of the constellated sky. But here we in fact have less to do with deconstructing than with reconstructing. As we have already pointed out, the sky tells us that the 'pluie', which had not 'chu', has now 'plu', and this achievement coincides with the calligram's having been 'lue(naire)'; and as we have also pointed out, the 'pluie' (/plчi/), whatever its burden of sorrows, can become the 'nuit' (/nчi/) in which raindrops turn to stars. Equally the 'nuage' which does not rain its fecundating rain, the cloud which flees not only leftwards, but also with the train, without regret, is the 'visage' of the newly married Marie, which he can no longer see; and yet through a 'voyage de Dante' the 'nuage' may become a 'visage' which has wept and now has its place in the firmament.

But it is not just by processes of repetition (assonance, rhyme) that language and meaning are reconstituted. It is also by processes of recombination (as we see in 'pluie' + 'chu' = 'plu') and dissemination. Thus the particular disposition of D $^O_{CE}$ U allows the 'où', 'ce', and 'du' of the train to abandon their lives of isolation and drudgery as grammatical tools, and participate in a semantics of quality, as well as reconciliation after rupture. 'Visage', on the other hand, undoes itself, not according to any known morphological principles, to reveal a 'vi(e)', a possessive adjective, a mutant form of poet's subjectivity /ʒə/. And this dissemination facilitates further combinations, e.g. 'visa' (p.h. of 'viser' or n.—where *were* the honeymooners going?), 'sage' (a wish for docility or wisdom achieved after tribulation). Explicit disseminations encourage the reader to find implicit ones—'étoiles' (et/toi/les), 'voyage' (vois/j/age). And as all this takes place, we have already been conditioned to shift, in self-reversing patterns, from literal to figurative, from figurative to literal: the 'nuage', represented graphically as literal, turned out to be a metaphor for 'amour', while similarly the 'oiseau', a metaphor for the 'télégraphe', is graphically represented as a literal bird. Or is it the other way round? All that is missing from the starlit sky is an Apollo, a sun, which would wed the 'nuit lu*naire*' with the poet.

This kind of analysis might be pushed further; but it is perhaps already sufficient to show that while passages of conventional rhythm can be recuperated from the text, as in 'Il pleut', and do add to the semantic productivity of the calligram, they are countervailed by an opposite pull in the direction of discontinuity and fragmentation. But where fragmentation had at best ambiguous implications in 'Il pleut', here it leads to a total revision, rewriting, of language, and thereby to a transfiguration of experience. Where 'Il pleut' imprisons the poet and *compels* the eye to move consistently and repeatedly downwards, 'Voyage' releases the poet and reader into the space of the poem and installs a real rhythmicity of the eye as it travels back and forth between phonemes, 'morphemes', lexemes, creating patterns of repetition, compounding and unravelling. In many senses, Dante's journey down the page has been a journey from an oral/ aural rhythm to a purely visual one, or at least a visual one which can alone activate the true, underlying acoustic relationships. In this sense, the image of this poem's rhythm is neither cloud, bird, nor train, but the constellated sky, that is to say something existentially and metaphorically other. This, too, then, like the poetry of Perse and Cendrars, is a voyage into language, in search of an appropriate rhythmicity. What this poem emerges with is not a rhythmicity belonging to voice, but one belonging to the eye scanning language, and scanning it in such a way that it is no longer prejudiced by the conclusions that voice would come to, by the kinds of segmentation that voice would engineer. We may want to argue that Apollinaire still keeps vocal and ocular rhythm in balance, that the sky presents a view of language which belongs more to concrete poetry than to Apollinaire; the fact remains that here, at least, this radically reimagined language releases the poet from the lyric trap and produces a manipulability into language which allows the recovery of an encompassing view.

My last example of an Apollinairean calligram, 'L'Éventail des saveurs', pursues the theme of opposed kinds of rhythmicity, but it does so by a rather different pictorial manœuvre. This is, of course, a war poem, from the final section of *Calligrammes*, 'La Tête étoilée', and as such it redefines what is at stake in the conflict of rhythmicities. Like 'Voyage' it is a composite calligram, made up of several parts, but at first sight at least it does not seem to enjoy the metonymic kinships enjoyed by the constituents of 'Voyage'. A cursory 'reading' of these figures suggests a pistol (Fig. A), an eye (Fig. B), a tail-less bird (Fig. C), a fan (Fig. D), and a mouth (Fig. E). Lockerbie and Greet (1980: 484–5) report that in manuscript the poem bore a longer title—'Éventail des saveurs de guerre par l'œil et le doigt jusqu'à la bouche'—and that Fig. D more clearly represented a fan; this orientated the poem more unequivocally towards parts of the body and the senses, and implied that Fig. D should act as the starting-point of reading; following the sequence of the original title, the reader would then move from Fig. A ('guerre'), down through Fig. B ('œil') and Fig. C ('doigt'), to arrive at Fig. E ('bouche'). Fig. C therefore is both the bird without a tail and the finger used as a substitute for a tail—this, of course, in no way invalidates the sexual pun pointed out by Lockerbie and Greet (1980: 486), whereby 'queue' = penis and 'oiseau' = maidenhead; on the contrary, it would only reinforce Fig. C's salaciousness.

Éventail des saveurs

Attols singuliers
de brownings quel
goût
de viv
re Ah! Fig. A

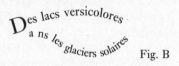

Fig. B

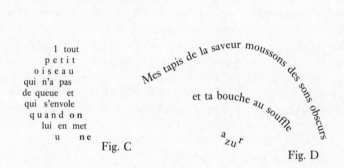

Fig. C

Fig. D

Fig. E

In fact the whole calligram could be sexualized: Figs. A and C (phallic), Fig. B (vaginal), Fig. D (mammary), Fig. E (labial, vulval), and such an interpretative move would endorse the suggestions made by Sacks–Galey (1988: 188) about the verbal meaning of Fig. E:

[Le cri] C'est le craquement d'une chaussure (sans doute un brodequin militaire) qui accompagne 'le pas', c'est le bruit d'un phonographe en marche, c'est la vibration qui émane du petit mirliton et c'est aussi le bruit de l'aloès qui éclate. Cet aloès évoque à la fois un phallus et un canon, et nous donne encore l'exemple d'un texte où la guerre et l'amour sont décrits dans des termes équivalents.

One might go on to argue that Fig. E is another image of sexual intercourse, where 'ouïs' functions as much as onomatopoeic cry as verb, where the phonograph is merely an accessory, part of an ill-defined interior, where 'le cri' and 'le petit mirliton' are sounds of sensual pleasure. And 'les pas'? Feet on the stairs, in the room above, etc.? The density of definite articles here would not make it difficult to suppose that this is a veiled reference to a particular occasion, shared affectively here by poet and addressee.

The shortening of the manuscript title and the increased abstractness of Fig. D lead Lockerbie and Greet (1980: 485) to conclude not only that 'éventail' now operates almost exclusively in its figurative sense ('scale', 'gamut') but also that the whole poem has a greater degree of ambiguity, that each figure is freer to acquire associations with more than one object. They themselves suggest that Fig. D may be another mouth (lips pursed perhaps to deliver its 'souffle azur'?) or, with its slight tipping to the right, an ear, in which case it would complement Fig. E: for while Fig. E is graphically mouth, but verbally about hearing, Fig. D would then be graphically ear, but verbally about sounds and breath.

Two further and more cohesive proposals should be made about the figures. By virtue of its position (centre top), Fig. A can operate as a prelude to the calligram as a whole: the 'attols singuliers' introduce that current of tropical imagery ('lacs versicolores'(?), 'tapis de la saveur', 'moussons', 'aloès') which polarizes against the featureless, dreary, battlefield landscape. They also introduce the sexual subtext to which we have alluded: the 'attols' are the destination of the 'revolver'. But they also, of course, introduce the battlefield itself: they are the craters large or small created by the impact of bombs, shells, and bullets, ridged holes in the soil or flesh. With this in mind, as our eyes scan the page, so they sketch in the whole battlefield; Fig. B is not an eye, or a lake, but a flying shell; Fig. D is an explosion, with shock-waves rising out of it; Fig. C is another shock-wave, or a soldier blown sideways, and Fig. E is an aerial view of trenches, or a water-filled crater. And the sounds of Fig. E immediately switch through from the sexual to the military; the 'cry' of boots, the scurry of footsteps, a phonograph in a dug-out, the aloe as howitzer, the 'petit mirliton' as the whine and whistle of a flying shell.

But if we have identified Fig. B as an eye and Fig. E as a mouth, why do we not go on from there? Fig. C is no bird but a stylized nose. Fig. D is the second eye closed now, and possibly upside down; or possibly it is the left ear. And the Browning is a cap, or hair with a provocative quiff. We find ourselves looking at a Cubist portrait, the image of a face which is not only the site of multifarious sensory experience, but also bears on it all the scars of the battlefield. The taste of death produces the taste for life, however much it has to be made of fantasy and memory; the weapons of destruction invert into images of intensified sexual desire.

But what of rhythmic matters? Here we need first of all to distinguish between, on the one hand, Figs. A and C, and, on the other, Figs. B, D, and E. Figs. A and C are examples of what Bohn, in his classification of calligrammatic types, calls 'shaped writing: (a) solid forms': 'A solid body of words, the text consists of a vertical series of horizontal verses whose individual lengths are varied to produce pictorial contours without the aid of outline' (1986: 51). Here, then, an image dictates a lineation, a lineation which can be experienced as a manifestation of the absurd, the arbitrary, the stultifying. The shape of the Browning in Fig. A threatens to fragment the 'goût de vivre' beyond all recognition, and the final exclamation 'Ah!' is not so much a crucial utterance of self-surrender, as a space-filler, a *cheville* with no purpose other than to 'describe' a pistol butt. In Fig. C we feel the same constrictions, the same danger that the visual image will stifle, mask, distort poetic discourse. The use of the arabic numeral, however much in keeping with Futurist policy of substituting signs for words whenever possible, is symptomatic of that kind of military mentality which reduces all phenomena to a purely statistical existence, which turns the events of the natural world into items on a list of sightings or of potential enemy activity. But in this figure we also feel some resistance to this mentality and to this condition of writing; the shape of the bird/nose/finger/crumpling soldier/shock-wave allows a gathering syllabic momentum as dissyllables shift to trisyllables:

1 tout	2
petit	2
oiseau	2
qui n'a pas	3
de queue et	3
qui s'envole	3
quand on	2
lui en met	3
u . ne	1

Here the typography is forced to make concessions to an increasing rhythmic necessity: the interruptive dissyllable 'quand on' is made to do service as three syllables by increased spacing between letters and heavier type. And this serves the expressive purposes of the poet, as the two syllables, extended, decelerated, capture that slow-motion stalking of the unsuspecting prey. Similarly, the single syllable 'une' is ruptured to make way not only for a tail but for missing syllables. In fact the line provides us with a nice example of what Morier calls *allongement*, that scansional process whereby one accentuated syllable is given the value of two (or presumably three in more comic or melodramatic contexts), by doubling (or tripling) its duration, thus

u—u—u—ne   3!

This rhythmic elasticity expresses the final climatic suspense, the reaching arm, the bated breath, before the 'fowler' makes his lunge to affix to the 'bird' his 'tail'. Thus the anti-expressive constraints of the solid form can be outwitted by the rhythmic flexibilities of humour, by the resourcefulness of the inventive poet. The triumph of discursive rhythm over the meaningless segmentations practised on language by the visual image as solid form is enacted in the reconversion of the Arabic numeral of the first line into the Roman alphabet of the last.

Figs. B, D, and E belong to what Bohn classifies as 'shaped writing: (b) outlined forms': 'Here the text is reduced to one or more lines that reproduce the contours of a given object. The closed forms tend to enclose large amounts of open space but may have a few additional words in their interior' (1986: 51). Fig. D is not quite as closed as Bohn's definition might wish it. The important thing is that the graphic images in these outlined forms are positively written into existence, rather than themselves bringing writing into existence. It is as if a particular image appears, not because it was preconceived, already drawn in, but because a certain quantity and distribution of writing involuntarily made it appear. It is therefore not surprising that these figures have the greater degree of traditional rhythmic coherence. In Fig. B, two hexasyllables radiate from the common initial D, complementing each other in their rhythmic segmentations

Des lacs versicolores   2 + 4
Dans les glaciers solaires.   4 + 2

And mirroring effects are further to be detected in the consonantal rhymes (/lɔR/ : /lɛR/), in the phonetic/graphic interchanges 'lacs'/'gla*ci*ers', -col-/sol-, and other phonemes and graphemes, such as /d/, /l/, /s/, /e/. This eye is full of linguistically generated imagery, and that is why perhaps the lakes are '*versi*colores' rather than, say, 'multicolores'. In this self-completing discourse, heat and cold, the monochrome and polychrome, the celestial and the terrestrial are drawn together in a scintillating pattern. Fig. D has something of the same characteristics, although it is both visually and rhythmically a looser structure:

Mes tapis de la saveur   1] 2 + 4
moussons des sons obscurs   2 + 4
et ta bouche au souffle azur   1] 2 + 4

It is less important that the last two 'lines' here rhyme on /yR/ than that the whole sequence of the five 'lines' of Figs. B and D close on the same tonality: vowel + R. In this way the sensations shared by the eyes have a kind of stereoscopic value. I have taken the liberty here of treating the first syllables of the first and third lines as *anacruses, extrametrical, line-initial upbeats; I feel justified in doing this not only to maintain the hexasyllabic configuration of the other 'eye', here treated as a repeated 2 + 4 sequence, not only because their shared /e/ seemed to warrant treating 'mes' and 'et' in the same way, but more particularly because the sequence 'tapis'/'moussons'/'ta bouche' has significance as a sequence: '*ta*pis' and 'm*ou*ssons' fuse to produce '*ta* b*ou*che'. This is, of course, only one dimension of the sound-patterning of a 'stanza' which, once again, seems to be self-generating and self-justifying: the /a/ of 'tapis' appears again in 'la' and 'saveur' in the first line and then, after exclusion from the second, reappears in 'ta' and 'azur'. The /u/ of 'moussons' and 'bouche', not heard in the first line, recurs in 'souffle'; and the 'sons' which are 'mous' in 'moussons' become 'obscurs' at the line's end.

The fact that Figs. B and D have a certain lyric charge, seem to form an acoustically woven network of private associations, should not blind us to the fact that they, too, may open on to an ever-present awareness of the war, on to a military subtext: 'ta bouche au souffle azur' may well be an artillery piece, the 'moussons des sons obscurs' may be the distant crump of shells at night, and 'mes tapis de la saveur' may be 'tapis de sol' or simply a patchwork of the bitter and sweet tastes of war, throwing an ironic sidelight on 'quel goût de vivre'. Likewise the 'lacs versicolores' may be shell-holes filled with a water coloured by oil, blood, and other effluent. It is important that the face carries the marks of its awareness of war. But despite this, these lines are willed, designed, express both sub-jective freedom and the ability to control discourse and harmonize ex-perience however discordant. This lyric persistence, shown as limiting and deserving of transcendence in 'Voyage', becomes itself the transfigur-ing vehicle and the moral comfort. How else is one, in time of war, to remain in control of one's moral destiny and cling on to one's perceptual rights, other than by writing?

But, as we have seen in other poems, the struggle between the rhythmic and the unutterable is never resolved. The dosages vary and the goal posts are moved. One might experience linguistic disaggregation as a non-compensated loss, as in 'Il pleut'; or such disaggregation might be the necessary route from the lexemic, through the 'morphemic', to the phonemic and a new mode of signifying, as in 'Voyage', where words, words of loss, impotence, and so on, are finally seen to be constellations of signifier-phonemes which can constantly reform and escape their destiny, which form new ocular rhythms across the calligrammatic page. In 'Éventail des saveurs', it is, appropriately, the mouth (Fig. E) in which this conflict is most acute. If, in Fig. C, a lyric guile comes to the aid of language to wrest it from the coercions of the solid form, in Fig. E the lyric freedom of the outlined form is put under pressure by staccato 'train' rhythms (the dissyllable) and an alien typography. By the latter I mean the typeface of 'nographe' and 'aloès', which is the typeface of the public announcement, the billboard poster, and the mail-order catalogue. This is the typeface which removes objects to the realm of public ownership and turns them into displayed commodities; all very well for the phonograph, perhaps, but for the aloe . . . Rhythmically the mouth begins by uttering a sequence of dissyllabic measures, framed at either end by a pair of 'ouïs'; this sequence involves unqualified monosyllabic nouns and the dismemberment of the phonograph. Only with the aloe, shaking off its typeface perhaps, does the trisyllable restore that extra syllable, so crucial in that it takes us from the mechanical off/on pattern to a group in which words can recover something of their diverse substance, and syntax can begin to formulate itself. So there is a new motor, room for the 'éclatement' of the aloe, room for the affectionate diminutive for 'mirliton'; the tetrasyllabic pattern of this last—'et le petit'—introduces that principle of variation without which rhythm cannot be said to exist and without which recurrent features cease to be *choices* and thus expressively significant:

l'aloès | éclater | et le petit | mirliton.   3 + 3 + 4 + 3

Without the evidence of the tetrasyllable, the run of trisyllables would be rhythmically little more 'speaking' than the string of dissyllables which precede them.

The calligram, it seems, provides Apollinaire with an infinite number of ways of exploring this fundamental collision between the rhythmic and non-rhythmic, discourse and image, an infinite number of ways of varying the mix, of responding to changing emphases. Apollinaire was able to adapt the Futurist 'words-in-freedom' programme to an essentially Cubist perceptual mode, and at the same time to hang on to the vocal coherence, albeit vestigial, of an earlier rhythmicity. In this way, in the

Calligrammes, this opposition is lived not as crisis, as it is in Cendrars's *Prose du Transsibérien*, compelling choice, but as simultaneous contrast, in which the poles of the opposition are mutually motivating and justifying; things exist, in a real and intense sense, only differentially. Cendrars was to find his solution, his brand of simultaneous contrast, in the collection published a year after *Calligrammes*, *Dix-neuf poèmes élastiques* (1919).

5

Blaise Cendrars, Dix-neuf poèmes élastiques *(1919)*
The Prosody of Orphism

THERE is an obvious sense in which Pound's 'In a Station of the Metro' is Orphic, if not Orphist: it is a trip to the underworld of the Métro in order to return, not with the crowd seen there, but with some insubstantial vision, the poem's second line. In *The Rhythms of English Poetry* (1982: 121) Derek Attridge scans this poem as an essentially dipodic structure:

> The apparition of these faces in the crowd;
>   o b oBo b o Bo b o B
> Petals on a wet, black bough
>   Bo b o B ô B ô B   [one might rather expect BoboBôbôB]

[Scansional code: B = primary beat; b = secondary beat; o = off-beat; ô = unrealized off-beat.]

What Attridge envisages here then is a duple metre (of alternating stress and non-stress, beat and off-beat, or vice versa), in which there is also an alternation in the strength of beats; the beats are alternately primary and secondary, so that duple feet pair in groups of four syllables. Attridge's point is that even behind the arras of the ostensibly non-metrical lurks the ghost of a traditional metrical frame. Such a view, however revealing, strikes me as mistaken, and for three reasons.

The first, and more general, reason is one already adverted to on several occasions. The real question for free verse is not whether a scansion fits or not, but what scansion is most appropriate. If a metrical set is a mental set, if a metrical set is an expressive set, and code of vocalization, then one must treat free verse's metrical/rhythmic vulnerability with circumspection. Indeed, part of the justification for free verse's rhythmic vulnerability is that the reader is given nothing, but must improvise his/her own reading, or scansion, and in so doing define a posture towards the text. Inasmuch as Pound's Imagistic epiphany, no less than the experience of reality provided by Delaunay's Orphism and pursued by Cendrars, is an exploration of the *profondeur* of perceiving consciousness, the reader/spectator's no less than the writer/painter's, then the discovery of a scansion is the discovery of one's psychophysiological relation to the world; rhythm is the experiential and existential dimension of utterance.

The second reason is connected with the assumption made in the first, that Pound's Imagism is closely affiliated with the Orphism of Delaunay and Cendrars. Attridge's scansion is a scansion of alternation: alternating beat and off-beat, alternating primary and secondary beat. Alternation is the metric of narration (the dipodic metres have intimate connections with the ballad) and discursive meditation. Orphism is not about alternation, but about (simultaneous) contrast and concentricity, the former developed in Delaunay's Window series of 1912, and the latter in his circular forms of 1913. If Orphism is served by any of Attridge's scansional moves, it is by his notation of implied off-beats, as we shall see.

The third reason is historical. When Pound first published 'In a Station of the Metro' in *Poetry* (Apr. 1913), he presented each line as three units, with spaces separating the units:

$$\times \times \quad \diagup \times \mid \times \times \quad \diagup \times$$
In a Station of the Metro
$$\times] \quad \times \times \diagup \times \quad \times \quad \times \diagup \times \quad \times \times \quad \diagup \quad (\times)$$
The] apparition   of these faces   in the crowd:
$$\diagup \times \quad \times \times \diagup (\times) \diagup (\times) \quad \diagup \quad (\times)$$
Petals   on a wet, black   bough.

[(×) = implied off-beats.]

What this reveals is a poem whose opening, particularly if one includes the title, is sustained by a third paeon, the rhythmic configuration ×× ⁄ ×. In order to regularize this pattern over the first line, I am treating the line-initial definite article either as an anacrusis (extrametrical upbeat) or as an elision ('Th'apparition . . .'). It is possible to imagine the spectral survival of the third paeon in the second line, in the phrase 'on a wet, black', if one imagines an off-beat rather than a beat (necessitating an *implied* off-beat between 'wet' and 'black') on 'black'. For my present purposes, namely the attempt to envisage a prosody of Orphism, both the context and the rhythmic disposition of this poem are important.

As mentioned, 'In a Station of the Metro' was first published in 1913, the year in which Apollinaire's 'Les Fenêtres' was published in the catalogue of Robert Delaunay's show in Berlin (January) and in which poems of Cendrars's particularly associated with the Delaunays were either published (*Prose du Transsibérien*, 'Tour') or written ('Journal', 'Contrastes',

'Hamac'). Pound's poem grew, or rather shrank, from an incident in Paris in 1911, when, emerging from the Métro at the place de la Concorde, he 'saw suddenly a beautiful face, and then another and another, and then a beautiful child's face, and then another beautiful woman, and I tried all that day to find words for what this had meant to me, and I could not find any words that seemed to me worthy, or as lovely as that sudden emotion'. Pound's account of the episode, which appeared in the *Fortnightly Review* (1 Sept. 1914—a shorter version had appeared in *T.P.'s Weekly*, 6 June 1913), goes on to describe how he found an equivalent of the experience in 'little splotches of colour', the germ of a new school of non-representative painting (an Orphist vision perhaps?). But the poem cost him greater effort: he started with a thirty-one-line draft, which six months later became something half that length, and, only a year after that, the poem we have before us. Pound emphasizes the need for empathy, if the poem is to be 'understood': 'I dare say it is meaningless unless one has drifted into a certain vein of thought'; and he adds: 'In a poem of this sort one is trying to record the precise instant when a thing outward and objective transforms itself, or darts into a thing inward and subjective.' What seems important to highlight in this account is the push towards an abstract equivalent of an acute sensory experience, which none the less maintains sensoriness, and the emphasis on the *dynamic* of transformation, movement as relation-in-change. The former of these is perhaps easier to associate with Orphism than the latter: Delaunay's cultivation of a non-objective art opens imaginative space up to the eye, which can now pass uninterruptedly from microcosm to macrocosm, from the occasional to the universal: 'This imaginative spaciousness of the Window pictures opens the way to a completely new dimension of consciousness for the painter: it throws open the door to the poetic-visionary realm' (Vriesen, in Vriesen and Imdahl 1967: 42).

The movement which carries the world of light and colour through the window of the eye to the soul in Delaunay's work:

Nos yeux sont les fenêtres de notre nature et de notre âme. C'est dans nos yeux que se passent le présent, la 'science mathématique' et par conséquent notre sensibilité. Nous ne pouvons rien sans la sensibilité, donc sans lumière. Par conséquent notre âme tient sa vie dans l'harmonie et l'harmonie ne s'engendre que de la simultanéité où les mesures et les proportions de la lumière arrivent à l'âme par nos yeux, sens suprême (Delaunay 1975: 159)

is vibratory and continuous, not descriptive and successive, as he would have us believe the dynamic of the Futurists is. But we may well feel that

Pound's outwardness 'darting' into inwardness has more in common with the transformations of external plastic infinity into internal plastic infinity described by Boccioni in his 'Technical Manifesto of Futurist Sculpture' (1912).

At all events, in a letter to Harriet Monroe of 30 March 1913 Pound observed: 'In the "Metro" hokku, I was careful, I think, to indicate spaces between the rhythmic units, and I want them observed.' Pound's spaces help us to latch on to the third paeon and to see the rhythmic cohesion of the title and the first line, based on the shared syntax of prepositional phrases. But while the title has two full third paeons, is purely notational or locational, is voice without expression, is no more than adverbial, the first line's paeons are shakier (anacrusis at beginning, truncation at end) and the notational style is invaded by perceptual ambiguity, sight by incipient vision: 'apparition' is both the passively seen and the actively appearing, something merely visible and something positively ghost-like (Kenner 1975: 184–5, is eloquent about the Hadean overtones of this line); 'these' introduces a subjective viewpoint and an attempt to fix and identify by deixis; the implied off-beat at the end of the line begins to introduce the rhythmic traces of the subject into the non-vocal, mental spaces between the units.

In the second line, the third paeon is only spectral. The marked syllabic reduction which has occurred between lines 1 and 2, from eleven or twelve syllables to seven, means a corresponding increase in implied off-beats, which insinuate themselves into every crevice of the line, engineering a subtext of tacit reverberation. The largely defined world of demonstratives and definite articles has become the unspecified mode of zero and indefinite articles. The notational style now belongs to an Orphist world, more abstract, expression without voice, a non-gravitational zone of measureless space.

But the poem does not merely describe an itinerary, a development. Its successiveness is undermined or counteracted by a powerful acoustic concentricity; the consciousness flickers back and forth between the circles of this urban hell as the inner ear picks up the echoes: 'station' 'faces' (/eI/); 'station', 'apparition' (/ʃən/); 'apparition', 'black' (/æ/); 'crowd', 'black' (/k/); 'crowd', 'bough' (/aʊ/); 'metro', 'petals', 'wet' (/ɛt/). A specific encounter/object (like Delaunay's Eiffel Tower in *Les Fenêtres*) is both the outer limit of all inner, psychic journeys, and the inner limit of all metaphysical ones. Pound's image which 'presents an intellectual and emotional complex in an instant of time' has deep affinities with Delaunay's Orphism. The sequential and successive become the kaleidoscopic, the multiple instant that gathers up spans of time and space.

Kenner is right to point out that 'In a Station of the Metro' is not formally a sentence, that its structure is typographic and metric (1975: 186–7), if he means that these lines tend towards the unspeakable, the unutterable, reject voice, in favour of language inhabited by movement, flow, inflexion. Pound's introduction of spaces between units is not a guide to uttering and pausing, but the installing of a distance, the provision of an option on disembodiment. The gaps allow the prepositions and propositions (nouns) degrees of absoluteness that aid autonomy, interchangeability and above all insistent presence, undifferentiated perspective, aura. The proposition that poetry constantly courts speech and experience in other modes, that it compels us to hear or perceive other kinds of existence even as we make sense of its words in terms of our own existence, will raise no eyebrows. Where is the language of poetry to be situated between sleeping and waking, between the will to speak and the will to hear, the will to speak and the will to be spoken (or verbalized), the will to control language (utter it) and the will to submit to it (assimilate it)? A poem is a transcript of a set of verbal events at a whole variety of possible levels of both the conscious and the unconscious. Implied beats and off-beats are one manner of multiplying the dimensions of the text and of experience, between the spoken and the heard, the superliminal and the subliminal, the manifest and the intuited; implied beats and off-beats are pure consciousness animated by the after-print of speech, the abstraction of the actualized. Too often they are thought of as purely metrical, a means of compensating for rhythmic incompleteness. But, as we see here, the implied off-beats of the second line are not filled metrical gaps so much as reverberations of preceding stresses, the inwardness of an outwardness, the moment when the spoken takes possession of itself as a kind of perception.

This is not the only means available in English poetry to establish the multidimensionality both of language and of the mechanisms of perception. Hopkins, for example, uses extrametricality to achieve this effect; he calls extrametrical syllables 'hangers' or 'outrides' precisely because 'they seem to hang below the line or ride forward or backward from it in another dimension than the line itself' (Author's Preface, 1883). And his own brand of essentialism, inscape, the thisness or selfhood of a thing, is apprehended through 'instress', or the stress of sprung rhythm, where stress for Hopkins is, among other things, 'the making of a thing more, or making it markedly what it already is; it is the bringing out of its nature' (letter to Patmore, 7 Nov. 1833). But just prior to World War I, the search for ways to open up temporality and space grew more urgent as multidimensional geometry, Bergsonian duration, and simultanism became crucial foundations for avant-garde aesthetics. This is certainly a central concern for Orphism.

Orphism as a term was invented by Apollinaire to identify a new departure in Cubism, and was first used by him of Kupka's work in October 1912. What most fundamentally distinguishes Orphism from Cubism is its preoccupation with colour, and more particularly colour contrasts, a continuation of the tradition leading from Chevreul's treatise of 1839, through Impressionism and Neo-Impressionism (Seurat was revealed to Delaunay in 1907–8 along with Chevreul; Cross had a retrospective in 1911 at the Salon des Indépendants) to Fauvism. Colour, inasmuch as it destroys line (spatial measurement), destroys the analytically successive and substitutes for it the 'deep' (immediate and total transparency—how 'deep' is colour?) and the simultaneous: '*La ligne c'est la limite. La couleur donne la profondeur* (non perspective, *non successive*, mais simultanée) *et sa forme et son mouvement*' (Delaunay 1957: 110). If we were crudely to tabulate what Delaunay himself sees as the principal differences between Cubism and Orphism, they would be these:

Cubism	*Orphism*
imitative/descriptive	representative/creative
linear/monochromatic	coloured
static	dynamic
opacity of objects	transparency of coloured surface
perspectival and gravitational	measureless space and antigravitational (rotational)
chiaroscuro and modelling	tonal modulation, complementarity of hue
analytic	synthetic
successive	simultaneous

Several of these distinctions might be quarrelled with; our own experience tells us that, at least in terms of its ocular elusiveness, Cubism is far from static, and that its awkward shifts in alignment and perspective make the notion 'successive' too simple, and its implication of 'consecutive' mistaken. Delaunay also taxed the Futurists with being descriptive and successive, as we have just seen; among other things, he finds their brand of simultaneity 'machiniste', in the way that chronophotography is:

La vision simultanée des futuristes est dans un tout autre sens. Je prends, par exemple, un titre de leur tableau: *Simultanéité*. Ce mot est étymologique en littérature, donc classique, passéiste. Dynamisme successif, machiniste en peinture, ainsi que cela ressort de leur manifeste. C'est un mouvement machiniste et non vivant. (Delaunay 1957: 110)

This is to take no account of the fact that the Futurist photographer Anton Giulio Bragaglia, in his manifesto of 'Futurist Photodynamism' (1911), took Marey to task for exactly the same failing:

To put it crudely, chronophotography could be compared with a clock on the face of which only the quarter-hours are marked, cinematography to one on which the minutes too are indicated, and Photodynamism to a third on which are marked, not only the seconds, but also the *intermovemental* fractions existing in the passages between seconds. This becomes an almost infinitesimal calculation of movement. (Apollonio 1973: 40)

But grafted on to the preoccupation with colour was a concern with non-Euclidean and particularly *n*-dimensional geometry, which Orphism shared with Cubism. This concern derived not only from the geometers themselves, from Riemann and Lobachevsky, Poincaré and Jouffret, via the Cubists' tame mathematician Maurice Princet, and the contemporary fad for science fiction, but from Cézanne and Japanese art.

Cézanne understood that space was a function of perception, and that perception itself was a dynamic activity involving constant readjustments of spatial dimension. What is more, the scanning movement of the eye is circular, so that the geometry most appropriate to it is not the flat planar geometry of the fifteenth century in which straight lines converge on a single vanishing point, but the non-Euclidean geometry of the curve. Furthermore, Cézanne's understanding of pictorial space as a construct of the perceiving subject squares very much with Poincaré's ideas about visual, motor, and tactile space, whereby space has as many dimensions as the spectator has muscles (for an absorbing history and treatment of non-Euclidean and *n*-dimensional geometry in the Cubist period, see Henderson 1975).

Japanese art had been instrumental in undermining mechanistic Renaissance perspective by offering a reversed view, a widening rather than narrowing perspective (one thinks back to the metaphysical rationale of the haiku and Pound's 'In a Station of the Metro'). But for all its liberation of the eye, 'perspective cavalière' is no more than a special dispensation from geometric perspective; its principles and means remain the same. Delaunay's quarrel with Cubism, as we have seen, was that Cubism perpetuates traditional perspectivism; it seems to introduce a new spatial language, it seems to liberate perception, but in fact it only tinkers with a system it does not abolish; it multiplies points of view within the system of point of view. We have seen, too, Cendrars's espousal of a new vitalistic mode of perceiving spatial relations. None the less, and Delaunay's objections aside, we should remember that reversed perspective was, for

Apollinaire at least, a way of making the fourth dimension available: he calls perspective a 'truc misérable . . . cette quatrième dimension à rebours . . . ce moyen de tout rapetisser inévitablement' (*Les Peintres cubistes*, 1913).

What made the Eiffel Tower such a potent symbol for Delaunay and Cendrars was not just what it meant as a symbol of modernity or of simultaneity (it had become a radio transmitter in 1909, sending messages across Europe and the Atlantic, as in Apollinaire's 'Lettre-Océan'), but what it meant as a structure which resisted depiction, which resisted depiction precisely because it was the figure of the unrepresentable, the structure which incorporated the curved and tapering planes of non-Euclidean geometry and the potential multi-dimensionality of *n*-dimensional space; as Cendrars puts it, in a lecture given on 12 June 1924 at Saõ Paulo on simultaneous contrast:

Aucune formule d'art, connue jusqu'à ce jour, ne pouvait avoir la prétention de résoudre plastiquement le cas de la tour Eiffel. Le réalisme rapetissait; les vieilles lois de la perspective italienne l'amincissaient . . . [Delaunay] désarticula la Tour pour la faire entrer dans son cadre, il la tronqua et l'inclina pour lui donner ses trois cents mètres de vertige, il adopta dix points de vue, quinze perspectives, telle partie est vue d'en bas, telle autre d'en haut, les maisons qui l'entourent sont prises de droite, de gauche, à vol d'oiseau, terre à terre . . . (Cendrars 1987: 79–80)

Not surprisingly, Delaunay's images of the destruction of the tower (1910) are more the images of the tower's destruction of old perceptual and constructional modes.

Juxtaposed, superimposed, and overlapping colour planes were one way that Delaunay could create multidimensional space: colours open the way to infinite depth, they advance and recede against each other, they attract and repel each other, vibrate, and the size and shape of colour areas dictate the degree of their influence and the direction of their activity. More basically, colour is the ground of all perceptual consciousness, the cross-over point between inner and outer states, and the source of all movement and simultanism. Through the contrastive play of complementary colours, of related and dissonant hues, slow and fast speeds are created ('les mouvements *lents*, des compléments, les mouvements *vites*, des dissonances', Delaunay 1957: 184). No colour can be perceived in isolation, but operates continuously and simultaneously with others, and in different ways for each: 'Tout par contraste a une valeur; il n'y a pas de couleur fixe, tout est couleur par contraste, tout est couleur en mouvement, tout est profondeur' (Delaunay 1957: 115). And beyond this pictorial simultaneity and mutual interdependence lies the interrelatedness of all being.

We have seen how the notion of simultaneous contrast might be applied to Apollinaire's *Calligrammes*; we have seen how Cendrars rejected the machinism of Futurism in favour of an organic 'chimisme', and adumbrated how a Futurist 'jusqu'au bout' might be replaced by an Orphist *profondeur*. It is to the relation between Orphism and Cendrars's *Dix-neuf poèmes élastiques* (1919) that we now turn, addressing ourselves, first of all, to 'Journal':

1. Christ
2. Voici plus d'un an que je n'ai plus pensé à Vous
3. Depuis que j'ai écrit mon avant-dernier poème Pâques
4. Ma vie a bien changé depuis
5. Mais je suis toujours le même
6. J'ai même voulu devenir peintre
7. Voici les tableaux que j'ai faits et qui ce soir pendent aux murs
8. Ils m'ouvrent d'étranges vues sur moi-même qui me font penser à Vous.

9. Christ
10. La vie
11. Voilà ce que j'ai fouillé

12. Mes peintures me font mal
13. Je suis trop passionné
14. Tout est orangé.

15. J'ai passé une triste journée à penser à mes amis
16. Et à lire le journal
17. Christ
18. Vie crucifiée dans le journal grand ouvert que je tiens les bras tendus
19. Envergures
20. Fusées
21. Ébullition
22. Cris.
23. On dirait un aéroplane qui tombe.
24. C'est moi.

25. Passion
26. Feu
27. Roman-feuilleton
28. Journal
29. On a beau ne pas vouloir parler de soi-même
30. Il faut parfois crier

31. Je suis l'autre
32. Trop sensible

There are immediately obvious ways in which 'Journal', written in
August 1913, just before the appearance of the *Prose du Transsibérien,* and
first published in *Les Soirées de Paris* (15 Apr. 1914), plays with radical
contrast: discursive autobiography collides with verbal eruption, and the
apostrophized Christ vies with the newspaper. Equally conspicuous is
the structural patterning, first pointed out by Flückiger (1977: 130): each
'Christ' apostrophe is followed by a seven-line development, and the
poem ends with a two-line self-definition, which gathers up indications in
lines 5, 13, and 24:

> 5. Mais je suis toujours le même   5 + 2

> 13. Je suis trop passionné   7 (2 + 5)[1]

> 24. C'est moi   2

These lines fall as follows: lines 5 and 13 are each the medial line of their
seven-line developments, and line 24 is the final line of its group. These
seven-line developments, as Flückiger has also observed (1977: 130–1),
move in concentric circles about their centres; once that centre has been
reached, one might therefore conclude, movement forward is always balanced by an equal and opposite movement backwards; reading is itself a
simultanizing process, a journey in Bergsonian *durée.*

   This notion of concentricity is worth picking out in more detail, since
it helps us understand the possible principles of lexical and acoustic
arrangement in the poem. Let us consider lines 2–8. Line 2, we notice,
already has its own concentricity: it begins and ends with a capitalized V;
'plus de' is answered by its negative counterpart 'ne . . . plus'; the nasal
/ã/ of 'an' is answered by 'pensé'; the line more or less pivots round the
coupled schwas 'que je'—I say 'more or less', because the medial point
is 'je', the seventh syllable in this thirteen-syllable line, just as the *self-*
centred lines 5 and 13 are the medial lines of their seven-line groups.

   The outer limits of this second line, /vwasi/ and /vu/, are also the
outer limits of the whole seven-line group (2–8), and indeed of the last
two lines of the group (7–8). The sense of this first stanza, therefore,
being a set of overlapping or interlocking planes is a fairly strong one.
And this pair—/vwasi/ and /vu/—also operate as the parameters of the
acoustic modulation /vwasi/ > /vi/ > /vuly/ > /vy/ > /uvR/ > /vu/,
so that, as the poet himself says in line 8, /vy/ makes him think of /vu/,

---

[1] Here, as elsewhere in this poem, I have opted for a careful reading (with diaeresis) of
-ion, in order to bring out structural parallels.

in a chain of purely abstract phonetic association (I leave out of account the sub-echoes in 'avant' and 'devenir').

But 'Voici' is not just the initiator of acoustic modulation; it also initiates patterns of modulation in grammatical function which lead us across the boundaries of the concentric circles, thus:

Voici (2) as temporal prep. (= il y a)	> Voici (7) deictic prep.
plus de (2)	> ne . . . plus (2)
depuis que (3) conj.	> depuis (4) adv.
le même (5) indef. pron.	> même (6) adv.
	> moi-même (8) adj.
faire (7) as action	> faire (8) as causative

There might be other such shifts of function to highlight, just as other acoustic chains—e.g. 'pense' > 'peintre' > 'pendent' > 'penser'—might be selected. What is important is that language begins to operate as a set of transparent planes through each of which one sees meaning, but by each of which, at the same time, one is handed on to another, contrasting, or adjusted, view. And these closely related, but divergent, grammatical colourings are there, like the absence of punctuation, to facilitate the passage of consciousness, to promote its unhindered, but vibrating circulation. Grammatical categories, just like acoustic tonalities, become a range of related or dissonant hues, varying the speed of assimilative movement, of reading.

Grammatical/syntactic structures can also, of course, contribute to the patterns of concentricity. In lines 2–8 the structures 'je' (or equivalent) + aux. ('avoir') and 'je' + pres. tense of 'être' create a chiastic arrangement:

2. je n'ai plus pensé
3. j'ai écrit
4. ma vie a changé
5. je suis le même
6. j'ai voulu
7. j'ai faits

which corresponds to the sequence: thinking—writing—change—no change—painting—thinking; or are part of a movement inwards from 'Vous' to 'je' followed by an outwards radiation, back towards the 'Vous' again. Paralleling these chiastic configurations is the pattern of syllabic contraction followed by a corresponding and equal expansion: 13 (2), 14 (3), 8 (4), 7 (5), 8 (6), 15 (7), 15 (8).

It is not, then, difficult to make the case for the presence of concentric and contrastive techniques which would relate this poem to Orphist

simultanism. Nor would it be impossible to argue that the prosody makes
its own contribution. The central prosodic contrast is that between long
and short lines. The syllabic spectrum within which French verse can be
properly metrical, visibly metrical, runs between 6 and 12, the hexasyllable
and the alexandrine, though one might argue between 4 and 12; in other
words, the poem provides us with examples of the prosodically infra-red
and the prosodically ultraviolet stringing out between them all the colours
of the spectrum. But beside this underlying polarized contrast, there is
contrast within the long line itself, as we shall see if we compare lines 3
and 7, which correspond to each other in relative length, in content, and
in their position in the seven-line sequence:

3. Depuis que j'ai écrit | mon avant-dernier   6 (2 + 4) + 7 (5 + 2) + 1
   poème | Pâques
7. Voici les tableaux | que j'ai faits | et qui   5 (2 + 3) + 3 + 4 + 3
   ce soir | pendent aux murs

There are basically two kinds of contrast within the long line: first, the
long line lends itself either to an intensive reading, as here line 7, with
a relatively high degree of primary accentuation and thus of expressive
insistence, or to an extensive reading, as in line 3, where the voice glides
over accent and encapsulates longer syllabic strings in more casual or
offhand discourse. So these longer lines set themselves at the crossroads
of the micro and macro perspectives, of proximity and distance. Secondly, the long line allows different degrees of metrical/rhythmic consistency and recognizability. Rhythmically, our two lines are worlds apart.
Line 3 is rhythmically inchoate; slack, long measures are capped by an
abrupt monosyllabic unit, creating an awkward juxtaposition of accents,
which in turn necessitates a pause, so that the title of the poem disengages
itself from the discourse; this is a line set in the temporal, and accompanied by vagueness and approximation. Line 7, one the other hand, seems
rhythmically altogether more purposeful; it has a spatial orientation, made
more specific by the deictics 'Voici' and 'ces', and is given order and
meaningful context by the relative clauses; and the recurrent trisyllabic
measure produces a certain stability at the same time as tautness and
control. Cendrars's vocation as a writer with a specifically spiritual quest
('Pâques') has led to a loss of Christ and a separation of himself from
his life. His attempts at painting, on the other hand, have produced
an *Auseinandersetzung* with himself which has opened up the route to
redemption.

The generating origin of the rhythmically infra-red (the monolexical

short line) in this poem is, of course, 'Christ' (/kRist/), also the generating origin of a suggestive lexical chain focused on the acoustic motif /i/:
'Christ—écrit—ma vie—la vie—lire—vie crucifiée—ébullition—cris—
passion—sensible'; and just as 'Christ' becomes 'cris' (as in /jezy kRi/),
so 'Christ' (/kRist/) is a fusion of 'cris' and 'triste'. The monolexical line
which has no rhythmic context, or is a protorhythmic cell available to all
contexts, is peculiarly both exclamatory—it must have an accent and a
line-accent at that—and unuttered. It has the irreducible urgency of an
interjection and the featureless presence of an item in a list. Thus polarized within it are the spoken and the written. Creating its own space of
discourse, it is a rhythmic zero, with a digital rather than analogue syllabic
contour; in other words, it is rhythmically abstract, non-figurative; it is
not embedded within a visible duration, but makes partially visible an
enigmatic and invisible duration to which it is somehow the key.

In the first sequence of these monolexical lines (17–22) Christ is cru-
cified in and by the newspaper, the new Bible, which also crucifies its
reader. This is the moment of Christ's disappearance, of his transformation
into 'Cris'; this is the moment at which the divine aviator of the Ascension becomes the falling Icarus of the foaming waves ('Envergures'?
'Ébullition'?). This is the moment, too, when the journal as organ of
public news reveals its other dimension, the intimate diary ('C'est moi').
Just as, just beyond the coloured shapes of Delaunay's windows, one may
suspect the presence of a city, its buildings and streets, so behind the
sequence of lines 19–22 one may suspect the continuing presence of the
newspaper, open, then closed, and then reopened: 'Envergures' (open,
as wings), 'Fusées' (closed, as a single narrow column), 'Ébullition' (the
rustling of the paper as another page is sought), 'Cris' (as the paper is
reopened and the headlines leap out at the reader). But this is a purely
potential reality, which is held back from us by virtue of the undetermined plurality of the nouns ('Ébullition' excepted). Equally these nouns
might be a set of mental processes: the flights of imagination ('Envergures'),
the soaring rockets of the exploration of *profondeur* ('Fusées'—'Le
simultané: mes yeux voient jusqu'aux étoiles', Delaunay 1957: 110), the
activity of the mind at boiling point ('Ébullition'), the moments of sharp
distress ('Cris'). It is perhaps no accident that, in describing Apollinaire's
encounter with Cendrars, Delaunay should have written in October 1913:
'Cette rencontre a donné une ébullition à Apollinaire . . .' (Delaunay 1957:
111).

The single-word lines at 19–22 occur in the syllabic sequence 3, 2, 5,
1. The next series, at lines 25–8, creates the sequence 3, 1, 5, 2. Thus

'Passion' = 'Envergures', 'Feu' = 'Fusées', but syllabically = 'Cris',
'Roman-feuilleton' = 'Ébullition', 'Journal' = 'Cris', but syllabically =
'Fusées'. At the same time singulars spark off plurals, literal shifts into
figurative and vice versa, and Christ, poet, and newspaper are caught up
in a vertiginous and inter-allusive web: 'Passion' refers back to 'Je suis
trop passionné', but also to Christ; 'Feu' reminds us of 'Tout est orangé',
but speaks, too, of death; 'Roman-feuilleton' trivializes perhaps the poet's
relationship with Christ, but also suggests that the serial can emerge from
the discontinuous and ephemeral. Goldenstein (1986: 27) reminds us, in
his excellent critical edition of *Dix-neuf poèmes élastiques*, that line 31 both
alludes to Nerval and adumbrates the theme of the double which will
recur in Cendrars's work, notably in *Moravagine* and *L'Homme foudroyé*.
But looking back to line 5, we must remember that the poet is as much
the same as he is the other, is as much the passionate (l. 13) as he is the
sensitive (l. 32), that, like his prosody and the lexical/grammatical structure,
he is the movement which emerges from simultaneous contrasts, from
complementarity and dissonance.

There is one further dimension of the monolexical line and its relation
to voice which we should explore, namely the monolexical line's necessary status as image. Just as the mechanism of primary rhythm can
threaten to reappropriate what the voice has assimilated and subjectivized
as secondary rhythm, so the image can likewise 'unvoice' itself if its origin
is seen to be not in the uttering imagination, but in visual or visualizing
perception; if, that is, it is not generated by language so much as merely
registered in it. This distinction is partly to do with the development of
the function of the image. The image which is called forth to illustrate,
decorate, or enhance a perception which is already in discourse will owe
much of its power, its functional efficiency, to the ease with which it
emerges from, and the degree to which it is assorted to, that same discourse.
In other words, the image's expressive efficiency is in large part rhetorical.
Not surprisingly, any image which appears in regular verse is subject to
the dominant discourse of the metre/genre and must, in that sense, always
be felt to be part of the uttering imagination, to be something called forth
by discourse itself and in conformity with the 'style' of that discourse.
Immediately one passes on to free verse, however, there are no rhythmic
guarantees about the source of the image and for that very reason the
function of the image is free to change. It is no accident that the ancestors
of Surrealist images are to be found in the poetic prose and prose poems
of Lautréamont and Rimbaud. The emergence of the 'new' imagery
coincides with the failure of discourse *qua* discourse, so eloquently ex-

plored by Hofmannsthal in the *Chandos Brief* (1902). What is the nature of the 'new' image? We might tentatively suggest the following character-istics: (1) it is bound into time and direct sensory experience, and lasts only a moment; (2) it is marked by revelatory speed (i.e. it is not rhetor-ically controlled) and may seem to come from anywhere; (3) it has a powerful attractive force (drawing together, synthesizing) and a powerful explosive force (ramifying association and connection); (4) it is a moment of existential or metaphysical illumination (epiphany); (5) it is autonomous, and can only occur in discontinuity (the 'absolute image' of German Expressionism).

It is to this brand of imagery that the monolexical line belongs, and its lack of status, or its totally problematic status, relates to its discontinuity and to its denudedness. Does it relate to what precedes or to what suc-ceeds? And if so, how? Is it sense-datum, a notation (Impressionism), or a metaphor, a hallucination (Expressionism), or an angle of vision (Cubism), or an object dynamized by its lines of force (Futurism), or is its meaning in the interval that lies between it and its context, in its very relationality (Orphism)? Is it third person (referential) or second person (conative), or even a persona of the first person (expressive)? If it is second person, for example, is it a simple vocative, or an apostrophe? That is, what kind of speech-act is it, what kind of illocutionary force does it have? When we say that these monolexical lines in 'Journal' polarize themselves as exclamation and item in a list, spoken and written, we should understand that the spoken is already at its limit: it is invol-untary speech, an act of merest identification, recognition, but at the same time the speech-act of fullest significance, naming; impotence and im-periousness catch us in another tension. And equally we are compelled to say that just as it is zero articled, so too it is zero rhythmed, or it is protorhythmic. Rhythm in this sense is a force of mediation, which negotiates between a vocal impulse and a word coming to meet that impulse, so that it is difficult to distinguish between inwardness and outwardness. In this catalytic or intermediary role, rhythm itself wins independence, or at least begins to exert its power as a free agent. Just as Delaunay's windows belong neither to the inside (subject) nor the outside (reality), and in that correspond to the eyes, or as Buckberrough (1982: 120) puts it:

our eyes are more than simply the filter through which the exterior reality becomes consciousness; they exist *independently* of both exterior nature and interior soul. Like the windows, our eyes are the neutral entities that allow the transcendence between the two to take place just so does rhythm belong neither to poet nor to language. To understand this fully, to be able to suggest that rhythm has become abstract, as abstract as the colour in a window, we have to understand the laws by which, in this instance, it comes into existence; it comes into existence neither as an imperative of syntactic segmentation or articulation (there is no syntax), nor as an imperative of expressivity (there is no expression); it comes into existence as an imperative of verse structure: the last (or only) word of a line of verse, whether regular or free, must carry an accent on its final accentuable syllable. This may sound as though abstract rhythm is in fact metrical, but it is not, because this law by itself is not metrical; it needs to be associated with syllabism before it can become metrical. In other words, and this is vital, lineation in free verse is not only a way of ensuring that rhythm belongs more meaningfully to the voice, can register more finely the voice's psychophysiological tremors; it is also a way of removing rhythm from the voice and from discourse, so that it can mediate not between an utterable text and utterance, but between a non-text, an anti-text, an unspeakable text (it can be spoken, but not in any meaningful discourse), and the voice. Concrete poetry (and indeed words-in-freedom) deals with uncontextualized, free-floating lexical items, but they do not engage the voice, so the voice, so the question of rhythm, does not arise (quite apart from the fact that our law of lineation does not apply). Cendrars's monolexical lines, on the other hand, still go 'à la marge/à la ligne' and collect their capitals, as part of an ongoing, developing structure. It is just that the rhythm of these lines is no longer the instrument of voice transforming text into inwardness and response, but is the interval between voice and linguistic entity, the vibration between them, so that because of rhythm neither can claim the victory. Rhythm is here purely an element of verse structure, and because of that it must be acceded to, 'Feu' must be 'Feú' and 'Journal' must be 'Journál'; but because of that, too, this mutual interrogation, of voice by word and word by voice, is worth while, for if rhythm holds the balance, it also guarantees the assimilation of text, not to voice, but to structure.

As we read 'Journal', then, we should be aware that we are passing through contrasting rhythms, not contrasting kinds of rhythm but contrasting perceptions of rhythm. The longer lines, which we have elsewhere called *palier* lines, draw elements back into discourse and make statements and declarations on the strength of them. The short lines throw discourse out, along with its perception of rhythm, as that which sustains and construes utterance; in its place they put words which displace the single viewing point of personal consciousness, and scatter it to the four corners of possible reality and its possible meanings. Rhythm is the agent of this dispossession; but it is also the agent of a vibratory dialogue between word and consciousness, the negotiator of their rival claims. In this sense, even as we read a sequence of short lines as a sequence of meanings (as we have done), we should remember that we are in fact reading, if only we could educate our desires to fit the model of perception, to fit, indeed, the facts, a sequence of suspensions of the process of reading; and by suspensions of reading, I do not mean deferrals of meaning, but the impossibility of knowing how to read, enunciate, articulate, motivate.

Delaunay concerned himself directly, if summarily, with what simultanism might mean in literature—'le simultanisme littéraire peut être donné par l'emploi des contrastes des mots' (Delaunay 1957: 112); and conversely, many of the terms he uses of the visual arts have powerfully literary connotations: in his essay on 'La Lumière' (pub. Jan. 1913), for instance, he writes, 'Le mouvement est donné par les rapports des *mesures impaires*' (Delaunay 1957: 146). Cendrars's 'Journal' is certainly rich in *vers impairs*, but this is not really the point, because Delaunay's 'mesures impaires' are contrasts of colour, and what contrast has meant in prosodic terms, so far, is the polarization of the ultraviolet and infra-red, and, within the ultraviolet, the polarization of intensive and extensive readings, of the rhythmically inchoate and the rhythmically cohesive, and within the infra-red the polarization of the written and spoken, the neutral item and the urgent exclamation. Finally, the polarization of ultraviolet and infra-red, long line and short, is the polarization of different ways of perceiving rhythm and rhythmic function.

In the course of our analysis of 'Journal' we have had ample cause to refer to the principle of concentricity, which relates directly to Delaunay's circular forms of 1913. Buckberrough (1982), like Spate (1979) before her, explores the celebration of the circular in early twentieth-century art, quoting in particular the lines from Jules Romains's *La Vie unanime* (1908):

> La roue de l'omnibus qui fait des étincelles,
> Et la roue du soleil qu'embourbent les nuages
> Donnent un rythme à ma pensée impersonnelle;
> Je suis un tournoiement majestueux d'images.

It is difficult to imagine, in the light of the *Prose du Transsibérien* alone, that Cendrars would not have heavily endorsed these lines, and scholars have paid much attention to the wheel in Cendrars's iconography—I

think particularly of Dupré (1977). The circle for Delaunay is the principle of the antigravitational, that which inextricably links centripetal and
centrifugal, that which ensures the simultaneous by being non-successive
and non-directional. It is an image of emanating consciousness achieving
universality. It is the form which maximizes the availability of colours to
each other, without any colour being lost from view. And most satisfying
of all perhaps, it is not the figure which rotates the colours, but the
movement of the colours which makes the figure rotate:

> On ne voit donc pas ici tourner un disque aux couleurs changeantes, on ne voit
> que des couleurs dont le rythme tend à devenir cyclique, des couleurs qui s'agrègent
> librement pour se cristalliser en rond, l'œil étant ramené de la sorte sans cesse de
> l'une à l'autre sans jamais pouvoir circonscrire leur mouvement dans un contour
> totalisant. (Le Bec 1985: 189)

It is from the point of view of the circular, of renewed concentricity, that
I wish to approach the fifth of *Dix-neuf poèmes élastiques*, 'Ma danse':

1. Platon n'accorde pas droit de cité au poète
2. Juif errant
3. Don Juan métaphysique
4. Les amis, les proches
5. Tu n'as plus de coutumes et pas encore d'habitudes
6. Il faut échapper à la tyrannie des revues
7. Littérature
8. Vie pauvre
9. Orgueil déplacé
10. Masque
11. La femme, la danse que Nietzsche a voulu nous apprendre à danser
12. La femme
13. Mais l'ironie?

14. Va-et-vient continuel
15. Vagabondage spécial
16. Tous les hommes, tous les pays
17. C'est ainsi que tu n'es plus à charge
18. Tu ne te fais plus sentir. . .

19. Je suis un monsieur qui en des express fabuleux traverse les toujours
    mêmes Europes et regarde découragé par la portière
20. Le paysage ne m'intéresse plus
21. Mais la danse du paysage
22. La danse du paysage
23. Danse-paysage
24. Paritatitata
25. Je tout-tourne

This poem is, as it were, made up of two laps of the same topoi, the second of which increases gradually in gyration, releasing stronger centripetal and centrifugal forces. The first part of the first lap is provided by lines 1–5, to which, in the second lap, correspond lines 14–18; the second part of the first lap is to be found in lines 11–13 and this is answered, in the second lap, by lines 19–25. Lines 6–10 operate as a counter argument or qualifying argument to lines 1–5, and allow the emergence of lines 14–18. The shift from the first circle to the second not only increases rotation but also provides a different range of colourings.

The poem opens with Plato's peremptory banishment of the poet from the Republic, because of his ability to arouse violent passions. The poet is thus cast as nomadic pariah, the wandering Jew condemned to walk the earth until the world's end for having abused Christ on his way to crucifixion, a Don Juan with a metaphysical rather than, or as well as, a sexual pruritus:

Je ne suis pas poète. Je suis libertin. Je n'ai aucune méthode de travail. J'ai un sexe. Je suis par trop sensible. Je ne sais pas parler objectivement de moi-même. Tout être vivant est une physiologie. Et si j'écris, c'est pêut-être par besoin, par hygiène, comme on mange, comme on respire, comme on chante. C'est peut-être par instinct; peut-être par spiritualité. (Cendrars 1987: 195)

The poet looks to his friends and those close to him for succour, but he has been culturally desocialized and has yet to create an alternative existential structure.

Lines 6–10 reverse this view in order to correct it. As tyrannical as Plato's banishment of the poet is the literary review's insistence on placing literature at the centre of urban existence. But literature is cultural hypocrisy. Cendrars creates a sequence of appositions which are self-inflating, up to the pentasyllable 'Orgueil déplacé', and then simply removes the carpet in the brusque, monolexical condemnation of 'Masque'. Or perhaps it would be more accurate to describe lines 7–10 as a movement of syllabic expansion, pretension—'Littérature' (4) > 'Orgueil déplacé' (5)— ghosted by a parallel movement of syllabic contraction and deflation— 'Vie pauvre' (2) > 'Masque' (1). Either way 'pauvre' justifies 'déplacé', and attracts to itself both literal and figurative interpretations. Lines 6–10, then, are a kind of small inner circle, which remind us that a literature which is fostered, pandered to, is no better than a literature out in the cold, and provide the poet with the salutary reminder that his casting himself as 'Juif errant' and 'Don Juan métaphysique' is no less a literary gesture, an act of literary self-inflation, than the behaviour encouraged by literary reviews; in fact, inasmuch as the two sequences parallel each other, 'Vie pauvre' corresponds to 'Juif errant', and 'Orgueil déplacé' corresponds to 'Don Juan métaphysique', and if this is so, there is some sense in which 'Masque' becomes a comment on 'Tu n'as plus de coutumes et pas encore d'habitudes'—the poet-as-exile survives no less on convenient personae than the metropolitan literatus. If lines 6–10 are an inner circle with a different set of hues, a different point of view—third person or impersonal rather then second person—its elements complement those of lines 1–5, and the circulation between the two colour sets is facilitated by lines like 2, 3, 7, 8, 9, and 10, which, because they have no articles, have no perspective, are available to all perspectives; we may learn to attribute a second-person perspective to 'Juif errant', for example, when we read line 5, but in itself it has no fixed perspective (first, second, third person, impersonal) at all.

By the time, therefore, that we reach the equivalent of lines 1–5 (plus 6–10) in the second concentric circle, at lines 14–18, the poet's view has undergone something of a sea-change: his nomadic existence is no longer cast in the form of personae, and literary archetypes at that, but in terms of movement itself, and, in the wry subtext of 'Vagabondage spécial' ('délit par lequel une personne aide, assiste ou protège le racolage en vue de la prostitution, pour en tirer profit'—*Le Petit Robert*, 1967), pretty downmarket movement, a movement not of self-affirmation, but of transaction, mediation, supplementation. It is, too, a vagabondage which has widened its affective horizons: the 'definite article line' which relates to audience and the poet's circle has been transformed from 'Les amis, les proches' to 'Tous les hommes, tous les pays'. If lines 14–15 parallel lines 2–3, and if line 16 develops line 4, then the two parts of line 5 now find their answer in lines 17–18. Upheld by the same second-person address and the same 'ne . . . plus' construction, lines 17–18 however present deprivation as liberation rather than loss; the poet who has no social place is now the poet who exerts no social (or moral) pressure, who has no social gravity and can thus enjoy an existential free-floatingness, expressed both by the stanza-terminal *points de suspension* and by the fact that, in these lines, one begins to feel the first urgings of purely linguistic generation:

Va-et-vient continuel   3 + 4
Vagabondage spécial   4 + 3

One notices here not only the shared /va/, /ʒ/, and /e/, but also the off-rhyme of the adjectival endings and the alternation of the distribution of rhythmic measures, pursued further in the line following:

Tous les hommes, tous les pays   3 + 4

The second segment of the first circle, lines 11–13, poses perhaps the greatest interpretational problems. What is one to make of the reference to Nietzsche? In his critical edition, Goldenstein (1986: 49–50) draws attention to the passage in *The Twilight of the Idols* in which Nietzsche speaks of the need to learn to see, think, speak, and write if one is to attain to a 'noble culture'; for Nietzsche the art of thought has to be learned, like the art of dancing. Goldenstein goes on to quote the closing lines of the section 'What the Germans are in the process of losing': 'C'est qu'il n'est pas possible de déduire de l'*éducation noble* la danse sous toutes ses formes. Savoir danser avec les pieds, avec les idées, avec les mots: faut-il que je dise qu'il est aussi nécessaire de le savoir avec la *plume*,—qu'il faut apprendre à écrire?', and to conclude that the dance celebrated by the poet, 'his' dance, is first and foremost the dance of writing, of the pen moving over the paper, as alluded to in the closing lines of 'F.I.A.T.' and 'Natures mortes'. This is, I am sure, very much to the point, but not to my mind an entirely satisfactory line of reasoning for the lines we have before us. Why? One of my structural assumptions is that the final two stanzas (ll. 14–18, 19–25) provide a second circle/lap for corresponding sections in the first stanza (ll. 1–5 (+ 6–10) and 11–13). The sections in the first stanza are given a completely new perspective in their second circle, are in a sense accelerated and given a direction, become movement rather than argument, movement rather than persona. Both principal sections in the first stanza take place under the aegis of a philosopher, but it is from the responsibilities of edicts, maxims, and tuition that the poet seems anxious to escape, in order to rotate, to slough off gravity. In this sense Nietzsche is no more preferable than Plato; even though both lines 11–13 and 19–25 have a first-person perspective, as opposed to the second-person perspective of lines 1–5 and 14–18, we should note that the Nietzsche lines concern a first-person *plural*, that is precisely the social dimension of the first person which the poet has, in different ways, dissociated himself from in lines 1–5 and 6–10. Furthermore, Goldenstein's suggestion does not sufficiently take into account the presence of 'la femme', who apparently supersedes or erases the dance, in line 11–12, so that she alone is left, and who is replaced, in the poet's quest for the dance, by 'le paysage'. This perhaps suggests that we would do better to look to Nietzsche's radical sexism for the sources of line 11, to remarks of the kind that appear in paragraphs 232–9 of *Beyond Good and Evil*:

That in woman which inspires respect and fundamental fear is her *nature*, which is more 'natural' than that of the man, her genuine, cunning, beast-of-prey suppleness, the tiger's claws beneath the glove, the naivety of her egoism, her ineducability and inner savagery, and how incomprehensible, capacious and prowling her desires and virtues are . . . (paragraph 239)

or those relating to the personification of life as woman in the Dance Songs of *Thus Spoke Zarathustra*:

Who would not hate you, great woman who binds us, enwinds us, seduces us, seeks us, finds us! Who would not love you, you innocent, impatient, wind-swift, child-eyed sinner! . . .
I dance after you, I follow you even when only the slightest traces of you linger. Where are you? Give me your hand! Or just a finger!

('The Second Dance Song')

Does not Cendrars wish to resist this kind of indoctrination, this kind of 'fossilized' view of human relations, as much as the dance of sexual seduction it dances? Does not philosophy, particularly of the moralizing Nietzschean kind, seek to fix us too narrowly, to assign roles to us merely so that a certain system of belief can keep itself in place? This is why Bergson is experienced as so liberating. Does not Cendrars, with his question 'Mais l'ironie', not only supply the perfect riposte to Nietzsche's gravity-heavy image of woman, but also commit himself to another kind of dance, that logopoeia defined by Pound as 'the dance of the intellect among words'? Irony is the consciousness that unceremoniously wrenches us out of fixation, mesmerization, the dance of idolatory. This breaking of a spell happens rhythmically as well as verbally. The long eleventh line leads us on through the by now familiar dissyllabic mechanism into a string of trisyllables which come back, in line 12, to the dissyllabic point of departure:

La femme, la danse que Nietzsche a voulu	$2 + 2 + 3 \,(?) + 3 + 3 + 3$
nous apprendre à danser	
La femme	2

The tetrasyllabic 'Mais l'ironie' provides the necessary rhythmic tangent to get out of the imprisoning circle.

Lines 19–25 trace the parturition of another kind of dance. Line 19 is like the negative of the experience described by Valéry Larbaud's 'Ode' (1908), and is as prolix as it is purposeless. Out of this grows a summarizing observation (l. 20) which takes up the 'ne . . . plus' construction we have met in the other concentric segments. But here it and 'le paysage' are countered by the adversative 'mais', just as 'la femme' was countered by this device. But whereas the 'Mais' of line 13 led to the relative dead end of an interrogative, the 'Mais' of line 21 is the starting-point of, supplies the leverage for, a self-intensifying, accelerating, increasingly vertiginous run at gyration, a progression registered in the now one-sided and now double-sided contractions of the rhythmic measures:

Le paysage ne m'intéresse plus	4 + 5
Mais la danse du paysage	3 + 4
La danse du paysage	2 + 4
Danse-paysage	1 + 3

Ironically, or fittingly perhaps, the poem ends with the dominance of the trisyllabic measure, casting a backward glance at line 11:

Paritatitata	6 (3 + 3) (possibly of course 2 + 2 + 2)
Je tout-tourne	3

We should not confuse line 24 with what we have had to say in Chapter 3 about the train, mechanical rhythm, and the stultification of meaning, for two reasons. First, 'Paritatitata' is neither proper noun, nor common noun, nor term of endearment; it is a new word, the resolving third term which grows out of the metaphoric friction of 'danse' and 'paysage' (though centred on Pari(s) we notice!). Secondly, it is encapsulated within, encompassed by, the spiritual transfiguration of the first-person subject, who opens this stanza in dejection and divagation, and closes it as the subject of movement itself, and, what is more, the subject of a movement which includes the object ('tout'), pre-empts the object. In becoming the wheel, the agent and patient of circularity, the poet has not surrendered consciousness, has not yielded linguistic meaning to primary rhythm. On the contrary, he has become consciousness both subjective and objective, both expressing and being expressed, not in sameness and mechanical uniformity (l. 19) but in rhythmic variety and semantic dynamism. 'Paritatitata' is a 'word-in-freedom' if you like, but a 'word-in-freedom' which affirms the creative consciousness.

We have already indicated the ways in which rhythm contributes to the various dynamisms at work in the overall structure of concentric circles: oscillation (ll. 14–16), converging acceleration (ll. 20–3), hypnotic gyration (ll. 11–12), inflation and deflation (ll. 7–10), slack and pointless traversal (l. 19: 5 + 8 (5 + 3) + 8 (2 + 6) + 7 (3 + 4) + 4). I would briefly like to return to the idea explored in our treatment of the monolexical line in 'Journal', that the function of rhythm and the kind of perception it engineers, the kind of point of view it provides, varies according to the syntactic developedness of the line. What Cendrars's elastic poems tend to do is ring the changes on certain basic structures, so that different kinds of rhythmic perception are built into the construction of the poem. At one extreme is the substantival monolexical line, already explored, which places rhythm as a third party between voice and language, neither of which is ultimately able to appropriate it or monopolize it. When the noun is accompanied by an adjective, the noun's perspectiveless nature may be qualified, particularly if the adjective is response-orientated (judgemental, evaluative, affective) (e.g. 'Orgueil déplacé'); in this case rhythm will gravitate towards voice and serve expressive colouring. If the adjective is object-orientated, inherent (descriptive, identifying), then it will gravitate towards language and become presentative, or cast the reader as its patient, as someone who undergoes its official status ('Va-et-vient continuel', 'Vagabondage spécial'). Sometimes it is almost impossible to choose between these two aspects, in which case an ambiguity arises, not in the rhythm itself, of course, but in rhythm's operation ('Juif errant', 'Don Juan métaphysique', 'Vie pauvre'). When the basic substantival element is determined by a definite or indefinite article, then the noun is mapped into patterns of expectation, function, familiarity, re-cognition, definition, and so on; the definite article, which is the only article we encounter in this context in 'Ma danse', confines things to the known, the classified, guarantees that they have a place and function; thus its rhythmic accompaniment will tend towards voice, but away from expressivity, towards a controlling subjective consciousness, but away from expressive manipulation; the definite article in rhythmic terms means *mere*, or minimal, possession of language by the voice. Crucial in 'Ma danse', therefore, is the change not just of rhythm, but of rhythmic perception, which accompanies the shift from 'La danse du paysage' to 'Danse-paysage', because while the former is still within the perspective of a particular viewer (who could point it out to someone else), is still anchored to an ultimately stabilizing horizon, is still grounded, can still be spoken as lyric utterance, 'Danse-paysage' has broken loose from voice, from horizon, and wheels in its own space as an erratic body, erratic in its relationship both to reality and the viewer. The 1 + 3 of 'Danse-paysage', therefore, is ontologically different from the 2 + 4 of 'La danse du paysage': we register the 2 + 4 as the measure of our measure of language, as a confirmation of our ability to speak it; the 1 + 3 of 'Danse-paysage', on the other hand, is a measure only of possi-bility, a transparent screen between reader and language which is where meaning relocates itself; that is, the meaning of 'Danse-paysage' is not so much a lexical question as a reader-relational question, expressed in the rhythmic configuration. The window in the surfeited traveller's 'portière' (l. 19) is a frame which merely returns to the viewer the (shallow) reality he has always known. Europe must always remain the same, if its reality remains untransformed. The window of rhythm through which the poet manages to look, however, reveals not the landscape, ever the same, but its dance, ever changing. Finally, at the other extreme from the monolexical line is the syntactically developed line of internal discourse, the line presided over by personal pronouns (e.g. ll. 5, 17, 18, etc.) or by subjects which can be assigned to verbs (e.g. ll. 1, 11, 20). The reading of 'Ma danse', therefore, is comparable to looking at Delaunay's circular forms in that the reader passes through different 'bands' of rhythmic perception, all in contact with each other, all involved with each other, in such a way that response to language *qua* language (as opposed to language as a set of specific words) shifts through different perceptual modes.

The final poem which I wish to examine in this brief foray into the Orphist rhythms of the *Dix-neuf poèmes élastiques* is the sixth, 'Sur la robe elle a un corps', which continues the dance theme, and which celebrates the vestimentary Orphism of Sonia Delaunay, his collaborator, of course, in the 'premier livre simultané', *Prose du Transsibérien*:

1. Le corps de la femme est aussi bosselé que mon crâne
2. Glorieuse
3. Si tu t'incarnes avec esprit
4. Les couturiers font un sot métier
5. Autant que la phrénologie
6. Mes yeux sont des kilos qui pèsent la sensualité des femmes
7. Tout ce qui fuit, saille avance dans la profondeur
8. Les étoiles creusent le ciel
9. Les couleurs déshabillent
10. ⟨⟨Sur la robe elle a un corps⟩⟩
11. Sous les bras des bruyères mains lunules et pistils quand les eaux se déversent dans le dos avec les omoplates glauques
12. Le ventre un disque qui bouge
13. La double coque des seins passe sous le pont des arcs-en-ciel
14. Ventre
15. Disque
16. Soleil
17. Les cris perpendiculaires des couleurs tombent sur les cuisses
18. ÉPÉE DE SAINT MICHEL
19. Il y a des mains qui se tendent
20. Il y a dans la traîne la bête tous les yeux toutes les fanfares tous les habitués du bal Bullier

21. Et sur la hanche
22. La signature du poète

In order to catch some of the underlying currents in this poem, we need to consult three sources. First, we need to alert ourselves more fully to the religious tonalities of the poem, most evident in the 'épée de Saint Michel', but to be heard too in 'Glorieuse' (possible to interpret as 'effulgent with divine splendour', as a synonym of 'rayonnement', thus also anticipating 'soleil' (l. 16)). The religious reading is borne out by the first manuscript version of the poem (Goldenstein 1986: 53–4), where the second and third lines of the final version are combined in the single:

Glorieux si tu [t'y] incarnes [ô St-Esprit]

If the wearing of one of Sonia Delaunay's Orphist dresses is the equivalent of a Pentecostal experience, if it produces the equivalent of the Revelation of St John the Divine (12: 7–9), the apocalyptic battle of good and evil in which colours have the penetrating lustrousness of St Michael's sword, then we should assimilate this text to another about the revelation of the feminine, 'La Roue', one of a cycle of three prose poems published in *Les Soirées de Paris* (no. 25, 1914) and dated 1912. This prose poem also helps to explain lines 19–20.[2] In it, a naked woman arises, whose beauty derives not from a corporeal beauty, but radiates from an inner nudity: 'Son rayonnement ne venait pas de sa beauté formelle. Il était intérieur, comme si, à travers son corps charnel, un autre corps eût lui, avec intermittences, dans un entrebâillement, idéal. Le Nu intérieur.' Suddenly a storm erupts. Lightning flashes at the woman. The lightning flashes are then perceived to be hands reaching out towards her:

Toutes ces mains se tendaient vers elle. Il y avait les mains maigres de l'artiste, les mains moites du banquier; celles, crochues, de l'avare et celles, gourdes, du

---

[2] The reference to the 'habitués du bal Bullier' in l. 20 brings to mind the passage from the *Mercure de France* (1 Jan. 1914) in which Apollinaire tells visitors to the bal Bullier, the popular dance hall in the place de l'Observatoire, what to expect in the way of a sartorial revelation: 'Il faut aller voir à Bullier, le jeudi et le dimanche, M. et Mme Robert Delaunay, peintres, qui sont en train d'y opérer la réforme du costume . . . Voici la description d'une robe simultanée de Mme Sonia Delaunay Terck: tailleur violet, longue ceinture violette et verte et, sous la jaquette, un corsage divisé en zones de couleurs vives, tendres ou passées, où se mêlent le vieux rose, la couleur tango, le bleu nattier, l'écarlate, etc, apparaissant sur différentes matières, telles que drap, taffetas, tulle, pilou, moire et poult de soie juxtaposés. . . . Et si, vous rendant à Bullier, vous ne les voyez pas aussitôt, sachez que les réformateurs du costume se tiennent également au pied de l'orchestre, d'où ils contemplent sans mépris les vêtements monotones des danseurs et des danseuses' (quoted Goldenstein 1986: 54).

vieillard; il y avait les mains timides du jeune homme, les mains adoratives du prêtre et les mains sacrilèges de l'assassin. Les mains de tous les hommes, les mains de toutes les générations se tendaient éperdues vers la Femme, la Prostituée. Il y avait aussi les mains hallucinées du Christ.

So the woman becomes the hub of the wheel of mankind, the centre of 'cette trombe de désirs déferlés dans l'au-delà'. This vision belongs as much to the nineteenth century as to the twentieth, to Cézanne's *L'Éternel féminin* (1875–7, where one sees 'toutes les fanfares' of l. 20) and Zola's *Nana* (1880, full of 'la bête' of l. 20!). But Sonia Delaunay is as much a *femme fatale,* if of a diviner kind, and as much a cosmic being, thanks to her dress, as the prostitute of 'La Roue'; and like the prostitute, her dress makes her radiant with an inner body.

This last idea is one that is also to be gathered from Robert Delaunay's notes on Sonia's 'tissus simultanés'. These notes are retrospective, dating from 1938, and may themselves owe something to the insights of Cendrars's poem. But they are carefully argued through, full of understanding of Sonia's vestimentary project, and illuminating for a reading of 'Sur la robe elle a un corps'. I quote only what seem to me two crucial extracts: 'Les robes n'étaient plus un morceau d'étoffe drapé selon la mode courante, mais un composé vu d'ensemble comme un objet, comme une peinture pour ainsi dire vivante, une sculpture sur des formes vivantes' (Delaunay 1975: 202). Just as the sculptor disengages form from the stone, meaning from matter, so the dress designer redefines the body, draws out another body from the one he or she clothes. 'Les couturiers font un sot métier' (l. 4) because they are concerned only with the body's surface and because they use the body as a hanger for clothes rather than designing clothes to redesign the body; clothes are the instrument of an almost religious transfiguration of the body:

On remarque dans l'ensemble de création de ces robes, une évolution: les couleurs au commencement sont très brisées, donnant au corps une trop grande mobilité visuelle, dans les dernières il y a un accord parfait, dans ce sens que les parties se combinent en hauteur ou de face et de dos, s'équilibrent dans une diversité d'imagination de la forme inédite et toujours variée—qui s'étire ou se rétrécit selon la femme qui la porte, selon que cette femme elle-même est faite—ce qui marque une authenticité et de la femme et de la robe. Ce n'est plus la chemise indifférente et morne, c'est la personnalité qui se dégage et se joue: des formes rentrantes et sortantes, selon que telle ou telle couleur est juxtaposée dans ses rapports immédiats ou dans l'ensemble de la composition. (Delaunay 1957: 202)

This second quotation gives us cause to confront an issue so far put aside: the 'elasticity' of *Dix-neuf poèmes élastiques* and the prosodic implications of this term. It should be said immediately that there is no reason to tie this term down to a particular origin, to Boccioni's *Elasticità* (1912), for instance. Elasticity is central to Bergson's insistence on the relativity and heterogeneous continuity of duration, to the distortions of space by moving bodies explored by non-Euclidians, to the lines of force and mutual interpenetrations of the Futurist world, to movement itself conceived of as an uninterrupted passage rather than as a sequence of intervals. Delaunay also implies an elasticity in Cendrars's *Prose du Transsibérien*, in the lexical latitude it allows: 'Transsibérien-Jehanne laisse la latitude [à] la sensibilité de substituer un ou plusieurs mots, un mouvement de mots, ce qui forme la forme, la vie du poème, le simultanisme' (Delaunay 1975: 112). Certainly all free verse is elastic in the sense that it encourages the improvisation of reading, the discovery of a reading cut to the proportions of the reader; free verse multiplies the structural coordinates at the reader's disposal, and extends the parameters of linguistic and paralinguistic option.

If we equate a Delaunay dress with a Cendrarsian text, then the reader, like the wearer, changes it shape, stretches it here, contracts it there, so that it snugly fits, thus authenticating text and reader reciprocally, in relation to each other ('ce qui marque une authenticité et de la femme et de la robe'). As this happens, of course, the elements of the text/dress change in configuration and relationship; when we say that a poem is different each time we read it, we merely mean that we as readers/wearers of the text have put on some weight, or lost it; the elastic poem merely builds this element of relativity into itself as a simultaneous co-existence of possible states, rather than as something developing through time.

An obvious example of this kind of elasticity is the option on combination provided by the absence of punctuation. Goldenstein's note on 'phrénologie' (l. 5) describes it as 'condamnée ici par Cendrars' (1986: 52), on the supposition that line 5 is to be read as a continuation of line 4:

> Les couturiers font un sot métier
> Autant que la phrénologie.

While it is true that the original manuscript seems to justify this connection (Goldstein 1986: 53), the syntax is extremely loose, inaccurate. I feel altogether happier reading:

> Autant que la phrénologie
> Mes yeux sont des kilos qui pèsent la sensualité des femmes.

After the phrenological palpation of the female body, or rather the female body as conceived in and palpated through the skull of the poet, his eyes undertake a similarly 'scientific' assessment of feminine sensuality: his eyes are the weights, or counterweights, on one side of the scales, while what he sees of feminine sensuality are the weights on the other. In my view, Cendrars celebrates the exact sciences of sensuality (phrenology, weighing), the sciences which project sensuality, as one might celebrate the laws (derived from Chevreul through Seurat) which produce the intoxicating effect of the colour of Orphism. One further reason for my desire to 'wear' the poem like this is that I wish to make a structural break after line 6, so I want a satisfying closing cadence, not an isolated sixth line. These six lines are the six lines of the poet as first person—when he reappears in the final line he is a third person; they shift from his mind to his eyes—the poem will end in his hand, caressing in writing. Lines 1 and 6 create a chiastic syntactic arrangement: 'Le corps de la femme > mon crâne > mes yeux > la sensualité des femmes'; in fact, the whole set of lines again create something approaching concentric circles, chiefly through rhyme or near-rhyme. If one turns to what might have been an original arrangement of these lines:

1. Le corps de la femme est aussi bosselé que mon crâne
2. Glorieuse si tu t'incarnes avec esprit
3. Les couturiers font un sot métier
4. Autant que la phrénologie
5. Mes yeux sont des kilos qui pèsent la sensualité des femmes

one finds that line 1 rhymes with line 5 (the /a/ : /a/ rhyme is treated as a full rhyme in classical prosody, cf. 'âme'/'femme', and Cendrars provides a nicely ironic reformulation of it); line 2 rhymes with line 4; and line 3 rhymes with itself ('couturier'/'métier') thus isolating itself as a parenthesized comment. And if one enquires why 'Glorieuse' has been detached, occupies its own line, it is not only in the interests of its own resplendence and the increased facility with which it can link up with 'Disque' and 'Soleil', but also because the octosyllable that it leaves behind ('Si tu t'incarnes avec esprit', 4 + 4) more noticeably allies it with the octosyllable that 'Autant que la phrénologie' (2 + 6) is. All these structural cogitations and propositions are like a series of adjustments the text has made so that it will fit me.

This problem of combination occurs at other points. We move out of the integrated sensuality of the first six lines into the more disembodied, abstract, coloured spaces of lines 7–17, where parts of the body ('bras', 'mains', 'dos', 'omoplates', 'ventre', 'seins', 'cuisses') float up among other images. Here it is difficult to know whether line 10, a quotation of the title, looks back and confirms line 9, or whether its 'Sur' looks forward to create a simultaneous prepositional contrast with the 'Sous' of line 11. And so on.

Obviously the most immediate way in which prosody is elastic lies in the handling of the *e atone* and cases of synaeresis and diaeresis. In a verse as syllabically various as Cendrars's it would be foolish to attempt to enunciate any principles. While

> Les couleurs déshabillent

is clearly 3 + 3, is the line preceding it—

> Les étoiles creusent le ciel

—also 3 + 3 or is it rather 3 + 2 + 3, where the *coupes enjambantes* 'hollow out' the interstices of the words, or is it, to catch the twinkle in the stars, *coupe lyrique* followed by *coupe enjambante*

> Les étoiles | creu: | sent le ciel   4′ + 1 + 3 or 4′ + 4?

These kinds of question can be asked about any number of Cendrarsian lines and it does not pay to attempt to 'solve' them, since each case may be judged on its own merits, and those merits themselves not be clear. I have, in my own scansions, taken a line of least resistance and tried to minimize immediate controversy. But the fact remains that margin of choice, or margin of error, is an in-built quality of this verse, which allows it actually to respond to the way the speaker speaks, to offer the kinds of enunciation most comfortable for him. And what we have said of the *e atone* holds equally well for the treatment of contiguous vowels (synaeresis, diaeresis). Do lines 19 and 20 begin /ilia/ or /ilja/? Would one be justified in saying /ja/ quite simply? Syllables are defined for the purposes of counting and hearing number. If one removes the necessity of number, what status does number have? Well, it certainly has the status of a scansional option, and thus the making of syllabic choices may still have significant consequences for the way a reader perceives a poem's organization. To read

> Les étoiles creusent le ciel

as 3 + 3 is to make it an event simultaneous with, or otherwise equivalent to,

> Les couleurs déshabillent.

These are both processes, one on a macrocosmic level, the other on a microcosmic one, one relating to 'pure' light, the other to prismatic light, whereby the transparency of colour allows infinite depth, and creates movements of infinite recession. If line 8, on the other hand, is read as an octosyllable, it might act as a bridge between Sonia's witty/spiritual incarnation (l. 3) and possibly the poet's signature (l. 22) if the 'e' of 'signature' is also articulated.

But more important still, perhaps, the *line* is elastic. In graphic terms it is demonstrably so. Each line we set out on relativizes itself in relation to its immediate context. That a line has eight syllables may relate it less significantly to other octosyllables than to, say, the decasyllable which precedes it and the trisyllable that follows it. This is, after all, one of the things we must mean by simultaneous contrast. To move from the fourteen (?)-syllable, triphrasal, first line to the three (or two)-syllable, monophrasal, second line is to shift instantaneously from a wry, self-mocking, worldly-wise stance to one of speechless (!), guileless wonderment. The first line proceeds by a process of steady addition in which each new segment is a new surprise knowingly engineered. The second line is a single, unconstructed, unavoidable illumination. In putting these two lines together we are beginning to negotiate the expressive range, the possible relationships, the modes of consciousness that the poem makes available. This is the phenomenon that Delaunay is referring to when he writes: 'des formes rentrantes et sortantes, selon que telle ou telle couleur est juxtaposée dans ses rapports immédiats ou dans l'ensemble de la composition.'

The line has an elasticity of another kind, the elasticity of its own increasing rhythmic ambiguation. Simply put, the longer a line is, the less sure we shall be of its rhythmic nature, both for the syllabic reasons outlined above, and for those reasons connected with intensive and extensive reading discussed earlier. However, the more rhythmically ambiguous a line is, the more it can belong to the reader, because the more room he has to make meaningful choices and consult his own interpretational interests. Ambiguity does not dispossess us of a text half as much as certainty does, simply because certainty belongs to too many and to nobody. Before a line has begun to stretch its elastic, in its opening measure, it occupies the realm of certainty; as we proceed into it, we increasingly have to create our own bearings. If I look down the opening measures of the lines in 'Sur la robe elle a un corps', I know where I am —where I do not, either repetition ('il y a') or isolation ('Glorieuse') makes the doubt relatively insignificant. Thus: 2.3.4.4.2.2.4.3.3.3.3.2.2.

1.1.2.2.2.2.(?).2(?).4.4. What such confidence means, of course, is that the poet can group his lines and give sequences cohesion 'from the front'; it means that the first measure of the line is peculiarly important as the locus where the readership comes briefly together as a community before departing once again on its separate ways. It coincides, too, with what we have been saying about the monolexical (substantival) line, in that because this line only has an initial measure, it is the line about which we have most 'rhythmic' confidence but which we possess the least, since, as we have said, the rhythm is more a given of the verse structure than something read or created by us. Equally then, the longer the line is, the more it will gravitate towards the voice, the more rhythm will recover the periodicity and the grounded horizon of discourse. A small example is provided by lines 12, 14–15; as monolexical lines 'Ventre' and 'Disque' are rhythmically unequivocal, as indeed is 'Le ventre' as the first measure of line 12; but thereafter possibilities multiply

Le ventre | un disqui bouge	$2 + 4$
Le ventre | un dis: | que qui bouge	$2 + 2 + 3$
Le ventre | un disque | qui bouge	$2 + 2 + 2$ or $2 + 3' + 2$
Le ventr'un disque | qui bouge	$4 + 2$ or $5' + 2$
etc.	

How indistinguishable does one want the 'ventre' and 'disque' to be? How fast does one want the rotation of the disc to be?

The Orphist dress not only adapts its designs to the occupying body, so that each new body can imprint its own 'interpretation' on the dress, construct its own version of the dress's elements, it also transfigures the body, transforms it into a cosmic matrix worthy of our obeisance. In lines 7–17 we see how elements of the human body become interfused with other forms of terrestrial and celestial being; we see, too, how the human body becomes a spatial figure stretching to infinity in all directions; this stretching is largely achieved by the perpetuation of acoustic echoes (/ɔ/: 'profondeur', 'robe', 'corps', 'omoplates', 'coque', 'soleil'; /o/: 'eaux', 'dos', 'glauques'; /u/: 'tout', 'couleurs', 'sous', 'bouge', 'double'; 'bras des bruyères'; 'lunules et pistils'; etc.). This is the section of the poem from which the poet is absent, in which metamorphosis seems to be delivered into the hands of language, and to follow its dictates. But the poet returns to repossess the poem and sign it. Wherever else language may come from, nothing is lost or surrendered as long as the poet's signature remains in place.

Goldenstein, with his eye principally on 'Titres', the sixteenth of the

Dix-neuf poèmes élastiques, believes that in this collection Cendrars really did go 'jusqu'au bout', but then called it a day:

Tout se passe comme si l'itinéraire poétique de Cendrars des Pâques aux *Dix-neuf poèmes élastiques*, et au-delà à *Documentaires*, avait donné lieu, au plan de l'écriture, à un mouvement de progression puis de régression. Progression: nous avons noté plus haut la graduelle émancipation à l'égard des formes constituées comme du vouloir-dire. Avec l'expérience des limites, la poésie élastique arrive à son seuil ultime d'étirement dans le collage et l'incohérence . . . Régression: techniquement parlant, Cendrars n'ira guère plus loin que les *Dix-neuf poèmes élastiques* mais reprendra les mêmes procédés avec les collages de Gustave Le Rouge dans *Kodak* (*Documentaires*). (1986: 178)

My view would be that Cendrars never went 'jusqu'au bout', but in the elastic poems found a way of incorporating an eruptive, abstract, mechanical, unrhythmed language into discourse, and into *his* discourse, into the autobiography of occasional poetry, 'des poèmes de circonstance' (quoted Goldenstein 1986: 108). What 'Dernière heure' and 'Mee too buggi', the two 'plagiarized' elastic poems, led him to wonder was whether his discourse could incorporate another's, whether he could 'sign' a text that was largely already there. Expressed in terms of the Orphist dress, where the dress is someone else's text, the questions run: Will my body give this dress a new shape? Will this dress adapt itself to my body, justify my signature? Will my body appear on this dress? We shall attempt to discover the answer to these questions in the analysis of *Documentaires* which follows.

6

Blaise Cendrars, Documentaires *(1924)*
The Prosody of Photography

I T was only in 1976 that Francis Lacassin was able to answer the challenge issued by Cendrars in *L'Homme foudroyé* (1945), in which he revealed that part of the purpose of *Documentaires* was to demonstrate to Gustave Le Rouge, the *roman-feuilletoniste*, that he, Le Rouge, was more a poet than he knew or would admit:

> j'eus la cruauté d'apporter à Lerouge un volume de poèmes et de lui faire constater de visu, en les lui faisant lire, une vingtaine de poèmes originaux que j'avais taillés à coups de ciseaux dans l'un de ses ouvrages en prose et que j'avais publiés sous mon nom! C'était du culot. Mais j'avais dû avoir recours à ce subterfuge qui touchait à l'indélicatesse—et au risque de perdre son amitié—pour lui faire admettre, malgré et contre tout ce qu'il pouvait avancer en s'en défendant, que lui aussi, était poète, sinon cet entêté n'en eût jamais convenu.
>
> (Avis aux chercheurs et aux curieux! Pour l'instant je ne puis en dire davantage pour ne pas faire école et à cause de l'éditeur qui serait mortifié d'apprendre avoir publié à son insu ma supercherie poétique.) (1945: 215)

Cendrars's 'supercherie poétique' might have been perpetrated by the poet Agenor Marmousier to divert his rich and world-weary patron Lord Burydan in the pages of Le Rouge's *Le Mystérieux Docteur Cornélius* (1912–13), for it was of 'cuttings' from this source that Cendrars composed forty-one of the forty-four titled poems of *Documentaires*, and indeed only fifty-six of the 790 lines involved in the forty-one poems belong exclusively to Cendrars (Lacassin 1976, 1979)—Yvette Bozon-Scalzitti has traced two of the remaining three poems ('Fleuve: Le Bahr-el-Zéraf' and 'Chasse à l'éléphant') to passages in Maurice Calmeyn's *Au Congo belge: Chasse à l'éléphant—Les Indigènes—L'Administration* (1912), following up the suggestion of Albert t'Serstevens, an intimate of Cendrars (1977: 297–309). In his 1976 article Lacassin published the first part of what would be a complete Cendrars–Le Rouge parallel text; this last appeared in its entirety only in 1986, in Lacassin's critical edition of Gustave Le Rouge's principal novels, under the provocative title 'Les Poèmes du Docteur Cornélius par Blaise Cendrars et Gustave Le Rouge' (pp. 1181–247).

Contemporary with the publication of Lacassin's findings was a revaluation of *Documentaires* (as indeed of 'Dernière heure' and 'Mee too buggi' of *Dix-neuf poèmes élastiques*) within an aesthetics of plagiarism. Henri Béhar (1976) sketches in the context for an art of the ready-made, of cultural detritus:

Il semble qu'arrivés à un certain stade de leur développement, les arts dits libéraux comme les sociétés avancées se rendent compte de l'énorme gaspillage d'énergie physique et intellectuelle entraîné par l'impératif du progrès et que soudain sans qu'aucune consigne n'ait été clairement formulée, on assiste à une vaste entreprise de récupération de déchets—ou de laissés pour compte. Tel peintre se contentera de clouer sur un cadre le chiffon qui lui sert à essuyer ses pinceaux; Kurt Schwitters édifiera, œuvre de sa vie, le Merzbilder, colonne de détritus, élan de matières rejetées; et par la vertu de son choix, Marcel Duchamp élèvera une carte postale ou un séchoir à bouteilles à la dignité artistique. Bien que moins connu, le mouvement est identique et simultané sur le plan littéraire, depuis les adaptations de Lautréamont, jusqu'aux 'pratiques sémiotiques' de Marcelin Pleynet, Jean-Pierre Faye, Michel Butor, Maurice Roche, etc. (pp. 102–3)

One may have some doubts about Béhar's conservationist interpretation of these phenomena, efficiency through recycling—they equally betray a crisis of values, are a polemical gesture, a utilitarian attitude to art which is also fundamentally anti-utilitarian. And it is perhaps this last paradox which we need to keep uppermost in our minds. An aesthetic of plagiarism might properly claim that it displaces the notion of authenticity from originality of production to the interpretation of the already existent, from the text to the author, now more reader than author. It is not so much the dress as the person who wears it; besides, the dress has no absolute or independent existence, it must always be *on* someone. This would coincide with Cendrars's declaration that he is a libertine rather than a poet, that he has no working method, that writing is an organic function as banal as eating.[1] This would coincide with Apollinaire's claim in 'Zone' that the only modern art is public, popular consumer art:

> Tu lis les prospectus les catalogues les affiches qui chantent
>   tout haut
> Voilà la poésie ce matin et pour la prose il y a les journaux

[1] This is in reference to a passage already quoted: 'Je ne suis pas poète. Je suis libertin. Je n'ai aucune méthode de travail. J'ai un sexe. Je suis par trop sensible. Je ne sais pas parler objectivement de moi-même. Tout être vivant est une physiologie. Et si j'écris, c'est peut-être par besoin, par hygiène, comme on mange, comme on respire, comme on chante' (1987: 195).

> Il y a les livraisons à 25 centimes pleines d'aventures
>   policières
> Portraits des grands hommes et mille titres divers

a claim frequently enough echoed by Cendrars and endorsed with a rejection of the poetical:

> Formes sueurs chevelures
> Le bond d'être
> Dépouillé
> Premier poème sans métaphores
> Sans images
> Nouvelles.

>   ('Titres', *Dix-neuf poèmes élastiques*)

Plagiarism also coincides with Walter Benjamin's view of history, in which 'official' history (tradition) is constantly being undone and its fragments, quotations, extracts, being reused in new configurations of meaning. The present is our reading of the past; the past reread in new ways can become newly instructive and purposeful. Phenomena belong to history in two senses: they belong to the time of their production (originality) and the time of their intelligibility (interpretation), the time of their being 'written' and the time of their being 'read'. Reading across genres is no different from reading across history; it involves similar processes of appropriation, interpretation, and remotivation. And this reading is a matter of construction rather than of creation: it concerns the arts of translation, montage, collage, adaptation, and its preoccupation is instructional and experimental rather than expressive. There is no medium which epitomizes the 'construction' mentality so much as photography. Photography not only democratizes art:

Anyone will be able to observe how much more easily a painting and above all, a sculpture, or architecture, can be grasped in photographs than in reality. The temptation is to attribute this to the decay of contemporary artistic perception. But preventing it is the recognition that at about the same time as the technology for reproduction the conception of great works was changing. One can no longer view them as the production of individuals; they have become collective images, so powerful that capacity to assimilate them is related to the condition of reducing them in size (Benjamin, 'A Short History of Photography' in Trachtenberg 1980: 212)

it is also the democratic art: anyone can become a photographer and thus a potential photographic artist, for photography does not necessitate the 'practising hand' so much as the complicity of subject and moment (the photogenic) and the efficient support of industry: 'No knowledge what-ever of Photography is required. No Dark Room or Chemicals. Three motions only: Hold it steady. Pull a string. Press a button. This is all we ask of *you*, the rest *we* will do' (advertisement for the Eastman Dry Plate and Film Co. in Ford 1989: 63). Plagiarism is the art of literature in the age of mechanical reproduction:

To pry an object from its shell, to destroy its aura, is the mark of a perception whose 'sense of the universal equality of things' has increased to such a degree that it extracts it even from a unique object by means of reproduction. (Benjamin, 'The Work of Art in the Age of Mechanical Reproduction', 1970/1936: 225)

These arguments are extremely helpful for an understanding of the spirit of Cendrars's *Documentaires*, but one should beware of falling a prey to their convenience. It is easy to follow on from the lines quoted above from Cendrars's 'Titres' to the linguistic grounds of his admiration for Le Rouge, as expressed in *L'Homme foudroyé*:

Au contraire, c'est dans ces publications populaires qu'il ne signait pas . . . qu'il se laissait aller à son démon, faisant appel à la science et à l'érudition, non par vain étalage encyclopédique . . . mais pour détruire l'image, ne pas suggérer, châtrer le verbe, ne pas faire style, dire des faits, des faits, rien que des faits, le plus de choses avec le moins de mots possible et, finalement, faire jaillir une idée originale, dépouillée de tout système, isolée de toute association, vue comme de l'extérieur, sous cent angles à la fois et à grand renfort de téléscopes et de microscopes, mais éclairée de l'intérieur. C'était de l'équilibrisme et de la prestidigitation. Ce jongleur était un très grand poète anti-poétique, et je donne la prose et les vers de Stéphane Mallarmé pour, notamment, une de ses plaquettes éphémères qui était intitulée *100 Recettes pour accommoder les restes* qui se vendait cinq sols, petit traité domestique à l'usage des banlieusards, précis d'ingéniosité utilitaire, parfait manuel du système 'D' et, en outre, le plus exquis recueil de poèmes en prose de la littérature française (1945: 207–8)

and from that to derive a ready-made critical position which emphasizes the *degré zéro* of Cendrars's writing and its disregard of all aesthetic considerations:

Le résultat de ces procédures est une prose poétique parfaitement lisse, sans style, sans rime, sans images ni rythme, l'élément lyrique provenant du fait brut, du vocable isolé. Langage de la dénotation par conséquent, aux antipodes de ce qu'on nomme habituellement poésie. (Béhar 1976: 109)[2]

---

[2] A similar view is expressed in Grojnowski (1988: 319): 'Dans le filigrane du poème apparaît un art d'écrire fait de propositions et de refus d'autant plus déroutants qu'ils demeurent implicites. Déperdition de la première personne, relégation des métaphores, abrogation d'une logique d'agencement—et prévalence d'une scansion en laquelle se résout pour une bonne part la fonction poétique.'

It is judgements like this which justify the comparison of *Documentaires* with the techniques of photography, or rather the techniques of photography according to a certain conception; we shall return to this question shortly. But these judgements are manifestly ill founded, as ill founded as Cendrars's own description of Le Rouge's style, which, on the contrary, is the style of popular melodrama, with plenty of adjectival intensification and adverbial ominousness. Besides, Cendrars's comments on Le Rouge themselves give the lie to the critical prejudice we have just outlined: Le Rouge's recipes may represent a 'précis d'ingéniosité utilitaire' but their utilitarian purpose is undermined by their self-justifying exquisiteness. Le Rouge may be concerned only with facts, may lead the assault against unnecessary decoration, but 'le plus de choses avec le moins de mots possible' sounds like a precept from the Imagist programme; and though originality may now be an intermittent, unsystematic affair, relating more to intellectual acrobatics than to genius, it is still prized, and prized as something which releases multidimensional vision and reveals the outer and inner as coextensive. We should take Cendrars at his word: he has set out to convince M. Jourdain/Le Rouge that all the time he thought he was speaking prose he was in fact speaking poetry; he has set out to show that poetry lurks in the most humble or banal environments; but to extract it you must know how to read. To insist that *Documentaires* belongs to an aesthetic of plagiarism is to distort the facts; Cendrars's art is an art of quotation, reconstruction, poeticization, and we need to see the full implication of those techniques of rewriting that Lacassin has so fully and helpfully outlined in his articles. Cendrars has 'imitated' Le Rouge in order to produce the inimitable, and at the same time to demonstrate that everyone can produce their own inimitability. Reproduction mythicizes its subject just as much as it reduces it, or makes it generally available, or neutralizes the cult of its uniqueness.

The poem 'Jeune fille', for example:

1. Légère robe en crêpe de Chine
2. La jeune fille
3. Élégance et richesse
4. Cheveux d'un blond fauve où brille un rang de perles
5. Physionomie régulière et calme qui reflète la franchise et la bonté
6. Ses grands yeux d'un bleu de mer presque vert sont clairs et hardis
7. Elle a ce teint frais et velouté d'une roseur spéciale
   qui semble l'apanage des jeunes filles américaines

derives from a description of Isidora Jorgell which occurs in the episode entitled 'L'Énigme du "Creek Sanglant" ' of Le Rouge's *Le Mystérieux Docteur Cornélius*:

La jeune fille portait *une robe de crêpe de Chine* bleuté qui accusait discrètement l'*élégance et* la *richesse* de ses formes.

Ses *cheveux d'un blond fauve*, dans lesquels *brillait un rang de perles*, encadraient harmonieusement une *physionomie régulière et calme*, où se *reflétaient la franchise et la bonté; ses grands yeux d'un bleu de mer presque vert étaient clairs et hardis* sans impudence et *elle* possédait *ce teint frais et velouté, d'une roseur spéciale, qui semble l'apanage de* certaines *jeunes filles américaines.* (Lacassin 1986: 54)

The mere device of lineation, the shift from a prose margin to a poetic one, has fundamentally transformed the activity of the language by transforming the mental set, the expectations and operations, we bring to bear on it:

Le langage poétique révèle ici . . . sa véritable 'structure', qui n'est pas d'être une *forme* particulière, définie par ses accidents spécifiques, mais plutôt un *état*, un degré de présence et d'intensité auquel peut être amené, pour ainsi dire, n'importe quel énoncé, à la seule condition que s'établisse autour de lui cette *marge de silence* qui l'isole au milieu (mais non à l'écart) du parler quotidien. (Genette 1969: 150)

Genette is no doubt right to emphasize 'état' over 'forme' since the text's degree of presence and intensity depends on the conditioning of the reader, on that receptive state of mind designed to maximize the semantic productivity of a text recognized as poetic. But, of course, in each instance, since it is a particular instance, matters of form will be important and particularly so where the text is reauthored, restyled, made differently inimitable. Here, for example, we might notice the inversion of the 'légère robe . . .' and the 'jeune fille', and the way in which it allows effect to precede cause, in Impressionist vein, the way in which it installs a more consistent progression from physical detail to abstract quality (l. 3) via the mediating girl, and finally the way in which it makes the three-syllable 'La jeune fille' the pivot or fulcrum of the longer lines (octosyllable, hexasyllable) which lie either side of her. We might note, too, the substitution in line 4 of 'où' for 'dans lesquels'; while the latter is more literal/specific, unequivocally plants the pearls within the hair, is in close-up, the former allows the pearls to become diadem if they wish (i.e. *on* the hair), allows the 'cheveux' to become 'chevelure', a total concept, and introduces distance by its ambiguity. The substitution of 'qui' for 'où' + reflexive in line 5, on the other hand, makes the abstract qualities ('franchise' and 'bonté') more intrinsic, more permanent an accompaniment, radiating spontaneously from within, rather than imposing themselves from without.

Lacassin has no doubt of Cendrars's poetic intentions. In his classification of Cendrars's revisions of Le Rouge, he attributes them to a poeticizing

enterprise either explicitly—'recherche d'un envol poétique par extension', 'recherche d'un envol poétique par déplacement'—or implicitly—
'Ils décuplent l'intensité d'une image' (insertion of adjectives), 'Le charme
est alors plus subtil' (alternate repetition). But in pursuing our analysis of
'Jeune fille', it is not just the question 'How poetic is this?' that we need
to ask; we need to address ourselves to the principal preoccupation of the
chapter, the relationship between *Documentaires* and photography, and ask,
'In what senses are these poems translations of the cinematic of narrative
into the snapshot of poem?'

When first published in 1924, *Documentaires* had for title *Kodak* with
the subtitle *Documentaires.* The title *Kodak,* whose repercussions for the
contemporary literary scene have been suggestively explored by Grojnowski
(1988), was dropped when a new edition of Cendrars's poems appeared in
1944, at the request of the Eastman Company; in introducing the new
edition, Cendrars quoted from the letter sent by the original publishers
(Éditions Stock): 'A la parution de *Kodak* de Blaise Cendrars nous avons
reçu un "papier timbré" de la maison américaine "Kodak Co" qui nous
expliquait que nous avions sans droit pris comme titre d'un de nos ouvrages
le nom de sa firme . . . etc' (1967: 133), and went on to comment:

Qu'importe un titre. La poésie n'est dans un titre mais dans un fait, et comme en
fait ces poèmes, que j'ai conçus comme des photographies verbales, forment un
documentaire, je les intitulerai dorénavant *Documentaires.* Leur ancien sous-titre.
C'est peut-être aujourd'hui un genre nouveau. (1967: 133)

In considering these poems as photographs, and especially as documentary photographs, I must emphasize that I am rejecting the cinematic
alternative; some critics (Béhar, for example) have treated the poems as
moving pictures; Cendrars's enthusiasm for and involvement in cinema
are, after all, well documented. But Grojnowski has argued convincingly
on three scores that the poems are conceived as still photographs: first, 'le
titre ne jouit donc nullement du prestige du cinématographe, il désigne
au contraire un appareil à la disposition du premier venu'; secondly,
Cendrars himself refers to them as 'verbal photographs' in his 1944
preface—and also in *Trop c'est trop* (1957: 254), where he adds that the
poems on elephant-hunting in *Documentaires* 'ne sont le produit ni du
chasseur d'images ni du cinéaste'—and as 'un album de mauvaises photographies' in a personal dedication; third, the only references to cameras
in the text, in 'Chasse à l'éléphant' in fact, are to single-image cameras
(1988: 318):

Je garde un homme avec moi pour porter le grand kodak

.   .   .   .

Quelle photo intéressante a pu prendre l'homme de sang-froid
qui se tenait à côté de moi (IV. 2, 8)

Et je m'avance seul avec mon petit kodak sur un terrain où je
puis marcher sans bruit

.   .   .   .

Une photo et le coup part   (VIII. 6; IX. 6)

I must also emphasize that the account of photography which follows is my version; photography has proved notoriously difficult to define and conceptualize, largely because of the multiplicity of its functions.[3]

In line with his previous practice, Cendrars omits punctuation from *Documentaires*, or, more properly, removes it from Gustave Le Rouge's text. This we may understand as part of the poetic project: 'effacement des relations grammaticales et tendance à constituer le poème, dans l'espace silencieux de la page, comme une pure *constellation verbale*' (Genette 1969: 151). Equally the removal of punctuation removes indicators of respiration, of spans of voice and pauses of juncture; that is to say, the poem is, to a certain extent at least, 'unvoiced'. We shall return to the implications of this, as to the implications of the removal of punctuation as the removal of a chronometric structure. For the moment I want to concentrate on the removal of punctuation as the obliteration of syntactical ordering, the obliteration of coherence/cohesion, and to consider this in conjunction with Cendrars's paratactic rendering of Le Rouge.

The very referentiality of a photograph makes it by nature incoherent; a photograph may offer all its evidence to the view, and immediately, a photograph may be totally visible, but there is no way that the spectator's knowledge is equal to this visibility. This disproportion between visibility and knowledge is the meaning of appearances. And the incoherence of the photographic image largely derives from the fact that it has lost the purposefulness, the 'plot', of continuity in time. (A corollary of this proposition is that the arbitrariness of a photograph is directly proportional to its historicity, is indeed the safeguard of that historicity, which is the more powerful, the less it can be recuperated.) And yet the photographic image is a picture; it is an incoherence existing within a convention that pledges significance. 'Jeune fille' is no longer Miss Isidora Jorgell, sister of the

---

[3] As Stephen Bann puts it: 'In the case of photography, many recent studies conspire to suggest that, in working on the photograph, we are not working on a distinct type of artefact but on the index or symptom of a cultural process which is heterogenous to itself' (1991: 3).

assassin Baruch Jorgell and wife-to-be of Harry Dorgan, whose portrait within the *roman-feuilleton* is both motivated and motivating. She is a portrait looking for the viewer who can reconstitute her, not as Miss Isidora Jorgell, but as at least a documentary image. In photography, it is a truth of the medium that the value of individual images becomes increasingly documentary; all photographs at least have documentary value. It is in her capacity as a typical 'jeune fille américaine' that Miss Isidora Jorgell will recover her photographic coherence. And it is in the last line of the poem, the line in which she becomes representative or exemplary, that a first-person consciousness most clearly intrudes, in the 'noticing' demonstrative 'ce', in the synthesizing speculation of 'semble', and indeed in the relative clause itself which, unlike those in lines 4 and 5, is restrictive, and thus both identifying and the sign of exploratory and interpretative looking.

This presence of a first person in filigree is, in some contexts, part of the moral and existential problematic of documentary photography. The documentary photographer must somehow be in the picture, committed as a social conscience, in order to answer the Sontag charge: 'Photographing is essentially an act of non-intervention . . . it is a way of at least tacitly, often explicitly, encouraging whatever is going on to keep on happening' (1978: 11–12). Don McCullin's 'Afterword' to *Perspectives* (1987) contains the statement: 'That wasn't a creative photograph. My photography's an expression—of my guilt, my inability to make a protest in another way' (p. 123). But it also contains the statement: 'I feel guilty, too, because they've been taken with the eye of a photographer and not with the concern of a social worker' (p. 144). This is the other dimension: in order not to appropriate the image for personal purposes, in order not to colonize it, the photographer must sustain the image's independence and the spectator's freedom to draw his/her own conclusions; and in order to do this he must sink personality as far as is consonant with maintaining coherence of vision: 'The photographer must have, and keep in him, some of the receptiveness of the child who looks at the world for the first time, or of the traveller who enters a strange country' (Bill Brandt, in Booth 1983: 45). Cendrars is a traveller in the country of Le Rouge; he maintains his own responsiveness to that journey by writing his own travel notes and by destroying Le Rouge's narrator; and he safeguards our journey in his text, safeguards our receptiveness, by providing an embryonic first person uninterfered with by a narrating first person, and by eliding the tendentious.

How does Cendrars destroy the narrator? By removing the interventionist articulation, pacing, priority-giving that punctuation is, by 'unvoicing' the poem. Brecht may tell us, rightly, that a photograph of the Krupp factory tells us nothing about the social conditions that underpin it; Benjamin may conclude that captions are necessary if photographs are to pull their political weight, that photographs must be 'voiced'. But captions belong to photojournalism and to photonarrative (e.g. Henry Peach Robinson), not to the documentary which thrives on the neutrality of the title.[4] Cendrars's reduction of articles (definite and indefinite) has the same effect; the features of the 'jeune fille' do not already have a purpose, are not instruments in a premeditated plot; they exist with a marvellous, unsustained randomness which only the poem, as realized in the reader, can make sense of; the non-restrictive relative clauses of lines 4 and 5 contribute to the accumulation of the dangerously circumstantial.

What Cendrars has also done is minimize the presence of the verb, and he has done this either by simply removing the verb ('portait', 'accusait', 'encadraient') or by banalizing it ('a' (l. 7) in place of 'possédait'). Le Rouge's verbs are all business without much internal dynamic, but narrative in this respect is like photojournalism. The journalistic photograph is a photograph of an act which is synecdochic of an action, an event, a situation; a documentary photograph, whether of an act, of people, of a scene, is synecdochic of a condition; the newspaper photograph is political and social, the documentary photograph is social and anthropological. One may of course have a documentary photograph of politicians (e.g. the work of Erich Salomon), but it does not interest itself so much in what they are doing, as in what they are being, in the kinds of behaviour that are characteristic of them, and of those who serve them.

One of the ways the incoherent photograph (documentary) becomes coherent, therefore, is in its ability to crystallize the typical. This is largely what Barthes means by *studium* (1980), our ability to interest ourselves in a photograph for cultural reasons. The *studium* factor is educative, and grows from the photographer's intentions. *Studium* is put into the picture. What also makes the photograph coherent is what the photograph surprises, catches unawares, improvises, rather than intends, namely what Cartier-Bresson calls the 'decisive moment': the narrative of

---

[4] The moral/aesthetic dilemma constantly undergone by the documentary photographer and exemplified in the commentary of Don McCullin is also apparent, briefly, among the photographic images of *Perspectives* (1987); consistently, these are *titled* images (e.g. 'Mother and son, Liverpool', 'Gravedigger, Bradford', 'Bradford Lady Drying Laundry'), but on p. 56 we encounter 'Uncomfortable, Unheated: Unjust'. That is a caption, the intervening voice of the photographer that can also just be heard in titles like 'Disturbed Exile in his Bradford Slum' (81) or 'Decayed Industrial Wasteland' (p. 91).

life, subject to the plotting of time, usually, if stopped, reveals relativity as fragmentation, cross-purposes, non-adaptation; but occasionally the point of time captures the concertedness of relativity, the vision of a possible integration and harmony:

We work in unison with movement as though it were a presentiment of the way in which life itself unfolds. But inside movement there is one moment at which the elements in motion are in balance. Photography must seize upon this moment and hold immobile the equilibrium of it . . . if the shutter was released at the decisive moment, you have instinctively fixed a geometric pattern without which the photograph would have been both formless and lifeless. (Cartier-Bresson in Weaver 1989: 266)

The same creed of the revelatory moment is to be found in the work of one of Cartier-Bresson's mentors, André Kertész; but in Kertész the reverberations of the moment are affective or *spirituelles* rather than existential or metaphysical. At all events, the photograph of the decisive moment combats the permanent distractedness of the cinematic, its theft of being by continuous anticipation, its constant narrative projection of itself into a temporal and spatial 'blind field', and tries to restore the unseen, the 'behind-the-scenes' of reality, which is vision. This behind-the-scenes' of reality, in the case of poetry, is rhythm.

It is noticeable that the poems of *Documentaires* do not resort to the polarization of long and short lines to the same degree as the *Dix-neuf poèmes élastiques* do; or more accurately, the long lines are frequently much longer, but they are only rarely answered by monolexical short lines; even in this sense, therefore, the poems are 'stiller', slower, more focused. To a large extent, also, as we have already intimated, the text is not only unnarrated but also unvoiced; first-person presence is minimized to allow the image to construct its own coherence, its own integrity. This coherence emerges from the cadence-accentual equilibriation of the text:

1. Légère robe | en crêpe de Chine

2. La jeune fille

3. Élégance | et richesse

4. Cheveux d'un blond fauve | où brille un rang de perles

5. Physionomie régulière et calme | qui reflète la franchise et la bonté

6. Ses grands yeux | d'un bleu de mer presque vert | sont clairs et hardis

7. Elle a ce teint frais et velouté | d'une roseur speciale | qui semble
   l'apanage | des jeunes filles américaines.

The poem falls into three parts, lines 1–3, 4–5, 6–7. It opens as we have already mentioned with an accelerated progression from the concrete/ sartorial to a pair of abstractions both literal and moral/spiritual; this immediately indicates the parameters of the portrait, while at the same time establishing the pattern of paired accents (often accompanied by a syntax of pairing which will govern the whole poem); one of the factors that gives variety to the doubling of accents is the play between doubling and redoubling, and between intra-phrasal and phrase-terminal accents. This initial three-line group is help together by insistent acoustic echoing.

$$\text{Légère robe} \mid \text{en crêpe de Chine}$$
$$\text{/le3εR/ /R/} \qquad \text{/Rε/} \qquad \text{/∫i/}$$
$$\text{La jeune fille}$$
$$\text{/3/} \quad \text{/i/}$$
$$\text{Élégance} \mid \text{et richesse}$$
$$\text{/ele/} \qquad \text{/Ri∫ε/}$$

Although there is some crossing of the frontier between left-hand and right-hand accent or accentual group, particularly by /R/ and /ε/, this acoustic echoing tends to underline the division (or balance) of one side against the other. So the left side has the /le/ and /3/ factors, while the right side has /i/ and /∫/. This separation the poem will go on to undo. Just as it will go on to establish the already common /ε/, particularly in the 'feminized' /εR/ form, as the dominant acoustic leitmotiv in the poem: 'Légère—crêpe—richesse—perles—régulière—reflète—mer— presque—vert—clairs—frais—américaines'.

The clearly contoured, focused, classical stillness of the first three lines, almost a poem in itself, and reminiscent of the haiku or Imagist poems to be found elsewhere in *Documentaires*, particularly in the Oriental 'Îles' section, reminiscent, too, of the menu poems, feasts for the eye as well as the palate, gives way to a certain rhythmic uncertainty, doubt, and tendency to triple, in lines 4–5. These two lines are further bound together by their common zero articles and relative clauses. I have scanned line 4 as though it belonged to the pattern of the first line: double accents in double measures; but the bracketed accents indicate the pressure of the triple, even if it is not realized. Line 4 is also susceptible of a redoubling of measures:

$$\text{Chev\'eux} \mid \text{d'un blo\'nd f\'auve} \mid \text{où br\'ille} \mid \text{un ra\'ng de p\'erles}$$

This would tend to silence the bracketed accents by gravitating unmistakably towards the classical tetrametric structure of the alexandrine. But the underlying syntax of the line is still binary (verbless main clause + relative clause); it is just that the overall and rather distanced view of the first three lines has given way to a more inquisitive, closer up, hesitant exploration of detail. The same is true of line 5, where the triple accentuation in each measure emerges more unequivocally. Here again a tetrametric reading might be applied:

Physionomíe | régulière et cálme | qui reflète | la franchíse et la bonté.

The increase in vocal segmentation and insistence, produced by the upgrading of the intra-phrasal accents of 'physionomie' and 'reflète' to phrase-terminal ones, increases the sense of the momentarily anxious interrogation of the single-accent measures ('Physionomie . . . (?)', 'qui reflète . . . (?)') being released in the confidently reassuring adjectival and substantival pairs; it also increases the mirroring effect, though it would be wrong to assume that Cendrars intends any neat equations between 'régulière' and 'franchise', or 'calme' and 'bonté'.

The tripling tendency reaches its climax in line 6, with its unmistakable triphrasality; it also relates back to the previous line, and to 'la franchise et la bonté' in particular, by the predominantly moral content of its paired adjectives 'clairs et hardis'. But it looks forward to line 7, too, in the re-establishment of accentual pairing, in its affirmation of the girl's presiding identity: '*Ses* grands yeux', 'Elle a ce teint frais', and its preoccupation with colour. Line 6 is a remarkable interweaving of sounds, which are passed on from one measure to the next and create a seamless wholeness, despite any rhythmic ambiguities:

Ses grands yeux | d'un bleu de mer presque vert | sont clairs et hardis
/jø/   /blø/   /ɛR/   /ɛR/   /ɛR/

The final line completes this process of return to synthesizing equilibrium, with its double accentuation and redoubled measures; it is a final statement which at one and the same time affirms the specificity of the girl, and her typicality, which completes the colour modulation ('blond fauve' > 'bleu-vert' > 'roseur') while privileging this final colour by its adjective, by its linguistic modernity ('roseur' is attested 1908 by *Le Petit Robert* and classified as 'rare'), and by its semantic range—while some colours have paired substantival forms ('rouge'/'rougeur', 'blanc'/ 'blancheur') which give them access to the figurative/spiritual as well as the literal/physical, 'fauve' and 'bleu' do not, and 'rose' had not, until 1908. The rhythmic patterns of 'Jeune fille', therefore, when seen in their totality, add up to a design, a design backed up by acoustic, lexical, and syntactic effects. The decisive moment is what the photographer sees in the temporally undifferentiated; the rhythm is what the poem reveals by having the particular kind of lineation it has. That lineation is chosen by the poet in rather the same way that the photographer chooses his point · of view, his pictorial elements, and manages the lighting and shutter speed. This is the 'first person' who makes the picture and who is just present in the picture; but this is not the 'first person' who constructs or unearths the coherence of the picture. The decisive moment is the revelation of the poetic in the quotidian; the documentary poem is the poem which lifts the rhythmicity of prose from its dormant, potential or inert state into an activating and motivating force, not merely *sustaining* language, or a narrative more interesting than it is, but replacing narrative with its own plot, a plot which allows language to re-cohere at a symbolic level, or at the level of the signifier, even as it continues to display a signified; it is in this same sense that the documentary photograph is both document (signified) and photograph (signifier), both addressing their claims for significance to the viewer.

If the incoherence of the photograph can be transformed into coherence by *studium* or the decisiveness of its moment, it can perhaps best engage the first-person of the viewer through an experience which Barthes calls *punctum*. The photograph distinguishes itself from normal vision by being monocular rather than binocular; framed rather than open to the peripheral; flat, windowed space rather than three-dimensional, inhabited space; and by being non-selective and non-generalizing, where normal vision both selects (for operative efficiency) and generalizes on the basis of the known; Kozloff (1979) expresses this last as: 'At a single stroke, the camera doses the visual field with that massive amount of discriminated material we miss at every blink, yet know to be there' (p. 102). He goes on to remind us that, paradoxically: 'This one, disinterested feature, completely uncharacteristic of our retinal activity, strikes us as a photograph's most clinching likeness of the way we see' (p. 102). It is not difficult to argue, in this light, that in rewriting Le Rouge Cendrars is simply shifting from normal to photographic vision; that while the reader of Le Rouge's omnibus novels skims, summarizes, concentrates, overlooks, by fits and starts, the reader of Cendrars is surprised to find his attention caught, or asked for, in relation to every item put in front of him. Cendrars has not only dropped those verbs with an attentional zero which threatens to infect their lexical environment ('portait', 'accusait', 'encadraient', 'possédait'), he has also cut those counter-productive adverbs which either muffle ('discrètement'), or discredit by inflation ('harmonieusement'), their lexical companions. Instead, and by skilful use of the unsettling variability of lineation, our reading of 'Jeune fille' is unremittingly alert and alerted. The visibility of the photograph, its total surrender of itself, provides us with more evidence than we know how to use; but it is also the superfluity of this evidence that provides us with the searing experience of *punctum,* that detail which does not produce the 'average' effect of *studium,* but pricks the individual viewer intensely. *Punctum* is uncoded, and Barthes leaves it fairly mysterious; sometimes it seems like a trigger of Proustian involuntary memory, with the same metonymic effect; sometimes, and this is important for our purpose, its action is comparable to that of a haiku (though not in a way that I would agree with):

the reading of the *punctum* (of the pricked photograph so to speak) is at once brief and active. A trick of vocabulary: we say 'to develop a photograph'; but what the chemical action develops is undevelopable, an essence (of a wound), what cannot be transformed but only repeated under the instances of insistence (of the insistent gaze). This brings the Photograph (certain photographs) close to the Haiku. For the notation of a haiku, too, is undevelopable: everything is given, without provoking the desire for or even the possibility of a rhetorical expansion. In both cases we might (we must) speak of an *intense immobility*: linked to a detail (to a detonator), an explosion makes a little star on the pane of the text or of the photograph: neither the Haiku nor the Photograph makes us 'dream'. (1984: 49)[5]

This is hard to believe, given Barthes's later description of the *punctum* as 'a kind of subtle beyond—as if the image launched desire beyond what it permits us to see' (1984: 59),[6] given that Barthes distinguishes the photograph from cinema by the room it creates for pensiveness (1984: 55), and given that the haiku is the verbal equivalent of the reversed perspective of the Japanese, where the vanishing point is not on the

---

[5] '. . . la lecture du *punctum* (de la photo pointée, si l'on peut dire) est à la fois courte et active, ramassée comme un fauve. Ruse du vocabulaire: on dit "développer une photo"; mais ce que l'action chimique développe, c'est l'indéveloppable, une essence (de blessure), ce qui ne peut se transformer, mais seulement se répéter sous les espèces de l'insistance (du regard insistant). Ceci rapproche la Photographie (certaines photographies) du Haïku. Car la notation d'un haïku, elle aussi, est indéveloppable: tout est donné, sans provoquer l'envie ou même la possibilité d'une expansion rhétorique. Dans les deux cas, on pourrait, on devrait parler d'une *immobilité vive*: liée à un détail (à un détonateur), une explosion fait une petite étoile à la vitre du texte ou de la photo: ni le Haïku ni la Photo ne font "rêver"' (1980: 81–2).

[6] 'une sorte de hors-champ subtil, comme si l'image lançait le désir au-delà de ce qu'elle donne à voir' (1980: 93).

horizon but in the centre of the spectator/reader.[7] Later in his essay Barthes generalizes a new *punctum* to all photographs (and presumably to all spectators), the ironic presence of time, the 'that-has-been' ('ça a été').

Barthes's confusion, or equivocations, about *punctum* are part of his desire to restore visceral experience to art, to escape the hermeneutic, which translates direct involvement into signification; and yet the draw of the hermeneutic is irresistible. What is important is that the *punctum* is already in the picture, but it is also added by the spectator (1984: 55); the available, the evident can become input and response. *Punctum* is the way the spectator is touched by the vulnerability of the photograph, immobilized in its Renaissance perspective, behind its window, the vulnerability of the photograph either as signified or as signifier. The vulnerability of the photograph as signified is in, say, the button-hole which condenses the picture's pathos, or the accidentally upturned collar which epitomizes the picture's rumbustious nonchalance and which we are somehow deeply familiar with, or the polished shoes which are not quite congruent with the village butcher, and which prevent his obliteration as recalcitrant eccentric by the codings and averagings of *studium*. In poetry, the vulnerability of the signified will normally be found in lexical items which momentarily disturb or mesmerize, as here the 'presque vert', which suggests an incipient transition into, or uncontrollable desire towards, a colour much less clearly coded than blue, or again the 'velouté' which has a depth of softness, a sensual palpability, a quality of self-awareness, not at all consonant with the less complex and altogether more epidermic 'frais'.

The vulnerability of the signifier, on the other hand, lies in its inability to determine the signified. Ian Jeffrey (1981: 189) points out that David Seymour's photograph of a crowd looking skyward, as a mother suckles her young child and a girl looks questioningly at the camera, is variously entitled 'A Public Meeting in Estremadura, just prior to the Outbreak of the Civil War: Spain 1936' or 'Air Raid over Barcelona, 1938'. The doubt about titles reveals the intrinsic incoherence of the picture (it is powerful

---

[7] In connection with haiku, we might also remember Pound's fascination with the decipherment of its cryptic messages, and with the challenge to reconstruct depth of semantic field out of its two-dimensional economies. In his footnote to his translation of Rihaku's (Li Po's) 'The Jewel Stairs' Grievance', he writes: 'Jewel stairs, therefore a palace. Grievance, therefore there is something to complain of. Gauze stocking, therefore a court lady, not a servant complains. Clear autumn, therefore he has no excuse on account of weather. Also she has come early, for the dew has not merely whitened the stairs, but has soaked her stockings. The poem is especially prized because she utters no direct reproach' (1968: 142).

merely as a page of studies of heads and expressions, or is it about that girl's lacerating look?) and the powerlessness of the photograph to make itself readable, to prevent manipulation—a title is a poor safeguard. The paradox of the photograph is that while we see much more, while much more is available to us in the field of vision, we also see much less, because that field of vision is so restricted, because we cannot see how the context projects the image (we can only see how the camera does). As we read a literary text, we read ourselves into a reading. When we cannot do that, we tend to look for the subtextual motivations for the surface text and often we will find these subtextual motivations in rhythm, or acoustic pattern, or syntactic configuration. The vulnerability of the signifier occurs when subtextual motivations themselves become doubtful, when we have to step in as midwife and assist at, or assist in, the labour of meaning, or meaning's projection. Let us return for a moment to the rhythm of line 5. We have presented this as a biphrasal line with triple accents in each 'hemistich'. We have also envisaged a tetrametric reading, and speculated about some of the expressive consequences of such a reading. If we now add to the ambiguities of the cadence-accentual version of the line syllabic considerations, we find our uncertainty compounded:

Physionomie régulière   et calme qui reflète   la   franchise
/fizjɔnɔmi/ /RegyljɛR/ /e/ /kalm/ /ki/ /Rəflɛt/ /la/ /f Rãʃiz/
     4   3   2   3   3
et la   bonté
/e/ /la/ /bɔ̃te/
     4

Here I experience three different kinds of possible rhythmic pressure I can exert on the way the line means. I can endorse the mirror effect by promoting a 4 + 3 + 2 + 2 + 3 + 4 chiastic arrangement, just by swallowing or darkening (making extrametrical) the relative pronoun:

Physionomie régulière et calme (qui) reflète la franchise et la bonté   (1)
        4   3   2   2   3   4

or alternatively by an *allongement* of 'et calme'

Physionomie régulière et ca-alme qui reflète la franchise et la bonté   (2)
        4   3   3!   3   3   4

An *allongement* of 'calme' would equally be part of an effort to privilege 'régulière' as the presiding rhythmic motor:

Physion'mie régulière et ca-alme qui reflète la franchise (et) la bonté   (3)
      3   3   3!   3   3   3

This involves a recessing of the second 'et' by slurring, or momentary *sotto voce*. The fourth alternative is to see 'et calme' as the spiritual destination of the line, a point of stillness and *recueillement*, an index of inner peace. The reading of the line would thus be accompanied by a deceleration and a gradual downcurve in pitch as the middle of the line is approached (against the generally expected rising pitch-curve towards the centre) followed by a momentary dead stop. For this reading, either version (1) or (2), with appropriate modifications of speed and pitch, would be suitable; but the segmentation would need to be altered so that a tetrametric structure, slightly different from the one already envisaged, could emerge, e.g.

Physionomie régulière | et calme ⌒ | (qui) reflète | la franchise et al bonté (4)

After the pause at 'et calme ⌒', the line would lift out of this trough, accelerate again, and 'open out' in the affirmation of the two abstract nouns.

The doubts and possibilities I have expressed here I would also identify as an experience of *punctum*, but at the level of the signifier. When we read a text or look at a photograph, we may be pricked by the defencelessness of its subject, by the way it cannot prevent the appropriation of the evidence it makes visible. And on this poignancy we feed dream and fantasy (even Barthes admits that the *punctum* has a blind field). But equally the prick may occur in the process of meaning itself, in what the signifier *might* offer. In looking at the photograph by David Seymour, I am pricked at the level of the signified, by the girl's face, or by the comb in the hair of the woman who has her back to us (the woman in the foreground suckling the child is all *studium*). At the level of the signifier, I am pricked by the fact that women could look up at a political speaker with the same mixture of expressions as they might look up at an air raid; or more poignantly vice versa. Similarly, in reading 'Jeune fille', and particularly in reading line 5, I am pricked by the portrait's inability to draw a portrait, by the unsteadiness of the contour and focus. In poetic terms I would be inclined to speak of polysemy, semantic abundance, fruitful ambiguity; in photographic terms I think of a line of verse, an evidence, which produces emotional disarray in the reader because of a kind of compassion for its inability to project its signified. That is to say that my compassion for the text is directly proportional to my power as a reader; the text surrenders to me, just as the motif must surrender to the aggressive hunter-photographer and to the voyeuristic spectator.

What is perhaps most disturbing about Barthes's account of *punctum* is the way in which he initially attaches it to the *being* of the photograph so that it can *become* something for the spectator, only to locate it, towards the end of his study, in the time of the 'that-has-been', in the cruelly inaccessible, in that which is being repeatedly taken away from the spectator. This latter emphasis on the pastness of the photograph, on its complicity with Death, is exaggerated; the less we know about a photograph the less we respond to its temporality; and there are a whole host of photographs which, for a variety of reasons, we can treat as contemporary with ourselves, which we look at in the belief that we could walk out and visit or verify their motifs. A totally historicized documentary photography would have archival rather than documentary interest; any engagement on the part of either photographer or spectator would be pointless. This is not so say that documentary photography does not have value as a 'that-has-been'; it is only to say that it is not its only value. The desires aroused by a pornographic photograph may have to be self-directed, because the model is not there, has been; but desire is aroused as part of a real possibility, as part of 'being' rather than 'has been'. I want to consider temporality in the documentary poem and to explore further the coexistence of the available (the possible) and the inaccessible, the for-ever-out-of-reach.

The kind of experience which Barthes associates with *punctum* as time is described by Proust, a shadowy but persistent presence throughout Barthes's *La Chambre claire*, in relation to the imperfect tense:

J'avoue que certain emploi de l'imparfait de l'indicatif—de ce temps cruel qui nous présente la vie comme quelque chose d'éphémère à la fois et de passif, qui au moment même où il retrace nos actions, les frappe d'illusion, les anéantit dans le passé sans nous laisser comme le parfait, la consolation de l'activité—est resté pour moi une source inépuisable de mystérieuses tristesses. ('Journées de lecture', 1971: 170)

The duration and iteration of the imperfect tense, condemned to illusoriness by the tense's very pastness, seem to recover some of their reality in the present tense. Cendrars's frequent transformation of the past tenses of Le Rouge into the present is noted by Lacassin, but described as a 'modification mineure'; it strikes me as crucial. In 'Pêche et chasse', for example:

1. Canards sauvages pilets sarcelles oies vanneaux outardes
2. Coqs de bruyère grives
3. Lièvres arctiques perdrix de neige ptarmigans

4. Saumons truites arc-en-ciel anguilles
5. Gigantesques brochets et écrevisses d'une saveur particulièrement exquise
6. La carabine en bandoulière
7. Le bowie-knife à la ceinture
8. Le chasseur et le peau-rouge plient sous le poids du gibier
9. Chapelets de ramiers de perdrix rouges
10. Paons sauvages
11. Dindons des prairies
12. Et même un grand aigle blanc et roux descendu des nuages

Cendrars combines two passages from *Le Mystérieux Docteur Cornélius*, one from 'L'Automobile fantôme', which describes the hunting and fishing activities of Lord Burydan, the Indian Kloum, the hunchback Oscar Tournesol, and the amnesiac Joe Dorgan, during their stay in Canada, at the Maison Bleue:

Les *canards sauvages*, les *pilets*, les *sarcelles*, l'*oie* du Canada, le *vanneau* et l'*outarde* y abondaient. Dans les bois les chasseurs rencontraient les *grives*, les *coqs de bruyère*, les *lièvres arctiques* et les *perdrix de neige* ou *ptarmigans*.

  La pêche fournissait des *saumons* superbes, des *truites arc-en-ciel*, des *anguilles*, de *gigantesques brochets et* des *écrevisses d'une saveur particulièrement exquise* (1986: 361)

the other from 'Le Cottage hanté', which is Fred Jorgell's Golden-Cottage near San Francisco and to which he has invited his various friends; the hunting party here consists of Lord Burydan, Kloum, Oscar, and the poet/factotum Agénor Marmousier:

La carabine en bandoulière, le bowie-knife à la ceinture, le lord excentrique et Agénor étaient . . . coiffés de larges chapeaux de paille mexicains. *Le bossu et le Peau-Rouge . . . pliaient sous le poids du gibier*. Ils étalèrent aux regards des jeunes filles, *des chapelets de ramiers et de perdrix rouges*, des *paons sauvages*, des *dindons des prairies* et jusqu' à un *grand* vautour *roux* que l'infaillible balle de Lord Burydan était allé chercher presque dans *les nuages*. (1986: 383)

In the first stanza, Cendrars has again removed what were redundant verbs ('abondaient' 'rencontraient', 'fournissait') given the 'plentifulness' of the enumeration; in the second, the imperfect tense 'pliaient' has become the present 'plient'.

  It is usual to speak of the atemporality of poems (e.g. Culler 1975: 162), in virtue of their textuality, their structural autonomy, alternative modes of meaning, loading in the direction of the signifier rather than the signified. But the physical process of reading draws the poetic text into the contingent and historical world of the reader, draws out strands of temporality which correspond to the temporality of reading. The present tense of the lyric is not just a conventional sign of the text's atemporality, it is a redrawing of the temporal contradiction inherent in all tenses, albeit along different axes. If the imperfect tense sets duration and iteration against pastness, the present tense sets punctuality (the *punctum* aspect of the present, the rich incoherence of the instantaneous, in which the mind can prospect for experience) against omnitemporality (the *studium* aspect of the present, the coherent, typical because permanent), the one which puts things within the reader's reach, the other which sets them in a more abstract, unusable world.

What kind of present is 'plient'? Action or image? First-person reading stance or third-person reading stance? We cannot really tell. We might argue that Cendrars's characteristic removal of determiners removes the time necessary to order responses; that is, the zero article produces the first-hand, the disorder of close-up experience, an absence of intellectual mediation. We might argue that the 'même' of the final line conveys that sense of coming across things, unprepared, in surprised encounter. We might argue that the indefinite article of the same line introduces that random element which has yet to find its function, the very spirit of the possible, the yet-to-be and the yet-to-signify. On the other hand, we might argue that the removal of articles removes context, removes intellectual or physical referentiality, and thus places all this game in the amber of a still life, beyond life, in a realm of the representative and represented; that the definite articles in lines 6–8 typicalize and genericize; this is just another photograph of a hunting party proudly displaying its bag, standing among the slaughtered and relating to them through the instruments of their destruction. And this doubt will either act retrospectively on the first stanza—is this a list of things that *can be* seen, from a guidebook, or that *can be* eaten, a menu, or, alternatively, is this a procession of sightings, of things actually *seen?*—or the first stanza will be felt to be temporally open, multidimensional, past, present, and future in all their aspects, something that a photograph simply could not be.

In outlining this ambiguity of the punctual and omnitemporal, we are not only expressing the ambiguity of the documentary photograph (personal involvement and typicality, camera as instrument of instantaneous response and camera as creator of durable image), and the tension between *punctum* and *studium*; we are also reviving a truth about the modern image, which we discussed in the previous chapter, and adding another facet to it. The modern image is bound into time and direct sensory experience, we said, and one of the concomitants of this proposition was that we can no longer distinguish between notation of sensory datum (Impressionism) and appearances that are vision (Expressionism). In other words, the 'modern' image is unimaginable: it cannot be anticipated, imagined, invoked, it can only be encountered; it is an image precisely by virtue of surprise. As we travel through the fauna of Manitoba and California, do we tick off Arctic hares and salmon on our check-list of Canadian facts, or do we recover these things in their exoticism (in Segalen's sense of 'otherness', the *divers*), both as signifiers and signifieds, in a repeated experience of dizzying defamiliarization? Are we tourists or adventurers? But this is not our only question, as the absence of monolexical lines with their displacement of rhythm makes clear. For another option lies before us, the option of engrossment, of 'discoursing' the list, of articulating it as groups of compound units, of periodizing it; thus, for example:

Canards sauváges | piléts sarcélles | oies vanneáux outárdes.

What I am doing is 'archaizing' the image, returning it to discourse and to the rhythms of voice which create a picture, make an image of images; now I am creating the effect on the birds, not vice versa. My mode of reading groups the ingredients of the list into attention fields, and as it does this it assigns differential accentuation. The list becomes a still-life arrangement in which the geese occupy the background, hardly visible behind the peewit in the middle ground, while the bustard occupies the foreground, a foreground it shares with the teal and the wild duck. Additionally, my segmentation institutes a progression, albeit a syncopated one: two words/one accent/one species > two words/two accents/two species > three words/two accents/three species; this last is the pleasure taken by the stylist(?) moulding his materials, invigorating his language by the way he rhythmically informs it; this is not the reader dumbfounded by an uncontrollable richness, subject to the text's materials, as it would be, if we read the line as a sequence of predominantly monolexical units:

Canards sauváges | piléts | sarcélles | oíes | vanneáux | outárdes
/kanaR/ /sovaʒ/   /pilɛ/ /saRsɛl/ /wa/   /vano/   /utaRd(ə)/

Here I submit to rhythm as the negotiator between a self-imposing text and the voice that wishes to inhabit it. Here the fowl are not 'discoursed', but collided with as phenomena seen and phenomena psychically, psychologically undergone. Rhythm transacts a dissyllabic measure, doubled in the first measure, but insists on monosyllabic focus, or suddenly narrowed perspective (distance), at 'oies'; this last may also be experienced as a kind of momentary psychic crisis. Part of the envocalizing of this unvoiced line also concerns the acoustic pattern. What the line lays out for us is a sequence of seven words, the first, middle, and last of which contain an /aR/ combination; the /a/ occurs in all words bar one, 'pilets', which, by virtue of this fact, may have something of the psychic relief of 'oies', though its isolation from /a/ is only recuperable retrospectively— in respect of its /lɛ/, on the other hand, it introduces the /ɛ/ of 'sarcelles'; just as the first and last words echo each other acoustically, so do the second and sixth; and more completely: with the chiastic arrangement /o/ /a/ /a/ /o/ and the mutually enjoyed support of /v/.

These acoustic patterns may lead us to believe that the line is not quite as innocent as it seems, particularly as there is no sign of /a/ in line 2. Indeed, we begin to feel that Cendrars's lineation is facilitating the emergence of his favoured movement of concentricity. There is probably much truth in this. Cendrars, in pitching his poem between *punctum* and *studium,* between first person and third person, is also pitching it between unvoiced and voiced, modern image and traditional image. And it is precisely variable lineation which allows him to create lines which have at once the imperious inevitability of spontaneous lexical production, and the arrangement of the controlled and formulated pattern. Our awareness of these two pressures as readers varies from line to line. What does seem to be clear from this poem, as from so many others in *Documentaires,* is that Cendrars wished to avoid the *unequivocal* moments of unvoicedness and displaced rhythmic operation to be found in the monolexical lines of *Dix-neuf poèmes élastiques.* Instead he leaves more undefined the line between the voiced and unvoiced, leaves them available to each other, as he does *punctum* and *studium.* So even where lines contain single noun phrases, the noun itself is qualified, substantiated, so that the voice equally has room for its respiration, room to impress its rhythmic trace. There are vocal satisfactions to be had in the $(1 + 2) > (2 + 3)$ progression of:

> Paons sauvages
> Dindons des prairies.

And characteristically, too, Cendrars introduces first-person perspective and discursive control in the last lines of both stanzas. I say 'characteristically' not only in the light of the examples we have already encountered, but also by virtue of the fact that, of the fifty-six lines identified by Lacassin as belonging exclusively to Cendrars, just under 50 per cent relate to the final lines of poems and stanzas. Here line 5 owes its shift in tonality to the appreciatively preposed 'Gigantesques' and to the marked deceleration, produced by the protraction of the adverb 'particulièrement' and the dwelling on the final adjective, stimulated by its being withheld; the effect of discursive control is increased by an acoustic mechanism similar to that already explored in line 1: the /i/ phoneme occurs at the beginning ('Gigantesques'), middle ('écrevisses'), and end ('exquise') of the line, where it is amplified by 'particulièrement'; and this structure of recurrence is accompanied by a more concentric configuration, the chiastic pattern: /ʒ/ (voiced) ('Gigantesques') > /ʃ/ (unvoiced) ('brochets') > /s/ (unvoiced) ('écrevisses', 'saveur') > /z/ (voiced) ('exquise'); one might also note the way in which the line is 'scandé' by /k/ ('gigantesques', 'écrevisses', 'particulièrement', and 'exquise'. Line 12, on the other hand, owes its broad discursive finality to the flow of the initial co-ordinating conjunction, the confident encapsulation of the double adjective ('blanc et roux') and the knowing play on 'descendu' whose semantic multiplicity implies a corresponding multiplicity of register ('shot down': colloquial; 'come down': neutral; 'descended from' ('a descendant of'): poetical) (we note that this is a lexical effect expressly introduced by Cendrars). Thus, whereas the first stanza ends with the sublime of the gustatory, the poem as a whole ends with the sublime of the ethereal; a hunting which has the stomach in mind becomes a hunting which has the soul in mind. It is hardly surprising that Cendrars should substitute 'aigle' for Le Rouge's 'vautour'. Once again we see an affirmation of the belief that writing/ speaking releases us from the potential stultification of the image, releases us into the image; the first person must reassert itself against the potential alienations of the third person.

If it is true to say that most of the *Documentaires* replace Le Rouge's past tenses with the present, and its fusion of punctual and omnitemporal, there are some instructive exceptions. 'Sur l'Hudson' is one of these:

1. Le canot électrique glisse sans bruit entre les nombreux navires ancrés dans l'immense estuaire et qui battent pavillon de toutes les nations du monde
2. Les grands clippers chargés de bois et venus du Canada ferlaient leurs voiles géantes
3. Les paquebots de fer lançaient des torrents de fumée noire
4. Un peuple de dockers appartenant à toutes les races du globe s'affairait dans le tapage des sirènes à vapeur et les sifflets des usines et des trains
5. L'élégante embarcation est entièrement en bois de teck
6. Au centre se dresse une sorte de cabine assez semblable à celle des gondoles vénitiennes.

This corresponds to the opening of the sixth chapter ('Sur l'Hudson') of the fourth episode ('Les Lords de la "Main Rouge"') of Le Rouge's *Le Mystérieux Docteur Cornélius*, in which Miss Isidora Jorgell, and her

Scottish companion Mistress MacBarlott, take a pleasure trip on the river, only to fall foul of the engineer Hardison's trials of his new torpedo. The relevant passages in Le Rouge are:

C'était *une élégante embarcation entièrement construite en bois de teck* et *au centre* de laquelle *se dressait une sorte de cabine assez semblable,* comme disposition, *à celles* qui l'on voit sur les *gondoles vénitiennes . . .*

Presque *sans bruit, le canot glissa entre les nombreux navires ancrés dans l'immense estuaire et qui* portaient *les pavillons de toutes les nations du monde. De grands clippers, chargés de bois et venus du Canada, ferlaient leurs voiles géantes. Des paquebots de fer lançaient des torrents de fumée noire,* tandis qu'*un peuple de dockers, appartenant à toutes les races* de l'univers, *s'affairait dans le tapage des sirènes à vapeur et les sifflets des usines.* (1986: 194)

(I have quoted Le Rouge in the order of his own text rather than in that of Cendrars's poem, as Lacassin does (1986: 1199), merely to show what rearrangement has been necessary for Cendrars to secure his last-line effect. Le Rouge has made clear that the 'canot' is 'électrique' in the first sentence of the chapter.)

Why then has Cendrars substitued the present tense for all that concerns the 'canot électrique' and yet maintained Le Rouge's imperfect tense for all the rest of the shipping on the Hudson? There seem to me to be four reasons. The first is in order to achieve a sense of movement: as the 'canot' slips down the river, it is one by one putting the other boats and activities behind it; if we believe that the very taking of a photograph is an act of consigning the motif to the past, then the electric boat is photographing everything it passes by. This temporal aspect of movement reveals the second reason: the poem is a kind of advertisement for a new type of river craft and for science's concern for the environment. As the 'canot' moves down the river, its very existence condemns all other kinds of craft to history, and a cumbersome, grubby, noisy history at that. What characterizes the clippers is their 'voiles géantes', this large, primitive, inefficient mode of locomotion; the funnels of the steamers, on the other hand, are belching forth great columns of dense, black smoke. And these two types of boat are tied to the industrial din of factory sirens, train whistles, and dock labour. The 'canot électrique', for its part, makes no noise, produces no pollution, is efficiently and invisibly powered; and not only that, but its contribution to the environment is aesthetic as well. As it passes, other craft become the design and engineering dinosaurs of the river. But the 'canot's' temporal difference from the rest of the shipping is also a difference in the order of its reality. Orson Welles tells us: 'The camera is much more than a recording apparatus, it is a medium via which messages reach us from another world, a world that is not ours and that brings us to the heart of a great secret' (quoted in Hiley 1982: 8). This quotation, reminiscent of that of Bill Brandt already quoted, draws our attention to a distinction which might be made between the tourist photograph and the documentary photograph of travel. Whereas the tourist photograph does not differentiate its monuments or beaches, but always tries to capture their average and transferable qualities (would it matter if the Eiffel Tower were in Cologne?), their third-personness, their being ever equal to themselves (by having myself photographed in front of the Eiffel Tower I in fact deprive the photograph of my first-personness; I merely turn myself into a third person), the documentary travel photograph interrogates the sight or site, demands that it historicize itself in the photographer's vision, that it becomes something for him, enters a reality other than its own. Whereas the tourist photograph becomes a substitute for contact, experience, a defence against reality, an absolution from enquiry and interest—

Travel becomes a strategy for accumulating photographs. The very activity of taking pictures is soothing, and assuages general feelings of disorientation that are likely to be exacerbated by travel. Most tourists feel compelled to put the camera between themselves and whatever is remarkable that they encounter. Unsure of other responses, they take a picture (Sontag 1978: 9–10)

—the documentary travel photograph is a contact with, a record of, the otherness of the motif, where otherness itself is embodied as a kind of response; the documentary travel photograph is not a substitute for another, unassimilable reality, but on the contrary the very place where another reality is made manifest as other, achieves its otherness. What is noticeable about the cosmopolitan river scene we have before us is that the multinationality of other craft is registered as muddled, undifferentiated, and essentially meaningless: 'qui battent pavillon de toutes les nations du monde' (l. 1), 'appartenant à toutes les races du globe' (l. 4). While the 'canot électrique' unmistakably represents the newness of the New World, it also represents the New World's ability to import the Old World, its style as well as its emigrants, and to synthesize them in ways that preserve their ethnic individuality and yet produce new species; the 'canot' has the electrical know-how of the USA, the hardwood of the tropics, and the artful elegance of Venice. In becoming this novel creation, the 'canot' floats in a world of dreamlike fantasy, aided by the apparent lack of any crew or passengers aboard her; even the 'assez' of the final line becomes less an indicator of careful comparative measurement and more an index of quizzical wonderment, reinforced by 'une sorte de'. This ghostly vessel, then, glides in and out of the scene almost unnoticed, an uncanny and fleeting presence, registered only by the photographer who is prepared to see; the present tense is, then, at one and the same time, the other which haunts this description, and the sign of the inwardness of the experience it produces.

This last observation leads into the fourth and final reason. The variation in tense allows a framing effect; the past tense of lines 2–4 lies within the present of lines 1 and 5–6. This creates not only a further sense of recession in the past tenses, as if they were almost parenthesized, but also embeds one kind of discourse, one kind of photography, within another. The first line leaves us still unenlightened as to the significance of the differentiation, partly because here, and here only, a present tense is applied to the other boats ('qui battent pavillon'), partly because the magical 'canot' is intermingled with the other craft, partly because it is difficult to derive any rhythmic hints from the line:

> Le canot électrique | glisse sans bruit | entre les nombreux navires |
>
> ancrés dans l'immense estuaire | et qui battent pavillon | de toutes
>
> les nations du monde

But there are hints here: the 'canot' occupies a biphrasal structure, with two accents per measure, while the rest of the scene occupies four measures with sometimes two, sometimes three accents in the measure (here alternating). What we need to emphasize is the fluency of the 'canot' ('glisse sans bruit'), a fluency which is connected not only with its motion through the water, but also with its motion through the imagination— 'canot electrique' > 'élégante embarcation' > 'gondole vénitienne'—and its motion in the voice. In order to wed the rhythm to the subject, we should, I think, repeat the pattern of the 'canot' in the first line when we arrive at lines 5–6, biaccentual, biphrasal:

> 5. L'élégante embarcation | est entièrement en bois de teck
>
> 6. Au centre se dresse une sorte de cabine | assez semblable à celle des
>
> gondoles vénitiennes.

What in fact happens in line 6 is that the biaccentuality is doubled, but the overall binary feel of the line is maintained by the facilitation of the pairing of accents by the syntax. This kind of fluency, not uneventful but controlled, elegantly symmetrical, even urbane, is not to be found in lines 2–4:

2. Les grands clippers | chargés de bois | et venus du Canada | ferlaient leurs voiles géántes

3. Les paquebots de fer | lançaient des torrents de fumée noire

4. Un peuple de dockers | appartenant à toutes les races du globe | s'affairait dans le tapage des sirènes à vapeur | et les sifflets | des usines | et des trains

This, on the contrary, is a prosody of 'affairement', bumpy and occasionally breathless. Number of phrases per line and accents per measure vary, and not with much pattern, apart from the virtual descent into chaos in line 4, where nouns quickly accumulate and measures contract to the staccato. This again sounds like the invasion of discourse by the imperious demands and clamour of a mechanized world. Line 3 at first, retrospectively, provides an ironic rhythmic parallel with line 5, but its significance needs to be seen within a larger pattern of activity and being: line 1 marks the movement of the 'canot' against the immobilization of the other shipping ('nombreux navires ancrés dans l'immense estuaire'); immobilization of the ships releases a countervailing activity (furling of sails, smoking of funnels, unloading of goods); in some senses this is a translation of being into movement, or a loss of being in dispersal and distraction. The 'canot' takes the opposite direction: its movements/activity ('glisse') silently transform themselves into being ('est', 'se dresse'), its linearity becomes a centredness ('Au centre'). Line 3 is in fact a mockery of line 5: against the integrated adjective + noun construction of line 5, where the preposing of the adjective signifies response (admiration), and the adjective's figurative and intrinsic qualities, the noun + noun complement construction of line 3 underlines the random or optional conjunction of the two nouns, unsupported by any acoustic affiliation (cf. /ele gɑ̃tɑ̃baRkasjõ/);

against the euphonic syllabic increase from 'L'élégante' (3) to 'embarcation' (4), we have a chopped contraction from 'Les paquebots' (3 or 4) to 'de fer' (2); against the balanced biaccentuality of the second measure of line 5, we have the destabilizing triaccentual pattern of the second measure of line 3; against the steamer's exhibitionist ('torrents') emptying of itself into the air in the second measure (l. 3), we have the self-collection in quiet integrity of the 'canot', in its second measure (l. 5). Finally we should note that the rhythmic chaos we have attributed to line 4 grows out of a change in line-initial grammar: the definite articles of an orchestrated, if unwholesome, set of activities have momentarily changed into an indefinite article, an open invitation to indiscipline.

Thus, from this poem emerge two voices, two modes of rhythm, the one belonging to the 'canot', the other to the other craft. The one emphasizes fluency, ease, but at the same time the acquisition of being and first-person responsiveness; the other is choppier, less predictable, a flirtation at one point with mechanized chaos, and tells of the disposal of being, the yielding of self to the third person. In some senses, therefore, one kind of rhythmic consciousness, that of the 'canot', belongs to the *punctum*, while the other, that of other shipping, belongs to the *studium*; put another way, we have, in another combination of rhythmic features, the two dimensions of the documentary photograph outlined at the outset.

It seems inadequate to me, therefore, to consider Cendrars's *Documentaires* exclusively in terms of an aesthetic of plagiarism. Berger argues that photographs quote from appearances (1982: 111); in parallel fashion we might argue that Cendrars quotes from Gustave Le Rouge. But this is to do both Cendrars and photography a profound injustice; the art of translation, which Berger reserves for painting, would be the fairer term, since such fundamental changes are undergone by the raw material in both cases. The lineation of free verse makes rhythmic, makes visible/audible, to degrees that quite transform it, linearly proceeding but non-lineated narrative prose. We operate with new spans of apprehension, and we segment language not according to the laws of continuity and plot, but according to principles of semanticization and symbolization; segmentation in free verse ravels up the signifier rather than unravelling the signified, as is necessary if reference is to become image. But more fundamentally still, reading becomes critical to perception; poetic texts, and free-verse ones in particular, problematize reading, make it the locus of the text's activity. In reading free verse, we have far more stops, in the musical sense, at our disposal: where to accentuate, where to slur, where to pause, where to introduce juncture, where to use synaeresis or diaeresis, where to use syncope or apocope, where to introduce an articulated *e atone*, which acoustic elements to foreground, what tone to use, what weight to attribute to the syllable and to number, where to locate the rhythmic principle, and so on; narrative prose might ask us similar questions, but it does not do so as a prerequisite of our understanding it; it is not in such questions that the meaning of narrative prose lies. Having chosen free verse as his medium, it was impossible for Cendrars to plagiarize Le Rouge; he could only translate him.

Another aspect of this translation is the translation of the journalistic photograph into the documentary photograph. Cendrars travels not in Gustave Le Rouge's prose so much as in the world that his prose makes visible; but in order to travel in this world and see it with his own eyes, he must destroy the narrator, the photograph's captional nature, its frenzied efforts to sell itself as news. Cendrars neither quotes Le Rouge (takes a tourist photograph of his text which changes nothing but merely reproduces the *Sehenswürdigkeiten*), nor does he perpetuate Le Rouge's spirit in a parallel pursuit of Le Rouge's 'action-with-local-colour' formula. Cendrars stands beside Le Rouge and looks at the same scenes and same events, but differently, not appropriating them for thrills or plot, but yielding to them, so that they can express themselves, and in so doing engage a response from him. This is documentary travel photography if you like; it is just that it is undertaken in a text rather than in a landscape.

7
Jules Supervielle, Gravitations
(1925/1932)
The Prosody of Displacement

YVES-ALAIN FAVRE'S listing of verse-forms in *Gravitations* (1981: 102–4) shows examples of alexandrine, decasyllable, octosyllable, heptasyllable, hexasyllable, heterometric structures, *vers libres*, and *versets*. Supervielle's cultivation of a multiform prosody is usually explained, and plausibly so, in terms of the existential range of his poetry, rather than as the fruit of any particular aesthetic pursuit:

> En fait, on constate chez Supervielle une lutte entre deux tendances contraires: un besoin de libre expansion qui correspond à un sentiment de l'espace cosmique et au désir d'un épanouissement sans limitation, et un désir de régularité qui rassure et réconforte. La première tendance incite à renouveler les mètres traditionnels, à les abandonner pour inventer une nouvelle métrique; la seconde, en revanche, entraîne un retour au vers régulier. (Favre 1981: 74–5)

If anything, Favre's account is still too much weighted in the direction of opposing forms. This is to be partly explained by his dramatization of Supervielle's imaginative life as 'une lutte entre deux tendances contraires' rather than as an oscillating dialectic in which one impulse constantly, but never definitively, gives way to its reverse, in which contrary impulses are indeed constantly synthesized. It is also partly to be explained, perhaps, as a perpetuation of that antagonism between the regular and free by which each is validated. But this position is essentially a polemical one, that is to say a position which derives its argumentative vigour from visions of rupture, revolution, and decline at the expense of those of development, unfussy continuity, and enrichment. Étiemble, a critic central to our understanding of Supervielle, has never been able to come to terms with free verse, and Supervielle's 'concessions' to it still look to him like the triumph of the arbitrary and modish:

> Quand vous aurez durement bataillé avec ces *vers* pour en chercher la raison d'être, vous ne pourrez plus vous en cacher le secret, à savoir que Supervielle, comme

tous les poètes du *vers libre*, découpe sa prose imagée en tronçons inégaux selon les mécanismes scolaires de l'analyse logique. (1960: 69)

It is with some satisfaction that Étiemble notes that while the poems in regular metre hardly undergo any revision from the 1925 to the 'definitive' 1932 edition, the free-verse poems 'souvent varient du tout au tout' (1960: 71) and thus 'trahissent l'embarras de celui qui ne sait à quelle discipline obéir' (1960: 75). What Étiemble does not envisage is that the very freedom of the verse *allows* a process of radical reimagining, encourages it, as one of its peculiar features. This is a point difficult to explore in an enquiry into the work of a particular poet: but the essence of free verse is its ability to combine elasticity—a margin of inclusion and exclusion (cf. Delaunay's words on Cendrars, quoted above p. 148), a margin of option in lineation and segmentation, a margin of margins, etc.—with the sense of the emergence of the indelible and inimitable 'chant profond' of a particular poet; put another way, the 'chant profond' of a particular poet is as relative as the poet; we never visit the same place twice, though we visit the same place twice.

Supervielle, for his part, experiences no awkward hiatus between the differing degrees of metricity, and would confirm what we have already proposed (1990: 295), that these different degrees and kinds 'constitute . . . a seamless continuum, and that one of the essential freedoms of free verse is the freedom to dip into that continuum at any point at any time according to the expressive needs of the moment'. Supervielle puts the matter with disarming simplicity:

Je me sers de formes poétiques très différentes: vers réguliers (ou presque), vers blancs qui riment quand la rime vient à moi, vers libres, versets qui se rapprochent de la prose rythmée. Aimant par-dessus tout le naturel, je ne me dis jamais à l'avance que j'emploierai telle ou telle forme. Je laisse mon poème lui-même faire son choix. Ce n'est pas là mépris mais assouplissement de la technique. Ou, si l'on préfère, technique mouvante qui ne se fixe qu'à chaque poème dont elle épouse le chant. Ce qui peut-être permet une grande variété d'inspiration. (1951: 66)

What is important for Supervielle is what was important for Saint-John Perse: not the ancestry or credentials of any particular form used, but its appropriateness to a subject, a mood, a tone. Form is not a sanctified something which is rolled into place, to give metrical status and generical kudos to a text waiting to be made; it is, as it were, a sudden, momentary encounter between utterance and its designated form, a form which was always possible given the range of technical resources. Perse's journey was a journey back to childhood in order to journey out of childhood, and therefore seemed to favour a prosody of boundaries, of expansion and contraction; boundary was experienced as colonialist authority, as security, as nostalgic fixation, but also as stagnation, or stimulus to a sensory dynamism. These same existential conflicts and concerns haunt Supervielle's poetry; but the dynamic of his verse is very different from Perse's. The extraterrestrial journeys of *Gravitations* do not generate such ostensible intensity; they proceed at a lower temperature and with greater gradualism, are not tempted by rupture, by traversal, are not egocentrically assertive, are not marked by the intoxication which cannot be withstood:

D'autres poètes, ses contemporains, nous ont frappés par leur puissance, leur ampleur, le déchaînement de leur lyrisme, les audaces et les nouveautés de leur forme. Aucun n'a eu cet accent, intime et humain à la fois, fraternel, qui nous émeut à la mesure de sa discrétion. (Arland, 1966: 8)

Much of the difference between Perse and Supervielle is to be explained by the difference of the forms of free verse they employ. But before we can discuss this difference, we should clear up a terminological dispute which gives rise to confusions.

With Favre's classification of the verse forms of *Gravitations* (1981: 102–4) I have two quarrels which amount to three. Favre distinguishes between 'poèmes en vers libres', namely 'La Belle au bois dormant', 'Tiges', 'Haut Ciel', 'Ascension', 'La Table', and 'Rêve', and other free-verse poems which he describes as 'versets'. Not only does Favre fail to establish the criteria by which this distinction is made—the whole point of Supervielle's versification, as I hope to show, is that one verse-form drifts, or 'gravitates', into another, without hiatus of any kind—but the term 'versets' is surely ill chosen. *Versets* conjure up a biblical connection, or at least a connection with litanic prose, and imply, if anything, (1) a cadence-accentual prosody (see our discussions of Claudel, 1990: 240–68, and Whitman, 1990: 98–110 and above, Chapter 3) and (2) a great degree of flexibility in relation to line-length, with a dominance of the longer over the shorter. While it may be appropriate to refer to several of the poems of *Débarcadères* (1922) as written in *versets* (e.g. 'Paquebot', 'Retour à l'estancia', 'La Métisse'), it seems to me positively misleading for *Gravitations*. For the Supervielle of *Gravitations* is a *verslibriste* of the line, that is to say, his free verse is essentially a sequence of congruities with, or approximations to, regular verse-lines, in which, consequently, the line continues to be the basic rhythmic unit, and a line defined by number of syllables rather than by number of measures.

Some of the blame for this terminological misapprehension must be borne by Supervielle himself; he refers to the *verset* more frequently than he is justified in doing, not only, for example, in the passage from 'En songeant à un art poétique' quoted above, but also in his correspondence with Étiemble:

j'ai un assez grand mépris de toutes les esthétiques et des techniques. Ce qui compte pour moi avant tout, c'est la substance poétique et suivant les jours je lui donne un moule ou un autre (vers réguliers, libres, assonancés, presque blancs, versets. (Supervielle and Étiemble 1969: 34)

It is not just that the term gives a false impression of the structure of his free verse, but it also implies a kind of movement which is alien to him. Perse's *verset* is a prosody of inflation, of chest or sail, inflation checked or turned in on itself perhaps, but informed by an impetuous dynamic. And each new *verset* reaffirms this possibility of setting out, or setting sail, whatever pressures it may subsequently yield to; it is a form potentially without boundary (how easily it could become a prose poem), and for that very reason it 'poses the question' about boundaries, since the more the *verset* expands, the greater the pressure to break boundaries and encapsulate ever larger spans of utterance. Supervielle's line-*verslibrisme*, on the other hand, is a priori limited, subject to boundary and a coming to completeness; the freedom to move lies within the form and it is a freedom which is essentially exercised by stealth and achieved through displacement.

Before looking more closely at these Superviellean strategies, we should make two fundamental points about his versification. This we can do in relation to the three-line poem 'Les Vieux Horizons', originally (1925) part of 'Sans murs', which will also serve to initiate our investigations into the notion of displacement. In his commentary on 'Les Vieux Horizons' Robichez (1981: 58) remarks: 'Pour le mètre, on observe, en réduction, le modèle qu'on retrouve dans bien d'autres poèmes du recueil: le passage à une cadence régulière, un vers sans mesure suivi de deux vers de quatorze syllabes.' Robichez's general point about the overall structure of many of Supervielle's poems ('passage à une cadence régulière') has much truth in it, but his comment about the first line of 'Les Vieux Horizons' ('sans mesure') is mistaken: this line conforms perfectly well to Supervielle's favoured binary, fourteen-syllable line:

Les vieux horizons déplacent les distances, les enfument,	$5 + 2 + 4' + 3$
Orgueilleux d'être sans corps comme Dieu qui les créa,	$3 + 4 + 3 + 4$
Jamais le marin de quart ne sait quand il les traverse.	$2 + 5 + 2 + 5$

Robichez has failed to note that Supervielle's verse depends a great deal on the expressive leverage provided by an expected medial articulation/ juncture/caesura (about which we shall have more to say in a moment); but more particularly he does not seem to have gathered that Supervielle employs a *césure épique or its equivalent, i.e. he treats any unelided *e atone* at the medial juncture (caesura) in the same way as one treats the line-terminal *e atone*, as extrametrical, as not counting in the syllabic total of the line, thus:

> Les vieux horizons déplac(ent) les distances, les enfument.

This habit seems also to have escaped Décaudin (1982), when he affirms: 'S'il sait appliquer les règles formelles de la prosodie, Supervielle ne fait pas de leur respect un principe absolu. Il procède, ou ne procède pas, à l'élision d'une syllabe, à la diérèse, selon les circonstances' (p. 63). About diaeresis we shall have cause to share Décaudin's doubts. But Supervielle's 'elision' of syllables is not so much a matter of particular contexts as of a principle consistently adhered to. In the two alexandrines that Décaudin picks out from 'Haut Ciel':

> Défendant aux étoil(es) de pousser un seul cri

and

> Dans le vertige de leur éternell(e) naissance

he is right to suppress the '-es' of 'étoiles', but for the wrong reasons, and wrong to select for omission the 'e' of 'éternelle', which is an intra-phrasal 'e' occurring at a point of secondary accentuation; he should have selected the 'e' of 'vertige', which occurs at a natural syntactic juncture and follows a primary accent; thus

> Dans le vertig(e) de leur éternelle naissance   4 + 5 + 3

rather than Décaudin's 4 + 6 + 2.[1] Similarly he should not be surprised

---

[1] Étiemble (1966: 316) has also failed to pick up this basic rule of Supervielle's metric; he, too, finds arbitrary practice in Supervielle's treatment of the unelided *e atone* because he does not distinguish between the structural significance of the medial juncture and that of the hemistich-internal *coupe*: 'Dans "Le Gaucho", écrit en quatorze syllabes selon toute vraisemblance, même hésitation: tantôt l'*e* moyen est compté pour un temps "Les chiens fauv*es* du soleil couchant harcelaient les vaches / Raboteus*e* comme après quelq*ue* tremblement de terre / Et les vach*es* ourdissaient un silenc*e* violent" tantôt l'*e* moyen s'escamote "Et tous les poils se brouillèr(*ent*) sous le hâtif crépuscule. / Toucha l'homme et ses ténèbr(*es*) dans la zone de son cœur." On le voit par ce vers, l'*e* moyen est si bizarrement traité que l'on ne sait s'il faut escamoter celui de "ténèbres" ou celui de "zone"; maint fois dans ce poème, on se trouve en butte à la même difficulté.'

to have to 'elide' the 'e' of 'rames' and 'escales', from the same poem, since they, too, occur at the medial juncture:

Tapis parmi les ram(es) d'un navire sans âge   2 + 4 + 3 + 3
Dans la nuit sans escal(es), sans rampes ni statues.   3 + 3 + 2 + 4

Décaudin's point about diaeresis is exemplified in the line

De soi-même prisonnières

where he feels obliged to treat 'prisonnières' as a tetrasyllable, rather than a trisyllable, in order to bring it into line with the three octosyllables by which it is immediately followed (in a sequence of three octosyllabic quatrains). Décaudin does not envisage, therefore, that, in the quatrain which follows, the line

L'impatience originelle

might be a heptasyllable rather than an octosyllable (/ɛ̃pasjɑ̃s/ rather than /ɛ̃pasiɑ̃s/), although he does point out (p. 64) that the heptasyllables of 'Ascension' are interrupted at the beginning of the third stanza by an octosyllable:

A ces arbrisseaux, ces arbustes

that 'Les Yeux de la morte' is composed of three heptasyllabic quatrains, apart from the line

De l'autre côté d'Altair   5 + 3

and that in 'Alarme', a poem exclusively in heptasyllables in the original edition (1925), the line

Fabricantes de l'oubli   3 + 4

was replaced in 1932 by

Où se développe l'oubli.   5 + 3

To this list, Décaudin later adds 'Commencements', an octosyllabic poem whose third stanza is none the less in heptasyllables, and whose fifth stanza contains the line

Virez beaux gestes sans bras.   2 + 2 + 3

If Supervielle equivocates about synaeresis and diaeresis, he does so, it seems, on purpose, as a matter of prosodic policy. What he wishes to achieve, it seems, is a prosody based on syllabic proximity rather than syllabic differentiation, and to complicate that prosody by blurring the line between immediately 'consecutive' metres (heptasyllables and octosyllables, for example). This is borne out by the fact that, of the seventy-two poems of *Gravitations*, sixteen are in octosyllables and eleven are in heptasyllables, which in turn bears out the suspicion that any classification of Supervielle's verse according to types is wrong-headed, since his verse slides, almost imperceptibly, across the range of available verseforms, and from one type to another.

What does seem odd, however, is that he should be at one and the same time a free-verse poet of the line, and of the caesura, and a poet of the syllabically scumbled, of the numerically easy-to-misapprehend. It is this apparent paradox which we will now go on to investigate, in a consideration of 'Apparition', a scansion of which is offered below:

1.	Où sont-ils les points cardinaux,	3 + 5
2.	Le soleil se levant à l'Est,	3 + 5
3.	Mon sang et son itinéraire	2 + 6
4.	Prémédité dans mes artères?	4 + 4
5.	Le voilà qui déborde et creuse,	3 + 5 / 3 + 3 + 2
6.	Grossi de neiges et de cris	4 + 4
7.	Il court dans des régions confuses;	2 + 6 / 2 + 4 + 2
8.	Ma tête qui jusqu'ici	2 + 5
9.	Balançait les pensées comme branches des îles	3 + 3 + 3 + 3
10.	Forge des ténèbres crochues.	1 + 4 + 3
11.	Ma chaise que happe l'abîme	2 + 6 / 2 + 3 + 3
12.	Est-ce celle du condamné	3 + 5
13.	Qui s'enfonce dans la mort avec toute l'Amérique?	3 + 4 + 3 + 4
14.	Qui est là? Quel est cet homme qui s'assied à notre table	3 + 4 + 3 + 4
15.	Avec cet air de sortir comme un trois-mâts du brouillard,	4 + 3 + 4 + 3
16.	Ce front qui balance un feu, ces mains d'écume marine,	2 + 5 + 2 + 5
17.	Et couverts les vêtements par un morceau de ciel noir?	3 + 4 + 4 + 3
18.	A sa parole une étoile accroche sa toile araigneuse,	4 + 3 + 5 + 3
19.	Quand il respire il déforme et forme une nébuleuse.	4 + 3 + 2 + 5
20.	Il porte, comme la nuit, des lunettes cerclées d'or	2 + 5 + 3 + 4
21.	Et des lèvres embrasées où s'alarment des abeilles,	3 + 4 + 3 + 4
22.	Mais ses yeux, sa voix, son cœur sont d'un enfant à l'aurore.	3 + 4 + 4 + 3

23. Quel est cet homme dont l'âme fait des signes   4 + 3 + 3 + 4
    solennels?
24. Voici Pilar, elle m'apaise, ses yeux déplacent le   4 + 4 + 4 + 4
    mystère.
25. Elle a toujours derrière elle comme un souvenir   4 + 3 + 5 + 3
    de famille
26. Le soleil de l'Uruguay qui secrètement pour nous   3 + 4 + 5 + 3
    brille,
27. Mes enfants et mes amis, leur tendresse est   3 + 4 + 3 + 4
    circulaire
28. Autour de la table ronde, fière comme l'univers;   2 + 5 + 1 + 6
29. Leurs frais sourires s'en vont de bouche en   4 + 3 + 4 + 3
    bouche fidèles,
30. Prisonniers les uns des autres, ce sont couleurs   3 + 4 + 4 + 3
    d'arc-en-ciel.
31. Et comme dans la peinture de Rousseau le   (2 + 5) + 3 + 4
    douanier,
32. Notre tablée monte au ciel voguant dans une   4 + 3 + 2 + 5
    nuée,
33. Nous chuchotons seulement tant on est près des   4 + 3 + 4 + 3
    étoiles,
34. Sans cartes ni gouvernail, et le ciel pour   2 + 5 + 3 + 4
    bastingage.
35. Comment vinrent jusqu'ici ces goélands par   3 + 4 + 4 + 3
    centaines
36. Quand déjà nous respirons un angélique oxygène,   3 + 4 + 4 + 3
37. Nous cueillons et recueillons du céleste romarin,   3 + 4 + 3 + 4
38. De la fougère affranchie qui se passe de racines,   4 + 3 + 3 + 4
39. Et comme il nous est poussé, dans l'air pur des   (2 + 5) + 3 + 4
    ailes longues
40. Nous mêlons notre plumage à la courbure des   3 + 4 + 4 + 3
    mondes.

[Note: Aside from the elision of line-medial *e atones*, every other 'e' is treated as
it would be in regular verse.]

It is no accident, perhaps, that when pressed by Robert Mallet to give
an example, from poetry, of the eloquence of simplicity, Supervielle
should quote the refrain from Baudelaire's 'L'Invitation au voyage'
(Étiemble 1960: 215):

> Là tout n'est qu'ordre et beauté,
> Luxe, calme et volupté.

The poem promises an elsewhere which moulds itself to the identity and desires of the traveller, and the heptasyllable is itself a metrical elsewhere which is also a metrical familiar: we find it in *Aucassin et Nicolette*, in Eustache Deschamps, in Charles d'Orléans, in the *vers mêlés of the seventeenth century, in La Fontaine, for example—and let us not forget Supervielle's admiration for him:

Je crois que l'auteur le plus souple, le plus 'disponible' de la littérature française, c'est La Fontaine. C'est lui qui passe le plus facilement de la prose aux vers, il n'est jamais si prisonnier de la prose qu'il ne puisse la quitter pour le vers ou réciproquement. C'est une force, c'est aussi un peu une faiblesse (Étiemble 1960: 213)

—in the *vers libéré* of Baudelaire, Mallarmé, Verlaine, and Rimbaud. But in what sense is the heptasyllable a metrical elsewhere? Partly by reputation, for if it is used by canonic poets, it is not itself a canonic form:

Les vers de sept et de cinq syllabes sont essentiellement des vers boiteux . . .
    Le premier est particulièrement rapide et le contraste de ses deux mesures sans cesse inégales lui donne une allure sautillante et saccadée, qui convient parfaitement à certaines poésies légères, surtout à celle dont le ton est badin ou ironique. (Grammont 1965/1908: 46)

Grammont's characterization of the heptasyllable is less sophisticated perhaps than Morier's when, in Henri de Régnier's poetry, he identifies 'le 7 agressif' (which he also attributes to Supervielle), 'le 7 défaillant', and 'le 7 dynamique' (1943–4: ii. 103–8), but both analyses imply something subversive about the line, and both locate this subversiveness in the line's expressivity. If the heptasyllable is a metrical elsewhere, then it is because it *is* subversive; but it is not ideologically subversive, so much as metrically subversive, and it is not so much subversive of other metres as of comfortable habits of reading. The heptasyllable is an intersticial metre, not just because it occupies the interstices between the octosyllable and the hexasyllable, but because it makes available an intersticial space of journeying.

In formulating an approach to Supervielle's love of the heptasyllable, we need to remember two basic mathematical truths about the *vers impair*:

1. Only in the *impair* can a *pair* measure be combined with an *impair* one.
2. Only in the *impair* can the constituent measures be immediately consecutive numbers.

These two characteristics are what identify the *impair*, not the oddness of its overall number. What I mean by that is this: it is extremely difficult to conceptualize the oddness of an odd number other than by declaring that half of it is a non-whole number (Cornulier 1989: 77); this is rhythmically meaningless. It is rhythmically meaningful, however, to say that *vers impairs* allow consecutive measures of consecutive syllabic values ($2 + 3$, $3 + 2$, $3 + 4$, $4 + 3$, $5 + 6$, etc.) and that these, as far as ease of reading is concerned, should be avoided. *Mètres pairs* allow a division into equal halves, repetition of measure ($3 + 3$, $4 + 4$, $6 + 6$); otherwise they compel a difference between their constituent measures of two syllables or more ($2 + 4$, $1 + 5$, $5 + 3$, $2 + 6$). When Leconte de Lisle affirms that 'le vers français vit d'équilibre, il meurt si on touche à sa parité' (Huret 1982/1891: 239), it should not be assumed that he is thinking only in terms of classical proportions and symmetry; the presence of 'équilibre' depends not on the fact of equilibrium, but on its perceptibility, and the parisyllabic line maximizes perceptibility by necessitating a certain minimum level of differentiation, unless of course all measures are equal. Cornulier (1989: 77–8) expresses this same truth in relation to stanzaic combinations of lines:

Dans la poésie classique, on ne rencontre pratiquement pas de quatrains mesurés en 8/7/8/7, ou en 7/6/7/6, alors qu'on en trouve en 8/6/8/6, en 7/5/7/5, ou en 7/4/7/4, par exemple: les deux types évités sont ceux où seraient mélangés deux mètres ne différant entre eux que d'une syllabe, le 8 et le 7, ou le 7 et le 6. D'une manière générale, les poètes classiques évitent, et certains métriciens proscrivent explicitement, le mélange de mesures ne différant que d'une syllabe, si elles ne sont pas inférieures à 5 ou 6 syllabes. En effet, plus deux réalisations voisines de mesures différentes tendent vers la longueur limite 8, plus il importe qu'elles soient nettement différentes l'une de l'autre, pour qu'il n'y ait pas d'effet de brouillage, et que chacune soit clairement et distinctement perçue dans son exactitude: c'est ce que j'appellerai la *Contrainte de Discrimination*, et qui peut avoir une influence sur le répertoire des mètres. (see also Cornulier 1982: 50–7)

Supervielle, then, with his fondness for mixing octosyllable and heptasyllable, and for exploiting the internal structure of the repeated heptasyllable, is working in the area where the risk of 'brouillage' is at its greatest. If we are going to justify the application of terms such as 'impalpable', 'insaisissable', or 'déséquilibré' to the *vers impair* (see argument, Chapter 1), then we will not do so on the basis of some aesthetics or metaphysics of oddness in numbers, but because the *impair must* combine like with unlike (odd with even) and *can* combine measures with only monosyllabic variation, so that the reader can never quite be sure.

If we return to 'Les Vieux Horizons', then, we can think of the heptasyllable as a line, or half-line, in which the horizon, the limit set by the first measure, undergoes, quite literally, a 'déplacement', a 'déplacement' so slight that the reader, however vigilant, hardly notices it:

> Jamais le marin de quart ne sait quand il les traverse.

But this scumbling of distances ('les enfument') is enough to regenerate or transform our sense of our relation to things. When at line 24 Pilar, the poet's wife, intervenes to quieten and calm, she does so again by a process of 'déplacement', by a momentary shift towards the octosyllable which allows the heptasyllable as if to reorientate itself in a less threatening, more confident atmosphere. Not surprisingly the line of her intervention brings with it a regularization of rhythm, the repeated tetrasyllable, a plateau of non-differentiated experience whose value is as much psychological as affective, since it is from this basis of non-differentiation, of the steady and always equidistant horizon, that the poet can re-embark on the journey of perpetual displacement, now with a restored trust, that will allow him into the interstices of existence where life meets death, and the celestial meets the terrestrial.

And there is another sense in which this line 24 is a displacement, for it echoes, in slightly different mode, the other line of repeated measures, line 9. Line 9 refers to a past that the poet has apparently been deprived of, a past when his mind was inhabited by equanimity, by ease and fertility of thought. The tropical overtones of 'branches des îles' become a lost sunlight, until Pilar restores the sun of Uruguay (l. 26). In some senses, then, the heptasyllable which takes possession of the poem from line 27 onwards is a combination of the poet's trisyllable of line 9 and Pilar's tetrasyllable of line 24, and the 'nous' of the last two stanzas is as much the couple as the family.

The shift from darkness to light, from anxiety to confidence, the reorientation of the heptasyllable, are not produced by rupture, but by stealth. When Robichez declares of 'Apparition': 'Grande netteté aussi de la métrique: les vers de huit ou de sept syllabes donnent une unité à chaque mouvement du poème, avec des effets de rupture très voulus et très riches de sens (vers 9)' (1981: 23) he gives a slightly false impression on two scores: the incidence of rupture to be found in Supervielle's verse, and the connection of metre with unity.

The first thirteen lines of the poem, predominantly in octosyllables, seem to draw a line between a 'jusqu'ici' (temporal) and a henceforth. In other words, there might be some justification in associating the octosyllable with both a lost past and a disturbingly changed present. And the dynamic which informs these lines is a kind of automatic or dead gravity: the pull of the earth downwards and inwards ('creuse', 'régions confuses' 'ténèbres crochues', 'abîme', 's'enfonce'), which is also a process of entombment—Robichez (1981: 23) suggests that lines 11–13 may relate to the sentencing to the electric chair of the Italian anarchists Sacco and Vanzetti in 1921 (they were to be executed in 1927). Not surprisingly, therefore, we are in the world of a *vers pair*, where the syllabic differential between the measures in any given line will produce a sense of things being sprung apart, polarizing themselves, losing contact with each other, enacting an enmity—the only instances of an immobilized balance of measures (ll. 4 and 6) are both past participial adjectival phrases, the one expressing a previous status quo (the preordained passage of the blood through the body), the other an ironic comment upon it, a new status quo in which the blood is going cold, being diluted, tormented.

All this no doubt has much truth in it. But it is an account which omits that kind of dazed or semi-conscious slippage characteristic of the movement of Supervielle's verse. Not only are there triaccentual alternatives ready to emerge from several of the biaccentual octosyllables (ll. 5, 7, 11, and possibly 6 (2 + 2 + 4)), but a heptasyllable is buried among them (l. 8), and another line (7) has one of those synaeresis/diaeresis dilemmas which could also produce an enneasyllable (/Reʒiɔ̃/ or /Reʒjɔ̃/?). The movement from a heptasyllable to an octosyllable, or from an octosyllable to an enneasyllable, is not experienced in Supervielle's verse as the leap from one metrical perspective to another so much as a wobbling of vision, or an unconscious adjustment, or a puzzling syncopation. The horizon shifts almost without the reader noticing it, so that the landscape, and the possibilities it offers, are constantly changing. Even the longer lines (9 and 13) grow out of the verse-texture as incidents of its flux, and of the temporal dimensions which that flux encompasses. The 'alexandrine' of line 9 is a backward glance over travelled roads, a briefly reinhabited golden age, metrically defunct now, vulnerable in its very lack of uncertainty, in its stability. And, ironically, line 13 is the looking forward, ironically, because the metre slips out of the octosyllable just at the point when the spirit reaches a nadir, just at the point where a condemnation to death condemns to death those who connive in it. True, we are still in the interrogative mode, a mode projected forward into the following sequence, up to line 23; true, the chair will turn out to be not that of the condemned man, but of the member of the 'tablée', the new space craft. But what is more important still is that one tetrametric structure (the alexandrine of l. 9) has been replaced by another, and this new tetrametric structure (joined heptasyllables) belongs to a world beyond our metrical ken, just beyond the limits of our knowledge, and has an unsteady metrical outline—the harder we listen the less sure we are of what we hear.

If Robichez sees rupture, Décaudin sees 'glissement', a 'glissement' which relates as much to rhyme as to syllabic number:

l'essentiel est que le traitement de la rime et celui du vers procèdent d'une même disposition où des schémas de type traditionnel se trouvent perturbés par un principe d'incertitude, qui n'est pas recherche d'un effet de rupture, mais glissement, lapsus à peine sensible. (1982: 64)

Unfortunately, Décaudin's purpose is to demonstrate that there is as much indifference in Supervielle's treatment of rhyme as there is in his treatment of metres, hence Décaudin's redefinition of 'glissement' as 'lapsus'. There is, however, every reason to suppose that Supervielle's apparently casual rhyming practices are an essential support of his metrical ones, and that the rhymes, and acoustics of half-rhymes, are as much an agent of 'déplacement' as monosyllabic variation. What follows is a far from comprehensive exemplification of how this works in 'Apparition'.

The poem opens with a pair of lines that do not rhyme—time and space have been emptied of their inherited *points de repère.* Lines 3–4, on the other hand, looking back to situation of programmed and secure existence, have a **rime suffisante* in /ɛR/ amplified by /t/ and a further /R/. This rhyme is of fundamental significance for the poem as a whole: it is the rhyme of inwardness, self, microcosm, which will become the rhyme of outwardness, others, macrocosm, in lines 27–8; the circulation of the blood becomes the circularity of the table and of the communication of those who sit around it, and we see how, by a slight acoustic 'déplacement' (/ɛR/ > /yR/), it relates to 'la courbure des mondes'. But the journey from lines 3–4 to 27–8 is not an untroubled one. If we look at lines 20–3, the closing lines of the description of the 'apparition', where the sense of threat is gradually diminishing, where communication is being established in that mixed mode so beloved of Supervielle, the childlike and the solemn, then we must assume a pattern of alternating rhyme—/ɔR/ > /ɛj/ > /ɔR/ > /ɛl/; the half-rhyme of 'abeilles' and 'solennels' is in a sense part of the enigma by which the mysterious figure, despite the positive signs, is still enveloped, and which necessitates the reformulation of the question at line 23. At this point Pilar intervenes as a catalyst, or agent of reorientation, and her line, line 24, with its syntactic self-sufficiency (full-stop) and self-insertive manner ('Voici Pilar') constitutes an extra line—lines 25–6 clearly institute a sequence of couplets that runs to the end of the poem. The 'déplacement' engineered by Pilar is not only a momentary sidestepping into octosyllables, but the undoing of the alternating rhyme and the installation of a couplet (ll. 23–4) whereby 'solennels' is allowed to jettison 'abeilles' in order to take on a new half-rhyming partner supplied by Pilar, namely 'mystère'. And what is important about this new /ɛl/ : /ɛR/ combination is that its two terms bifurcate to create the pairs 'circulaire'/'univers' (ll. 27–8) and the immediately following 'fidèles'/'arc-en-ciel' (ll. 29–30). Just as the alternating pattern was an unproductive scheme that Pilar needed to correct, so equally 'abeilles' was not the partner which would launch 'solennels' into the right kind of stratosphere or moral field.

If we now return to the opening thirteen lines, we discover from line 5 onwards something like acoustic disarray. Does 'creuse' rhyme with 'cris' (/kR/) or 'confuses' (/k . . . z/)? Does 'cris' rhyme with 'jusqu'ici' or 'îles' or 'abîme' or 'Amérique', or with all four? Does 'confuses' rhyme with 'creuse' or with 'crochues' (/k . . . y/)? Does 'condamné' rhyme with nothing, or are we meant to hear a dying echo of its accentuated final syllable in the unaccentuated medial syllable of 'Amérique'? The spiritual and intellectual helplessness betokened by this set of unanswerable questions about acoustic structure continues with the arrival of the mysterious guest and up to Pilar's intervention; lines 20–3, as we have seen, constitute a quatrain in *rimes croisées*; lines 18–19 are clearly a couplet, whose /ɸz/ rhyme calls up some of the negative qualities of 'creuse' (l. 5); lines 14–17, on the other hand, are something of a puzzle: is this an *xaxa* scheme, where the rhymes are in /aR/, or is this a monorhymed quatrain in /a/, often supported by /R/, in which, however, one of the rhyme-words ('marine') rhymes on its unaccentuated rather than its accentuated syllable (in the manner of 'condamné'/'Amérique'?)? This is the negative dimension of slippage or 'déplacement', when the horizon is not seen to shift but is gradually erased altogether, and the mind wanders randomly and without reference point in an unresolvable mid-air.

But sometimes underlying this confusion is a pattern we could not apprehend, because we could not achieve the right 'déplacement', could not think quite laterally enough. Perhaps the most delightful lines from a rhyming point of view are lines 37–8, because they demonstrate the knowledge that the terrestrial traveller has achieved, but which the reader may still be short of. Strictly speaking, of course, these two lines:

> Nous cueillons et recueillons du céleste romarin,
> De la fougère affranchie qui se passe de racines

do not rhyme—/Rɛ̃/ : /sin/—or if they do, they rhyme very distantly on /R/ and unaccentuated /a/. The truth of the matter is, of course, that they rhyme both very distantly, across wide galactic spaces, and very intimately. And the intimacy of their rhyming depends on our knowing that Supervielle rhymes masculine forms with feminine ones—as in 'circulaire'/'univers' or 'fidèles'/'arc-en-ciel'—and that a necessary feminine form (/in/) is available in the masculine (/ɛ̃/). Is this another way of declaring the male/female poet/Pilar partnership? Is this a way of installing the masculine, the poet, in a world that is otherwise solicitously feminine (all other rhymes of ll. 35–40 are feminine), in just the same way that the mysterious masculine stranger has been familiarized, assimilated into the family, by Pilar? Perhaps, more important still, 'romarin' is the common element that binds lines 35–8 together inasmuch as /ɛ̃/ is not only the masculine form of /in/, but also of /ɛn/ (ll. 35–6). At all events it would be as unwise to assume that there is no method in Supervielle's rhyming, as it would be to assume that his heptasyllables are the products of chance; faced with the careful inversions in lines like

> Et couverts les vêtements par un morceau de ciel noir

and

> Et comme dans la peinture de Rousseau le douanier

we cannot but believe that Supervielle had both syllables and rhyme-words in mind.

This takes us back to that other proposition, in Robichez's remark quoted above, namely that metrical consistency (of octosyllable or heptasyllable) gives unity to each movement of the poem. Not only does this imply that each movement of the poem is circumscribed and formally complete—our analysis of the rhymes above would lead us to doubt that—but that the purpose of metre, and metrical variation, is aesthetic. But what we have been at some pains to suggest is that rhythm, even when wrought up to some metrical consistency, is the way we read, is the mental set of the reader, and the way the subject *is*, has being, rather than a pattern from the metrical pattern-book designed to generalize the particularity of the verse-instance into some aesthetically satisfying principle. The heptasyllable is not what unifies the text; it is the way the reader journeys through the text, responds to it, semanticizes it. We have already tried to show that the poem is not easily sectionable, at least in terms of its rhythmic and acoustic workings. We might add to the evidence already offered the fact that, in the 1925 edition, the Pilar passage (ll. 24–30) was separated from the preceding lines by a space and enclosed in brackets. We might also point out that, just as line 8 is a heptasyllabic infiltration of octosyllables, so the second hemistich of line 18 is the reverse—indeed this momentary incursion of an octosyllabic structure, acting in concert with the rhyming echo of 'creuse'/'araigneuse', further darkens this couplet with reminiscences of the spiritual state of the first thirteen lines. It is left to Pilar to redeem the octosyllable and at the same time remotivate the heptasyllable, and this she does with remarkable deftness: having created the temporary plateau of recurrent measures at line 24, which gives a very different complexion to the octosyllable, and harks back to the internal order of line 4, she then instigates a couplet in which heptasyllable and octosyllable are discreetly combined; as the heptasyllable changes the order of its measures ($4 + 3 > 3 + 4$), the octosyllable holds steady at $5 + 3$, laying the spectre of the $5 + 3$ at line 18, binding together the family with the unwavering, if inconspicuous, light of its past.

There are two further points to be made about the way the heptasyllable affects our reading mentality, the one of a more speculative kind, the other focal and unmistakable. First, if we were to propose that our sense of syllabic number can be undone by syntactic variation unless the syllabic numbers of consecutive measures within a hemistich are noticeably similar (equal) or noticeably different (by two syllables or more), then we would have to propose the converse, namely that when there is no significant likeness or difference between the syllabic numbers of consecutive measures within a hemistich, then syntactic structure is a prominent indicator of relative rhythmic weights and durations. This is an argument I would like only to introduce for consideration. Little is understood at present about the relationship between rhythm, syntax, lexical structure, and semantics, or more especially about the ways in which syntactic significance, length of word, importance of meaning affect our perception of rhythmic values. If we select a sequence of trisyllables from 'Apparition', such as 'Où sont-ils', 'le soleil', 'monte au ciel', 'Quand déjà', 'pour nous brille', 'de Rousseau', are we predisposed by their trisyllabicity to overlook their syntactical, semantic, and lexical differences? Or are there conditions in which we are more likely to hear their syllabicity than others, for example, when they are combined with other trisyllables:

Quand déjà le soleil monte au ciel de Rousseau

or when there is a clear syllabic differentiation between them and adjacent measures:

> . . . comme un souvenir de famille
> . . . qui secrètement pour nous brille?

And conversely, are there situations in which, because of the numerical proximity of consecutive measures (monosyllabic variation), we perceive the numbers themselves as approximate and thus pay more heed to the way the duration and intensity and pace of a measure is generated by syntax, lexis, and semantics? Would it be true to say, for instance, that in line 30:

> Prisonniers les uns des autres, ce sont couleurs $3 + 4 + 4 + 3$
> d'arc-en-ciel

the syllabic inferiority of 'Prisonniers', in relation to 'les uns des autres', does not strike us so forcibly as its semantic superiority, as its syntactic pre-eminence, since it is the noun which triggers the prepositional construction? And would it be equally true to say that the syntactically and semantically neutral, colourless 'ce sont couleurs' yields its nominally greater syllabic weight to the eye-catching scintillations of 'd'arc-en-ciel', with its compounding of two nous and the accentual reinforcement supplied by rhyme? In circumstances such as these, syllabic differentiation, already minimal, sinks into insignificance, and measures are related to each other by a highly complex set of variables. While these may be features of the reading of $3 + 4$ or $4 + 3$ heptasyllables, that is to say that while it may be a characteristic of such heptasyllables that the reading of them involves a frequent abandonment of metrical reference points— this is a sense in which the free verse of the line may be freer than you think—their metrical foundation cannot ultimately be denied, and it is safer to account for the hesitations and uncertainties inherent in the reading of heptasyllables in syllabic terms, rather than in the speculative and unquantifiable ones outlined above.

Journeying, in Supervielle's verse, is not a grand adventure, or daring enterprise, powered by a marked dynamic. It is more a question of a continual and imperceptible altering of states, so that one finds oneself at a destination without being quite sure how one got there. Exile from cosmic beatitude may bring its sorrows, even anger, and the prospect of being afloat in the tractless expanses of space may induce agoraphobic anxieties, but the actual transit from earth to empyrean is more like a transition, accomplished as soon as embarked upon. The spatial dimension is much easier to inhabit than the temporal, and 'Apparition', and the spiritual journey it recounts, is about the transformation of the one into the other: the 'jusqu'ici' of line 8, a temporal notation which cuts the poet off from the past and leaves him stranded in the chaos of the present, becomes the 'jusqu'ici' of line 35, a notation of spatial achievement, which is temporally a 'déjà' (l. 36), time experienced as a completely painless traversal. Robichez (1981: 23) tells us that no specific picture of Rousseau's corresponds to lines 31–4, but suggests that Supervielle may have in mind *Une noce à la campagne, La Carriole du Père Juniet(r), Réunion de famille, La Famille;* but perhaps, too, Supervielle was thinking of those pictures of 1908, like *View of the Bridge of Sèvres,* or *The Quay of Ivry* or *The Fisherman and the Biplane,* in which the inventions of modern aviation are seen to pass through a frictionless, wonderfully smooth atmosphere, with the same kind and degree of motion as Rousseau's clouds. Like Rousseau's world, Supervielle's is domestic, slow-moving, and decorative. But then, as the title of the collection indicates, motion is not impelled by motor-mechanisms but by gravitations, by mysterious laws of attraction, and it is these that the heptasyllable enacts.

In lines such as:

Nous cueillons et recueillons du céleste romarin $3 + 4 + 3 + 4$
De la fougère affranchie qui se passe de racines $4 + 3 + 3 + 4$

how easily does the reader lose syllabic bearings, begin to even out the inconsistencies? How far are syllabic differences isolatable and reducible to linguistic elements which only have a marginal role to play? For gravitation to work must we feel similarity to the same degree that we feel difference? How easy is it to read these lines as:

Nous cueillons (et) recueillons du célest(e) romarin
D'la fougère affranchie qui se pass(e) de racines

so that syllabic variation is already below the threshold of full consciousness? And in the line

Sans cartes ni gouvernail, et le ciel pour bastingage $2 + 5 + 3 + 4$

is not the difference between the syllabic differential in each hemistich ironed out by an underlying similarity of nominal structure and lexical weight:

Sans cart(es) . . . gouvernail . . . le ciel . . . bastingage?

Elements like the articulated 'e' and doubts about synaeresis and diaeresis allow the reader to float a little between fairly narrowly defined syllabic margins. What we feel at work are the pressures towards equalization and equivalence at the same time as we may be reminded of slight incompatibilities and 'déplacements'. Indeed those very sources of uncertainty which instigate a gravitation towards may in other contexts work to engineer a gravitation away: line 28 for example:

Leurs frais sourires s'en vont de bouche en bouche fidèles   4 + 3 + 4 + 3

may come to us as the even more differentiated

Leurs frais sourir(es) s'en vont | de bouche en   4 + 2 + 4 + 2
    bouch(e) fidèles

or be reduced in consciousness still more:

. . . frais sourir(es) s'en vont | . . . bouch(e) . . . bouch(e) fidèles

that is to say, as a gravitation away followed by a gravitation back together again. But what is important is that the rhythmic structure of the line keeps the mechanisms of apprehension in a state of fairly consistent doubt, instability, which is at the same time availability and the desire to transact equivalences or see differences. In this sense, the heptasyllable, by the very fragility of the monosyllabic variations it thrives on, keeps the mind in a state of readiness, and accustoms it to adjustments of perception; this in turn means that the relationships described by the lines are never really more than potential, truths half-glimpsed. Supervielle's cosmic spaces are inhabited not only by the winged, but also by the unrooted.

The kind of fluid apprehensions and gravitational movements we have just explored lead one to wonder whether Supervielle's free verse is best identified as a free verse of the line *tout court*, or as a free verse of the line which produces cadence-accentual reading habits. In other words, as a result of reading a sequence of heptasyllables paired in fourteen-syllable lines, do we rely more and more on the basic perception of the tetrametric (four-accent) structure of the line, as our sense of the number of syllables of which those four measures are composed gets fuzzier and fuzzier? Put in the terms in which movement operates in Supervielle, does his free verse itself gravitate across or between kinds, does it gravitate towards or away from a free verse of the line? Given the remark already quoted from Robichez about the characteristic structure of the Superviellean free-verse poem—that they often begin 'sans mesure' and gradually accede to a 'cadence régulière' (1981: 58)—the question is in two parts: Does the Superviellean free-verse poem characteristically shift from a cadence-accentual prosody to a free verse of the line? Does that free verse of the line, once established, maintain a significant contact with cadence-accentual prosody?

In order to answer these questions, I would now like to turn to a consideration of 'Le Survivant', which I scan as follows:

1. Lorsque le noyé se réveille au fond des mers et $5 + 3 + 4 + 4$
   que son cœur
2. Se met à battre comme le feuillage du tremble $4 + 5 + 3$
3. Il voit approcher de lui un cavalier qui marche $5 + 2 + 4 + 4$ /
   l'amble $2 + 5 + 4 + 4$
4. Et qui respire à l'aise et lui fait signe de ne pas $4 + 2 + 4 + 7$
   avoir peur.
5. Il lui frôle le visage d'une touffe de fleurs jaunes $3 + 4 + 3 + 4$
6. Et se coupe devant lui une main sans qu'il y ait $3 + 4 + 3 + 4$
   une goutte de rouge. $+ 3 + 3$
7. La main est tombée dans le sable où elle fond $5 (2 + 3) + 3 + 4 + 4$
   sans un soupir
8. Une autre main toute pareille a pris sa place et les $4 + 4 + 4 + 4$
   doigts bougent.
9. Et le noyé s'étonne de pouvoir monter à cheval, $4 + 2 + 5 + 3$
10. De tourner la tête à droite et à gauche comme $5 + 5 + 5 + 5$
    s'il était au pays natal,
11. Comme s'il y avait alentour une grande plaine, la $6 + 3 + 6' + 4$
    liberté,
12. Et la permission d'allonger la main pour cueillir $6 + 5 + 3 + 5$
    un fruit de l'été.
13. Est-ce donc la mort cela, cette rôdeuse douceur $5 + 2 + 4 + 3$
14. Qui s'en retourne vers nous par une obscure $4 + 3 + 4 + 3$
    faveur?
15. Et serais-je ce noyé chevauchant parmi les algues $3 + 4 + 3 + 4$
16. Qui voit comme se reforme le ciel tourmenté de $2 + 5 + 2 + 5$
    fables.
17. Je tâte mon corps mouillé comme un témoignage $2 + 5 + 5 + 2$
    faible
18. Et ma monture hennit pour m'assurer que $4 + 3 + 4 + 3$
    c'est elle.
19. Un berceau bouge, l'on voit un pied d'enfant $5' + 2 + 4 + 3$
    réveillé.
20. Je m'en vais sous un ciel qui semble frais $3 + 4 + 2 + 5$
    inventé.
21. Alentour il est des gens qui me regardent à peine, $3 + 4 + 4 + 3$
22. Visages comme sur terre, mais l'eau a lavé leurs $2 + 5 + 5 + 2$
    peines.
23. Et voici venir à moi des paisibles environs $5 + 2 + 3 + 4$
24. Les bêtes de mon enfance de le Création $2 + 5 + 7$

25. Et le tigre me voit tigre, le serpent me voit serpent,	3 + 4 + 3 + 4
26. Chacun reconnaît en moi son frère, son revenant.	5 + 2 + 2 + 5
27. Et l'abeille me fait signe de m'envoler avec elle	3 + 4 + 4 + 3
28. Et le lièvre qu'il connaît un gîte au creux de la terre	3 + 4 + 2 + 5
29. Où l'on ne peut pas mourir.	5 + 2

One of my reasons for choosing this poem is that its structure in many respects resembles that of 'Apparition': it opens with an encounter with a mysterious stranger, through whom a set of fears are lived through and finally exorcized; the early sections are metrically changeable, diverse, and it is only at line 13 that paired heptasyllables finally establish themselves; the emergence of the heptasyllable coincides, or almost, with the emergence of couplets: the first eight lines are made up of a quatrain in *rimes embrassées*, followed by an *xaxa* quatrain; at line 9 couplets begin to make their appearance. There are, of course, differences: where 'Apparition' is a progression from a first-person singular via the mysterious stranger and Pilar to a first-person plural, 'Le Survivant' passes from a third-person singular ('le noyé') via the mysterious 'cavalier' to a first-person singular; where 'Apparition' describes a flight from the earth into which the poet initially is being increasingly sucked, 'Le Survivant' describes a kind of return to earth, in resurrection, which is not however a return to earth ('Visages comme sur terre').

Another reason for choosing this poem is that Yves-Alain Favre has produced what is in essence a cadence-accentual reading of the first eight lines:

Outre ces effets de concordance entre la métrique et la syntaxe, il faut noter la distribution harmonieuse des accents toniques, qui s'opère en relation étroite avec le sens. Là encore, le rythme contribue à renforcer la signification. Dans les quatre premiers versets du 'Survivant', on a

3/1
1/2
2/2
2/2

Une discordance initiale (3/1) marque le réveil brusque du noyé qui sent son cœur battre de nouveau; il s'en suit un rythme régulier (2/2) qui correspond à la fois au rythme cardiaque redevenu normal et au pas du cavalier qui s'avance calmement. Les quatre versets suivants sont ainsi rythmés:

2/2
3/3
3/2
3/1

Après un rythme régulier qui s'élargit très légèrement, on observe une première discordance, puis une seconde beaucoup plus nette (3/1): elle correspond précisément au moment où les doigts se mettent à bouger; cette brusque défaillance du nombre d'accents indique et tente d'exprimer la rupture de l'équilibre et le commencement du mouvement. (1981: 69–70)

As will be apparent, there is little difference between Favre's account of the accentuation and my own—the only difference, in fact, is his greater confidence in the accent on the 'main' of the seventh line: 'La maín est tombée.' Where we might differ more fundamentally would be in the placement of the 'caesura' which makes this verse binary. A cadence-accentual reading will place this juncture where the syntax dictates, since in cadence-accentual prosody syntax is the sole source of rhythmic interval; thus the first line is segmented

Lorsque le noyé se réveille au fond des mers | et que son cœur

and the eighth line:

Une autre main toute pareille a pris sa place | et les doigts bougent.

If I am to argue that these lines are *metrically* controlled, by paired octosyllables, then they will be segmented:

Lorsque le noyé se réveille | au fond des mers et que son cœur

Une autre main toute pareille | a pris sa place et les doigts bougent.

What exactly is at stake? First, even though the problem does not arise here, the treatment of the articulated 'e': if Supervielle treats unelided 'e' occurring at the medial juncture in the same way as line-terminal 'e', then the location of that medial juncture is of some significance. If, for example, we applied a cadence-accentual principle to line 19, we would derive this reading:

Un berceau boug(e), | l'on voit un pied d'enfant réveillé   4 + 2 + 4 + 3

with a 1/3 accentual pattern, rather than the 2/2 segmentation I would propose, with the consequent counting of the e of 'bouge':

Un berceau bouge, l'on voit | un pied d'enfant réveillé.   5′ + 2 + 4 + 3

Secondly and relatedly, we forget all too easily that the reading of verse, as a linear unfolding in time, is not just a process of registering a conformation; it is as beset with the tensions of expectation, speculation, disappointment, surprise, as the reading of a novel, but more intensively and more expressively so; and rhythm is the way in which the turmoil of the reader's inner life is regulated. The rhythm that yields to the authority of the syntax is a rhythm in danger of becoming an inert accompaniment, in danger of abandoning its role as mediator between text and reading psyche, text and subjectivity, and of becoming something purely linguistic. Enjambement is one of the means by which rhythm is constantly compelled to stand off from the syntax and become the agent of a curiosity, an impatience, a fearful apprehension. One of the characteristic *loci* of enjambement is just before or just after the verb, when the subject is looking for a function, or destiny, or when the verb is looking for a target or a context. Part of the expressive force of the first line of 'Le Survivant' depends on the counterpointing between the line-terminal juncture, which occurs before the verb, and the line-medial juncture which occurs just after the verb: the drowned sailor (unexpectedly) awakens (the hope, that he is safe, and out of the water, dashed by) at the bottom of the sea (so nothing is changed) and his heart (is waterlogged? no longer feels? not at all!) begins to beat . . . If we read this as Favre does:

Lorsque le noyé se réveille au fond des mers | et que son cœur

then we will tend to make the confirmatory, even tautological, connection between 'le noyé' and 'au fond des mers', and 'se réveille' will lose its dramatic leverage and become something more decorative or metaphorical. Similarly, in this atmosphere of recurrent 'étonnement', the cavalier, conjuror in body parts and transplant specialist, produces his substitute hand with magical suddenness:

Une autre main toute pareille | a pris sa place et les doigts bougent;

and the short, final co-ordinate clause participates in the achievement of the verb preceding it, grows directly out of it. To read:

Une autre main toute pareille a pris sa place | et les doigts bougent

on the other hand, would be to make the marvellous matter-of-fact, would disengage the reader, and identify the co-ordinate clause as an afterthought, or make it more surprising than the transplant itself. Besides, because the dynamic of the verse is low-powered, gravitational, because of the generally prosaic quality of the discourse, this medial articulation, this moment of metrical vigilance and tension, is crucial to the purposefulness of the verse.

Thirdly, once one admits a metrically motivated medial juncture, one must also admit the significance of the measures which project it, or are affected by it. In this way, when two lines are joined to form a single unit, a new kind of interest attaches to the final measure of the first and the first measure of the second, for these are the measures involved in the negotiation of the juncture between them. It is no longer sufficient to say that the line is binary, with two major accents in each half; we must also know what kinds of pressure are being put on the juncture and how these relate to syntax and rhythmic structure. Sometimes the juncture is 'uneventful', occurring, for example, between major clauses, as in lines 6 (clause of negative consequence) and 7 (relative clause), where syllabic fluctuation between the second and third measures remains minimal; if anything, in these two cases, the post-junctural tetrasyllabic measure 'soothes' the preceding trisyllable, discharges some of its upgathering. Perhaps the most extreme case of this kind, in the first twelve lines at least, is at line 10, where one reads across the juncture into the 'comme si' clause with that lack of perturbation which characterizes this liberating line as a whole (which is not to say that lines with minimal syllabic fluctuation cannot have dramatic medial junctures if the syntax engineers it, as we saw in l. 8—here the regular tetrasyllable expresses the 'tout pareille' and diverts the drama into a mode of reassuring fantasy). Interestingly, line 10 is followed by a line in which there is some polarization of measures, even though the 'comme si' construction is repeated; the extensiveness of the verbal section suddenly condenses in the adverbial insert 'alentour' and is then released again as an extensiveness in space. In rather the same way, in line 9, the drowned man, momentarily taken short by surprise, relaxes back into recovered powers in the pentasyllable following the juncture. And line 12 presents this movement in reverse— the expansive and magnanimous nature of the measures before the juncture contract to a trisyllable in the suddenly intimate and careful gesture of picking fruit.

If this kind of evidence were not sufficient to convince us that even in these rhythmically disordered opening lines a cadence-accentual reading is inadequate, that the full flavour of these lines will only emerge if they are read as metrically constructed, then we should recognize that these lines are about a recovery, a difficult emergence, a recuperation of familiar and novel powers. This process of recovery is a metrical one, not only in the gradual accession to the couplet, but also in the disengaging of the heptasyllable from other rhythmic flotsam. One line is a straightforward adumbration of the paired heptasyllable (l. 5), another is a paired heptasyllable which has misjudged its horizon (l. 6), another is a heptasyllable that is displaced to an octosyllable (l. 3), others are paired octosyllables (ll. 1, 7, 8). These opening lines also allow the pentasyllabic measure, of such significance when the distichs get under way, to establish itself, and that with increasing insistence.

My answer to our first question ('Does the Superviellean free-verse poem characteristically shift from a cadence-accentual prosody to a free verse of the line?') is therefore 'no', at least on this evidence; from the outset his is a free verse of the line. If it were not so, we would not experience the metrical disorientations as disorientating, but simply as inchoate; we would not be able to measure the process of recovery; we would not have access to those junctural mechanisms which dramatize the verse; the degree of our rhythmical engagement would be less. The second question ('Does that free verse of the line, once established, maintain a significant contact with cadence-accentual prosody?') is not prejudiced by the answer to the first, so much as by the pentasyllabic measure, of which we have just been speaking; it is this latter feature which metrically distinguishes 'Le Survivant' from 'Apparition'.

As the drowned man enters into the repossession of his kingdom, he fuses with the 'cavalier' figure:

> Et serais-je ce noyé chevauchant parmi les algues
> Qui voit comme se reforme le ciel tourmenté de fables.
>
> (ll. 15–16)

The drowned man is not taken away from himself, but rather restored to himself in a way that runs counter, as Robichez points out (1981: 30), to the tradition adhered to by Bürger's 'Lenore' and Verlaine's 'Cauchemar' (*Poèmes saturniens*). But this resurrection seems to necessitate the monosyllabic variation of the 3 + 4 / 4 + 3 heptasyllable being offset by the 5 + 2 / 2 + 5 variety, and as the distichs proceed it is this latter variety which increasingly has the last word. The pretty continuous presence of this pair of measures, with their trisyllabic differential, has two principal effects. First, it motivates the medial juncture in ways already explored: syllabic variation in measures around the juncture will tend to produce effects associated with enjambement. In the distichs, it is particularly effects of revelation, of seeing with new understanding, which are emphasized:

Est-ce donc la mort cela, cette rôdeuse douceur

(l. 13)

Qui voit comme se reforme le ciel tourmenté de fables

(l. 16)

Un berceau bouge, l'on voit un pied d'enfant réveillé

(l. 19)

Chacun reconnaît en moi son frère, son revenant

(l. 26)

This last line discloses the second effect. The self of the poet is no longer a body gravitating elsewhere, but itself the centre of attraction, that towards which all identities gravitate:

Et le tigre me voit tigre, le serpent me voit serpent.

The poet is no longer sitting at a table, occupying a circular periphery, but is now the still centre out of which an 'alentour' radiates, around which an 'alentour' gravitates. And it is the confidence generated by this centring process that allows him to follow any direction, respond to any invitation, as occurs in lines 27–8. Uncentred gravitation is a risk taken, which may lead to the desolately nomadic, the orphaned, the kind of condition explored in 'Naissance':

A peu de distance gravitent
Les astres pauvres et soumis
Qui depuis avant Jésus-Christ,
Sans défaillir, cherchent un gîte.

Un chien en retrait, les yeux clos,
Devine que nait à ses pieds
Jusqu'aux trébuchants horizons
Une terre désespérée.

There is a world of difference between horizons which 'se déplacent' and those which 'trébuchent'. By resorting to a hemistich composed of fairly polarized measures, Supervielle creates a clear field of vision, a rhythmic decisiveness which ensures that the more undiscernible and indeterminate gravitations of 3 + 4 and 4 + 3 do not deteriorate to a groping uncertainty. The 2 + 5 and 5 + 2 heptasyllables, therefore, tend to prevent the reader from 'simplifying' the 3 + 4 and 4 + 3 combinations into a cadence-accentual pattern where doubts about the exact number of syllables in each unit are less crucial. There is, of course, a very general sense in which free verse creates scansional anxiety, and part of the journey out of that anxiety may be the espousal of the cadence-accentual. If the answer to the second question must, in the case of 'Le Survivant', be 'no', this is not to disqualify its validity in other verse-contexts, and in other verse-contexts of *Gravitations*. Here Supervielle has ballasted and validated the monosyllabic displacement of the $3 + 4 / 4 + 3$ heptasyllable by providing an accompaniment of the rhythmically cut-and-dried. Elsewhere cadence-accentual scansion may be a necessary refuge from rhythmic vertigo and perplexity.

In my questioning of opinions and propositions about the nature of Supervielle's prosody, I would like to investigate briefly one last view, that expressed by Décaudin about the poems which go to make up the 'Poèmes de Guanamiru' section of *Gravitations*:

Mais il faut attendre la dernière partie de *Gravitations*, les 'Poèmes de Guanamiru' . . . pour assister à un emploi non plus épisodique et quasi accidentel, mais constant de ce type de vers ou de verset [dépourvu de toute organisation]. Cette fois, c'est le mètre auquel nous étions habitués, celui de sept ou de huit syllabes, qui est exceptionnel, et le vers dont la seule mesure est d'ordre syntaxique ou sémantique, qui est la règle. Tout se passe comme si l'explosion libératrice que représente dans l'imaginaire de Supervielle la création de Guanamiru s'était accompagnée d'un éclatement de ses structures prosodiques fondamentales. (1982: 67)

I want to test this view against the last poem of the section, and of the collection, 'Terre':

1. Terre lourde que se disputent les cadavres et les arcs-en-ciel,	$3 + 5 + 3 + 6$
2. Des statues au nez brisé sous le soleil d'or incassable	$3 + 4 + 4 + 4$
3. Et des vivants protestataires levant leur bras jusqu'aux nues	$4 + 4 + 4 + 3$
4. Quand c'est leur tour de s'offrir à tes abattoirs silencieux,	$4 + 3 + 5 + 4$ (3)
5. — Ah! tu fais payer cher aux aviateurs leurs permissions de vingt-quatre heures,	$1 + 5 + 5 + 5 + 4$
6. A trois mille mètres de haut tu leur arraches le cœur	$5 + 3 + 4 + 3$
7. Qui se croyait une fleur dans la forêt du ciel bleu	$4 + 3 + 4 + 3$
8. Serons-nous longtemps pasteurs de ta bergerie de nuages,	$5 + 2 + 5 + 3$
9. De tes monts chercheurs de ciel, des fleuves chasseurs de lune,	$3 + 4 + 2 + 5$
10. De tes océans boiteux qui font mine d'avancer	$5 + 2 + 3 + 4$
11. Mais vont moins vite sur les plages	$4 + 4$

12. Que des enfants titubant avec des pleins seaux de sable?   4 + 3 + 5 + 2

13. Aurons-nous encore du tonnerre dans cent quatre-vingt-dix mille ans,   5 + 4 + 8

14. La foudre, les quatre vents qui tournent sans rémission,   2 + 5 + 2 + 6 (5)

15. Les hommes nus enchaînés dans leurs générations   4 + 3 + 7 (6)

16. Et les roses pénitentes à genoux dans leur parfum?   3 + 4 + 3 + 4

17. Maudite, tu nous avilis à force de nous retenir,   3′ + 5 + 2 + 6

18. Tu nous roules dans la boue, pour nous rendre pareils à elle   3 + 4 + 6 + 2

19. Tu nous brises, tu nous désosses, tu fais de nous de petits pâtés,   3 + 5 + 4 + 5

20. Tu alimentes ton feu central de nos rêves les plus tremblants.   4 + 5 + 3 + 5

21. Prends garde, tu ne seras bientôt qu'une vieillarde de l'espace,   3′ + 6 + 4 + 4

22. Du plus lointain du ciel on te verra venir faisant des manières   4 + 2 + 4 + 2 + 5

23. Et l'on entendra la troupe des jeunes soleils bien portants: 5 + 2 + 5 + 3

24. ⟨⟨C'est encore elle, la salée aux trois-quarts,   4 + 3 + 3

25. La tête froide et le ventre à l'envers,   4 + 3 + 3

26. La tenancière des quatre saisons,   4 + 3 + 3

27. L'avare ficelée dans ses longitudes!⟩⟩   2 + 4 + 5

28. Et plus rapides que toi s'égailleront les soleils   4 + 3 + 4 + 3

29. Abandonnant derrière eux des éclats de rires durables   4 + 3 + 5 + 3

30. Qui finiront par former des plages bruissantes d'astres.   4 + 3 + 2 + 5

31. Prends garde, sourde et muette par finasserie,   3′ + 4 + 6

32. Prends garde, à la colère des hommes élastiques,   2 + 4 + 2 + 4

33. Aux complots retardés de ces fumeurs de pipes,   3 + 3 + 4 + 2

34. Las de ta pesanteur, de tes objections,   1 + 5 + 6 (5)

35. Prends garde qu'ils ne te plantent une paire de cornes sur le front   2 + 5 + 6 + 4

36. Et ne s'embarquent le jour de la grande migration   4 + 3 + 3 + 5 (4)

37. Aimantés par la chanson d'une marine céleste   3 + 4 + 4 + 3

38. Dont le murmure déjà va colonisant les astres.   4 + 3 + 5 + 2

39. Des trois-mâts s'envoleront, quelques vagues à leurs flancs,   3 + 4 + 3 + 4

40. Les hameaux iront au ciel, abreuvoirs et lavandières,   3 + 4 + 3 + 4

41. Les champs de blé dans les mille rires des coquelicots,   4 + 5 + 6

42. Des girafes à l'envi dans la brousse des nuages,	3 + 4 + 3 + 4
43. Un éléphant gravira la cime neigeuse de l'air,	4 + 3 + 5 + 3
44. Dans l'eau céleste luiront les marsouins et les sardines	4 + 3 + 3 + 4
45. Et des barques remontant jusqu'aux rêveries des anges,	3 + 4 + 5 + 2
46. Des chevaux de la Pampa rouleront de pré en pré	3 + 4 + 3 + 4
47. Dans la paille et le regain des chaudes constellations	3 + 4 + 2 + 6 (5)
48. Et même vous, ô squelettes des premiers souffles du monde,	4 + 3 + 4 + 3
49. Vous vous émerveillerez de vous trouver à nouveau	7 + 4 + 3
50. Avec cette chair qui fit votre douceur sur le globe,	5 + 2 + 4 + 3
51. Un cœur vous rejaillira parmi vos côtes tenaces	2 + 5 + 4 + 3
52. Qui attendaient durement un miracle souterrain	4 + 3 + 3 + 4
53. Et vos mains onduleront comme au vent les marguerites!	3 + 4 + 3 + 4

Where is the lack of metrical organization in this poem? True, and in distinction from our previous poems, 'Terre' does not make much effort to rhyme; we may notice a *rimes croisées* sequence in lines 4–7 of /ɸ/ : /œR/ : /œR/ : /ɸ/, the 'nuages'/'plages' of lines 8, 11 as a failed attempt at *rimes embrassées* (or does 'plages' rhyme with 'sable' on /a/?), and a sort of scheme of *rimes embrassées* at lines 13–16: /ɑ̃/ : /sjɔ̃/ : /sjɔ̃/ : /œ/, and so on; but these do not seem to serve any expressive or structural purpose, and such echoes seem to grow fewer in number as the poem proceeds. On the other hand, a first draft of the poem, published in the *Nouvelle Revue Française* (1 Sept. 1922), presents us with a sequence of thirty-nine alexandrines in **rimes plates*; traces of this original survive in the alexandrines at lines 32–4, although, as so often happens in Supervielle, they are slid into through the rhythmically problematic line 31; this line is clearly trimetric and for this reason it is difficult to know whether to treat the junctures as 'caesural' (i.e. leave the 'e' of 'garde' and 'muette' out of the scansion), and thus notate the line as 2 + 4 + 5, or whether to treat the junctures as *coupes* and scan as I have. A further complicating factor is the syllabic value of 'muette' (synaeresis or diaeresis?). The line could after all be a decasyllable (2 + 3 + 5) or an alexandrine (3′ + 3 + 6).

A similar problem occurs in lines 24–7, where the young suns address the earth with their mockeries. I have identified these lines as a sequence of three decasyllables, all with the same rhythmic configuration, followed by a hendecasyllable, so that the sense of slippage and displacement is terminating rather than initiating. But this has involved a possibly devious procedure on my part; because of the clarity of the syntactic break at

'elle' and 'froide' in lines 24–5, I have counted it as a caesural juncture
and thus dismissed the 'e' of 'elle'. In lines 26–7, the breaks after 'tenancière'
and 'avare' have been treated as *coupes* and the final 'e' retained. A more
consistent and 'metrical' reading of these lines would be

$$4 + 3 + 3$$
$$4 + 3 + 3$$
$$4 + 2 + 3$$
$$2 + 3 + 5$$

In other words, the 'déplacement' would occur at the third line and
'explain' the rather disorderly nature of the decasyllable with which the
group ends.

As we have seen, Supervielle uses 'glissement' to keep his metric in
movement, fragile, provisional. His alexandrines or his fourteen-syllable
lines are only just what they are, only just manage to be themselves, and
that for no more than a moment. He is not particularly interested in the
dynamic effects of sudden and resolute change; his verse gives that impression of being in constant transition, even when it is apparently at its
most stable; and occasionally, as in the case of the 'romarin'/'racines'
rhyme of 'Apparition', we feel that certain kinds of manipulative device
are available to us, which, however, we hesitate to use.

A metrical example of this last—besides those I may already have
seemed to use in my scansion of lines 24–7—occurs at line 41. Immediately mankind has taken the decision (or been imagined to take the decision)
to migrate from earth, at line 36, paired heptasyllables take control and
run through to the end of the poem, almost without hiccough. I say
'almost without hiccough' because some reduction of diaeresis to synaeresis
is necessary at lines 36 and 47, because there is a momentary deviation
into octosyllable in the second hemistich of line 43, just to remind us
that we achieve heptasyllables only on sufferance,[2] and because line 41
remains obstinately resistant to rhythmic assimilation. If, however, we
rigorously applied the metrical rules we have deduced from Supervielle's
paired heptasyllabic practice, we would obtain the following result:

Les champs de blé dans les mill(e) | rires des coquelicots $4 + 3 + 1 + 6$

that is the metrically acceptable enforcing the syntactically nonsensical.
But then we see, suddenly, that this new formulation is splendidly

---

[2] Presumably there is some affectionate humour in this interpolated octosyllable as well.
The elephant presumably does not find the snowy peaks of the air easy going, and the slight
syllabic extension of the first measure of the second hemistich, along with the two
articulated 'e's, convey some of the labour of plodding through the yielding snow.

triumphant, amplified, explosive. The now immediately adjacent accents on 'mille' and 'rires' compel an intensification of the accent on 'rires' so that the voice can continue its journey along an upward pitch curve and justify the slight hesitation before the final ascent. Because of its accent and the suspension after it, 'mille' becomes the mode of the superlative and assertive rather than the mode of the numerical and notative. And the 'rires' themselves become irrepressible, unanimous, bursting in unison. Without a sense of potential metrical imperatives, this insight into line 41 would simply not be available to us, and we would lose all sense of the tensions and conditions which make gravitation perceptible and make the shifting of horizons possible.

If we have found sequences of alexandrines, decasyllables, and four-teeners, we might also make mention of the seventeen-syllable lines 19–22, the central section of the indictment of Earth by Supervielle's persona Guanamiru (ll. 17–23) before the young suns have their say (ll. 24–7). Once again this short sequence is introduced by 'approximate' lines of sixteen and fifteen syllables, before moving into the chiastic rhythmic arrangement of lines 19–20. Then, when the speaker moves on to his imperative of warning, a new rhythmic register is engaged, one which might lead us to rethink line 22: perhaps the hexasyllabic measure re-quires that we read line 22 as a *trimètre*:

Du plus lointain du ciel | on te verra venir | faisant des manières   6 + 6 + 5

This makes the line a better integrated whole, and dispels the impression that it is a regular (tetrametric) alexandrine with a pentasyllabic supple-ment, unless, of course, one feels that the whole point of the line is precisely that: laggard and misshapen rhythms for laggard and misshapen heavenly bodies.

One final observation should be made about the heptasyllable. In this poem it serves the Promethean revolt against Mother Earth, is the vehicle of the migration to other worlds, and the instrument of the resurrection of the dead (ll. 48–53). We meet it intermittently in the opening sixteen lines, too, as an expression of the human condition:

> Des tes monts chercheurs de ciel, des fleuves chasseurs de lune,
> De tes océans boiteux qui font mine d'avancer
> Les hommes nus enchaînés dans leurs générations
> Et les roses pénitentes à genoux dans leur parfum.

We hear it in the fall of the aviators who have sold out to the Earth in their day-long leaves; we hear it in the pitiful efforts of natural phenomena to establish contacts with the cosmos; we hear it in the recurrent pantomime of mutual sexual dependence. The heptasyllable is, then, the clay out of which the totality of Supervielle's poetic universe might be moulded; it is the continuum that runs from imprisonment and exasperation, through release, to a restless gravitational movement which might as much be homelessness and instability as renewed communication with all beings, both terrestial and celestial. In short, what marks the heptasyllable, and particularly the 3 + 4 and 4 + 3 varieties, is restlessness, unsettledness, that same force which sets all Supervielle's poems in motion, whether they are in heptasyllables or not. The heptasyllable lets us hear all the voices of displacement, unease, not being at home in the inhabited world, as well as renewal of perspective, sideways shifts into parallel realities, and those slightly irregular movements which give us access to things normally out of reach. But the gravitational potential of the heptasyllable would not be available without the careful measurement of movement, and the redrawing of space would be impossible without a clear idea of the horizons which might be displaced. All this argues for the treatment of Supervielle's free verse as a free verse of the line, albeit based on the improvised metric of longer verse-lines; the freedom of the verse lies not only in the freedom of variation, but in the fact that Supervielle's 'metrical' lines belong to a breed with which we are not really familiar.

The lexis and thematics of Supervielle's verse have been well served by criticism, in the work of, among others, Greene (1958), Blair (1960), Hiddleston (1965), Vivier (1971), Favre (1981), Viallaneix (1982); his versification, on the other hand, has been strangely taken for granted, or treated rather cavalierly. Some critics have pointed to his textual revisions to demonstrate that content matters more than metrics to Supervielle, and it seems easy, given Supervielle's declaration to Nadal (1964: 266)— 'Je laisse à ce qui est à dire le soin de choisir sa forme'—to come to the conclusion that Vivier does (1971: 176); 'Elle [sa métrique] est très variée, libre plutôt. Il ne s'astreint pas à une règle, et semble n'avoir pensé au problème du vers que par intermittences.' I think there is every reason to believe the opposite, and that for all the transparency of Supervielle's favouring of the heptasyllable, and indeed the octosyllable, there is much we do not understand about his metrical craft. We are very poor readers of Supervielle's rhythms.

8

Pierre Reverdy, Sources du vent *(1929)*
The Prosody of Cubism

FOR Supervielle, the reading aloud, the 'diction', of verse is almost a condition of its achieving a full and substantial existence:

Ce n'est pas un simple jeu de la vanité pour le poète que de dire ses vers en public. A la projeter ainsi devant soi dans une épreuve redoutable, il n'est pas fâché de sentir si son œuvre est vraiment transmissible et achevée ou si quelque défaut ne viendra pas se retourner en l'air même, contre lui. (1951: 68)

Although Supervielle sees the benefits of eye reading—the silent and unmediated communion, the concentration made precious by the unwitnessed exaltation it may lead to—he insists that reading aloud alone releases the text from the page, and allows it to participate in the circumambient reality:

Mais le vers n'est-il pas fait surtout pour la vie vocale, n'attend-il pas que la voix de l'homme vienne le délivrer des caractères d'imprimerie, de leur poids, leur silence, leur geôle, de leur indifférence apparente?
   La voix humaine, si elle est compréhensive, donne au vers un véhicule quasi métaphysique. N'est-elle pas la fusion du corps et de l'esprit, un fluide qui s'évade dans l'air tout en se révélant. (1951: 68–9)

To support his argument, Supervielle calls Bergson to witness: according to the philosopher, recitation is not an ornament of learning, a supplementary skill, but a fundamental support on which all else is constructed; we only understand and intimately know what we have had, in some measure, to reinvent. Recitability, therefore, is a safeguard against opacity and untransmissibility; and textual transparency, which the voice vouches for and actualizes, is that sign by which we know that a poem is, like all other recitable poems, a repetition, a representation, of an original act which restores the terrestrial paradise prophesied by Isaiah (11: 6–10):

La poésie est pour les poètes l'art de ne se priver de rien et, par cela même, de nous combler de tout. Ils en arrivent à se prendre pour le Créateur et ce comble est qu'ils n'ont pas tout à fait tort puisqu'on retrouve dans leur univers toutes les bêtes du paradis terrestre voisinant avec quelques monstres qui leur sont particuliers. (1951: 70)

On the evidence of the previous chapter, we might propose that Supervielle's poetry is not as rhythmically transparent as he might wish, or that the semantic transparency is not borne out by the rhythms. The truth of the matter is that Supervielle's poems are gravitations towards a desired truth, without guarantee of achievement. None the less, we may suppose that the act of reading, of rhythmic inhabitation of the text, is an espousal or appropriation of the experience of the poet/persona.

Such a view is almost diametrically opposed to that expressed by Reverdy in his reply to the survey into 'la diction poétique' carried out by the Cahiers d'Études de Radio-Télévision in 1956. Reverdy anathematizes the attempt to naturalize and recuperate the poetic text by reciting it, largely because any reading is a deformation of the text, necessarily brings to the text something which is not there, namely the reader:

Je ne pense pas que la diction d'un poème puisse, ou même ait à lui apporter une valeur nouvelle. De la tête au papier c'est tout le trajet nécessaire; et, dans celui-là du moins s'il y a quelque chose à perdre, il y a aussi quelque chose à gagner. Le poème intérieur devient le poème extérieur et communicable à autrui. Si l'on pense à ce que cet autre en fera déjà, en l'intégrant par la lecture silencieuse par l'œil, cela fait déjà assez de déformation. Tout ce que la diction apporte au poème ce n'est pas ce qui serait inexprimé sous sa forme écrite, mais quelque chose d'étranger à lui-même, surajouté et qui peut changer du tout au tout selon le diseur et même selon le moment et les circonstances où le diseur dit ou redit le même poème. (1974: 243)

There is nothing uncharacteristic about Reverdy's insistence on the recalcitrant otherness of the work of art here; he would argue, I think, that the reality of the work of art is directly proportional to its capacity to resist the reader, to remain opaque. What will seem stranger to the reader of Reverdy's contributions to *Nord–Sud*, which he edited 1917–18, are his intentionalist convictions: 'Il n'y a qu'une intervention de la voix humaine admissible à la rigueur après qu'un poème a été écrit, celle de l'auteur—encore que la plupart du temps, la pauvreté des moyens de l'auteur pour ce genre d'exercice le rende plutôt désastreux' (1974: 244). What makes this sound oddly is Reverdy's earlier eschewal of anything that smacks of *communicative* intentions on the part of the author. One of the drawbacks of reading verse aloud is that it invites the reader to imagine a coherent psychological presence behind the poem, whose spiritual autobiography he then attempts to reconstitute. But poetry has nothing to do with describing or recounting, according to Reverdy; indeed one of its functions is to make the author an irrelevance, to transcend him. The paradoxical corollary of this is to say, of Mallarmé, for example: 'Son *intention* est plus importante que son œuvre' (1975: 121); for if the particular poem as achieved aesthetic object transcends those authorial feelings and that authorial psychology that give birth to it, so the general intention of the author, that is to say not his communicative intention, but his aesthetic or contractual intention, transcends any particular work; what the author intends to make has a significance far surpassing anything he intends to say; indeed to approach the writing of a poem with the intention to say is sure to adulterate it. In his reply here, Reverdy seems to speak of intentionality in its communicative aspect, at least momentarily; more in keeping is the passage which follows almost immediately:

Ce que l'on oublie c'est que le poète en écrivant ne peut pas, ne doit pas penser à l'effet que son poème produira sur quelqu'un d'autre, à moins d'être un faiseur; la source de la poésie exclut tout souci de cet ordre sous peine de fausser et de compromettre l'essentiel. (1974: 245)

If, for Reverdy, the desire to read poems aloud betrays a fundamental misunderstanding of what poems are, it equally betrays a disregard of the movement of history, a movement which has perfected the written existence of the poem and correspondingly signed the death warrant of lyricism: 'Le mot écrit est à mon sens, à son point extrême de perfection. La poésie lyrique est morte dans une interminable agonie depuis l'invention de la typographie' (1974: 246). About typography, we shall have more to say in a moment. About lyricism, we should again be careful to distinguish. Reverdy here, as elsewhere (1975: 183–5), means by lyricism that voice-derived emotion which leads poetry back to its origins in song, but which more recently is associated, to use Mallarmé's terms, with the 'direction personnelle enthousiaste de la phrase' ('Crise de vers', 1945/ 1896: 366). Lyricism too easily presupposes a necessary vocal presence in the poem, as though the written were the record of the spoken; but there is clearly a huge difference, not frequently enough perceived perhaps, between the spoken language and the oral production of a written text which does not have a previous or prior oral existence. The lyricism of the written is not to be found, therefore, in the sustaining, domineering, intoxicating breath of the enraptured utterer, but in the contact with words:

Enfin, je ne crois pas qu'on puisse raisonnablement se proposer d'emporter l'âme d'un lecteur, d'un auditeur, dans un grand courant d'air, mais plutôt qu'il s'agit de la toucher au point le plus sensible d'un coup sec qui saura l'émouvoir. Le choc n'a l'air de rien, mais l'émotion s'étend ensuite, augmente, s'irradie, ou conquiert la sensibilité entière, brusquement. (1975: 184)

Crucial, then, to the reading of verse, for Reverdy, is solitude, silence, intimacy, meditation, and this last necessitates the ability to pace one's reading, to interrupt, to go back, to accelerate and decelerate: in many senses, the reading aloud of poetry destroys reading, inasmuch as reading is not verbalization, actualization, but pondering a text, assimilating a text, creating a dialogue of the eye with it. And one might propose straightaway that one of the functions of typography in Reverdy's work is precisely to create this unevenness, to dissuade us from what is too conveniently problem-solving in fluency, to remind us of the asperities and obstacles of a reality that the voice wants pre-digested.

If Reverdy insists that intention should be regarded more as a matter of contract than of communication, more as a matter of the way the poet conditions the reader to read than of what he offers to be read, then we would do well to approach Reverdy's Cubist intentions in the same spirit. When a critic sets out to demonstrate what one art owes to another, it is easy for him to suppose that the plausibility of his case will depend on the detail and comprehensiveness of the evidence, that is to say on the data of style. If Cubism is multi-perspectival, for instance, in what senses can the language of the poetry contemporary with it equally be described as multi-perspectival? If analytic Cubism cultivates the monochromatic, in what sense can a particular use of language be regarded as uncoloured, or colourless? These kinds of equivalence can be the subject of fascinating, and often illuminating, speculation. But what is important for Reverdy in Cubism are its aesthetic premisses, which are to be applied to other arts—though in 'Le Cubisme, poésie plastique' (*L'Art*, Feb. 1919) Reverdy claims that poetry has historical priority in these matters; and the under-lying premiss is that each art must develop and be faithful to the means peculiar to it; in some senses, presumably, this is bound to force the arts apart, at least as far as stylistic borrowings are concerned.[1] This belief is the foundation of Reverdy's insistence on poetry's becoming, if anything, more written, rather than less so: '*Le propre d'une œuvre d'art littéraire est de ne pouvoir être conçue et réalisée autrement qu'écrite*' (1975: 53–4).

[1] As Reverdy himself puts it: 'Aussi bien, s'il est difficile de trouver des moyens nouveaux dans un art, il n'est méritoire que de les trouver propres à cet art et non pas dans un autre. C'est-à-dire que les moyens littéraires appliquées à la peinture (et vice versa) ne peuvent que nous donner une apparence de nouveauté facile et dangereuse' (1975: 16).

On the purification of the means of its particular art depends the work's capacity to achieve autonomy, to become a reality in the world on an equal footing with all other realities. What the work must avoid at all costs is the derivative, in all its forms—imitation, description, transcription, recounting, representing—because the derivative inevitably concedes its reality to that from which it is derived:

Il faut préférer un art qui ne demande à la vie que les éléments de réalité qui lui sont nécessaires et qui, à l'aide de ces éléments et de moyens nouveaux purement artistiques, arrive, en ne copiant rien, en n'imitant rien, à créer une œuvre d'art pour elle-même. Cette œuvre devra avoir sa réalité propre, son utilité artistique, sa vie indépendante et n'évoquera rien autre chose qu'elle-même. (1975: 45)

Cubism has achieved this independence for its works, is an art of creation, rather than of reproduction or interpretation. Reverdy's assessment of Cubism is thus very different from that of Delaunay, explored in Chapter 5; whereas Delaunay taxes Cubism with being too preoccupied with the object (and thus too imitative), and still embroiled in a perspectival and volumetric way of seeing, Reverdy specifically rebuts such charges: 'Comme la perspective est un moyen de représenter les objets selon leur apparence visuelle, il y a dans le cubisme les moyens de construire le tableau en ne tenant compte des objets que comme élément et non au point de vue anecdotique' ('Sur le cubisme', 1975: 18). For Cubism *vraisemblance* is an irrelevant concern. But some critics, while in agreement with this statement, would still argue that Cubism is aiming at 'total representation' or at 'stereometric' or 'synthetic' reproduction (i.e. implying a representational rather than conceptual approach); in Reverdy's eyes, Cubism has passed beyond this: 'Les objets n'entrant plus que comme élément on comprendra qu'il ne s'agit pas d'en donner l'aspect mais d'en dégager, pour servir au tableau, ce qui est éternel et constant (par exemple la forme ronde d'un verre, etc.) et d'exclure le reste' (1975: 19). Objects are no longer iconic signs, but compositional elements, relating neither to the anecdotal (the 'having-been-seen') nor to the temporal (viewing positions in time). Conceptualization and the reduction to 'primary' qualities are thus means to achieve not a new mode of representation, but a new conception of the status of the artistic product. Not surprisingly, then, Reverdy insists that 'Cubism' and 'portraiture' are mutually exclusive terms. He summarizes his argument thus:

Nous sommes à une époque de création artistique où l'on ne raconte plus des histoires plus ou moins agréablement mais où l'on crée des œuvres qui, en se détachant de la vie, y rentrent parce qu'elles ont une existence propre, en dehors

de l'évocation ou de la reproduction des choses de la vie. Par là, l'Art d'aujourd'hui
est un art de grande réalité. Mais il faut entendre réalité artistique et non réalisme;
c'est le genre qui nous est le plus opposé. (1975: 20)

Throughout Reverdy's reflections, it is impossible to tell what kind of
Cubism he has in mind, or what artists, although his fondness for Picasso
and Gris in particular is well known. This fact, in itself, should discour-
age us from hunting too zealously for 'textual' parallels. How far does
Reverdy engage with the techniques of Cubism at all? We know that a
representational work of art is always false (1975: 134); we know that
reality does not motivate art, but rather that art starts out from life only
to achieve its own alternative reality in the real world (1975: 117); we
know, correspondingly, that a work of art is born of one set of emotions
only to give birth to another set, that the emotion that results is very
different from the emotion which produces (i.e. a work of art comes to
produce its own emotions and not to communicate someone else's) (1975:
134). But exactly how are these things accomplished? What techniques
are necessary to make the work of art, and the Cubist work of art in
particular, a locus of transformation?

The answers to these questions are largely to be found in two passages
from 'Le Cubisme, poésie plastique'. As adumbrated earlier, Reverdy in
this essay argues that the poets of the late nineteenth century (Rimbaud,
Mallarmé) preceded the painters in creating a non-descriptive art, in re-
conquering the purity of their own means. One of the things the painters
derived from these poets was the visual equivalent of image-making:

Dégager, pour créer, les rapports que les choses ont entre elles, pour les rapprocher,
a été de tous temps le propre de la poésie. Les peintres ont appliqué ce moyen aux
objets et, au lieu de les représenter, se sont servis de rapports qu'ils découvraient
entre eux. Il s'ensuit une reformation au lieu d'une imitation ou d'une interprétation.
C'est un art de conception: ce que fut de tout temps l'art poétique. La reformation de l'objet équivaut à la création poétique de la phrase non descriptive. (1975:
144)

We hardly need reminding of Reverdy's formula for the image, so enthu-
siastically adopted by the Surrealists:

L'image est une création pure de l'esprit.

Elle ne peut naître d'une comparaison mais du rapprochement de deux réalités
plus ou moins éloignées.

Plus les rapports des deux réalités rapprochées seront lointains et justes, plus
l'image sera forte—plus elle aura de puissance émotive et de réalité poétique.
(1975: 73)

What we do need reminding of, however, are the fundamental ways in which the Reverdyan image is to be dissociated from the Surrealist one. For Reverdy the image is not a product of chance or perceptual disorder, its function is not shock or stupefaction, its status is not self-justifying; rather, the image is important as the most effective, and economical, means whereby reality can be changed into poetic reality, whereby objects drawn from the real world can, by interaction, become elements in a new construction ('C'est au moment où les mots se dégagent de leur significa- tion littérale qu'ils prennent dans l'esprit une valeur poétique', 1975: 107). Furthermore, in the final paragraph of his definition, we should emphasize 'justes' quite as much as 'lointains'; Reverdy is not on the look-out for the brutal and fantastic, for the force of the image is located in the emotion it arouses, not in the colourfulness of its constituents.

Reverdy's rejection of comparison in his aesthetics of the image would seem to relate to what we said about the modern image and its unvoicing in Chapter 5; comparison is a discursive form of imagery in which resem- blance is vocally/syntactically guaranteed; the image is something already given and thus, again, participates in the recounted rather than presented. Just as the Cubists by a process of *rapprochement* of objects, or of facets of objects, oust spectatorial possibility, so the Reverdyan image erases the possibility of its being spoken; in other words, while the Cubists start from things seen only to create canvases which are beyond the bounds of normal perceptual possibility (we can view the canvas but we could not view its contents were they to be removed from it, to be returned to real space), so the poetic image takes the spoken only to render it unspeakable. And the way these things are achieved is described, if only sketchily, in a paragraph a little further on in 'Le Cubisme, poésie plastique':

Au point de vue plastique, Cézanne est aussi un précurseur. Mais à cause de lui on a classé parmi leurs préoccupations celle de figurer les objets en volumes, ce dont il ne fut jamais sérieusement question. Il s'agit seulement d'une figuration dans l'espace sans l'aide de la perspective; de l'utilisation de la matière sans l'atmosphère qui l'enveloppe, et au total d'une création à l'aide d'objets reformés et conçus par l'esprit, d'une œuvre qui est le résultat d'une émotion au lieu d'en être la répétition; c'est par là que les œuvres qu'apporte cette esthétique nouvelle constituent des réalités en elles-mêmes. (1975: 145-6)

Reverdy is nothing if not insistent about the autonomy of the work of art; but his technical remarks are nothing if not sparse and elusive. Neverthe- less from these remarks we can infer further grounds for a comparison of the methods of Cubism with those of Reverdy. I say 'further' grounds because it is clear that Reverdy's conception of the poetic work of art is based very much on his reading of Cubism; it is clear, too, that he reads his own aesthetic of the image into Cubism, so that he can derive that aesthetic from it; it is, finally, evident, although we have only adverted to it in passing, that the 'primary' language of Cubism, that language that makes it 'éternel et constant', the language which is one of the sparest and most repetitive in the arts, coincides very much with the kind of poetic lexis canvassed by Reverdy in 'Poésie' (*Le Journal littéraire*, 7 June 1924):

. . . seulement, parmi tous les phénomènes sensibles, le poète choisit ceux qui participent strictement du réel. Il faut entendre, par là, toutes choses simples, profondes, constantes, que le temps n'apporte ni n'emporte, aussi essentielles à l'être humain que ce dernier peut être indispensable à lui-même (Le nuage et la table sont, comme le soleil, la pluie et l'ombre des réalités; la forme particulière d'un vêtement est irréelle, la réminiscence livresque visitée en poésie reste dans l'irréalité). (1975: 205–6)

The 'further grounds' relate to a version of Cubism in which visual illusionism is systematically removed from the canvas. Not only is the Cubist painting unlit, not only does it abandon spatial depth, and the sense of mass which produces weight, not only does it inextricably enmesh its subject in the painted context, and either drastically limit, or equally drastically extend, the 'natural' colour range, but it reforms, reconstitutes, the objects which are ostensibly its subject. All this produces a 'figuration dans l'espace' which is peculiar to it, and the absence of an atmospheric envelope.

If Cubism is out to remove visual illusionism from painting, then Reverdy is correspondingly bent on removing vocal illusionism from poetry. Where the Cubists replace the ordered, three-dimensional space of modelling and perspective with the problematized, near two-dimensional space of juxtaposed and overlapping planes of varying sizes, Reverdy replaces the illusion of the linear voice, with its implication of an integral uttering presence, produced by punctuation, with an uncohesive, layered writtenness, inaccessible to the voice, produced by typographic variety. Reverdy makes it absolutely clear that the disappearance of punctuation and the development of new typographical resources are causally related:

La ponctuation est un moyen infiniment utile pour guider le lecteur et rendre plus facile la lecture des œuvres de forme ancienne et de composition compacte. Aujourd'hui chaque œuvre porte, liée à sa forme spéciale, toutes les indications utiles à l'esprit du lecteur. (1975: 62)

He makes equally clear his distaste for calligrammatic experiments of the kind undertaken by Apollinaire (though he is not otherwise stinting in his

praise for Apollinaire), which produce 'une difficulté de lecture déplorable'
(1975: 122), and justifies his own practice thus: 'je me créais une disposition dont la raison d'être purement littéraire était la nouveauté des
rythmes, une indication plus claire pour la lecture, enfin une ponctuation
nouvelle, l'ancienne ayant peu à peu disparu par inutilité de mes poèmes
(1975: 122). Additionally he defends the new typography as a much more
satisfying rationalization of the page than free verse presented 'à la ligne/
à la marge', disturbing in its asymmetry. More important still, the new
typography is an index of the novelty of the syntax, indeed the creator of
that novelty: 'La syntaxe est un moyen de creation littéraire. C'est une
disposition de mots—et une disposition typographique adéquate est
légitime' (1975: 82). Reverdy's syntax in itself is new only in its cryptic
brevity, in its paratactic opacity; it has none of Mallarmé's distortions of
grammatical function, anacolutha, ellipses, and convolutions. But typography itself begins to function as a system of hypotaxis even though the
margins it operates with may not coincide with clausal junctures; in the
absence of punctuation, capitals and lower-case letters also take on a
syntax-implying role which may complicate expected relationships. But
of this we shall have more to say in a moment.[2]

Does the transformation of which we have spoken, from reality-derived
to reality-creating, from voiced to unvoiced, take place in the course of
reading, as a result of the poem's refusal to be other things that we might
wish it? Or do we from the outset know that we are in another world, that
there is no point in trying to put together an *isotopie, or that if we do put
one together, we shall end up with another of those shadowy, but desolate,
existential conditions which haunt Reverdy's poetry and which seem a
peculiarly inadequate way of reading? But can one read *towards* an object,
read towards the written, read towards the unreadable? Would not this
make reading simply a movement of reconstitution, of reconstituting the
poem's recalcitrance? Let us begin by taking a look at 'Derrière la gare':

1.	Un nuage descend tout bas	$3 + 5 / 6 + 2 /$
		$3 + 3 + 2$
2.	Là où il y a un vide	$1 + 4 + 2$
3.	Près de moi	3

---

[2] Far more thorough accounts of the theoretical bases of Reverdy's poetics and its
connection with Cubism are to be found in Greene (1967) and Rothwell (1989). Rothwell,
in particular, explores the links between Reverdy's anti-mimeticism and a spatialized syntax, as they are expressed through the metafigure of 'atmosphere'. Other works comment on
different aspects of Reverdy's relationship with Cubism; for the purposes of this study, one
might mention Milhau (1982) and Hubert (1982).

4.	Un trou	2
5.	Au loin quelque chose finit	5 + 3 / 2 + 6 / 2 + 3 + 3
6.	Un grand bruit	3
7.	s'éteint	2
8.	Et je vois du monde	3 + 2
9.	Dans ma tête il y a un monde fou	3 + 3 + 4
10.	C'est toi	2
11.	Et je ne reconnais personne	6 + 2
12.	quelle vie	3
13.	Ce n'est pas encore fini	5 + 3
14.	Une ride profonde au front	3 + 3 + 2 / 6 + 2
15.	C'est transparent comme du cristal	4 + 5
16.	Quelque chose au bout des doigts qui me fait mal	3 + 4 + 4
17.	Quand je t'ai connue	5
18.	Quand je t'ai tenue	5
19.	Certainement quelque chose tombait	4 + 3 + 3
20.	Une fausse parure	3 + 3
21.	Et tu ne voyais même pas ma figure	5 + 3 + 3
22.	La porte tournait	2 + 3
23.	Quelqu'un riait	4
24.	C'était si loin	4
25.	Où pourrait-on aller se perdre maintenant	4 + 2 + 2 + 4

I would like, as a first move, to disregard Reverdy's ambitions for poetry and treat this as though it were the equivalent of what should not exist, but does, the Cubist portrait. In Picasso's portrait of Daniel-Henry Kahnweiler (1910), for instance, the title itself not only guarantees that the picture has a subject, and a subject with a specific referent, but it also indicates to us what kinds of sign to look for. As a face emerges from the shallow, faceted three-dimensionality of the canvas, we can use some of our conventional spatial orientations to locate the folded hands at the base of the picture, the watch-chain, a button. We can also deduce a sitting posture: the diagonals at the bottom left suggest crossed legs, and the still life just above the 'knees' places an occasional table. Golding (1959: 89) also identifies one of the New Caledonian sculptures owned by Picasso, at the top left of the canvas. A portrait made of half-glimpsed features, clues, as if only imperfectly remembered—Golding also reports (1959: 89) that although Kahnweiler submitted to about twenty sittings, the painting was actually based on a photograph.

Likewise, moving out from Reverdy's title, we might feel justified in finding in the poem an anecdote from the poet's sentimental life, the account of a meeting off a train. The cloud which descends is smoke from the train, coming to fill, as it were, the void at the poet's side. The hubbub of the train's arrival and of the disembarking passengers gradually fades, either literally or in the poet's mind. People emerge from the station (l. 8). His mind is in confusion, as though this same crowd were tramping through it, but wildly (l. 9). He tricks himself with a moment of recognition 'C'est toi', but this is no more than a mirage. The reverberations of the train's arrival and of his own disappointment are not yet over (l. 13); his own despondency and carewornness (l. 14) are transparently obvious, are suffered as an intensified vulnerability (l. 15). The absence of the hoped-for arrival is now experienced as the pain of an empty hand (l. 16). The poet takes refuge in the past, in a relationship described in general temporal terms (perfect, ll. 17–18), but then moves to another encounter, the fatal one perhaps, another meeting off a train perhaps: something fell, it could have been jewellery (or was it night and the coming of the stars?), and caused a distraction (l. 21), an unseeingness which ran much deeper, which was like the death-knell of the relationship. There were other, scattered events: someone passing through the revolving door, someone laughing; but these seemed to belong to another world and, besides, are already so far back in memory. Indeed the imperfect tenses in these lines embody the indeterminate temporality of memory, or the protractedness of the pain caused by the events recounted. In any case, the poet was left alone, it was the end of something. Where now could he go to bury his solitude?

This interpretation may seem ludicrous in its literality, and in its dependence on the text as a producer of reliable data. Part of what makes it ludicrous is its need to know, its need to find a coherence, not in the language and structure of the poem itself, but in the *fait divers* which lies beyond it. Many things might be different: the hoped-for arrival did actually arrive (l. 10), but the waiting poet no longer recognized her as someone he knew. Or did she walk straight by him? The imperfect tense, which monopolizes the poem from line 19, is not a previous occasion, but the present occasion of lines 1–16 remembered afterwards. Indeed the whole of my preliminary reading would be much more convincing if formulated in the mode of memory: this poem is not about the time the poet turned up to meet his girlfriend off the train, only to realize that his relationship had come to an end; it is about the tricks, distortions, shifted emphases, omissions, recuperations produced by memory when it confronts particularly painful experience: the dying hubbub on the station, for instance, is experienced almost as something apocalyptic (ll. 5–7); sorrow crystallizes in the momentary focus of one tell-tale feature:

Une ride profonde au front

just like Kahnweiler's hands or watch-chain emerging from the welter of superimposed planes or from that peculiar emptiness at the centre of his stomach; one is not quite sure whether sensations have physical origins or not (l. 16).[3]

But what ultimately makes such an interpretation untenable? What creates the obstacle to its satisfying realization? We might begin by saying 'The very device which seems to validate it', namely the title. Where is 'derrière la gare'? Is it the same kind of planar behindness we find in 'Descente':

> La monde qui se fond
> Derrière ce tableau?

Or is it the kind of behind we find in 'Dernière Heure':

> On n'ose pas crier
> Derrière l'arbre ou la lampe
> Il s'est mis à prier

where it seems less like a place and more like the spatial modality of praying (or crying out).[4] At least in these two poems, this behind is answered by an in-front ('Finir devant la haie'; 'Les lèvres s'avancent'); in 'Derrière la gare', on the other hand, this counter-movement does not seem available; the coordinates, the axes which would allow the plotting of a location, seem to be missing. The only coordinates we have in fact are 'près de' and 'au loin', but what kinds of space and distance do these describe? And besides the spatial dimension of 'Au loin' acquires a possibly temporal dimension in the line

> C'etait si loin.

In short there is no place in which this anecdote can be. Like Picasso's Kahnweiler, the personal pronouns of 'Derrière la gare' do not exist in space by any rights bestowed by mass or perspective; they are themselves constitutive of space, or what Reverdy calls 'une figuration dans l'espace';

---

[3] These kinds of doubt are equally to be found in Reverdy's syntax of spatial relations; Cardonne-Arlyck (1989: 90) comments: 'Reverdy's marked attentiveness to spatial configurations can be correlated to his attempt, from poem to poem, to oppose a given, tangible reality to the mind's fluctuating movements. His multiple but disconnected use of spatial relations signals the mind's contradictory thrusts toward and away from reality, the object of desire and resentment.'

[4] The absence of punctuation makes it impossible to tell whether 'Derrière l'arbre ou la lampe' acts as an adverbial phrase for the line preceding it, or, rather, for the line following it. I tend to conclude the latter, because both lines are on the same margin.

directions are generated out of them, proximities and distances are trian-
gulations on the basis of impressions, response, fear, hope. That volume,
that presence by virtue of the occupation of space, which Kahnweiler
seems to be aiming at, particularly through the featuring of his face,
seems suddenly to be erased, as space itself eases him out of its designs,
as it comes to his midriff. Does not the 'I' of the poet have the same
difficulty in achieving opacity (l. 15), in holding out against the 'vide', the
'trou' which seems to be encroaching on him?[5] If being is pain, it is
preferable to the spatial effacement that the poet ironically invokes in the
last line of the poem. In the end, then, whatever the poem may appear to
recount, there is hardly anyone, or hardly anything of anyone, to participate in it, wherever it is.

But this is not all. Reverdy, in the same paragraph from which we
have just quoted, speaks of 'l'utilisation de la matière sans l'atmosphère
qui l'enveloppe', in Cubism's overturning of Impressionist and Post-
Impressionist principles. Part of our difficulty in finding a spatial setting
for human subjects is the fact that space itself is not 'inflated' by any
circulation of air, nor illuminated, shown, given contour and extent by
any source of light. Kahnweiler's watch-chain is not seduced into wonderful contingency, does not stand as a monument to that particular time,
or moment of being, thanks to the impatient temporality of light. The
watch-chain loses it power to historicize, and Kahnweiler becomes less
portrait than still life; in so becoming, the image delivers what Bryson
(1989: 233) defines as still life's third insult to the human subject: 'the
subject who looks out at the scene of still life is made to feel no bond of
continuous life with the objects that fill the scene, it proposes and assumes
a viewing subject who looks at things *without* from a field *within* the self,
and experiences disconnection.' This objectification of Kahnweiler, this
cutting him off from our space and time, or from our spatiality and
temporality, coincides with his iconic death (*nature morte*) and his resurrection as alternative reality. But we must accept that we can no more
express ourselves through the spectation of the picture than we can
recover the pre-pictorial Kahnweiler. The picture mediates nothing; it is
its own destination.

Reverdy's poem, too, is without atmosphere, the coherent atmosphere
of orality, of discourse, and this absence of atmosphere equally cuts the
poem off from historicity, in three senses. First, as we have seen, al-

---

[5] The typographical implications of this existential problem are investigated by Michel
Collot (1982), particularly as they are manifest in Reverdy's revisions, a line of enquiry
initiated by Eliane Formentelli.

though the poem has tenses, it has no *temps d'histoire*, no reconstructible chronology; the present tense of lines 1–16 might equally precede or succeed the imperfect tense of 19–24. And if the present precedes the imperfect, then the element of presentness in the perfect tenses of lines 17–18 defines a new present which is occupied only by these auxiliaries, and these two instances of 'je', but by no other circumstances, detail, or setting. And this multiplication of temporal dimensions without sequence means that the poem exists in no time, that is to say, not outside time, but not in time either, rather at the intersection of all available and possible times, in a kind of temporal blank. This feature is brought home by the last line of the poem, in which a conditional (future in the past) is present-directed ('maintenant').

If we are denied a reconstructible *temps d'histoire*, if we have no access to an event which unfolded in a certain order within a certain time-span, then perhaps we have a *temps de récit*, a time which belongs to telling. Just as we may say that the poem is not about an event but about the way we remember an event, so the time is not of the event but of its recuperation. Indeed the plot is in the writing, is in the verbal, and its peripeteia are enacted by the typography. The present tense of lines 1–16 is not the present of a recounted event but the present of the recounting, of the words following each other across the page:

Un nuage descend tout bas (yes, the 'nuage' is on the ground–
        horizontal of the written line)
Là où il y a un vide (yes, the line *produces* the 'vide' of a terminal
        blank space)
    Près de moi (yes, 'vide' is close to 'moi' as is the
        blank space which surrounds this phrase)
        Un trou (the 'trou' is in its 'o', which is also at the heart of 'moi')
Au loin quelque chose finit (as the line finishes)
Un grand bruit (which is the very presence of graphemes on a white
        ground)
        s'éteint (here the disappearance of the graphic is aided
        by the lower-case initial letter).

This is the crudest of analyses, but serves to demonstrate the way in which the 'three-dimensional' and referential is 'lifted' to the surface of the page to become the self-generating two-dimensionality of writing, or the extremely shallow three-dimensionality of meta-discourse. But even here temporality is not historicized, cannot exist as chronology, partly because the past tense once again produces unreadable overlaps and insertions and deletions. It is all very well to claim that a line like:

Quelque chose au bout des doigts qui me fait mal

initiates its own meaning, that the 'quelque chose' cannot be named as an object precisely because 'quelque chose' are the words at the 'end' of the fingers which hurt: 'qui me fait mal'; but in lines 17–18:

> Quand je t'ai connue
> Quand je t'ai tenue

the graphemically enacted meaning 'Quand je t'ai' (i.e. a 'te' caught between and indeed contracted by, reduced by, two first-person elements, both as it were in the present of writing) is cancelled by the past participles which follow, erased. Similarly the imperfect tenses which follow make possible alternative readings, both of which undo the presence of the text as an unfolding temporal present: either these imperfect tenses refer back to a text prior to lines 1–16, which is no longer available and cannot be verified, so that the textuality of 'Derrière la gare' becomes increasingly spectral and unlocatable; or these imperfect tenses refer back to lines 1–16 and 'fill out' the earlier text in retrospect, or overlap with it. In this latter case, the gaps in lines 1–16 are failures of memory or failures of certainty which the last seven lines come to supplement, though they are powerless to complete, in a roughly reverse pattern. Thus (and again I apologize for the crassly rudimentary way I do this):

> .   .   .   .
> Au loin quelque chose finit. C'est si loin
> Un grand bruit
>   s'éteint
> La porte tourne. Et je vois du monde
> Quelqu'un rit. Dans ma tête il y a un monde fou
> C'est toi. Certainement quelque chose tombe.
> Une fausse parure Et tu ne vois même pas ma figure
> Et je ne reconnais personne etc.

I certainly do not wish to imply that this version of the jigsaw is the right one; I merely wish to demonstrate the possibility of the principle. Reverdy's typography creates a sense of textual gaps, of textual absences, which are certainly part of a graphemically orientated meaning, but which also invite us to fill them with other textual material, taken from other moments of the text. If Reverdy's text does not belong in time, it is once again because the *temps de récit* is also intersectional, or a precipitate of different textual times. If there is some truth in the idea that the latter part of 'Derrière la gare' folds back on the first sixteen lines and either overlaps with them or fills out their textual gaps, then the final line has as much irony in it as it has pathos: Reverdy has, by 'plugging up' retrospectively the holes in his own text, denied himself that blank space which is the necessary bolt-hole.

That we are right to think of Reverdy making his textual space more 'shallow', reducing the three-dimensionality of referential illusion to the near two-dimensionality of a text executing its meaning in its writtenness, in its graphic choreography, is reinforced by the almost imperceptible way that metatextual elements slip into his poems. We have already had occasion to quote from 'Dernière Heure' where we find the lines:

> L'animal est un cadavre grotesque
> Un abreuvoir en encrier ou les mots sont pris
> Les lèvres s'avancent
>
> .   .   .   .
>
> La porte
> Le livre
> Minuit

We might equally, for example, cite lines from 'L'Ombre', such as:

> La porte tranche le mot

or

> Un mot doucement reste comme un oiseau.

But it is not just at the level of the *temps de récit* that the Reverdyan text has no atmosphere, has no time, no history; it is at the level of the **temps de lecture*, too. We have already seen one of the ways in which this might be so; we find ourselves reading the text back into itself, so that we can at no point take readerly control, we can at no point imprint a discourse on the text, moving through time and tied to our subjective history. Earlier we hinted that just as Cubist painting transforms what may possibly have been seen into the unseeable, so that the spectator is ousted from the canvas's inner space, must view it from the outside,[6] so Reverdy ousts the reader of the text from a 'speaking' position within it. Without making his text into a purely visual experience—his texts are not calligrams and their acoustic structure is of much importance, as we shall see— Reverdy thwarts its orality, its amenability to discursive assimilation. He does this in two ways additional to the one just explored.

---

[6] Some would disagree with this view. I think of Hockney, for example: 'Cubism moved the viewer into the picture, pushing him, pulling him in' (Joyce 1988: 124).

One reason why the Reverdyan poem is quite simply unreadable is its Cubist structure of 'plans superposés'. The Reverdyan poem is a complex system of competing structurations all of which overlap with each other. The sources of these structurations are margins, rhythm, syntax, acousticity. Rather like Apollinaire's 'poème-conversation', the Reverdyan poem tempts us to unravel various concurrent threads, to discover different itineraries of continuity through the poem. If, for example, I identify the pentasyllable as one route through 'Derrière la gare', I will conjoin in the same discourse unit 'Près de moi' and 'Un trou', and equally 'Un grand bruit' and 's'éteint'; but, by the same token, I shall find myself wishing to combine 'c'est toi' and 'quelle vie' which involves me in, as it were, reading behind, or in front of, 'Et je ne reconnais personne'. I then move on to lines 17–18 and finally line 22. Left unsolved by this reading, however, is whether pentasyllabic elements from other, longer lines (e.g. ll. 1, 2, 5, 13, 14, and so on) should be included, or at least affiliated to this reading. Left unsolved, too, is how the reader should cope with the complication of this pentasyllabic chain by the competing claims of margin. The poem has five margins, one of which suggests that I should place lines 17–18 not in a sequence of pentasyllables, but in another sequence which runs: 'Dans ma tête il y a un monde fou . . . quelle vie . . . Quand je t'ai connue . . . Quand je t'ai tenue . . . Une fausse parure'. Syntactically, I might feel some pressure to group all lines which begin with the co-ordinating conjunction (8, 11, 21), or with indefinite articles (1, 4, 6, 14, 20). Acoustically, there are not only the connections created by rhyme (usually couplets), but the whole complex addition of line-internal echoes as well: 'vide > vie > ride' (and all other /i/ phonemes); 'monde > profonde > front'; 'moi > toi > vois > doigts'; etc.

As well as expressively organizing the space of the page, and placing text at different levels of consciousness, or encouraging different intensities of utterance, multiple margin, then, also operates a structural distribution of the text. But it does something more: it determines the *temps de lecture.* What the single margin does is guarantee a certain consistency of duration and pacing in the text. We feel confident, for example, in assuming that the next line begins almost immediately after the previous line has ended; we know, too, thanks to this continuity, what our intonational bearings are; we imagine that lines with the same margin all last for about the same amount of time. The single 'margin' ensures the consistency of the reading atmosphere, is a safeguard against the reading space's being invaded by temporal relativities, which would eject the reader from an inhabitable temporality; of course the reader is free to develop his own relativities; this after all is exactly what reading and the orality of text is about, but we can only do this within a framework of temporal stability; if the text imposes, or even just implies, its own relativities then the reader cannot read himself into the text. And of course this last is precisely the effect that multiple margin has, and particularly a multiple margin which also allows variations in capital and lower-case initial letters. When I meet the lines:

> Et je ne reconnais personne
> quelle vie
> Ce n'est pas encore fini
>
> (ll. 11–13)

I find my own voice being neutralized by my doubts about intonation, pause, tempo, all those paralinguistic features in fact by which I am accustomed to make a text peculiarly mine, part of my voice, in the reading. The orality of a written text, crudely put, is to be found in those paralinguistic features which denote vocal possession, the subjective atmosphere of discourse. How much time takes place between lines 11 and 12, what has happened in this intervening space, what change of perspective (or even speaker) has occurred, what tone is to be adopted, what kind of temporal space does line 12 lead into? We must suspect Reverdy of being disingenuous when he claims of his typography: 'je me créais une disposition dont la raison d'être purement littéraire était la nouveauté des rythmes, une indication plus claire pour la lecture, enfin une ponctuation nouvelle' (1975: 122). About the 'novelty of the rhythms' we shall have more to say in a moment. But we can only accept 'une indication plus claire', if 'claire' means the transparency of the non-atmospheric. In reality, Reverdy's typography tends to disinform us, to imply a hidden agenda or rationale which only makes the reader less sure of himself and more sure of the inaccessibility of the 'first cause'. In these conditions, orality, attempted orality, has no point. In Picasso's portrait of Kahnweiler, we have to live with the idea that the painting is offering something to be seen, and to be seen more fully than it might be if the traditional rules of single-point perspective were adhered to, at the same time as the composition of the picture seems to be one of strenuous and repeated concealment; looking at the portrait we know that all that we see is all that we shall ever be able to see, the painted surface could not be more candid, and yet it seems to imply that we should try to see more. Reverdy likewise indicates to the reader by typographical means, but what he indicates is one of his own 'quelques choses'. And if we define the functions of punctuation as syntactic ordering, regulation of respiration, and expressivity, then we would have to conclude that Reverdy's typography has only the last function and that this yields its priority to a purely structural function. In many senses, punctuation is the presence of the paralinguistic in the written, the presupposition that the voice will come to inhabit the text. Removal of punctuation is a first step towards increasing the writtenness, or non-orality, of text. And far from replacing punctuation as an equivalent notation, Reverdy's typography disarticulates the text, problematizes juncture, and relativizes linguistic values preemptively, thus further intensifying the opacity of the text's writtenness.

If then we wished to identify those factors in Reverdy's verse which produce that conceptualization of the motif characteristic of Cubism— 'Ce qui différencie le cubisme de l'ancienne peinture, c'est qu'il n'est pas un art d'imitation, mais un art de conception qui tend à s'élever jusqu'à la création' (Apollinaire, 'Les Peintres cubistes', in Décaudin 1966: 24)— one would point to this writtenness and to the verbalization of the subject, the transformation of reference (out into reality) into verbal modality, of language as utterance (expression) into language as analysis, creating its own linguistic space, its own linguistic assumptions and imperatives. We have looked at how language exploits its own graphic identity, without however passing over into the imitatively pictorial; we have gained a passing sense of how language will develop its own acoustic structures (this is familiar enough, anyway). Perhaps some mention should also be made of language's location of meaning in the modalities of its grammar.

The reader of 'Derrière la gare', nonplussed at the level of the signified and any reference to an event or events beyond that, will not find it difficult to disentangle certain recurrent grammatical elements. From the first line, what the poem goes on to consolidate, or activate, are indefinite articles and intransitive verbs. Unlike the definite article, the indefinite article has an option on momentariness; something not seen before, unfamiliar, comes into the sensory field, and may leave just as immediately; for this reason, it is peculiarly geared to historicity, to the chances of temporality; its very contingency gives it a kind of uniqueness in time. But in Reverdy's non-atmospheric, devoiced world, this feature of the indefinite article is missing, and it is left nursing its randomness, its fund of possible existences, without being able to 'stick' in a narrative. The pervasiveness of the indefinite article in this poem makes the definite article of line 22 startlingly dramatic (I leave out of consideration those definite articles of parts of the body, in ll. 14 and 16, where there is no significant choice); this is the decisive moment, the moment at which one particular agent is somehow recognized, predestined, the master of ceremonies. Is this the door that separates the couple? Is this the door of the turning world which assigns all encounters to oblivion? Is this the door that produces all encounters, indifferently? Is this the door through which the solitary lover departs, a door which leads straight into the question of line 25, lines 23–4 providing only a circumstantial parenthesis?

The intransitive verb develops into a more varied environment. Things happen without establishing contacts or having consequences. In a strange world in which agents perform inscrutable acts and there are no patients, how will any relationship ever be established? The intransitive develops through the minimally presentative form ('il y a', cf. 'c'est' and 'c'était' forms) to the reflexive, in which the agent becomes its own patient in solipsistic isolation. It is hardly surprising, then, that when more or less genuine transitive verbs arrive, the verbs of the poet's contact with the world, and with the woman (and vice versa), they are scotched either by indetermination (l. 8), negativization (ll. 11, 21) or by unfulfilled subordination (ll. 17, 18). Intransitive verbs, unqualified, without a future, duly return (ll. 19, 22, 23), condemning to helpless pathos another feature of the majority of the transitive verbs, the co-ordinating conjunction 'et' (ll. 8, 11, 21), which attempts to give transitivity some impetus, to create the illusion of sequence and consequence around these verbs of potential contact. The last line combines, with wonderful finality, a modal in the conditional, an intransitive infinitive ('aller') and a reflexive infinitive ('se perdre'). What a crushing of the implied expectancy in 'maintenant' this is!

I do not wish to pursue this analysis any further. But it is evident that a reading like this would also comment on the impersonals, the failure of reference ('Quelque chose', 'Quelqu'un', 'Ce'), adverbs and prepositions of proximity and distance, pronouns as shifters. The poem does not give us an account of an experience, but the texture of experience, all those elements of verbal modality which, when juxtaposed, superimposed, repeated, submerge event in the play of their surfaces.

We need to understand rhythm, too, as part of the conceptualizing process. As we have already made clear, rhythm is no longer to be understood in rhetorical terms, as the way the reading subject inscribes himself in the text and communicates the text, either back to himself or to others. Rhythm, therefore, is not periodization, synthesis, sustenance, of linguistic flow. On the contrary, it is analysis, something that produces segmentation as part of the transformative process whereby what might be too easily naturalized by the human voice, as real speech, is restored as a facet of textuality. It is as if the scansional process never culminated in, or derived from, a production of the text by the voice. Instead the rhythmic structure of the poem invites us to build up an image of the poem, in which measures are the elements constitutive of the construction that the text is, rather than the accidents of an utterance, or factors which prove the poem's assimilability to a kind of speech which exists outside it. Just as Reverdy seeks that elementary, elemental lexis, based in reality, but susceptible of a new kind of essentialization which serves the reality of the work in which it finds itself, so, correspondingly, he uses the 'prime numbers' of rhythm to translate what otherwise would be potential orality into the designs of the written. This is what he means, I take it, by 'la nouveauté des rythmes', reinforced by a typographical disposition which helps to bring out their graphic relationships rather than their significance as an interval of speech-flow.

It will be seen from my notation of the 'rhythms' of 'Derrière la gare' that I have counted and elided the *e atone* in the traditional way. My reasons for doing this are threefold. It is a common critical practice as far as Reverdy's verse is concerned (see, for example, Deguy 1971 and Collot 1982), borne out by his cultivation of familiar lines and units. Secondly, inasmuch as Reverdy's purpose is to frustrate any attempt to naturalize his poems back to a spoken language in which some ordinary event might be related, it is understandable that he should cling to a diction which has an existence peculiar to verse and to the writtenness of verse (it is the writtenness of verse which minimizes the archaic quality of the *e atone* as speech). Let us reiterate that, even when verse is recited, it is the orality of the written language we hear, not the spoken language. Finally, the *e atone*—and I mean particularly the unelided, line-internal *e atone*, falling just after an accentuated syllable—is a moment of verbal overlap, the invasion of a measure by a word which does not really belong in it. In other words, the post-accentual unelided *e atone* produces variation in the nature of the measure and in the way in which it lies in the line, and relates to its verbal context. Conversely, the word which ends in an *e atone* will have a varying relationship with the barrier of the *coupe*.

In calling Reverdy's rhythms analytic, I mean, among other things, that rhythm selects lexical items and kinds of grammar in its process of segmentation, and assigns them to a certain syllabic category. The nature of each category will then vary according to its position in a chain of measures. Thus, for example, in the poem's final line:

Où pourrait-on aller se perdre maintenant $4 + 2 + 2 + 4$

the two infinitives are selected as dissyllabic measures, at the heart of an alexandrine, flanked by tetrasyllabic measures. The infinitive, of course, has a peculiar poignancy in Reverdy's verse, being that suspended, non-verbal part of the verb in which action exists as something potential, or something stifled by circumstance. The infinitive is the prison of the infinitely non-finite. It is fitting, then, in the plot of the poem's structure that the dissyllable should have moved, as it were, to the centre, for here it is both an end (of the first hemistich) and a beginning (of the second). Hitherto the text has treated us either to dissyllabic ends or beginnings, but never both together, and never middles. When the dissyllable occurs as a terminal unit, it has unmistakably dispiriting associations; the 'tout bas' of the first line affiliates that line with Baudelaire's 'Spleen':

Quand, le ciel bas et lourd pèse comme un couvercle;

the 'personne' of line 11 identifies the 'du monde' of line 8 as faceless strangers; even the 'au front' of line 14 is experienced as burden, since it bears the stigma of the 'ride profonde'. And here, too, the margin helps us to identify the dissyllabic lines as essentially terminal or initial in nature—'un trou' is clearly terminal, answering the terminal 'un vide', as is 's'éteint'. 'C'est toi' (l. 10), on the other hand, is initial and has in it that glimmer of hope, of real possibility, which is characteristic of the dissyllable in this position: a moment of recognition, the promise of an alternative space, an escape from abysmal proximity ('Au loin', l. 5), and opening either to or from somewhere ('La porte', l. 22). What may give line-initial or, in line 25, hemistich-initial dissyllables particular modal intensity is a post-accentual *e atone*:

La por: | te tournait
. . . se per: | dre maintenant

The dissyllable yearns forward, beyond barriers, or at least tries to leak out of the confinement of its inertia. Reverdy's analytic rhythms increase the presence of barrier, the peremptoriness of *coupe*, and enact that fundamental preoccupation of his verse:

'Ce mur si lisse, si épais, si haut, si calme . . . , cet effroyable mur' (R.P., 192), 'toujours ce mur, cet immense mur' (R.P., 189) dont tant de poèmes recommencent le cauchemar, et contre lequel s'arrête notre 'inutile essor' (F.V., 8), cette paroi multiforme qui est, selon les cas, haie ou rivière, cloison ou porte, rue interposée, fenêtre close, rideau de pluie ou de brouillard, nuage, c'est la nature elle-même devenue pour nous obstacle et refus. (Richard 1964: 14)

The traditional treatment of the *e atone* is crucial to his prosody as the instrument of the 'inutile essor', the last signs of aspiration and longing in a world without the atmosphere or the temporal punctuality to give them substance.

In this poem, the combination of 2 with 4 in the last line betokens a new departure, for the dissyllable most frequently finds itself in the company of the trisyllable, to constitute the pentasyllable to which we have already referred. It is not surprising, given what we have described as the decisive moment of the only definite article, that line 22 marks the final and culminating appearance of the pentasyllable, before the poem pans away in tetrasyllabic measures, with, as we have said, the dissyllable, now in a new modal landscape, still caught in its spiritual paralysis.

In further exploring the pentasyllable, I would like to concentrate on the articulation of its parts. We have already indicated how the order of constituents—2 + 3 or 3 + 2—might be significant; to this, variable margin adds further resources of relationship. What, for example, is the consequence of the typographical differences between

> Près de moi
> Un trou
>
> (ll. 3–4)

and

> Un grand bruit
> s'éteint?
>
> (ll. 6–7)

Clearly, in lines 3–4, the capital letter of 'Un trou' allows an amplification of 'un vide' of line 2. But more important, perhaps, it presents itself as something which the trisyllable (3) cannot assimilate, something which has the same existential status as the trisyllable, something which occurs at the same level of consciousness and on the same spatial plane as the trisyllable, something which is almost created by the very insurmountability of the barrier which exists between the two elements. Lines 6 and 7 on the other hand engineer a greater continuity, thanks to the syntax, the lower-case initial of line 7, and its partial overlap, and have a more imitative function: as the noise dies away, it both becomes more distant and drops in level. To these two versions of the pentasyllable we can add the 'divided' pentasyllable of lines 10 and 12, to which we have already made reference and whose measures are quite literally driven apart by an intervening observation, distracting the poet from the woman and generalizing her into a condition ('quelle vie') in which a fruitful encounter is unimaginable. There are also, of course, 'complete' pentasyllables like those in lines 17–18, in which it seems for a moment that connected discourse can be initiated, that a story can be told, that lessons can be learned; the very presence of the conjunction at the beginning of these lines betrays their hypotactic ambitions, or illusions. These hypotactic ambitions may surface in an unelided *e atone*, when the pentasyllable seeks to generate further measures, as in line 13:

Ce n'est pas enco: | re fini   5 + 3

How long can the pentasyllable prolong this 'encore' before the negative of the verb is contradicted by the arrival of the past participle? What a pitiful clinging on there is in these *e atones*. Viewed from the other end, the pentasyllable becomes a kind of product of the *e atone*, since it is this last which initiates the measure:

Un nua: | ge descend tout bas

I suppose we might begin to hear a new verb form, or at least a palimpsestic presence, here: 'je descends tout bas.' But we also hear lexical dissolution, a powerlessness to prevent unwanted permeations, the negative version of aspiration. Is this really a pentasyllabic measure? Well, only as an enforced condition, compelling that 3 + 2 division which spells out the existential dead end. It is as if the second part of this line is powerless to prevent the falling cloud; its barriers are not sufficiently syllable-tight.

Not only does Reverdy vary the nature and expressive implications of measures by varying margin and exploiting the *e atone*, he can also enmeasure a recurrent lexical item, so that its changing role in the pattern of modalities can be rhythmically registered.

In 'Derrière la gare', 'quelque chose' is just such a lexical item; it is a trisyllable with an available *e atone*. In line 5, it works in rather the same way that 'encore' does in line 13. Both of these lines are octosyllables in which an initial pentasyllable tries to prolong itself in the face of a verb, 'finir', which already condemns its impulse to extinction. In other words, the 'quelque chose' of line 5 is experienced as an 'encore', as an essentially temporal plea, as a something which claims duration because it may thereby define itself, identify itself as something specific and desired. As one can see from the table of measures, line 5 is in many senses the reverse of line 1: a liberating adverb at the beginning rather than a damning one at the end, distance rather than proximity, an *e atone* of escape, extension, rather than of invasion and alienness; the unnameability of 'quelque chose' is a safeguard of its promise. Line 19 has very much the same syntactic structure as line 5, adv. + 'quelque chose' + verb, but the rhythm is different, as is the modality of the adverb. The certainty that something fell is more important than what, which can then be dismissively identified in the line following. The activated *e atone* of 'quelque chose' is both an ironic adumbration of the (pretentious?) fulsomeness of the 'e's in line 20:

Un*e* fauss*e* parur(*e*)

and an inability to prevent the falling. 'Certainement' itself belongs to the tetrasyllabic orientation, the hope given up, of the poem's final lines. The 'quelque chose' of line 16 is something different again. With its 'e' elided, it has a greater hardness, a greater resistance, an effect increased by its syllabic incompatibility with the rest of the line; with its 'e' elided, it is not inhabited by any trace of a subjectivity; it is that recalcitrant otherness which hurts by its otherness.

This survey of some of the rhythmic features of 'Derrière la gare' may serve to persuade us that, although Reverdy may at first sight seem to be, like Supervielle, a free-verse poet of the line, he is in fact a free-verse poet of the measure within the line. Given his desire to suppress orality, and what we have described as his conceptualizing attitude towards language, this is not surprising. The line, after all, is the span of voice in poetry; any sapping of that ascendancy, particularly in verse of a still recognizably metrical complexion, will constitute a threat to voice. Measures for Reverdy are not instruments of pacing and proportion, part of the eventfulness of utterance; they are the construction kit for a text, those planes which go to constitute the space peculiar to the particular linguistic canvas. By now, too, I think we shall be persuaded of the complexity of Reverdy's poetic means generally, and that the function of these means is to thwart the referential and naturalizing urges of the reader, and to encourage him to transform these urges into an appreciation of the ways in which the text is self-generating, self-sustaining, and, for those reasons, in Reverdy's case at least, ultimately unreadable/unspeakable.

In my final analyses, I would like to take all the moves and strategies we have explored in 'Derrière la gare' as read, and concentrate as exclusively as possible on a consolidation of the prosodic findings which have emerged. First, I would like to push a little further our study of the relationship between measures and margin, and of the way in which margin can diversify the rhythmic impact of measures apparently identical with each other. To do this, I have chosen 'Descente':

1. Eau			1
2.	gaze		1
3.		étoile	2
4.	Halo		2
5. Tout ce qui est mort sur la toile			5 + 3
6.	La grotte à l'horizon		2 + 4
7.		Le ruisseau	3
8.	Le monde qui se fond		2 + 4
9.		Derrière ce tableau	2 + 4
10.		Finir devant la haie	2 + 4
11. Pas plus loin que l'endroit où le chien regardait			3 + 3 + 3 + 3
12. Le ciel plein de lueurs qui saignent			2 + 4 + 2
13.		Le chemin sous la pluie	3 + 3
14.		Tes cheveux embrouillés	3 + 3
15.	Les arbres qui se plaignent		2 + 4

This eight-margin poem seems to be an attempt to establish a close and inhabitable space against the two-dimensionality of distance. The enumerated items of the first four lines, the first three of which combine to produce the fourth, establish the underlying hexasyllable, but do so in the least dynamic, most incoherent way possible. These four items are those things which are described as inert, the still life of the 'toile' which is a 'toile de fond'. Behind the surface or plane, which the 'toile'/'tableau' is, everything is merged together by the rain and distance. The items can be named as known constituents of the landscape, as concepts, but they cannot act, relate, even really be perceived. At line 10, the poem moves in another direction, towards an 'in-front', a proximity. This proximity is not an abstract image, but a space with a history ('où le chien regardait') and in which the rain is not experienced as mere obliteration, polarizing concept (the known object) and percept (the object made invisible by the screen of gauze/rain), but as an environment which changes things, gives them new kinds of life, offers event. This side of the hedge is demonstrated to be inhabitable by a human presence ('Tes').

Looking at the tabulation of measures, we might suppose that the change of direction at line 10 coincides pretty well with a change from a 2 + 4 hexasyllable to a 3 + 3 one. This certainly has some truth in it. What we find in the first part are odd 3s but significantly not joined with other 3s. Instead we find 2s, taking up the random, undetermined 2s of 'étoile' and 'halo', and more or less polarized against tetrasyllables which provide qualification without supplying purpose; the same rhythmic gesturing is merely repeated. What is noticeable about the second part

on the other hand (ll. 10–15) is a greater concertedness, a closer syllabic
kinship of elements (the trisyllabic measures, the symmetrical arrangement
of l. 12). The definite article, which in lines 6–8 denoted the constituents
of the 'toile' and was no more than deictic, becomes, in lines 10–15, the
guarantee of a purposiveness, of something predestined and loaded with
meaning. Can we tell what drama took place in this forward-placed landscape? No, we cannot. But at least we feel that a drama did take place, or
is taking place, and one whose colours are essentially tragic, as befits the
rain ('qui saignent', 'qui plaignent').

This account, however, leaves us to explain away lines 10 and 15,
precisely the lines which frame this second part. Of course we might
argue that line 10 is a line of transition bound to the following alexandrine
of trisyllables by the rhyme 'haie'/'regardait', the passage out of the
background into the foreground; thus the overall structure from line 6
onwards is: *rimes croisées* (ll. 6–9) > *rimes plates* (ll. 10–11) (transition) >
rimes embrassées (imperfect) (ll. 12–15); the indifferent alternation of rhymes
is replaced by the more tactical arrangement of enclosed rhymes, with
their greater finality. But we should notice that line 10 no longer falls
on either of the two margins established by the preceding four lines. Its
2 + 4 is on a slightly different plane, is a displacement of the previous
2 + 4s. This new margin has the effect not only of encouraging us to
rethink the modality of 2 + 4 but also of liberating the margin of 2 + 4:
lines 12 and 15 may still have essentially the same syntactic structure as
line 8, but they have very different graphic projections. Line 12 begins at
the first margin, thus allowing it to comment ironically on the octosyllable
of line 5 and to align itself with the alexandrine which precedes it: we may
indeed be surprised to discover, so accustomed are we to the paratactic
autonomy of Reverdy's lines, that line 12 is a possible grammatical object
of line 11's 'regardait', and that therefore 'qui saignent' is in fact a relative
clause within a relative clause (creating, momentarily, a linguistic third
dimension, and the space of a discursive atmosphere). Line 15, for its
part, falls at the second margin and is the only line which occupies it (just
as l. 10 is the only line to occupy the sixth margin); that is to say, it does
not undergo the margin, accede to a fixed place on a 'toile', but rather
places itself in relation to the other *données*, chooses its perspective. Of
course 2 + 4 will carry forward into the second half some of its first-half
afflictedness; but here the affliction is not inflicted, and it can express
itself relative to other phenomena. Variability of margin allows relation
and dissociation; it is not for nothing that lines 13–14 are on the same
margin as, and therefore proffered as an answer or invitation to, lines 7

and 9, particularly as line 7 is already made up of an unpaired trisyllable. So line 15, with all its Verlainian overtones ('L'ombre des arbres dans la rivière embrumée', 'Ariettes oubliées IX') claims its 2 + 4 as somehow uniquely its own, not merely by virtue of its unique combination of features—plurality, *coupe enjambante*, feminine rhyme whose accentuated syllable also includes 'plaie', the imperfect ending, and opening consonants of 'pluie'—but also because it is constructing an image rather than representing it.

The other structural feature, besides margin, which has some bearing on the way in which rhythmic units vary their tonality, or modality, is rhyme, and for an exemplification we can look to 'Un seul moment':

1.	Aucun souffle sous l'occident	3 + 5
2.	Les notes viennent de plus loin	4 + 4
3.	Tous ceux qui meurent	2 + 2
4.	Dans le lointain	4
5.	Au même instant	4 (2 + 2)
6.	Tous ceux qui pleurent	2 + 2
7.	Des voix passent comme le vent	3 + 5
8.	On regarde sans rien voir	3 + 4
9.	Devant soi	3
10.	L'air même devient noir	2 + 4
11.	Il n'y a plus qu'une étincelle	4 + 4
12.	Au ciel	2
13.	Une flamme pareille	3 + 3
14.	Et ton regard	4
15.	La lampe et la soirée	2 + 4
16.	Que l'on éteint plus tard	4 + 2

This poem has only three margins, but like 'Descente' it has a clearly bipartite structure. The first part, which runs from lines 1 to 7, and is framed, at 1 and 7, by 3 + 5 octosyllables, concerns the auditory: voices, like music, come through the breathless air from great distances, voices which are a synthesis of the voices of all those dying and lamenting in a particular instant of time. Morbid though they may sound, these are lines of advent, visitation, passage, communication, of rich simultaneity. In the second part, lines 8–16, we shift to the sense of sight, but a sense of sight under threat from encroaching darkness, witnessing the extinction of the last traces of light, re-entering a state akin to non-being. If the first part has a spatial orientation ('sous l'occident', 'de plus loin', 'dans le lointain', 'passent'), the orientation of the second part is temporal ('devient', 'il n'y a plus que', 'plus tard').

Structurally, the first part is relatively straightforward. As already mentioned, it is framed by two 3 + 5 octosyllables rhyming in /ɑ̃/. The lines of the owners of the voices (3 and 6) both fall on the second margin, rhyme in /œR/, and share the same syntax and rhythmic pattern. Originally, it seems, these lines were designed to alternate with a pair of 4 + 4 octosyllables rhyming in /ɛ̃/. But with wonderful appropriacy, 'Au même instant' (l. 5) comes to create a turbulence in the rhythmic air; it abbreviates the partner line for line 2 to the four syllables of 'Dans le lointain', as though distance were being denied, and inserts its own 'completion' of the octosyllable, supplying a third destabilizing rhyme in /ɑ̃/ and aligning itself fittingly on the second margin, so that it not only does act as the bridge between 'Tous ceux qui meurent' and 'Tous ceux qui pleurent', binding their voices together, but also tends towards their 2 + 2 version of the tetrasyllable.

But it is not on this first part that I wish to concentrate, so much as on the second, which is made up of a series of triplets (ll. 8–10, 11–13, 14–16). These triplets are all different kinds of distribution of their common syllabic total, sixteen syllables (i.e. the equivalent of two octosyllables, the underlying 'metric' of the first part); lines 8–10 and 11–13 are each composed of two tetrasyllables, two trisyllables, and one dissyllable; lines 14–16, on the other hand, are made up of three tetrasyllables and two dissyllables—the trisyllable has been removed. What these permutations reveal is a set of measures trying out new roles for themselves, trying to find different ways of living with each other.

The first triplet (ll. 8–10) rhymes in /wa(R)/ and like the others combines two lines of two measures each, with one of one (l. 9). What is noticeable here is that the terminal tetrasyllables have dark colorations, and, as the carriers of the rhyme, force the 'soi' into the admission of blackness, into an acceptance of their final /R/ ('soi' becomes 'soir'). The trisyllable for its part is experienced as a destabilizing factor, as an element of transition between 2 and 4; had line 10 contained a trisyllable, then line 9 might have had some function as fulcrum; as it is, it operates more as an instrument of syllabic disarray. This has its tragic overtones, since the trisyllable is the representative of the interests of the impersonal human presence ('on', 'soi'). Line 10 sees the tetrasyllable consolidating its partnership with the dissyllable.

Lines 11–13 function very differently and an impression of unanimity emerges. As in lines 8–10, the single measure line falls at the centre of the triplet, but here it is genuinely pivotal, having at each side a doubled measure. One might argue, indeed, that the function of the 3s and 4s is purely structural in these lines, not at all expressive; they are called upon simply to make up the syllabic total of sixteen in the most balanced way possible. These are three lines of light holding out against the invasions of the darkness; the tetrasyllables affirm a star, the trisyllables, perhaps carrying forward some of their human connotations, a lamp(?) (see l. 15).

The final triplet takes up the three elements already explored, the 'regard' (ll. 8–10), the lamp (l. 13), and the star ('soirée' referring back to ll. 11–12), and assists at their ultimate extinction. Given what has been said about the 2 + 4 of line 10, it is not surprising that these two measures should preside at the end, that the trisyllable should be ousted. But things are not quite as straightforward as that. Why does not line 15 rhyme? It does not rhyme because the fitting rhyme, already prefigured in line 9, is refused. The rhyme sound of lines 14–16 /aR/ echoes the rhyme of lines 8–10 /wa(R)/, and not surprisingly since, after the last glimmers of light of lines 11–13, the pall of darkness is finally being surrendered to. But the spirit of these last lines is different from the disorderly defeat of lines 8–10. If 'soir' is refused as the rhyme in line 15, it is not merely to prevent a final incursion of the trisyllable, but to redefine the tetrasyllable as benignly protractive, as solicitous—'soirée' is to be distinguished from 'soir' as something with implications of festivity, as something which views evening as 'déroulement', from within, rather than as unit of time, from without, as something which begins with the fading of the light and ends at midnight, rather than as the already dark. This same kind of conversion has taken place in line 14 also. The previous occurrence of 'regarder', at line 8, was both trisyllabic and impersonal; in line 14 it is personalized in 'ton', and its 'extra' syllable, which we might reckon to be the syntactically unnecessary 'Et', provides that smoothness of entry, that lack of hiatus and jolt, which again give the tetrasyllable a smiling, if melancholic, demeanour. And these colourings it carries with it, even when it seems most unequivocally hostile, in line 16; in fact 'Que l'on éteint' has the air of a benediction. As the companion of the tetrasyllable, the dissyllable provides the equally soothing balance of alternating position (2 + 4 / 4 + 2), letting the directness, the peremptoriness, of its notations either melt into, or more gently qualify, the longer measure.

In this poem, in which one of those rare entries of punctual time, of historicity, into Reverdy's poetry is registered in rhythmic perturbation, and in which there is a close correspondence between rhyme formation and the varying ways in which a basic vocabulary of rhythmic measures means, one can see, as indeed one can see in the other Reverdyan poems we have investigated, two related truths. First, and in accordance with his

Cubist principles, the source of meaning in Reverdy's poems is in verbal surface rather than referential depth, is in structural relationships rather than content, is more abstract and conceptual than it is concrete and 'autobiographical'. One of the principal contributors to the structural systematization of meaning is rhythm, that is, rhythm conceived not as the presence of the reading subject in the poem, not as the inscription of voice in the text, but as the text's self-analysing and self-organizing mechanism which we in fact apprehend more as scansion than as rhythm. Reverdy is a free-verse poet of the elementary, non-discursive constituent, the measure, rather than of the line, that translation of linguistic units into language, into voiced discourse. And this leads to the second truth: namely that Reverdy's opaque, elusive, disorientating texts, at least at lexical and syntactic levels, are remarkably transparent and legible at the rhythmic level, and that criticism itself has been incomprehensible in its single-minded neglect of this key which can open, this lamp which can illuminate, Reverdy's 'chambres closes' (1975: 206).

Conclusion

THE underlying conclusion of the foregoing chapters is a rudimentary one: we can only read by continually learning to read, and each new poem challenges us afresh to learn to read it. But in affirming this, we must understand what we mean, in two respects: first, 'learning to read' means flexibly maximizing the resources we already have at our disposal and creating others in response to the instigations of a particular text; it also means recognizing the relativity of reading, recognizing that each reader has a voice, or a voicing, which implies an equally idiosyncratic or idiomatic mode of rhythmic perception. The reader does not actualize a text, but completes it. To return to the Orphist dresses of Sonia Delaunay, we might say that the text is a dress which each wearer wears differently; the dress is the same, but its configuration on the body varies infinitely, even if infinitesimally. And we should remember Robert Delaunay's comment that dress and woman (wearer) are mutually authenticating, and add that this reciprocal authentication is itself wholly dependent on the relativity of the partners and their partnership. The preceding chapters present models of rhythmic analysis, often based on the contemporary visual arts; but they are not intended as models in the sense of exemplary solutions, but rather in the sense of ways of imagining rhythmic activity.

In our first chapter we indicated the way in which generative metrics has been instrumental in removing rhythm from consciousness, by subsuming it within metre. This is something more than a cosmetic move, in that the generative proposal of a set of rules which can predict all possible manifestations of a certain metre, that is, a set of rules which apparently governs all verse instances, effectively pre-empts any discoveries that the process of reading might make. But, in many senses, reading, and 'reading the rhythm' in particular, is the only way that the poem can be invested and informed by a subjectivity. And I do not use the term 'informed' lightly, since in our experience of free verse at least, the rhythmic choices available to the reader are varied enough to warrant the claim that the reader bestows structure on the poem. What we find in generative theory is a metric which is almost exclusively stress-related— when it interests itself in juncture it is to refine the rules of stress—and in which the potential expressivity of stress must yield to a linguistic determination. In effect, much of generative metrics is not about reading at all.

Generative metrics invites us, and for good reason, to be interested in the degrees of complexity possible in a given metre, which will allow us to go on to further stylistic taxonomies of that metre. But our initial encounter with a poem is not an encounter with a specimen, species, or data-source. What the generativists do not do is assess the complexity that a reader is confronted with even in the least controversial example of a metre, the complexity of the act of self-relation, since the reader is at stake as much as the poem he is reading. Generative metrics may teach us what kind of conclusions to draw (i.e. how to rationalize its own arbitrariness—why do we need rules rather than our own ears to judge what is metrically acceptable, and I mean 'judge' and not 'describe', since, as we have already intimated, generative rules often permit versions of a metre which are unknown and unimaginable in reality?); but it does not teach us how to read. And a fundamental prerequisite of any prosodic theory must be that it contributes to the perceptivity of the reader; a prosodic description is important more for what it can tell us of the expressive resources of a rhythmic structure than for merely measuring degrees of conformity or deviation. Every new poem requires some adjustment of expectations, or of the habits we read by, or of rhythmic focus. Unfortunately we are usually too lazy to make the adjustment, and metrical theories, in their devotion to the unitary and categorical, only endorse that laziness.

If generative metrics is hostile to reading, if only by omission, so too, ironically, is the prestige enjoyed by ambiguity and polysemy. Instead of taking the wealth of connotations, structural equivocations, allusions, as read, as the *ground* of reading, as the inevitable concomitant of all verse structure, we feel bound to foreground them. In doing so, we outlaw choice. The poem must remain suspended in the amber of its own potentiality, of its own textuality. This is perhaps all very well if we wish to locate virtue in the text, and in a selection of particular texts; it then becomes sufficient to find out which texts are the chosen ones and to commune with them, and thus a canonizing criticism is born. Such an approach has, for the reader, two drawbacks. First, it limits his role to establishing the text. No text can exist until it has been read; reading is thus merely a process by which the text is brought into existence. Having read it through, we are free to decode, admire, itemize, its linguistic constituents. Clearly this divorce of language from reading runs the risk, as a creed at least, of alienating us from our products. The danger is that we do an injustice not to the text, but to the reader, since, conversely, it is the text which brings the reader into existence as a reader. Proust's observations have lost none of their relevance:

En réalité, chaque lecteur est, quand il lit, le propre lecteur de soi-même. L'ouvrage de l'écrivain n'est qu'une espèce d'instrument optique qu'il offre au lecteur afin de lui permettre de discerner ce que, sans ce livre, il n'eût peut-être pas vu soi-même. (1954: iii. 911)

Reading, indeed, is a process of self-interrogation, whereby the question 'What mode of reading makes this text work most convincingly for me?' involves or implies the question 'What kind of reader am I and what form of self-expression is reading, for me?' But Proust's remarks need to be filled out with the corollary of the second sentence of this quotation: the reader is a kind of optical instrument, a perceptual configuration, by which a text can come to an understanding of itself, of its function.

Secondly, the critical perceptions of ambiguity and polysemy that justify the textualization of text are themselves text-based; in other words, ambiguity and polysemy are treated as essentially semantic by nature and lexical by location. The danger of reading a text, in the sense of realizing the text in the voice rather than 'reading it through', consequent on such a view, is that reading enjoins choice and choice 'flattens' the text out into a single dimension. For his part, the reader feels denied by the text. In fact, however, the reading of a text relocates ambiguity and polysemy. The question/observation 'What does this mean?'/'This means many things' becomes not 'How should I say it (to myself) if I am to maintain its plurisignificance?' but 'How do I express, in reading, the ambiguities this text awakens *in me*?' In making rhythmic choices, in learning to read the text, the reader tests his responses and tries to find those mechanisms, those principles of organization, which bring the text into closest synchrony with his own metabolism, and vice versa. The ambiguity of the text expands from its purely lexical location to embrace the multiple impulses of the responsive subjectivity. Reading is as much like smoking a cigar (Mallarmé's 'Toute l'âme résumée') as it is like wearing a dress.

To say that each reader wears the text differently is not merely to say that each reader performs the text differently in the unmonitored area of paralanguage, with different paralinguistic decoration, as though the essential linguistic data were reliable, ascertainable, and unchanged by incidental improvisations. We do not improvise reading alone, we improvise texts, and simply for this reason: linguistic data could only be reliable if the text were completely comprehensible (whatever that means); but since, by definition, verse texts are never comprehensible—because structural and linguistic input is so multiform—so their linguistic data can never be verified beyond a doubt. It would be wrong, however, to propose that the paralinguistic should therefore be unconditionally admitted. For one thing, we have few accessible methods of measuring it, of coping with its diversity and variability. But we should at least enunciate, emphatically, this principle: the more that the process of reading is admitted as itself the source of both linguistic and paralinguistic features, the more resources of analysis and measurement the reader will have at his disposal. Put negatively, the dissociation of analysis from reading to be found in the linguistic approach to text of structuralists and generativists alike tends to produce an unjustifiably exclusive view of what constitutes rhythmic analysis. This lack of justification is made particularly evident by the existence of free verse. What the history of prosodic analysis has seen is the evolution of *metrical* theory as an account of rhythm, and, within the parameters of a metrical account, the privileging of certain features, such as stress or syllable, to the virtual exclusion of others. If we accept the reading process as a highly relativized one, we shall also accept that no prosodic analysis can lay claim to a stable hierarchy of values.

It will be clear that the rhythmic analyses undertaken in this book set themselves, ideologically at least, against a distributional approach that treats the poem as a static construction, whose patterns can best be retrieved in a spatial dimension, against an approach which implies that the poem manifests itself not in its 'being-read' but in its 'having-been-read'. I say 'ideologically at least' because criticism has yet to find a way of presenting language as a dynamic of changing relationships. The very discourse of criticism is bound into that spatialized, retrospective kind of reading which produces an idealized image of the poem (as something functioning consistently and equally on a number of perfectly reconciled and interrelated levels—phonic, morphological, syntactic, rhythmic, etc.). We may have to operate with the method, but this does not necessitate a compliance with its implications. A relativized process is inevitably a dynamic one, and the conventions of literary criticism compel us to recuperate the text in highly inauthentic ways; the more so in the case of free verse, which guarantees no retrievable metrical deep structure, which exists, on the contrary, to deny a metrical retrievability, and whose performative nature is inscribed in its very typography.

But my ideology is also determined by historical pressures, inasmuch as free verse is a historical product and itself proposes a shift in our ways of envisaging the nature and function of rhythm. Free verse is more an assault on the hegemony of metrical thinking than it is on regular verse. But it helps less to regard it as free by virtue of its anti-metricality than by virtue of the choices about metricity and rhythmicity it makes available to its readers. It has been my contention that, with each new poem, free verse offers a renegotiation of terms and a re-evaluation of factors and features to be taken into account. For this reason, one of the immediate tasks of the verse-analyst is to uncover, for the general benefit, those structures which might, in one reading or another, accede to the status of presiding rhythmic principle. Our experience in the preceding chapters has shown that, in many cases, the poem will situate itself within the parameters of the verse-types—free verse of the measure, free verse of the line, cadence-accentual free verse—I explored in *Vers Libre* (1990). But, even so, the ways in which these verse-types may be qualified or supplemented are innumerable, and these qualifying or supplementary factors need not be linguistic in origin, but rather originate in the mental set of the reader, in a certain perception of the poem's expressive landscape.

Before proceeding to a summary of the rhythmic 'qualifiers' and 'supplements' we have encountered in the course of our enquiries, I would mention one other sense in which the account of verse analysis proposed here is historically constrained. One of the curious features of the early development of French free verse is the speed with which it was, in some respects, superseded. In fact, we would have to say that free verse's validity remained unproblematic only between its emergence in 1886 and 1914. Free verse had already begun to feel Marinetti's derision in 1913, the year in which Apollinaire began publishing the poems to be collected in *Calligrammes* (1918), poems which, as we have seen, he described as an 'idéalisation' of free verse at a time 'où la typographie termine brillamment sa carrière'. Parallel with, and closely related to, the development of Marinetti's 'words-in-freedom' and Apollinaire's calligrams, there occurred a change in the nature of the image, and in its function within, and effect on, poetic discourse; this change was, in its turn, connected with the mechanization of movement and the reduction of secondary rhythms to primary ones. We have only investigated this constellation of shifts in a sketchy fashion; it deserves a thorough history. But even though free verse happily survived, it had been knocked off course, in the sense that its original *raison d'être*, the expression of an inimitable self caught in all its variability and elusive relativity:

Chaque homme est selon son moment dans le temps, son milieu de race et de condition sociale, son moment d'évolution individuelle, un certain clavier sur lequel le monde extérieur joue d'une certaine façon. Mon clavier est perpétuellement changeant et il n'y en a pas un autre identique au mien. Tous les claviers sont légitimes (Laforgue 1903: 141)

had to make way for kinds of writing which were neither voice-derived nor voice-intended nor voiceable. This theft of voice from text, this eruption of the non-discursive into discourse, was effected by the 'new' image, and by the incursions of the mechanical and the visual. Rhythm consequently found itself registering not only all the modulations of restless subjectivity, all the psychophysiological motions of the poetic persona, but also the intrusions of machine-sound and language dislocated from utterance. It is fitting that the above quotation from Laforgue appears in his essay on Impressionism, for it was with Impressionism perhaps that the first signs of this schism appeared; the Impressionist canvas, particularly as represented by Caillebotte and Degas, both parades the subjectivity of its view and at the same time threatens to oust the spectator, by a series of obstructive devices (close-up, spectators with a better view within the picture, diagonal composition, spatial ambiguity, obstacles to vision, etc.).

But both by virtue of its in-built appetite for change and endless permutation, and by virtue of the condition of harassment through which it survives, free verse has never tired of multiplying rhythmic resources and diversifying their combinations. In the course of the preceding chapters, we have begun to uncover some of these resources, and it is with a summary of these that I would like to conclude.

SUMMARY OF FINDINGS

1. The stanza/strophe as the metrical/rhythmic field. This ensures some developmental, dynamic perspective on rhythm and draws rhythmic description out of its normal confinement to the single line. It also allows a fuller view of the translinear acoustic and syntactic influences on rhythmic arrangement. This approach might usefully be applied to regular verse, in order to discover what is *sui generis* about the apparently standard metricity of a particular poem.

2. The rhythm of junctures or boundaries. Where rhythm unfolds over longer verse-spans, as in the *verset*, and thus tends to lose contour, the reader may refocus rhythmic awareness at junctures or boundaries, indeed may perceive a rhythm *of* junctures. The interpretative freedom of the reader is exercised in decisions not only about the nature of the

boundary (we suggested three types: ˥, ⌒, and –), but also about where they fall (Perse).

3. Concomitantly with the above, the treatment of the *e atone* may become more rhythmically decisive, as a free resource available to the reader in any of its guises, both line-internally and line-terminally (Perse).

4. Combining (1) and (2) above, we may arrive at a rhythmic principle whereby junctures 'organize' the contextual acoustic landscape. In other words, recurrent phonemes are either foregrounded or recessed according to their position relative to the major accents associated with junctures. A rhythm of phonemes results (Perse).

5. Measures as amplifications and contractions of a chosen 'core' measure. This develops the notion of a free verse sustained by a recurrent *constante rythmique*. The *constante rythmique* is now no longer an intermittent rhythmic *point de repère*, but rather an informing and consistent presence against which all other measures are measured, as rhythmic expansions or contractions (Perse).

6. Variation on above. The selection of a sustaining 'core' measure with which other measures are roughly equalized (made isochronous), largely by paralinguistic means, and notably by changes of tempo, drawling or slurring, pausing, silent syllables, and even silent accents (Perse).

7. In cadence-accentual free verse the sense-accent (primary or nuclear accent) need not coincide with the tonic accent. Degrees of accent can be more freely redistributed, and this produces the possibility of rhythmic 'distortions', Futurist and Expressionist perception, a direct contact with psychic response (Cendrars).

8. Rhythmic structure may have a thematic function. In the *Prose du Transsibérien*, biphrasality is associated with the train as locomotive and triphrasality with the train as journey into consciousness (Cendrars).

9. Length of line may be structurally significant. Many of Cendrars's stanzas gravitate around a long line, a *palier* line, whose position in the stanza may also be of structural significance (Cendrars).

10. Free verse allows the intrusion of machine-rhythms, the reduction of secondary rhythm to primary rhythm. This has the effect of transforming language from the symbolic into the imitative, of desemanticizing it (Cendrars).

11. Similar consequences for rhythm attend the intrusions of the visual, unless the visual itself is a source of expressive rhythmicity (Apollinaire).

12. The calligram conjoins the verbal and visual to the degree that it polarizes them. But this polarization is something more than a polarization of the spoken and the written, for the visual may as much be the

source of paralinguistic information as that which makes language un-speakable (Apollinaire).

13. Rhythm in free verse is meaning not in the sense of signification but in the sense of illocutionary act (Apollinaire).

14. At the limit of the textual disaggregation which takes place in the calligram is the textual constellation in which language can be multiply reconstructed by the new reading rhythms of the eye. No longer bound to a left-to-right, top-to-bottom itinerary, the reading eye can move in any direction and in any spatial plane (Apollinaire).

15. Free verse is able to occupy the prosodically infra-red and the prosodically ultraviolet. The ultraviolet (long line) polarizes intensive and extensive readings, the rhythmically purposeful and the rhythmically inchoate. The infra-red (monolexical short line) polarizes the written and the spoken, the unuttered item and the exclamation, the accusative and the vocative (Cendrars).

16. There is another sense in which the monolexical short line is a special case: it is necessarily an image, situated between notation and hallucination. Rhythm becomes an autonomous, mediating, or catalytic agent, which negotiates between a vocal impulse and a word coming to meet that impulse, between inward and outward (Cendrars).

17. Voiced rhythm and unvoiced rhythm can constitute different kinds of rhythmicity in the same poem. In this sense, there can, in free verse, be a rhythm not only of different rhythms but also of different concep-tions or perceptions of rhythm (Cendrars).

18. The free-verse line is elastic not merely because of its overall rhythmic ambiguity, but because of its increasing rhythmic ambiguation. The further we read into a free-verse line the less sure we can be of its rhythmic constitution. But there are compensations: the reader has cor-respondingly more freedom of choice, more opportunity to consult his interpretational interests, the further he reads (Cendrars).

19. Rhythm in free verse, by virtue of its flexibility, can mediate be-tween first-person response and third-person typicality, between the 'de-cisive moment' of a vision of coherence and the temporally undifferentiated, between alertness to the specific and generalization, between the punctual and the omnitemporal (Cendrars).

20. Rhythmic elasticity produces a vulnerability in the signifier which is tantamount to a surrender to the reader. Free verse is given power to project its signifieds only by the intercession of the reader, for without the reader, and in a very real sense, rhythm does not exist (Cendrars).

21. Rhythmic *brouillage* (scrambling/scumbling) created by measures

or larger units of numerically consecutive numbers of syllables. This involves a destabilization of rhythmic 'horizons', so that the reader almost imperceptibly shifts rhythmic ground. Here, rhythm operates as a series of perceptual displacements (of which rhyme is another instrument) (Supervielle).

22. Ironically, the above depends on a heightened, if troubled, syllabic awareness, and this in turn re-establishes the caesura as a structural and rhythmic crux, not only in terms of the treatment of the *e atone* (*césure épique*), but more especially in the way it increases tensions between the measures on either side of the caesura (Supervielle).

23. Rhythmic *brouillage* may also have the effect of promoting syntactical, lexical, and semantic features as rhythmic determinants. If rhythmic distinctions cease to work at the syllabic level, or become approximate, because of the near-equality of measures, then the relative and comparative weight of measures will be determined by other criteria, syntactical, lexical, or semantic (Supervielle).

24. Analytic rhythmicity, or rhythm as scansion. Rhythm as a purely written phenomenon, destroying rather than creating vocal illusionism and the atmospheric envelope of reading. Rhythm as non-temporal (Reverdy).

25. Rhythm as one element, along with margins, syntax, acousticity, and typography, designed to create a system of competing structurations within the poem, a series of overlapping planes. In other words, rhythm does not create cohesion or coherence within the text, but rather adds to its imbrications (Reverdy).

26. Typography working in conjunction with standard scansion to produce a rhythm of grammatical categories (Reverdy).

27. The use of variable margins and/or rhyme to diversify the impact of measures apparently identical with each other. The interlinear connections created by multiple margin and (non-systematic) rhyme can help recurrent rhythmic measures to vary their tonality or modality (Reverdy).

Appendix I
Glossary of Technical Terms

acatalectic Line of verse in which there are no unfilled metrical positions, no implied beats or off-beats, no missing syllables or feet, in short, a line without catalexis (q.v.).

accent d'impulsion The way the voice inhabits and projects rhythm, colours accent, and bestows a dynamic on rhythmic measures. The *accent d'impulsion* is the expressive and psychophysiological dimension of the *accent tonique* (q.v.), turning the tonic accent into a speech-act, a linguistic function.

accent d'intensité This term has two meanings: (1) it may refer to an *accent tonique* (q.v.) whose principal characteristic is its strength (stress) as opposed to its duration or pitch; (2) it may refer to an accent allocated to a non-tonic syllable for expressive or rhetorical purposes; in this sense it is synonymous with the *accent oratoire* (sense (2)) (q.v.).

accent oratoire This term also has two meanings: (1) in the theoretical texts of de Souza and Mockel it is synonymous with Kahn's *accent d'impulsion* (q.v.); (2) in modern prosodic parlance, it is an accent allocated to a non-tonic syllable for expressive or rhetorical purposes; its point of impact is the consonant(s) before the vowel, but it reverberates through the vowel to produce a properly syllabic accent, e.g.:

> Contemple-les, mon âme; ils sont *vrai*ment affreux!
>
> (Baudelaire, 'Les Aveugles')

It should be emphasized that this kind of *accent oratoire* is not an *accent tonique* (q.v.), not part of the rhythmic/metrical structure of the line; it is a paralinguistic, recitational accent. The tonic accents in the line quoted create a 4 + 2 + 4 + 2 rhythmic configuration.

accent tonique (tonic accent) The accent which falls on the last accentuable syllable of the word or word-group and thus creates the rhythmic measure. This is a properly linguistic accent; it inheres in, and organizes, linguistic structure, and is not supplied, on an occasional basis, by the expressive impulses of the reader (cf. *accent oratoire*, sense (2)).

alexandrine The 'national' French line (enjoying the same prestige as the iambic pentameter in English verse), twelve syllables long, with, in its regular form, a fixed medial caesura (q.v.). It may have as few as two accents (on syllables 6 and 12), but usually has four. The classical proportions and rhythmic equilibrium of the regular alexandrine were undermined in the nineteenth century by the development of the *trimètre* (q.v.), and by an increasing incidence of enjambement, both at the caesura and at the line-ending.

alexandrin trimètre *see trimètre*

allongement The scansional device whereby one syllable is made the equivalent of two by doubling its duration (scansional mark: an exclamation after the newly increased measure). Thus what at first sight might look like, say, a trisyllabic measure may be scanned and enunciated as 4!.

anacrusis Extrametrical syllable or syllables, occurring before the metre proper is under way and acting as an upbeat. In Anglo-German versification, anacrusis always involves line-initial unstressed syllables.

apocope (cf. syncope (q.v.)) The non-pronunciation (metrical deletion) of an unelided, word-terminal *e atone* (q.v.), e.g. 'un(e) blanch(e) main': /yn blɑ̃ʃ mɛ̃/. Apocope should not be confused with the standard elision of a word-terminal *e atone* before a following vowel or mute 'h'.

ballade Old French fixed form, dominant in the fourteenth and fifteenth centuries, in which the number of lines in the stanza usually corresponds with the number of syllables in the line. The most common type of ballade is made up of three eight-line octosyllabic stanzas rhyming *ababbcbC* and a four-line *envoi* (address to patron or to subject of poem) rhyming *bcbC*. As the capital letter indicates, the last line of the first stanza serves as a refrain. The decasyllabic ballade is usually composed of three ten-line stanzas (*ababbccdcD*), with a five-line *envoi* (*ccdcD*).

caesura The major metrical/rhythmic juncture within lines of nine syllables or more, which usually, but not necessarily, coincides with a significant syntactical juncture. In the regular alexandrine (q.v.) the caesura is medial and fixed (at the sixth syllable), and thus a metrical feature of the line. In other lines (hendecasyllable, decasyllable, enneasyllable) the position of the caesura is determined by the particular verse-context and achieves metrical status only by virtue of its regular recurrence at that position.

catalexis In Anglo-German usage catalexis usually refers to the omission, at the end of a line, of one or more unstressed syllables (particularly in trochaic and dactylic metres). In more extreme instances (e.g. irregular ode) catalexis may involve the omission of whole feet. The reader is reckoned to compensate for these shortfalls by pausing, silent beat, silent stress, or other mental events.

césure enjambante (cf. *coupe enjambante* (q.v.)) This occurs when a word 'straddles' the caesural *coupe* (q.v.), that is, when an accentuated syllable at the caesura (q.v.) is immediately followed by an unelided *e atone* (q.v.); the accentuated syllable belongs in the first hemistich (q.v.), the *e atone* in the second. The *césure enjambante* is a rare phenomenon:

Le silen: | ce, les clo: | | ches, le silence | encore

(Séverin, 'Le Rêve du voyage')

césure épique In modern prosody an unelided *e atone* (q.v.) falling immediately after the accentuated syllable at the caesura (q.v.) may be treated in the same

Appendix I

way as a line-terminal *e atone*, i.e. as extrametrical, not counted as a syllable in the scansion of the line. This is called a *césure épique*, because it was standard practice in medieval epics, the *chansons de geste*.

cheville A word or phrase (interjection, discourse filler, pleonasm) called upon, not for any semantic or expressive reason, but merely to satisfy a metrical demand, whether it be to fill out the required number of syllables in a line, or to extricate the poet from a rhyming problem.

clausule The closing line of a stanza, or closing measure of a line, or the final clause/phrase of an oratorical period.

constante rythmique A measure which recurs with sufficient frequency within a passage of verse to constitute a rhythmic leitmotiv, a structuring principle. The term was coined by Duhamel and Vildrac (1910).

coupe The 'bar-line' which usually falls immediately after an accentuated syllable and divides one measure from the next:

Ainsi, | toujours poussés | vers de nouveaux | rivages   2 + 4 + 4 + 2

(Lamartine, 'Le Lac')

The *coupe* is a purely scansional device, an aid to prosodic description, and has no bearing on the enunciation of the line, other than in the cases of the *coupe enjambante* (q.v.) and the *coupe lyrique* (q.v.). The caesura (q.v.) is a *coupe*, and something more: a crucial metrical articulation which combines measures into larger units (hemistichs (q.v.)), and acts as a fulcrum about which the semantic energies of the line play.

coupe enjambante When an accentuated syllable is immediately followed by an unelided *e atone* (q.v.), it is usual to place the *coupe* (q.v.) after the accentuated syllable, so that the word 'straddles' the *coupe* and so that the *e atone* is counted as the first syllable of the measure following:

J'ai: | me de vos longs yeux | | la lumiè: | re verdâtre   1 + 5 + 3 + 3

(Baudelaire, 'Chant d'automne')

This is the *coupe enjambante*. But, for expressive or syntactic reasons, it may be desirable or necessary to place the *coupe* after the *e atone*, so that the *e atone* is included in the measure of the accentuated syllable, rather than initiating the measure following. This is the *coupe lyrique*, which is indicated by an apostrophe in the tabulation of measures:

Mais parle: | de son sort | qui t'a rendu | l'arbitre?   3′ + 3 + 4 + 2

(Racine, *Andromaque*, v. iii)

coupe lyrique see coupe enjambante

diaeresis (cf. synaeresis (q.v.)) The pronunciation of two contiguous vowels as two distinct syllables (separation of the elements of a diphthong): e.g. suicide (/syisid/); diamant (/diamã/).

dipode A compound 'foot' made up of a pair of feet in which one stress is primary (thesis) and the other is secondary (arsis). A sequence of dipodes will, therefore, create a rhythm not only of alternating strong and weak syllables, but also of alternating stronger and weaker stresses. When thesis precedes arsis, then the dipode is 'falling'; when the arsis is following by the thesis, then the dipode is 'rising'.

e atone A more appropriate term for the so-called 'e mute', since in verse—and in regular verse particularly—an unelided 'e' is by no means mute; *atone* (atonic) reminds us that the 'e' (/ə/) cannot be accentuated under any circumstances, whereas other word-terminal syllables will be either accentuated (tonic) or not (non-tonic) depending on the specific verse-context. Word-terminal 'e' is elided (neither counted nor pronounced) when it is followed by a vowel or mute 'h'; it is not elided (both counted in the scansion and articulated to a greater or lesser degree) when it is followed by a consonant or aspirate 'h'. In regular verse an *e atone* at the end of the line is not counted in the scansion, though it may attract some articulation in reading; it serves principally to identify the rhyme as feminine.

emboîtage (cf. *remontage* (q.v.)) The process whereby two or more metrical entities are combined, often with some overlap, to form a single longer line.

hemistich Each of the pair of half-lines created by a caesura (q.v.). Although the very definition 'half-line' naturally associates the hemistich with a medial caesura (as in the regular alexandrine (q.v.)), it is also frequently used where the 'half'-lines are unequal, as, for example, in a 4 ‖ 6 decasyllable.

iambe Satiric poem of variable length in *rimes croisées* (q.v.), in which alexandrines (q.v.) alternate with octosyllables throughout. Cultivated particularly by André Chénier and, in the nineteenth century, by Auguste Barbier.

incise An interpolated phrase or clause, usually of a parenthetical or incidental nature.

isochronous The principle whereby the recurrent units in a metrical/rhythmic pattern (syllables, feet, measures, lines) are deemed to be of equal duration. If such units are ostensibly unequal, certain compensatory mechanisms (pause, increased accentuation, silent time-marking, etc.) may be activated to restore isochronicity to the sequence.

isosyllabic The metrical principle whereby poems are constructed of lines each with the same number of syllables. If a poem consists of a sequence of heterosyllabic stanzas, then the same syllabic structure must be exactly repeated in each stanza.

isotopie Term coined by Greimas to describe the semantic field or thematic reference created by a set of semantic components.

palier Coinage to describe a long line which, occurring in a context of predominantly shorter lines, acts as breathing space, a relaxation of tension, an opportunity to re-establish developed discourse and rhythmic continuity and coherence.

remontage   If *démontage* is the process whereby a larger rhythmic unit is sub-divided and presented as separate, smaller ones (e.g. a decasyllable presented as a tetrasyllabic line followed by a hexasyllabic one, or as two pentasyllabic lines), then *remontage* is the reconstruction of the 'original' larger unit out of the smaller ones.

rimes croisées   Alternating rhyme: *abab*.

rimes embrassées   Enclosed rhyme: *abba*.

rimes plates   Couplets: *aabbcc* etc.

rime suffisante   In the French system of differing degrees of rhyme, *rime suffisante* is produced by the homophony of two phonemes in the rhyme (i.e. tonic vowel + one consonant, preceding or succeeding the tonic vowel: 'père'/'frère', 'assauts'/'vermisseaux'). *Rime suffisante* is thus stronger than *rime pauvre* (homophony of one phoneme, the tonic vowel: 'bonté'/'aimé'), but weaker than *rime riche* (homophony of three or more phonemes, tonic vowel + two or more consonants: 'marche'/'arche', 'rêve'/'trêve').

synaeresis (cf. diaeresis (q.v.))   The pronunciation as one syllable (diphthong) of two contiguous vowels; that is, one of the vowels—usually the first—is treated in pronunciation as a semi-consonant, e.g. 'lumière' (/lymjɛr/); 'nuit' (nɥi).

syncope (cf. apocope (q.v.))   The non-pronunciation (metrical deletion) of a word-internal *e atone* (q.v.): 'vêtements' (/vɛtmã/).

temps de lecture or *temps de la lecture*   Time necessary for reading the text, or time taken to read the text, or the reader's experience of time while reading.

temps de récit or *temps du récit* or *temps de la narration* or *temps racontant* or *temps de l'écriture*   The time of telling, the time that belongs to the process of narrating rather than to what is narrated, textual time.

temps d'histoire or *temps de l'histoire*   Recounted or represented time, the time of the story, of the events narrated.

terza rima   An Italian verse-form (Dante uses it in his *Divina Commedia*), quickly adopted by other European poets, it consists of interlinked tercets in which the second line of each tercet rhymes with the first and third lines of the one following: *aba bcb cdc*, etc. The sequence of tercets formed in this way may be of any length, and is brought to an end by a single final line which rhymes with the second line of the tercet preceding it: *yzy z*.

trimètre   A line of three measures and, more especially, the three-measure alexandrine (q.v.) popularized by Hugo and the Romantic poets. The (*alexandrin*) *trimètre* disregards the sanctity of the medial caesura (q.v.) and the four-measure structure it usually begets (*tétramètre*) and, instead, produces a central syntactical group which straddles the caesura, deaccentuates the sixth syllable, and creates rhythmic configurations such as $4 + 4 + 4$, $3 + 5 + 4$, $4 + 5 + 3$.

verset   A verse-line of the late nineteenth and twentieth centuries, deriving from the short numbered paragraphs ('verses') of the Bible and from similar paragraphs in other sacred books. It is the most elastic of rhythmic units, ranging in length from just one syllable to seventy syllables or more. It owes its rhythmic cohesion to a variety of possible sources: to patterns of parallelism and repetition, to the combination of familiar metrical entities, to the ordered variation of respiratory spans, to a recurrent number of accents per *verset*, to the rhythm of its boundaries (junctures), or to a blend of these elements.

vers libéré   A 'liberated' form of regular verse, which came into its own in the latter half of the nineteenth century. *Vers libéré* makes free with the rules of rhyme, and destabilizes the line's rhythmic structure by exploiting the asymmetries of the *trimètre* (q.v.), the equivocations of the *impair*, and the disarticulations of enjambement. But, for all its liberties, *vers libéré* maintains the principle of isosyllabism (q.v.) and the indispensability of rhyme.

vers mêlés   Also called *vers libres classiques* and *vers irréguliers*. A kind of verse current in minor or hybrid genres (verse-epistle, fable, madrigal, idyll, epigram) of the seventeenth and eighteenth centuries, in which lines of different length, though regular in their internal construction, are irregularly and unpredictably combined. Isosyllabism (q.v.) gives way to heterosyllabism, and a single, repeated rhyme-scheme is replaced by a free-rhyming structure, still subject, however, to the rule of alternating masculine and feminine rhyme-pairs.

Appendix II

Full Texts of Poems Analysed

1. Saint-John Perse, Éloges (Chapter 2)

(a) Écrit sur la porte

J'ai une peau couleur de tabac rouge ou de mulet,
J'ai un chapeau en moelle de sureau couvert de toile blanche.
Mon orgueil est que ma fille soit très-belle quand elle commande aux
femmes noires,
    ma joie, qu'elle découvre un bras très-blanc parmi ses poules noires;
    et qu'elle n'ait point honte de ma joue rude sous le poil, quand je   5
rentre boueux.

Et d'abord je lui donne mon fouet, ma gourde et mon chapeau.
En souriant elle m'acquitte de ma face ruisselante; et porte à son
visage mes mains grasses d'avoir
éprouvé l'amande de kako, la graine de café.
Et puis elle m'apporte un mouchoir de tête bruissant; et ma robe de
laine; de l'eau pure pour rincer mes dents de silencieux:
    et l'eau de ma cuvette est là; et j'entends l'eau du bassin dans la   10
case-à-eau.

Un homme est dur, sa fille est douce. Qu'elle se tienne toujours
à son retour sur la plus haute marche de la maison blanche,
et faisant grâce à son cheval de l'étreinte des genoux,
il oubliera la fièvre qui tire toute la peau du visage en dedans.

J'aime encore mes chiens, l'appel de mon plus fin cheval,   15
et voir au bout de l'allée droite mon chat sortir de la maison en
compagnie de la guenon . . .
    toutes choses suffisantes pour n'envier pas les voiles des voiliers
    que j'aperçois à la hauteur du toit de tôle sur la mer comme un ciel.

(b) Pour fêter une enfance I

Palmes . . . !
Alors on te baignait dans l'eau-de-feuilles-vertes; et l'eau encore était
du soleil vert; et les servantes de ta mère, grandes filles luisantes,
remuaient leurs jambes chaudes près de toi qui tremblais . . .

(Je parle d'une haute condition, alors, entre les robes, au règne de
tournantes clartés.)
   Palmes! et la douceur
   d'une vieillesse des racines . . . ! La terre   5
alors souhaita d'être plus sourde, et le ciel plus profond où des
arbres trop grands, las d'un obscur dessein, nouaient un pacte
inextricable . . .
   (J'ai fait ce songe, dans l'estime: un sûr séjour entre les toiles
enthousiastes.)

   Et les hautes
   racines courbes célébraient
   l'en allée des voies prodigieuses, l'invention des voûtes et des nefs,   10
   et la lumière alors, en de plus purs exploits féconde, inaugurait le
blanc royaume où j'ai mené peut-être un corps sans ombre . . .
   (Je parle d'une haute condition, jadis, entre des hommes et leurs
filles, et qui mâchaient de telle feuille.)
   Alors, les hommes avaient
   une bouche plus grave, les femmes avaient des bras plus lents;
   alors, de se nourrir comme nous de racines, de grandes bêtes   15
taciturnes s'ennoblissaient;
   et plus longues sur plus d'ombre se levaient les paupières . . .
   (J'ai fait ce songe, il nous a consumés sans reliques.)

   2. *Blaise Cendrars*, Prose du Transsibérien et de la petite Jeanne de France
                              (Chapter 3)

En ce temps-là j'étais en mon adolescence
J'avais à peine seize ans et je ne me souvenais déjà plus de mon
      enfance
J'étais à 16.000 lieues du lieu de ma naissance
J'étais à Moscou, dans la ville des mille et trois clochers et des sept
      gares
Et je n'avais pas assez des sept gares et des mille et trois tours   5
Car mon adolescence était si ardente et si folle
Que mon cœur, tour à tour, brûlait comme le temple d'Éphèse ou
      comme la Place Rouge de Moscou
Quand le soleil se couche.
Et mes yeux éclairaient des voies anciennes.
Et j'étais déjà si mauvais poète   10
Que je ne savais pas aller jusqu'au bout.

Le Kremlin était comme un immense gâteau tartare
Croustillé d'or,

Avec les grandes amandes des cathédrales toutes blanches
Et l'or mielleux des cloches . . .   15
Un vieux moine me lisait la légende de Novgorode
J'avais soif
Et je déchiffrais des caractères cunéiformes
Puis, tout à coup, les pigeons du Saint-Esprit s'envolaient sur la
    place
Et mes mains s'envolaient aussi, avec des bruissements d'albatros   20
Et ceci, c'était les dernières réminiscences du dernier jour
Du tout dernier voyage
Et de la mer.

Pourtant, j'étais fort mauvais poète.
Je ne savais pas aller jusqu'au bout.   25
J'avais faim
Et tous les jours et toutes les femmes dans les cafés et tous les verres
J'aurais voulu les boire et les casser
Et toutes les vitrines et toutes les rues
Et toutes les maisons et toutes les vies   30
Et toutes les roues des fiacres qui tournaient en tourbillon sur les
    mauvais pavés
J'aurais voulu les plonger dans une fournaise de glaives
Et j'aurais voulu broyer tous les os
Et arracher toutes les langues
Et liquéfier tous ces grands corps étranges et nus sous les   35
    vêtements qui m'affolent . . .
Je pressentais la venue du grand Christ rouge de la révolution russe . . .
Et le soleil était une mauvaise plaie
Qui s'ouvrait comme un brasier.

En ce temps-là j'étais en mon adolescence
J'avais à peine seize ans et je ne me souvenais déjà plus de ma   40
    naissance
J'étais à Moscou, où je voulais me nourrir de flammes
Et je n'avais pas assez des tours et des gares que constellaient mes
    yeux
En Sibérie tonnait le canon, c'était la guerre
La faim le froid la peste le choléra
Et les eaux limoneuses de l'Amour charriaient des millions de   45
    charognes
Dans toutes les gares je voyais partir tous les derniers trains
Personne ne pouvait plus partir car on ne délivrait plus de billets
Et les soldats qui s'en allaient auraient bien voulu rester . . .
Un vieux moine me chantait la légende de Novgorode.

Moi, le mauvais poète qui ne voulais aller nulle part, je pouvais aller   50
    partout
Et aussi les marchands avaient encore assez d'argent
Pour aller tenter faire fortune.
Leur train partait tous les vendredis matin.
On disait qu'il y avait beaucoup de morts.
L'un emportait cent caisses de réveils et de coucous de la Forêt-Noire   55
Un autre, des boîtes à chapeaux, des cylindres et un assortiment de
    tire-bouchons de Sheffield
Un autre, des cercueils de Malmoë remplis de boîtes de conserve et
    de sardines à l'huile
Puis il y avait beaucoup de femmes
Des femmes des entre-jambes à louer qui pouvaient aussi servir
Des cercueils   60
Elles étaient toutes patentées
On disait qu'il y avait beaucoup de morts là-bas
Elles voyageaient à prix réduits
Et avaient toutes un compte-courant à la banque.

Or, un vendredi matin, ce fut enfin mon tour   65
On était en décembre
Et je partis moi aussi pour accompagner le voyageur en bijouterie qui
    se rendait à Kharbine
Nous avions deux coupés dans l'express et 34 coffres de joaillerie de
    Pforzheim
De la camelote allemande 《Made in Germany》
Il m'avait habillé de neuf, et en montant dans le train j'avais perdu un   70
    bouton
— Je m'en souviens, je m'en souviens, j'y ai souvent pensé depuis —
Je couchais sur les coffres et j'étais tout heureux de pouvoir jouer
    avec le browning nickelé qu'il m'avait aussi donné

J'étais très heureux insouciant
Je croyais jouer aux brigands
Nous avions volé le trésor de Golconde   75
Et nous allions, grâce au transsibérien, le cacher de l'autre côté du
    monde
Je devais le défendre contre les voleurs de l'Oural qui avaient
    attaqué les saltimbanques de Jules Verne
Contre les khoungouzes, les boxers de la Chine
Et les enragés petits mongols du Grand-Lama
Alibaba et les quarante voleurs   80
Et les fidèles du terrible Vieux de la montagne
Et surtout, contre les plus modernes

Les rats d'hôtel
Et les spécialistes des express internationaux.

Et pourtant, et pourtant   85
J'étais triste comme un enfant
Les rythmes du train
La 《*moëlle chemin-de-fer*》 des psychiatres américains
Le bruit des portes des voix des essieux grinçant sur les rails congelés
Le ferlin d'or de mon avenir   90
Mon browning le piano et les jurons des joueurs de cartes dans le
      compartiment d'à côté
L'épatante présence de Jeanne
L'homme aux lunettes bleues qui se promenait nerveusement dans le
      couloir et qui me regardait en passant
Froissis de femmes
Et le sifflement de la vapeur   95
Et le bruit éternel des roues en folie dans les ornières du ciel
Les vitres sont givrées
Pas de nature!
Et derrière, les plaines sibériennes le ciel bas et les grandes ombres
      des Taciturnes qui montent et qui descendent
Je suis couché dans un plaid   100
Bariolé
Comme ma vie
Et ma vie ne me tient pas plus chaud que ce châle
Écossais
Et l'Europe tout entière aperçue au coupe-vent d'un express à toute   105
      vapeur
N'est pas plus riche que ma vie
Ma pauvre vie
Ce châle
Effiloché sur des coffres remplis d'or
Avec lesquels je roule   110
Que je rêve
Que je fume
Et la seule flamme de l'univers
Est une pauvre pensée . . .

Du fond de mon cœur des larmes me viennent   115
Si je pense, Amour, à ma maitresse;
Elle n'est qu'une enfant, que je trouvai ainsi
Pâle, immaculée, au fond d'un bordel.

Ce n'est qu'une enfant, blonde, rieuse et triste,
Elle ne sourit pas et ne pleure jamais;   120

Mais au fond de ses yeux, quand elle vous y laisse boire,
Tremble un doux lys d'argent, la fleur du poète.

Elle est douce et muette, sans aucun reproche,
Avec un long tressaillement à votre approche;
Mais quand moi je lui viens, de-ci, de-là, de fête,   125
Elle fait un pas, puis ferme les yeux — et fait un pas.
Car elle est mon amour, et les autres femmes
N'ont que des robes d'or sur de grands corps de flammes,
Ma pauvre amie est si esseulée,
Elle est toute nue, n'a pas de corps — elle est trop pauvre.   130

Elle n'est qu'une fleur candide, fluette,
La fleur du poète, un pauvre lys d'argent,
Tout froid, tout seul, et déjà si fané
Que les larmes me viennent si je pense à son cœur.

Et cette nuit est pareille à cent mille autres quand un train file dans la   135
    nuit
— Les comètes tombent —
Et que l'homme et la femme, même jeunes, s'amusent à faire l'amour.

Le ciel est comme la tente déchirée d'un cirque pauvre dans un petit
    village de pêcheurs
En Flandres
Le soleil est un fumeux quinquet   140
Et tout au haut d'un trapèze une femme fait la lune.
La clarinette le piston une flûte aigre et un mauvais tambour
Et voici mon berceau
Mon berceau
Il était toujours près du piano quand ma mère comme Madame   145
    Bovary jouait les sonates de Beethoven
J'ai passé mon enfance dans les jardins suspendus de Babylone
Et l'école buissonnière, dans les gares devant les trains en partance
Maintenant, j'ai fait courir tous les trains derrière moi
Bâle–Tombouctou
J'ai aussi joué aux courses à Auteuil et à Longchamp   150
Paris–New York
Maintenant, j'ai fait courir tous les trains tout le long de ma vie
Madrid–Stockholm
Et j'ai perdu tous mes paris
Il n'y a plus que la Patagonie, la Patagonie, qui convienne à mon   155
    immense tristesse, la Patagonie, et un voyage dans les mers du Sud
Je suis en route
J'ai toujours été en route
Je suis en route avec la petite Jehanne de France

Le train fait un saut périlleux et retombe sur toutes ses roues
Le train retombe sur ses roues   160
Le train retombe toujours sur toutes ses roues

《Blaise, dis, sommes-nous bien loin de Montmartre?》

Nous sommes loin, Jeanne, tu roules depuis sept jours
Tu es loin de Montmartre, de la Butte qui t'a nourrie du
    Sacré-Cœur contre lequel tu t'es blottie
Paris a disparu et son énorme flambée   165
Il n'y a plus que les cendres continues
La pluie qui tombe
La tourbe qui se gonfle
La Sibérie qui tourne
Les lourdes nappes de neige qui remontent   170
Et le grelot de la folie qui grelotte comme un dernier désir dans
    l'air bleu
Le train palpite au cœur des horizons plombés
Et ton chagrin ricane . . .

《Dis, Blaise, sommes-nous bien loin de Montmartre?》

Les inquiétudes   175
Oublie les inquiétudes
Toutes les gares lézardées obliques sur la route
Le fils télégraphiques auxquels elles pendent
Les poteaux grimaçants qui gesticulent et les étranglent
Le monde s'étire s'allonge et se retire comme un accordéon qu'une   180
    main sadique tourmente
Dans les déchirures du ciel, les locomotives en furie
S'enfuient
Et dans les trous,
Les roues vertigineuses les bouches les voix
Et les chiens du malheur aboient à nos trousses   185
Les démons sont déchaînés
Ferrailles
Tout est un faux accord
Le *broun-roun-roun* des roues
Chocs   190
Rebondissements
Nous sommes un orage sous le crâne d'un sourd . . .

《Dis, Blaise, sommes-nous bien loin de Montmartre?》

Mais oui, tu m'énerves, tu le sais bien, nous sommes bien loin
La folie surchauffée beugle dans la locomotive   195
La peste le choléra se lèvent comme des braises ardentes sur notre
    route

Nous disparaissons dans la guerre en plein dans un tunnel
La faim, la putain, se cramponne aux nuages en débandade
Et fiente des batailles en tas puants de morts
Fais comme elle, fais ton métier . . .   200

《Dis, Blaise, sommes-nous bien loin de Montmartre?》

Oui, nous le sommes, nous le sommes
Tous les boucs émissaires ont crevé dans ce désert
Entends les sonnailles de ce troupeau galeux Tomsk
Tchéliabinsk Kainsk Obi Taïchet Verkné Oudinsk Kourgane   205
    Samara Pensa-Touloune
La mort en Mandchourie
Est notre débarcadère est notre dernier repaire
Ce voyage est terrible
Hier matin
Ivan Oulitch avait les cheveux blancs   210
Et Kolia Nicolaï Ivanovitch se ronge les doigts depuis quinze
    jours . . .
Fais comme elles la Mort la Famine fais ton métier
Ça coûte cent sous, en transsibérien, ça coûte cent roubles
En fièvre les banquettes et rougeoie sous la table
Le diable est au piano   215
Ses doigts noueux excitent toutes les femmes
La Nature
Les Gouges
Fais ton métier
Jusqu'à Kharbine. . .   220

《Dis, Blaise, sommes-nous bien loin de Montmartre?》

Non mais . . . fiche-moi la paix . . . laisse-moi tranquille
Tu as les hanches angulaires
Ton ventre est aigre et tu as la chaude-pisse
C'est tout ce que Paris a mis dans ton giron   225
C'est aussi un peu d'âme . . . car tu es malheureuse
J'ai pitié j'ai pitié viens vers moi sur mon cœur
Les roues sont les moulins à vent du pays de Cocagne
Et les moulins à vent sont les béquilles qu'un mendiant fait
    tournoyer
Nous sommes les culs-de-jatte de l'espace   230
Nous roulons sur nos quatre plaies
On nous a rogné les ailes
Les ailes de nos sept péchés
Et tous les trains sont les bilboquets du diable
Basse-cour   235

Le monde moderne
La vitesse n'y peut mais
Le monde moderne
Les lointains sont par trop loin
Et au bout du voyage c'est terrible d'être un homme avec une　　240
　　femme . . .

«Blaise, dis, sommes-nous bien loin de Montmartre?»

J'ai pitié j'ai pitié viens vers moi je vais te conter une histoire
Viens dans mons lit
Viens sur mon cœur
Je vais te conter une histoire . . .　　　　　　　　　　　　　　245

Oh viens! viens!

Aux Fidji règne l'éternel printemps
La paresse
L'amour pâme les couples dans l'herbe haute et la chaude syphilis rôde
　　sous les bananiers
Viens dans les îles perdues du Pacifique!　　　　　　　　　　250
Elles ont nom du Phénix, des Marquises
Bornéo et Java
Et Célèbes à la forme d'un chat.

Nous ne pouvons pas aller au Japon
Viens au Mexique!　　　　　　　　　　　　　　　　　　255
Sur ses hauts plateaux les tulipiers fleurissent
Les lianes tentaculaires sont la chevelure du soleil
On dirait la palette et les pinceaux d'un peintre
Des couleurs étourdissantes comme des gongs,
Rousseau y a été　　　　　　　　　　　　　　　　　　260
Il y a ébloui sa vie
C'est le pays des oiseaux
L'oiseau du paradis, l'oiseau-lyre
Le toucan, l'oiseau moqueur
Et le colibri niche au cœur des lys noirs　　　　　　　　　　265
Viens!
Nous nous aimerons dans les ruines majestueuses d'un temple aztèque
Tu seras mon idole
Une idole bariolée enfantine un peu laide et bizarrement étrange
Oh viens!　　　　　　　　　　　　　　　　　　　　270

Si tu veux nous irons en aéroplane et nous survolerons le pays des
　　mille lacs,
Les nuits y sont démesurément longues
L'ancêtre préhistorique aura peur de mon moteur
J'atterrirai

Et je construirai un hangar pour mon avion avec les os fossiles de   275
   mammouth
Le feu primitif réchauffera notre pauvre amour
Samowar
Et nous nous aimerons bien bourgeoisement près du pôle
Oh viens!

Jeanne Jeannette Ninette nini ninon nichon   280
Mimi mamour ma poupoule mon Pérou
Dodo dondon
Carotte ma crotte
Couchou p'tit-cœur
Cocotte   285
Chérie p'tite chèvre
Mon p'tit-péché mignon
Concon
Coucou
Elle dort.   290

Elle dort
Et de toutes les heures du monde elle n'en a pas gobé une seule
Tous les visages entrevus dans les gares
Toutes les horloges
L'heure de Paris l'heure de Berlin l'heure de Saint-Pétersbourg et   295
   l'heure de toutes les gares
Et à Oufa, le visage ensanglanté du canonnier
Et le cadran bêtement lumineux de Grodno
Et l'avance perpétuelle du train
Tous les matins on met les montres à l'heure
Le train avance et le soleil retarde   300
Rien n'y fait, j'entends les cloches sonores
Le gros bourdon de Notre-Dame
La cloche aigrelette du Louvre qui sonna la Barthélemy
Les carillons rouillés de Bruges-la-Morte
Les sonneries électriques de la bibliothèque de New-York   305
Les campagnes de Venise
Et les cloches de Moscou, l'horloge de la Porte-Rouge qui me
   comptait les heures quand j'étais dans un bureau
Et mes souvenirs
Le train tonne sur les plaques tournantes
Le train roule   310
Un gramophone grasseye une marche tzigane
Et le monde, comme l'horloge du quartier juif de Prague, tourne
   éperdument à rebours.

Effeuille la rose des vents

Voici que bruissent les orages déchaînés
Les trains roulent en tourbillon sur les réseaux enchevêtrés   315
Bilboquets diaboliques
Il y a des trains qui ne se rencontrent jamais
D'autres se perdent en route
Les chefs de gare jouent aux échecs
Tric-trac   320
Billard
Caramboles
Paraboles
La voie ferrée est une nouvelle géométrie
Syracuse   325
Archimède
Et les soldats qui l'égorgèrent
Et les galères
Et les vaisseaux
Et les engins prodigieux qu'il inventa   330
Et toutes les tueries
L'histoire antique
L'histoire moderne
Les tourbillons
Les naufrages   335
Même celui du *Titanic* que j'ai lu dans le journal
Autant d'images-associations que je ne peux pas développer dans mes
      vers
Car je suis encore fort mauvais poète
Car l'univers me déborde
Car j'ai négligé de m'assurer contre les accidents de chemin de fer   340
Car je ne sais pas aller jusqu'au bout
Et j'ai peur.

J'ai peur
Je ne sais pas aller jusqu'au bout
Comme mon ami Chagall je pourrais faire une série de tableaux   345
      déments
Mais je n'ai pas pris de notes en voyage
《Pardonnez-moi mon ignorance
《Pardonnez-moi de ne plus connaître l'ancien jeu des
vers》
Comme dit Guillaume Apollinaire
Tout ce qui concerne la guerre on peut le lire dans les *Mémoires* de   350
      Kouropatkine
Ou dans les journaux japonais qui sont aussi cruellement illustrés
A quoi bon me documenter

Je m'abandonne
Aux sursauts de ma mémoire . . .

A partir d'Irkoutsk le voyage devint beaucoup trop lent   355
Beaucoup trop long
Nous étions dans le premier train qui contournait le lac Baïkal
On avait orné la locomotive de drapeaux et de lampions
Et nous avions quitté la gare aux accents tristes de l'hymne au Tzar.
Si j'étais peintre je déverserais beaucoup de rouge, beaucoup de jaune   360
    sur la fin de ce voyage
Car je crois bien que nous étions tous un peu fous
Et qu'un délire immense ensanglantait les faces énervées de mes
    compagnons de voyage
Comme nous approchions de la Mongolie
Qui ronflait comme un incendie.
Le train avait ralenti son allure   365
Et je percevais dans le grincement perpétuel des roues
Les accents fous et les sanglots
D'une éternelle liturgie

J'ai vu
J'ai vu les trains silencieux les trains noirs qui revenaient de   370
    l'Extrême-Orient et qui passaient en fantômes
Et mon œil, comme le fanal d'arrière, court encore derrière ces trains
A Talga 100.000 blessés agonisaient faute de soins
J'ai visité les hôpitaux de Krasnoïarsk
Et à Khilok nous avons croisé un long convoi de soldats fous
J'ai vu dans les lazarets des plaies béantes des blessures qui   375
    saignaient à pleines orgues
Et les membres amputés dansaient autour ou s'envolaient dans l'air
    rauque
L'incendie était sur toutes les faces dans tous les cœurs
Des doigts idiots tambourinaient sur toutes les vitres
Et sous la pression de la peur les regards crevaient comme des abcès
Dans toutes les gares on brûlait tous les wagons   380
Et j'ai vu
J'ai vu des trains de 60 locomotives qui s'enfuyaient à toute vapeur
    pourchassées par les horizons en rut et des bandes de corbeaux
    qui s'envolaient désespérément après
Disparaître
Dans la direction de Port-Arthur.

A Tchita nous eûmes quelques jours de répit   385
Arrêt de cinq jours vu l'encombrement de la voie
Nous le passâmes chez Monsieur Iankéléwitch qui voulait me donner
    sa fille unique en mariage

Puis le train repartit.

Maintenant c'était moi qui avais pris place au piano et j'avais mal aux
dents

Je revois quand je veux cet intérieur si calme le magasin du père et les
yeux de la fille qui venait le soir dans mon lit

Moussorgsky

Et les lieder de Hugo Wolf

Et les sables du Gobi

Et à Khaïlar une caravane de chameaux blancs

Je crois bien que j'étais ivre durant plus de 500 kilomètres

Mais j'étais au piano et c'est tout ce que je vis

Quand on voyage on devrait fermer les yeux

Dormir

J'aurais tant voulu dormir

Je reconnais tous les pays les yeux fermés à leur odeur

Et je reconnais tous les trains au bruit qu'ils font

Les trains d'Europe sont à quatre temps tandis que ceux d'Asie sont
à cinq ou sept temps

D'autres vont en sourdine sont des berceuses

Et il y en a qui dans le bruit monotone des roues me rappellent la
prose lourde de Maeterlinck

J'ai déchiffré tous les textes confus des roues et j'ai rassemblé les
éléments épars d'une violente beauté

Que je possède

Et qui me force.

Tsitsika et Kharbine

Je ne vais pas plus loin

C'est la dernière station

Je débarquai à Kharbine comme on venait de mettre le feu aux
bureaux de la Croix-Rouge.

O Paris

Grand foyer chaleureux avec les tisons entrecroisés de tes rues et tes
vieilles maisons qui se penchent au-dessus et se réchauffent

Comme des aïeules

Et voici des affiches, du rouge du vert multicolores comme mon passé
bref du jaune

Jaune la fière couleur des romans de la France à l'étranger.

J'aime me frotter dans les grandes villes aux autobus en marche

Ceux de la ligne Saint-Germain–Montmartre m'emportent à l'assaut
de la Butte

Les moteurs beuglent comme les taureaux d'or

Les vaches du crépuscule broutent le Sacré-Cœur

O Paris

Gare centrale débarcadère des volontés carrefour des inquiétudes
Seuls les marchands de couleur ont encore un peu de lumière sur leur
  porte
La Compagnie Internationale des Wagons-Lits et des Grands Express
  Européens m'a envoyé son prospectus
C'est la plus belles église du monde   425
J'ai des amis qui m'entourent comme des garde-fous
Ils ont peur quand je pars que je ne revienne plus
Toutes les femmes que j'ai rencontrées se dressent aux horizons
Avec les gestes piteux et les regards tristes des sémaphores sous la
  pluie
Bella, Agnès, Catherine et la mère de mon fils en Italie   430
Et celle, la mère de mon amour en Amérique
Il y a des cris de sirène qui me déchirent l'âme
Là-bas en Mandchourie un ventre tressaille encore comme dans un
  accouchement
Je voudrais
Je voudrais n'avoir jamais fait mes voyages   435
Ce soir un grand amour me tourmente
Et malgré moi je pense à la petite Jehanne de France.
C'est par un soir de tristesse que j'ai écrit ce poème en son honneur
Jeanne
La petite prostituée   440
Je suis triste je suis triste
J'irai au *Lapin agile* me ressouvenir de ma jeunesse perdue
Et boire des petits verres
Puis je rentrerai seul
Paris   445
Ville de la Tour unique du grand Gibet et de la Roue.

Bibliographical References

APOLLONIO, UMBRO (1973) (ed.), *Futurist Manifestos* (London: Thames & Hudson).

ARLAND, MARCEL (1966) (ed.), *Jules Supervielle: 'Gravitations' précédé de 'Débarcadères'* (Paris: Gallimard).

ATTRIDGE, DEREK (1982), *The Rhythms of English Poetry* (London: Longman).

—— (1989), 'Linguistic Theory and Literary Criticism: *The Rhythms of English Poetry* Revisited', in P. Kiparsky and G. Youmans (eds.), *Phonetics and Phonology*, I: *Rhythm and Meter* (San Diego: Academic Press), 183–99.

BANN, STEPHEN (1991), 'Photography and Genre: A Project for Cultural Studies', in G. Clarke (ed.), *Images of England: The Photograph in Context* (Canterbury: Centre for Modern Cultural Studies, University of Kent), 3–5.

BARTHES, ROLAND (1980), *La Chambre claire: Note sur la photographie* (Paris: L'Étoile, Gallimard, Seuil).

—— (1984), *Camera Lucida: Reflections on Photography*, trans. R. Howard (London: Fontana).

BATEMAN, JACQUELINE (1976), 'Questions de métrique persienne', in *Cahiers du 20e siècle: Lectures de Saint-John Perse* (Paris: Klincksieck), 7: 27–56.

BÉHAR, HENRI (1976), 'Débris, collage et invention poétique', *Europe*, 54/566: 102–14.

BENJAMIN, WALTER (1970), 'The Work of Art in the Age of Mechanical Reproduction', in *Illuminations*, ed. H. Arendt, trans. H. Zohn (London: Jonathan Cape), 219–53 (1st pub. 1936).

BERGER, JOHN (1982), 'Appearances', in J. Berger and J. Mohr, *Another Way of Telling* (London: Writers & Readers), 81–129.

BERGSON, HENRI (1983), *Le Rire: Essai sur la signification du comique* (Paris: PUF) (1st pub. 1900).

BLAIR, DOROTHY (1960), *Jules Supervielle: A Modern Fabulist* (Oxford: Blackwell).

BOBILLOT, JEAN-PIERRE (1990), 'L'Élasticité métrico-prosodique chez Apollinaire: Une lecture formelle des "Colchiques" ', *Poétique*, 21/84: 411–83.

BOCHNER, JAY (1978), *Blaise Cendrars: Discovery and Re-creation* (Toronto: University of Toronto Press).

BOHN, WILLARD (1986), *The Aesthetics of Visual Poetry 1914–1928* (Cambridge: Cambridge University Press).

BOOTH, PAT (1983) (ed.), *Master Photographers: The World's Great Photographers on their Art and Technique* (London: Macmillan).

BOZON-SCALZITTI, YVETTE (1972), 'Blaise Cendrars et le Symbolisme: De *Moganni Nameh* au *Transsibérien*', *Archives des lettres modernes*, 137.

—— (1977), *Blaise Cendrars, ou La Passion de l'écriture* (Lausanne: L'Âge d'Homme).

BRYSON, NORMAN (1989), 'Chardin and the Text of Still Life', *Critical Inquiry*, 15: 227–52.

BUCKBERROUGH, SHERRY A. (1982), *Robert Delaunay: The Discovery of Simultaneity* (Ann Arbor, Mich.: UMI Research Press).

CAIZERGUES, PIERRE (1983), 'Blaise Cendrars, poète du voyage et voyageur de l'écriture', in C. Leroy (ed.), *Blaise Cendrars 20 ans après* (Paris: Klincksieck), 57–74.

CARDONNE-ARLYCK, E. (1989), 'Reverdy's Swerving Syntax', trans. G. Wells, *Nottingham French Studies*, 28/2: 84–92.

CENDRARS, BLAISE (1945), *L'Homme foudroyé* (Paris: Denoël).

—— (1957), *Trop c'est trop* (Paris: Denoël).

—— (1967), *Du monde entier: Poésies complètes 1912–1924* (Paris: Gallimard).

—— (1987), *'Aujourd'hui 1917–1929' suivi de 'Essais et réflexions 1910–1916'*, ed. M. Cendrars (Paris: Denoël).

CHAMPIGNY, ROBERT (1963), *Le Genre poétique: Essai* (Monte Carlo: Regain).

CHATMAN, SEYMOUR (1965), *A Theory of Meter* (The Hague: Mouton).

CHOMSKY, NOAM, and HALLE, MORRIS (1968), *The Sound Pattern of English* (New York: Harper & Row).

CLAUDEL, PAUL (1963), 'Réflexions et propositions sur le vers français', in *Réflexions sur la poésie* (Paris: Gallimard), 7–90 (1st pub. 1928).

COCTEAU, JEAN (1920), *Carte blanche* (Paris: La Sirène).

COLLOT, MICHEL (1982), 'L'Horizon typographique dans les poèmes de Reverdy', *Littérature*, 46: 41–58.

CORNULIER, BENOÎT DE (1981), 'La Rime n'est pas une marque de fin de vers', *Poétique*, 12/46: 247–56.

—— (1982), *Théorie du vers: Rimbaud, Verlaine, Mallarmé* (Paris: Seuil).

—— (1989), 'Metre "impair", métrique "insaisissable"? Sur les "derniers vers" de Rimbaud', in M. Dominicy (ed.), *Le Souci des apparences: Neuf études de poétique et de métrique* (Brussels: Université de Bruxelles), 75–91.

CULLER, JONATHAN (1975), *Structuralist Poetics: Structuralism, Linguistics and the Study of Literature* (London: Routledge & Kegan Paul).

CURETON, R. D. (1985), 'Rhythm: A Multilevel Analysis', *Style*, 19: 242–57.

DEBON, CLAUDE (1982), 'L' "Écriture cubiste" d'Apollinaire', *Europe*, 60/638–9: 118–27.

DÉCAUDIN, MICHEL (1966), *Œuvres complètes de Guillaume Apollinaire*, iv (Paris: Balland & Lecat).

—— (1982), 'Sur la prosodie de *Gravitations*', *Revue d'histoire littéraire de la France*, 82: 61–9.

DEGUY, MICHEL (1971), 'Préface', *Pierre Reverdy: 'Sources du vent' précédé de 'La Balle au bond'* (Paris: Gallimard), 9–19.

DELAUNAY, ROBERT (1957), *Du cubisme à l'art abstrait*, ed. P. Francastel and G. Habasque (Paris: SEVPEN).

DUHAMEL, GEORGES, and VILDRAC, CHARLES (1910), *Notes sur la technique poét* (Paris: Champion).

DUPRÉ, N. (1977), 'La Roue du "Transsibérien" ', *Recherches et travaux* (Greno Université de Grenoble, UER de Lettres), 15: 60–106.

DURRY, MARIE-JEANNE (1964), *Guillaume Apollinaire: 'Alcools' II* (Paris: SEDF

EASTHOPE, ANTHONY (1983), *Poetry as Discourse* (London: Methuen).

ERKKILA, BETSY (1980), *Walt Whitman among the French: Poet and Myth* (Prince NJ: Princeton University Press).

ÉTIEMBLE, RENÉ (1960), *Supervielle* (Paris: Gallimard).

—— (1966), 'Évolution de la poétique chez Supervielle entre 1922 et 19 *Poètes ou faiseurs? Hygiène des lettres*, iv (Paris: Gallimard), 298–322.

FAVRE, YVES-ALAIN (1977), *Saint-John Perse: Le Langage et le sacré* (Paris: Co

—— (1981), *Supervielle: La Rêverie et le chant dans 'Gravitations'* (Paris: Niz

FLÜCKIGER, JEAN-CARLO (1977), *Au cœur du texte: Essai sur Blaise Cend* (Neuchâtel: La Baconnière).

FORD, COLIN (1989) (ed.), *The Story of Popular Photography* (London: Centu

GATES, ROSEMARY (1985), 'The Identity of American Free Verse: The Proso Study of Whitman's "Lilacs" ', *Language and Style*, 18: 248–76.

GENETTE, GÉRARD (1969), *Figures*, ii (Paris, Seuil).

GOLDENSTEIN, JEAN-PIERRE (1986), *Dix-neuf poèmes élastiques de Blaise Cend* (Paris: Méridiens Klincksieck).

GOLDING, JOHN (1959), *Cubism: A History and an Analysis 1907–1914* (Lond Faber).

GRAMMONT, MAURICE (1965), *Petit Traité de versification française* (Paris: Co (1st pub. 1908).

GREENE, ROBERT (1967), *The Poetic Theory of Pierre Reverdy* (Berkeley, Ca University of California Press).

GREENE, TATIANA W. (1958), *Jules Supervielle* (Geneva: Droz).

GROJNOWSKI, DANIEL (1988), 'Poésie et photographie: *Kodak* de B. Cendra *Poétique*, 19/75: 313–23.

GUYARD, M.-FRANÇOIS (1959), 'De Patmore à Claudel: Histoire et nature d' influence', *Revue de littérature comparée*, 33: 500–17.

HALLE, MORRIS, and KEYSER, SAMUEL (1970), 'Chaucer and the Study Prosody', in D. Freeman (ed.), *Linguistics and Literary Style* (New York: H Rinehart & Winston), 366–426 (1st pub. 1966).

HENDERSON, LINDA D. (1975), 'The Artist, "The Fourth Dimension", and n Euclidean Geometry 1900–1930: A Romance of Many Dimensions', unp doctoral thesis, Yale University.

HIDDLESTON, J. A. (1965), *L'Univers de Jules Supervielle* (Paris: Corti).

HILEY, MICHAEL (1982) (ed.), *Bill Brandt: Nudes 1945–1980* (London: Gord Fraser).

HUBERT, ÉTIENNE-ALAIN (1982), 'Pierre Reverdy et la "poésie plastique" de s temps', *Europe*, 60/638–9: 109–18.

HURET, JULES (1982), *Enquête sur l'évolution littéraire*, ed. D. Grojnowski (Vanves: Thot) (1st pub. 1891).

JEFFREY, IAN (1981), *Photography: A Concise History* (London: Thames & Hudson).

JOYCE, PAUL (1988), *Hockney on Photography: Conversations with Paul Joyce* (London: Jonathan Cape).

KAHN, GUSTAVE (1897), 'Préface sur le vers libre', in *Premiers poèmes* (Paris: Mercure de France), 3–38.

KENNER, HUGH (1975), *The Pound Era: The Age of Ezra Pound, T. S. Eliot, James Joyce and Wyndham Lewis* (London: Faber).

KIPARSKY, PAUL (1975), 'Stress, Syntax, and Meter', *Language*, 51: 576–615.

—— (1977), 'The Rhythmic Structure of English Verse', *Linguistic Inquiry*, 8: 189–247.

KNODEL, ARTHUR (1966), *Saint-John Perse: A Study of his Poetry* (Edinburgh: Edinburgh University Press).

KOZLOFF, MAX (1979), *Photography and Fascination* (Danbury, NH: Addison House).

LACASSIN, FRANCIS (1976), 'Gustave Le Rouge: Le Gourou secret de Blaise Cendrars', *Europe*, 54/566: 71–101.

—— (1979), 'Gustave Le Rouge ou le gourou secret de Blaise Cendrars', *Passagers clandestins*, i (Paris: Union Générale d'Édition), 283–335.

—— (1986) (ed.), *Gustave Le Rouge: 'Le Mystérieux Docteur Cornélius', 'Le Prisonnier de la planète Mars', 'La Guerre des vampires', etc.* (Paris: Laffont).

LAFORGUE, JULES (1903), *Mélanges posthumes* (Paris: Mercure de France).

LE BEC, JEAN-YVES (1985), 'Le Verbe coloré: Cendrars et ses peintres', in J.-M. Debenedetti (ed.), *Blaise Cendrars* (Paris: Henri Veyrier), 159–206.

LITTLE, ROGER (1973), *Saint-John Perse* (London: Athlone Press).

LOCKERBIE, S. I., and GREET, ANNE HYDE (1980) (eds.), *Guillaume Apollinaire: 'Calligrammes'* (Berkeley, Calif.: University of California Press).

McCULLIN, DON (1987), *Perspectives* (London: Harrap).

MAGNUSON, KARL, and RYDER, FRANK G. (1970), 'The Study of English Prosody: An Alternative Proposal', *College English*, 31: 789–820.

—— —— (1971), 'Second Thoughts on English Prosody', *College English*, 33: 198–216.

MALLARMÉ, STÉPHANE (1945), 'Crise de vers', in *Œuvres complètes*, ed. H. Mondor and G. Jean-Aubry (Paris: Gallimard), 360–8 (1st pub. 1896).

MATHEWS, TIMOTHY (1987), *Reading Apollinaire: Theories of Poetic Language* (Manchester: Manchester University Press).

—— (1988), 'Apollinaire and Cubism?', *Style*, 22: 275–98.

MILHAU, DENIS (1982), 'Lecture du cubisme par deux poètes: Apollinaire et Reverdy', *Europe*, 60/638–9: 44–50.

MILNER, JEAN-CLAUDE (1974), 'Réflexions sur le fonctionnement du vers français', *Cahiers de poétique comparée*, 1/3: 2–21.

MITCHELL, W. J. T. (1986), *Iconology: Image, Text, Ideology* (Chicago: University of Chicago Press).

MOCKEL, ALBERT (1962), 'Propos de littérature', in *Esthétique du symbolisme*, ed. M. Otten (Brussels: Palais des Académies), 70–173 (1st pub. 1894).

MOREAU, FRANÇOIS (1987), *Six études de métrique: De l'alexandrin romantique au verset contemporain* (Paris: SEDES).

MORIER, HENRI (1943–4), *Le Rythme du vers libre symboliste et ses relations avec le sens*, 3 vols. (Geneva: Les Presses Académiques).

—— (1975), *Dictionnaire de poétique et de rhétorique*, 2nd edn. (Paris: PUF).

NADAL, OCTAVE (1964), 'Conversation avec Supervielle', in *A mesure haute* (Paris: Mercure de France), 257–68.

NOULET, ÉMILIE (1965), 'L'Octosyllabe dans *Amers*', in J. Paulhan (ed.), *Honneur à Saint-John Perse* (Paris: Gallimard), 316–26.

PATMORE, COVENTRY (1894), 'Essay on English Metrical Law', in *Poetical Works*, ii (London: George Bell), 215–67 (1st pub. 1878).

PERSE, SAINT-JOHN (1972), *Œuvres complètes* (Paris: Gallimard).

POUND, EZRA (1968), *Collected Shorter Poems* (London: Faber).

PROUST, MARCEL (1954), *A la recherche du temps perdu*, ed. P. Clarac and A. Ferré, 3 vols. (Paris: Gallimard).

—— (1971), *'Contre Sainte-Beuve' précédé de 'Pastiches et mélanges' et suivi de 'Essais et articles'*, ed. P. Clarac and Y. Sandre (Paris: Gallimard).

RENAUD, PHILIPPE (1969), *Lecture d'Apollinaire* (Lausanne: L'Âge d'Homme).

REVERDY, PIERRE (1974), *Cette émotion appelée poésie: Écrits sur la poésie (1932–1960)* (Paris: Flammarion).

—— (1975), *Nord–Sud, Self-Defence et autres écrits sur l'art et la poésie (1917–1926)* (Paris: Flammarion).

RICHARD, JEAN-PIERRE (1964), *Onze études sur la poésie moderne* (Paris: Seuil).

ROBICHEZ, JACQUES (1977), *Sur Saint-John Perse: 'Éloges', 'La Gloire des rois', 'Anabase'* (Paris: CDU/SEDES).

—— (1981), *'Gravitations' de Supervielle* (Paris: SEDES).

ROSKILL, MARK (1985), *The Interpretation of Cubism* (Philadelphia: Art Alliance Press).

ROTHWELL, ANDREW (1989), *Textual Spaces: The Poetry of Pierre Reverdy* (Amsterdam: Rodopi).

ROUBAUD, JACQUES (1971), 'Mètre et vers: Deux applications de la métrique générative de Halle-Keyser', *Poétique*, 2/7: 366–87.

—— and LUSSON, PIERRE (1974), 'Mètre et rythme de l'alexandrin ordinaire', *Langue française*, 23: 41–53.

SACKS-GALEY, PÉNÉLOPE (1988), *Calligramme ou écriture figurée: Apollinaire inventeur de formes* (Paris: Minard).

SCOTT, CLIVE (1986), *A Question of Syllables: Essays in Nineteenth-Century French Verse* (Cambridge: Cambridge University Press).

—— (1990), *Vers Libre: The Emergence of Free Verse in France 1886–1914* (Oxford: Clarendon Press).

SCOTT, DAVID H. T. (1988), *Pictorialist Poetics: Poetry and the Visual Arts in Nineteenth-Century France* (Cambridge: Cambridge University Press).

SONTAG, SUSAN (1978), *On Photography* (London: Allen Lane).

SOUZA, ROBERT DE (1892), *Le Rythme poétique* (Paris: Perrin).

SPATE, VIRGINIA (1979), *Orphism: The Evolution of Non-figurative Painting in Paris 1910–1914* (Oxford: Clarendon Press).

SUPERVIELLE, JULES (1951), *'Naissances' suivi de 'En songeant à un art poétique'* (Paris: Gallimard).

—— and ÉTIEMBLE, RENÉ (1969), *Correspondance 1936–1959*, ed. J. Étiemble (Paris: SEDES).

TRACHTENBERG, ALAN (1980) (ed.), *Classic Essays on Photography* (New Haven Conn.: Leete's Island Books).

TRAGER, GEORGE L., and SMITH, HENRY LEE (1951), *An Outline of English Structure*, Studies in Linguistics Occasional Papers, no. 3 (Norman, Okla.: Battenberg Press).

VALÉRY, PAUL (1957), 'Le Retour de Hollande', *Œuvres*, i, ed. J. Hytier (Paris: Gallimard), 844–54 (1st pub. 1926).

VANDERHOFT, CLAIRE (1989), 'Problèmes de métrique dans la poésie unanimiste: La Théorie des accords', in M. Dominicy (ed.), *Le Souci des apparences: Neuf études de poétique et de métrique* (Brussels: Université de Bruxelles), 93–119.

VAN RUTTEN, PIERRE-M. (1975), *Le Langage poétique de Saint-John Perse* (The Hague: Mouton).

VARNEDOE, KIRK (1989), *A Fine Disregard: What Makes Modern Art Modern* (London: Thames & Hudson).

VERLUYTEN, PAUL (1989), 'L'Analyse de l'alexandrin: Mètre ou rythme?', in M. Dominicy (ed.), *Le Souci des apparences: Neuf études de poétique et de métrique* (Brussels: Université de Bruxelles), 31–74.

VIALLANEIX, PAUL (1982), 'La Poétique de l'espace dans *Gravitations*', *Revue d'histoire littéraire de la France*, 82: 46–60.

VIVIER, ROBERT (1971), *Lire Supervielle* (Paris: Corti).

VRIESEN, GUSTAV, and IMDAHL, MAX (1967), *Robert Delaunay: Light and Color* (New York: Harry Abrams).

WEAVER, MIKE (1989) (ed.), *The Art of Photography 1839–1989* (London: Royal Academy of Arts).

WHEATLEY, J. R. (1988), 'Metre, Metrics, Constraints and the Alexandrine', *Australian Journal of French Studies*, 25: 290–9.

YOUMANS, GILBERT (1989), 'Introduction: Rhythm and Meter', in P. Kiparsky and G. Youmans (eds.), *Phonetics and Phonology*, i: *Rhythm and Meter* (San Diego: Academic Press), 1–14.

Further Bibliography

ASHOLT, WOLFGANG, 'Avant-garde et guerre: Quelques remarques à propos de poèmes d'Apollinaire, de Cendrars et de Reverdy', *Romanistische Zeitschrift für Literaturgeschichte*, 11 (1987), 401–29.

BERRY, DAVID, *The Creative Vision of Guillaume Apollinaire: A Study of Imagination* (Saratoga, Calif.: Anma Libri, 1982).

BIGEL, JEAN-PIERRE, 'Le Paradis perdu: Étude de la structure et analyse d'*Éloges*', in P.-L. Assoun, P. Berthail, *et al.* (eds.), *La Nostalgie: Analyses et réflexions sur Saint-John Perse, 'Éloges'* (Paris: Édition Marketing, 1986), 85–94.

BISHOP, MICHAEL, 'Eyes and Seeing in the Poetry of Pierre Reverdy', in R. Cardinal (ed.), *Sensibility and Creation: Studies in Twentieth-Century French Poetry* (London: Croom Helm, 1977), 57–71.

BLAIR, DOROTHY, 'Jules Supervielle and the Myth of the Creation', *Durham University Journal*, 75/2 (1983), 77–88.

BOCHNER, JAY, 'Cendrars—Surprise', *Sud*, 18 (1988), 35–54.

BOCHOLIER, GÉRARD, *Pierre Reverdy: Le Phare obscur* (Paris: Champ Vallon, 1984).

BOHN, WILLARD, 'Landscaping the Visual Sign: Apollinaire's "Paysage" ', *Philological Quarterly*, 65 (1986), 345–69.

—— 'Poésie critique and poésie visuelle: Apollinaire's "Les Lunettes" ', *Neophilologus*, 72 (1988), 34–43.

BRÉDA, FRANÇOIS, 'Blaise Cendrars, *Dix-neuf poèmes élastiques*', *Recherches sur l'imaginaire*, 13 (1985), 111–35.

CAILLOIS, ROGER, *Poétique de Saint-John Perse* (Paris: Gallimard, 1954).

CAIZERGUES, PIERRE, 'Cendrars et Apollinaire', *Sud*, 18 (1988), 71–102.

CARDINAL, ROGER, 'Pierre Reverdy: Reading the Natural Sign', *Nottingham French Studies*, 28/2 (1989), 75–83.

CAWS, MARY ANN, 'Blaise Cendrars: A Cinema of Poetry', in *The Inner Theatre of Recent French Poetry* (Princeton, NJ: Princeton University Press, 1972), 26–51.

—— *La Main de Pierre Reverdy* (Geneva: Droz, 1979).

CHADOURNE, JACQUELINE, *Blaise Cendrars poète du cosmos* (Paris: Seghers, 1973).

CHEFDOR, MONIQUE, *Blaise Cendrars* (Boston: Twayne, 1980).

CHIPP, HERSCHEL B., 'Orphism and Color Theory', *Art Bulletin*, 40 (1958), 55–63.

COLLOT, MICHEL, *Horizon de Reverdy* (Paris: Presses de l'École Normale Supérieure, 1981).

COOK, ALBERT, 'The Windows of Apollinaire', *Figural Choice in Poetry and Art* (Hanover, NH: University Press of New England, 1985), 64–85,

COTONEA, MARIE-LINE, 'Étude du seuil et de l'attente: *Sources du vent* (Pierre Reverdy)', *Recherches sur l'imaginaire*, 11 (1984), 30–4.

DEBON, CLAUDE, *Guillaume Apollinaire après 'Alcools' I: 'Calligrammes': Le Poète et la guerre* (Paris: Minard, 1981).

EDSON, LAURIE, 'A New Aesthetic: Apollinaire's "Les Fiançailles" and Picasso's "Les Demoiselles d'Avignon" ', *Symposium*, 36 (1982), 115–28.

FARASSE, GÉRARD, 'Mots à decouvert ou le langage d'*Éloges*', in P.-L. Assoun, P. Berthail, *et al.* (eds.), *La Nostalgie: Analyses et réflexions sur Saint-John Perse, 'Éloges'* (Paris: Édition Marketing, 1986), 159–72.

GOLDENSTEIN, JEAN-PIERRE, 'Quelques vues successives sur la simultanéité', *Sud*, 18 (1988), 55–69.

HENRY, ALBERT, 'Les "Images à Crusoé" et la méthode philologique', *Travaux de linguistique et de littérature*, 9 (1971), 329–46.

HERMANS, THEO, 'Pierre Reverdy: The Poem as Object', in *The Structure of Modernist Poetry* (London: Croom Helm, 1982).

HOUSTON, J. P., 'Cendrars's Modernism', *Southern Review*, 6 (1970), 561–5.

JACARET, GILBERTE, *La Dialectique de l'ironie et du lyrisme dans 'Alcools' et 'Calligrammes' de G. Apollinaire* (Paris: Nizet, 1984).

JACOBUS, EVERETT F., 'Cendrars's Variegated Poetic Persona: Seduction and Authenticity in *Prose of the Transsiberian* and *Nineteen Elastic Poems*', *Studies in Twentieth-Century Literature*, 3 (1978–9), 153–71.

JAUSS, HANS ROBERT, '1912: Threshold to an Epoch: Apollinaire's "Zone" and "Lundi rue Christine" ', *Yale French Studies*, 74 (1988), 39–66.

JULIO, MARYANN DE, 'The Drama of Self in Apollinaire and Reverdy: Play of Light and Shadow', *French Forum*, 6 (1981), 154–62.

LEVILLAN, HENRIETTE, *Le Rituel poétique de Saint-John Perse* (Paris: Gallimard, 1977).

—— and SACOTTE, MIREILLE (eds.), *Saint-John Perse: Antillanité et universalité* (Paris: Éditions Caribéennes, 1988).

LITTLE, ROGER, 'The Image of the Threshold in the Poetry of Saint-John Perse', *Modern Language Review*, 64 (1969), 777–92.

—— 'Language as Imagery in Saint-John Perse', *Forum for Modern Language Studies*, 6 (1970), 127–39.

—— *Apollinaire* (London: Athlone Press, 1976).

—— 'The World and the Word in Saint-John Perse', in R. Cardinal (ed.), *Sensibility and Creation: Studies in Twentieth-Century French Poetry* (London: Croom Helm, 1977), 122–35.

LOVEY, JEAN-CLAUDE, *Situation de Blaise Cendrars* (Neuchâtel: La Baconnière, 1965).

MARTIN, GRAHAM DUNSTAN, 'Jules Supervielle: A Poetry of Diffidence', in R. Cardinal (ed.), *Sensibility and Creation: Studies in Twentieth-Century French Poetry* (London: Croom Helm, 1977), 103–21.

NYKROG, PER, 'A la veille du grand adieu sur les "idéogrammes lyriques" d'Apollinaire', *Romanic Review*, 80 (1989), 109–23.

PARENT, MONIQUE, *Saint-John Perse et quelques devanciers: Études sur le poème en prose* (Paris: Klincksieck, 1960).

PARENT, MONIQUE, 'La Fonction poétique dans deux textes de Saint-John Perse', *Travaux de linguistique et de littérature*, 9 (1971), 347–57.

PEAN, VALÉRIE, 'La Dynamique spatiale dans les calligrammes de G. Apollinaire: De l'envol à la chute', *Recherches sur l'imaginaire*, 13 (1985), 91–110.

PERLOFF, MARJORIE, ' "Mouvences des midis": Les *Poèmes élastiques* de Blaise Cendrars et Frank O'Hara', in M. Chefdor (ed.), *Blaise Cendrars*, ii: *Cendrars et l'Amérique, Revue des lettres modernes* (Paris: Minard, 1989).

POUPON, MARC, 'Apollinaire et Cendrars', *Archives des lettres modernes*, 103 (1969).

REVERDY, PIERRE, *En vrac: Notes* (Monaco: Le Rocher, 1956).

RINSLER, NORMA, 'The War Poems of Apollinaire', *French Studies*, 25 (1971), 169–86.

ROBICHEZ, JACQUES, 'Portrait de Supervielle dans *Gravitations*', *Revue d'histoire littéraire de la France*, 82 (1982), 41–5.

ROTHWELL, ANDREW, 'Reverdy's *Les Jockeys camouflés*: From Aesthetic Polemic to Art *poétique*', *Nottingham French Studies*, 28/2 (1989), 26–44.

RUSSELL, CHARLES, 'The Poets of Time: Apollinaire and the Italian Futurists', *Poets, Prophets, and Revolutionaries: The Literary Avant-Garde from Rimbaud through Postmodernism* (New York: Oxford University Press, 1985), 62–95.

SACOTTE, MIREILLE, 'Paroles d'îles', in P.-L. Assoun, P. Berthail, *et al.* (eds.), *La Nostalgie: Analyses et réflexions sur Saint-John Perse, 'Éloges'* (Paris: Édition Marketing, 1986), 113–27.

SCHROEDER, JEAN, *Pierre Reverdy* (Boston: Twayne, 1981).

SELLIN, ERIC, 'The Esthetics of Ambiguity: Reverdy's Use of Syntactical Simultaneity', in M. A. Caws (ed.), *About French Poetry from Dada to 'Tel quel': Text and Theory* (Detroit: Wayne State University Press, 1974), 112–25.

SIDOTI, ANTOINE, 'Genèse et dossier d'une polémique: *La Prose du Transsibérien et de la petite Jehanne de France*: Blaise Cendrars—Sonia Delaunay nov.–dec. 1912–juin 1914', *Archives des lettres modernes*, 224 (1987).

SOMVILLE, LÉON, 'Pierre Reverdy', in P. Brunel, J. Burgos, *et al.* (eds.), *L'Esprit nouveau dans tous ses états: Mélanges Décaudin* (Paris: Minard, 1986), 401–9.

STALLONI, YVES, 'Éloges du corps/Le Corps dans *Éloges*', in P.-L. Assoun, P. Berthail, *et al.* (eds.), *La Nostalgie: Analyses et réflexions sur Saint-John Perse, 'Éloges'*, (Paris: Édition Marketing, 1986), 135–41.

TACONET, NOEL, *Lectures de 'Éloges' de Saint-John Perse: La Nostalgie* (Paris: Belin, 1986).

TAYLOR, JOSHUA, *Futurism* (New York: Museum of Modern Art, 1961).

TAYLOR-HORREX, SUSAN, 'Cendrars, Delaunay et le simultanéisme: Évolution de l'esthétique simultanéiste', in J.-C. Flückiger (ed.), *Cahiers Blaise Cendrars*, iii: *L'Encrier de Cendrars* (Neuchâtel: La Baconnière, 1989), 209–17.

THIBAULT, JEAN-FRANÇOIS, 'Simultanéisme et poésie: *La Prose du Transsibérien*, poeme visuel', in P. Crant (ed.), *French Literature and the Arts* (Columbia, SC: University of South Carolina, 1978), 49–65.

UMLAUF, JOACHIM, 'Blaise Cendrars et les Delaunay', *Annali di Ca' Foscari*, 27 (1988), 355–61.

VALETTE, BERNARD, 'Introduction à la poétique de Saint-John Perse', in P.-L. Assoun, P. Berthail, *et al.* (eds.), *La Nostalgie: Analyses et réflexions sur Saint-John Perse, 'Éloges'* (Paris: Édition Marketing, 1986), 73–8.

WHITE, KENNETH, 'L'ABC du monde', *Sud*, 18 (1988), 11–33.

WINSPUR, STEVEN, *Saint-John Perse and the Imaginary Reader* (Geneva: Droz, 1988).

Index